Human Subjects Research Regulation

Basic Bioethics
Arthur Caplan, editor

A complete list of the books in the Basic Bioethics series appears at the back of this book.

Human Subjects Research Regulation

Perspectives on the Future

edited by I. Glenn Cohen and Holly Fernandez Lynch

The MIT Press
Cambridge, Massachusetts
London, England

© 2014 Massachusetts Institute of Technology

All rights reserved. No part of this book may be reproduced in any form by any electronic or mechanical means (including photocopying, recording, or information storage and retrieval) without permission in writing from the publisher.

MIT Press books may be purchased at special quantity discounts for business or sales promotional use. For information, please email special_sales@mitpress.mit.edu.

This book was set in Sabon LT Std by Toppan Best-set Premedia Limited, Hong Kong. Printed and bound in the United States of America.

Library of Congress Cataloging-in-Publication Data

Human subjects research regulation : perspectives on the future / edited by I. Glenn Cohen and Holly Fernandez Lynch.
    pages cm – (Basic bioethics)
  Includes bibliographical references and index.
  ISBN 978-0-262-02746-5 (hardcover : alk. paper) – ISBN 978-0-262-52621-0 (pbk. : alk. paper) 1. Human experimentation in medicine–Evaluation. 2. Human experimentation in medicine–Law and legislation. 3. Medical ethics. 4. Clinical trials. I. Cohen, I. Glenn. II. Lynch, Holly Fernandez.
  R853.H8H863 2014
  174.2'8–dc23
  2013047483
ISBN: 978-0-262-02746-5 (hardcover)—978-0-262-52621-0 (pbk.)

10 9 8 7 6 5 4 3 2 1

to Philippe and Jason
—IGC

to Liza Dawson and Seema Shah, for introducing me to the world of human subjects research ethics
—HFL

Contents

Series Foreword xi
Acknowledgments xiii

Introduction 1
I. Glenn Cohen and Holly Fernandez Lynch

1 Setting the Stage: The Past and Present of Human Subjects Research Regulations 9
Amy L. Davis and Elisa A. Hurley

I Regulation of Risk

Introduction 27
Nir Eyal

2 *De minimis* Risk: A Suggestion for a New Category of Research Risk 31
Rosamond Rhodes

3 Risk Level, Research Oversight, and Decrements in Participant Protections 45
Ana S. Iltis

II Protection of Vulnerable Populations

Introduction 61
Patrick Taylor

4 Classifying Military Personnel as a Vulnerable Population 65
Efthimios Parasidis

5 Children as Research Partners in Community Pediatrics   79
Adam Braddock

6 Back to the Future? Examining the Institute of Medicine's Recommendations to Loosen Restrictions on Using Prisoners as Human Subjects   93
Osagie K. Obasogie

III Redefining the Participant–Researcher Relationship and the Role of IRBs
Introduction   109
I. Glenn Cohen

7 Toward Human Research Protection That Is Evidence Based and Participant Centered   113
Michael McDonald, Susan Cox, and Anne Townsend

8 Outsourcing Ethical Obligations: Should the Revised Common Rule Address the Responsibilities of Investigators and Sponsors?   127
Seema K. Shah

9 Subjects, Participants, and Partners: What Are the Implications for Research as the Role of Informed Consent Evolves?   143
Alexander Morgan Capron

10 Democratic Deliberation and the Ethical Review of Human Subjects Research   157
Govind Persad

11 IRBs and the Problem of "Local Precedents"   173
Laura Stark

IV Specimens, Data, and Privacy
Introduction   189
Jeffrey Skopek

12 Biospecimen Exceptionalism in the ANPRM   193
Ellen Wright Clayton

13 Biobanking, Consent, and Certificates of Confidentiality: Does the ANPRM Muddy the Water?   207
Brett A. Williams and Leslie E. Wolf

14 Mandating Consent for Future Research with Biospecimens: A Call for Enhanced Community Engagement   221

Carol Weil, Hilary Shutak, Benjamin Fombonne, and Nicole Lockhart

15 Take Another Little Piece of My Heart: Regulating the Research Use of Human Biospecimens   237

Gail H. Javitt

16 Reconsidering Privacy Protections for Human Research   251

Suzanne M. Rivera

17 In Search of Sound Policy on Nonconsensual Uses of Identifiable Health Data   265

Barbara J. Evans

V   Paradigm Shifts in Research Ethics

Introduction   281

I. Glenn Cohen

18 What Is This Thing Called Research?   285

Zachary M. Schrag

19 What's Right about the "Medical Model" in Human Subjects Research Regulation   299

Heidi Li Feldman

20 Three Challenges for Risk-Based (Research) Regulation: Heterogeneity among Regulated Activities, Regulator Bias, and Stakeholder Heterogeneity   313

Michelle N. Meyer

21 Protecting Human Research Subjects as Human Research Workers   327

Holly Fernandez Lynch

22 Getting Past Protectionism: Is It Time to Take off the Training Wheels?   341

Greg Koski

Appendix: Regulatory Changes in the ANPRM: Comparison of Existing Rules with Some of the Changes Being Considered   349
Contributors   359
Index   363

Series Foreword

I am pleased to present the forty-third book in the Basic Bioethics series. The series makes innovative works in bioethics available to a broad audience and introduces seminal scholarly manuscripts, state-of-the-art reference works, and textbooks. Topics engaged include the philosophy of medicine, advancing genetics and biotechnology, end-of-life care, health and social policy, and the empirical study of biomedical life. Interdisciplinary work is encouraged.

Arthur Caplan

Basic Bioethics Series Editorial Board
Joseph J. Fins
Rosamond Rhodes
Nadia N. Sawicki
Jan Helge Solbakk

Acknowledgments

Putting together a volume with thirty-three cross-disciplinary authors from around the world is no easy feat. The task was made much easier by the help of others. We, of course, extend sincere thanks to each of our authors for their superb contributions and dedication to this effort. Stanley Chen, Jesse King, and Ethan Prall acted as "deputy editors," helping us line edit each of the chapters. Kaitlin Burroughs beautifully managed the inflow and outflow of chapters and helped administer this project more generally. Karl Kobylecki also provided additional research assistance. Kathy Paras and Shannon Sayer helped us mount the May 2012 conference that served as the basis for this volume. That conference was sponsored by the Petrie–Flom Center for Health Law Policy, Biotechnology, and Bioethics at Harvard Law School and the Harvard University Program in Ethics and Health, with financial support from the Oswald DeN. Cammann Fund for Law and Medicine at Harvard University, which we also thank. Finally, Glenn Cohen thanks the Radcliffe Institute for Advanced Studies and the Greenwall Foundation Faculty Scholars Program in Bioethics for support during the editing of this volume.

Introduction

I. Glenn Cohen and Holly Fernandez Lynch

Tens of billions of dollars are spent each year on clinical research of investigational treatments in the United States and around the world (Getz 2010), but clinical trials represent only the tip of the iceberg when it comes to human subjects research. From the scientists involved in multimillion dollar clinical trials of potential HIV vaccines, to the university anthropologist who wants to conduct interviews in Chile of shamans in the Mapuche tribe (or nation as they prefer to be called) to understand the ways in which they attach mystical significance to legal texts, to the psychology graduate student studying how other students allocate funding in a simulated charity, all of these disparate researchers have to wrestle with largely the same framework for regulating human subjects research.

The history and details of this framework—which entails elements of both paternalism and preservation of individual autonomy—are described in greater depth in the next chapter and many of the subsequent ones. In the United States it emerged out of the horrors of the Nazi experiments, confronted by the world in the Doctors' Trials at Nuremberg following World War II, as well as the now-infamous Tuskegee syphilis study conducted by government researchers on poor black men in Alabama from 1932 to 1972. The framework has gone through a number of iterations since the initial regulations for protecting human subjects in research supported or conducted by the Department of Health, Education, and Welfare (the precursor to today's Department of Health and Human Services) were first promulgated in 1974 (Porter and Koski 2008), but its foundational essence has remained largely intact since then.

As the authors in this volume catalog, however, the US regulatory system governing human subjects research has a number of major deficiencies: it is slow, it is expensive, it is inconsistent in part due to its decentralized review system, it fetishizes the formalities of informed consent, and it overprotects patients from small potential risks while failing to compensate them for more serious injuries sustained during research, among many other problems. In general, it seems poorly equipped to deal with the realities of human subjects research in the twenty-first century.

When we first gathered these contributing authors together for a conference at Harvard Law School in May 2012, the system seemed poised for its most significant change since the early 1990s, and perhaps since its inception. In July 2011, DHHS had released a much-touted Advanced Notice of Proposed Rulemaking (ANPRM) titled "Human Subjects Research Protections: Enhancing Protections for Research Subjects and Reducing Burden, Delay, and Ambiguity for Investigators" (DHHS 2011a).[1] This ANPRM proposed to substantially amend the main federal regulations governing human subjects research (known as the "Common Rule") for the first time in more than twenty years. When the public comment period ended, the Department had received more than 1,100 submissions over the course of only three months, signaling the high level of interest in this issue. In addition, in September 2011, President Obama's Commission for the Study of Bioethical Issues made a number of recommendations to improve the regulatory protection of subjects in federally funded research (DHHS 2011b). When combined with the increasing globalization of human subjects research and the attendant need to harmonize divergent approaches, the more frequent conduct of multiregional clinical trials, and increasing research on biospecimens, it appeared that we were at a moment when the regulatory scheme was ripe for a major course correction.

As we write this introduction approaching autumn of 2013, however, the future of the ANPRM looks much less certain, and there has been no additional movement from the government in more than two years. Dr. Jerry A. Menikoff, the current director of the Office for Human Research Protections at DHHS, and the man charged with reconciling the hundreds of comments received on the ANPRM and the views of the multitude of government agencies directly impacted by any change, has tried to put a brave face on the matter, stating that "[t]his is, of course, a complicated undertaking, as was stated from the outset, and it takes time" (Basken 2013). But J. Thomas Puglisi, a former division chief in the same office, was more pessimistic in a commentary he wrote in *The Hastings Center Report*, suggesting that the initiative had "become stalled, at least for the foreseeable future, if not permanently. Given the current political climate and the often divergent interests of the seventeen agencies that adhere to the rule, meaningful systemic modernization of the Common Rule is not likely to occur any time soon." Nonetheless, Puglisi maintained that modernization is "desperately needed" (2013, S40).

Other than Menikoff and Puglisi's vague and somewhat elliptical statements, no one "in the know" has gone on record to explain why the ANPRM process seems to be in paralysis at the moment—if not completely dead. Of course, we can speculate as to why this initiative stalled. Perhaps it was because the interests of those potentially affected by the proposed changes were too heterogeneous. On this line of thought, the ANPRM might have opened up the sutures in the Common Rule that bound together disparate fields of research in terms of methods and values. While these various communities had learned to grudgingly live with the existing Common Rule system, when the opportunity for change arose, it is possible that anything short of a complete overhaul left all parties dissatisfied—and although the ANPRM proposed some substantial change, it is far from a comprehensive rethinking of the current approach to human subjects research regulation. A second and quite different story that might be told has to do with sequestration. In the face of huge cuts to science funding already destabilizing the research community, the powers that be might have decided that reformation of the research ethics rules (which would entail potentially costly training and compliance efforts) should be put off. A third possibility is that the ANPRM's scope was too ambitious, and that some of the issues it aimed to cover—biospecimens, for example—proved to be the third rail of reform and made it difficult to move forward even though many other reforms would have been welcome and uncontroversial had they been separated out. Finally, there is a cynical explanation: everyone is unsatisfied with the existing regulations but there is disagreement as to what type of change is in order, so the ANPRM was just a bone to chew on with no real hope or anticipation of actual change. Indeed there is already an entire industry built on the existing regulations and change would be quite disruptive.

None of these possible explanations are anything more than speculative, and it may be years, if ever, before the inside story of the ANPRM's demise (or at least slumber) will be told. But whatever the reason, the pressing question remains: Where do we go now?

Using the proposed changes suggested by the ANPRM as their launching (and sometimes counter) point, the twenty-two chapters in this volume seek to offer a fresh outlook on the regulatory framework for human subjects research fit for the realities of the twenty-first century university-industrial research complex. Some seek to capitalize on and refine the directions charted by the ANPRM, others seek to show why they are wrongheaded, and still others seek to reengineer human subjects research regulation in entirely new terms, taking analogies from contract, employment law, and medical malpractice.

In our book's first chapter, Amy L. Davis and Elisa A. Hurley set the stage for the rest of this volume by reviewing the history of the US research regulations and the six key changes proposed in the ANPRM:

1. A new approach to calibrate the review process to the level of risk posed by a particular research project.

2. Facilitating the use of a single IRB for multisite research.

3. Changing the requirements for documenting and waiving informed consent.

4. Putting in place mandatory data security protections for identifiable data, including from biospecimens.

5. Harmonizing disparate systems for adverse event reporting and facilitating the aggregation of such reports.

6. Extending the regulations to all research at all facilities that receive federal funding from an agency that requires compliance with these protections, rather than exclusively for the research that these agencies actually fund.

Davis and Hurley then describe the specific public comments on the ANPRM that were submitted to the government by their organization, Public Responsibility in Medicine and Research (PRIM&R), a nonprofit educational organization committed to advancing the highest ethical standards in the conduct of biomedical and social science/behavioral research.

The rest of this volume is divided into five parts, each with its own introduction by an eminent scholar, representing a different avenue for concern about or revision of the existing regulatory structure.

The first part focuses on regulation of risk, and the question of how to strike the appropriate balance between protecting subjects and allowing important research to proceed without unnecessary hindrance. At root, research risks—physical, emotional, and social—are one of the primary reasons that research is regulated at all, but if risk could be eliminated entirely or reduced to negligible levels, a number of questions arise. For example, should consent still be treated as absolutely essential? Should researchers be granted greater discretion and less oversight? Do subjects have other interests that remain in need of protection? Rosamond Rhodes and Ana K. Iltis tackle these issues and others in their chapters comprising part I, ultimately reaching divergent conclusions as to whether the Common Rule is over- or appropriately protective.

The authors in part II, Efthimios Parasidis, Adam Braddock, and Osagie K. Obasogie, bring us back to the historical genesis of the current regulatory framework, namely attempts to develop the appropriate governance structure for research involving vulnerable populations. Here we have a Goldilocks inquiry from the trio, as we are asked to consider whether existing regulations protect various vulnerable groups—military personnel, children, and prisoners—just right, too much, or not enough. Again, identifying the appropriate balance between protection and overprotection emerges as an important theme.

In part III, Michael McDonald, Susan Cox, Anne Townsend, Seema K. Shah, Alexander Morgan Capron, Govind Persad, and Laura Stark introduce the complex cast of characters involved in human subjects research, including subjects themselves, investigators, sponsors, and institutional review boards. At present, the regulations treat subjects in a largely passive way, but several chapters in this section suggest that this approach is mistaken, urging greater attention to the subjects' perspective in research development and oversight, and exploring some specific ways to do so. We are, however, cautioned against some potentially negative consequences of the trend toward conceptualizing subjects as active "participants," and encouraged to impose responsibilities not only on IRBs (who are themselves encouraged to take steps toward greater regulatory consistency) but also on those involved in directly conceiving of and conducting the research. Each chapter in this part raises important questions as to whether the current division of labor contemplated by the existing regulatory structure is the right one.

Part IV's authors, Ellen Wright Clayton, Brett A. Williams, Leslie E. Wolf, Carol Weil, Nicole Lockhart, Hilary Shutak, Benjamin Fombonne, Gail H. Javitt, Suzanne M. Rivera, and Barbara J. Evans, examine data privacy with a particular focus on biospecimens and tissue banking. The authors in this section review the existing regulations governing the use of biological samples and the case law that got us there, confront the clash of paradigms (e.g., property versus privacy), and evaluate the proposed ANPRM approach, in several cases critiquing the ANPRM's emphasis on mandatory general consent for research as both overprotective and potentially meaningless. These authors examine how serious the risk is that information gleaned from de-identified biospecimens could, in accordance with existing law, be re-linked to a particular individual, as well as ways in which the advent of a self-disclosing Facebook generation may alter the balance of interests. Finally, the authors develop potential solutions to some of the privacy concerns at work, including certificates of confidentiality, tiered consent processes, enhanced education, and collaboration with participant communities.

Part V concludes with several fundamental challenges to the current regulatory paradigm, lobbed by Zachary M. Schrag, Michelle N. Meyer, Holly Fernandez Lynch, and Greg Koski, as well as one bid at a partial defense from Heidi Li Feldman. Here, on the one hand, several of our authors see the ANPRM as a possible opening for fundamental regulatory restructuring and throw some new "hats" into the ring for consideration: assume researchers are inherently good, stop treating every attempt to gather information as research, allow subjects more freedom to accept risks according to their own preferences, and start to recognize problematic inconsistencies between the regulatory protections offered to human research subjects and those offered to more traditional workers. On the other hand, we have an argument not against restructuring per se, but more narrowly against the common complaint that social and behavioral research ought to be regulated differently from biomedical research, refocusing the problem human subjects research regulation is aimed at solving as the deprivation of subject autonomy. Taken together, the chapters in this section push us to consider whether the regulatory system we have is one that we should salvage or scrap—a particularly compelling question in light of the way in which the US regulations have been exported, directly and indirectly, around the globe.

After absorbing the many insights offered in the chapters that follow, the hope is that our readers will experience that feeling captured so well by T.S. Eliot in *Little Gidding* (1944, 48):

We shall not cease from exploration
And the end of all our exploring
Will be to arrive where we started
And know the place for the first time.

The fundamental issues at stake are the same as they have always been—balancing protectiveness against autonomy, risks against benefits, efficiency against deontological concerns. But several decades after the current human subjects regulatory framework was first adopted, as the authors in this volume agree, it is not well-suited for the reality of much of the research that will emerge in the twenty-first century and the institutions that will be conducting it; indeed several argue that the framework has had important flaws for quite some time. The attempt to promulgate the ANPRM is a sign that even the regulators in Washington recognized the need for action, and we hope that this once-in-a-generation willingness to seriously contemplate change will be able to overcome the inevitable lethargy that accompanies any attempt to rework a complex system with multitudes of diverse stakeholders. The chapters that follow chart a path toward where we should be going, offering the regulators creative solutions to the most serious infirmities of the existing system, as well as pleas to keep "unfixed" what is not broken.

Moving from the theoretical to the political, what are the key lessons for getting reform through that might be culled from our authors' analyses and the regulators' delay in moving beyond the ANPRM? First, future reforms would do well to package reforms into smaller "chunks" than the ANPRM. While horse trading and compendium bills sometimes have great success in Congress—where one can swallow the bitter if there is enough sweet—the fate of the ANPRM might suggest that when it comes to human subjects research regulation, less may be more and the affected communities can only take so much change at once. Second, the notice-and-comment process for the ANPRM appears to have been more intense than many informed observers, including the progenitors of the reform, might have anticipated. In some ways the comments and viewpoints expressed during this process are the kinds of information that one might have wanted *before* the ANPRM was issued, so that the actual notice-and-comment process could have been quicker and less adversarial. In some ways, President Obama's experience with health reform might have proved useful as a playbook (though not, to be sure, its subsequent implementation). There the Administration rolled out a "charm offensive" with stakeholders, and cut deals in sequence with the most powerful "spoilers" (the insurance and pharmaceuticals industries) at the very start of the process, a kind of divide-and-conquer strategy. Is this the ideal way to do ethics and protect subjects? Not by a long shot, but one of the abiding lessons of the ANPRM process is that reasoned elaboration and analysis may sometimes have to yield to Realpolitik.

At a time when unprecedented amounts of funding, both public and private, are flowing into human subjects research, when the promise of genomics research has never been closer, and when we have finally confronted the ghosts of research ethics violations past (whether in Germany, Guatemala, or on our own soil), we need a regulatory framework that is up for the challenge. Whatever happens with the ANPRM, at the very least, it started a conversation—a conversation that we aim to continue in this volume.

Note

1. For ease of reference, a summary of the key changes proposed by the ANPRM is included as an Appendix to this volume.

References

Basken, Paul. 2013. Federal overhaul of rules for human research hits impasse. *Chronicle of Higher Education*, March 7, 2013. http://chronicle.com/article/Overhaul-of-Rules-for-Human/137811/?cid=at&utm_source=at&utm_medium=en.

Department of Health and Human Services (DHHS). 2011. Advance Notice of Proposed Rulemaking. Human subjects research protections: Enhancing protections for research subjects and reducing burden, delay, and ambiguity for investigators. *Federal Register* 76 (143): 44512–31.

Department of Health and Human Services. Presidential Commission for the Study of Bioethical Issues. 2011b. *Moral Science: Protecting Participants in Human Subjects Research*. Washington, DC: DHHS.

Eliot, T. S. [1944] 1971. Little Gidding. In *Four Quartets 39*. New York: Harcourt Brace Jovanovich.

Getz, Kenneth A. 2010. Sizing up the clinical research market. *Applied Clinical Trials Online*, March 1. http://www.appliedclinicaltrialsonline.com/appliedclinicaltrials/CRO%2FSponsor/Sizing-Up-the-Clinical-Research-Market/ArticleStandard/Article/detail/660749.

Porter, John P., and Greg Koski. 2008. Regulations for the protection of humans in research in the United States. In Ezekiel J. Emanuel, Christine Grady, Robert A. Crouch, Reidar K. Lie, Franklin G. Miller, and David Wendler, eds., *The Oxford Textbook of Clinical Research Ethics*. Oxford: Oxford University Press, 157.

Puglisi, Tom. 2013. Reform within the Common Rule? *Hastings Center Report* 43: S40–42.

1
Setting the Stage: The Past and Present of Human Subjects Research Regulations

Amy L. Davis and Elisa A. Hurley

On July 26, 2011, the Department of Health and Human Services (DHHS) and the Office of Science and Technology Policy (OSTP) issued an Advanced Notice of Proposed Rulemaking (ANPRM) titled, "Human Subjects Research Protections: Enhancing Protections for Research Subjects and Reducing Burden, Delay, and Ambiguity for Investigators." The ANPRM requested public comment on how the current regulations for protecting human research subjects might be modernized and revised to improve efficiency and enhance protections.

The ANPRM represents the first potential revision of the regulations governing federally funded human subjects research in over twenty years; it is no surprise, then, that its publication caused a sensation within the human subjects research community, spawning a mini-industry of analysis, criticism, and speculation over the following year. During the three months the ANPRM was open for comment, DHHS received over 1,100 responses, some exceeding 100 pages in length. Comments came from universities, nonprofit organizations, professional societies, pharmaceutical companies, independent review boards, hospitals, and individuals. Many provisions of the ANPRM were controversial enough to generate equal numbers of supportive and oppositional responses.

During the months since its publication, numerous meetings, conferences, presentations, and papers have critically examined both the general strategy and potential consequences of the ANPRM's proposals. Such controversy increases the challenge of revising the Common Rule.

In this introductory chapter, we set the stage for those that follow by providing a summary of the major regulatory changes proposed in the ANPRM and placing those changes in context. We begin by reviewing the milieu in which the current regulations were developed nearly forty years ago in light of the ANPRM's objective to create a research oversight system better adapted to twenty-first century research and thereby improve protections for human subjects while reducing burdens and ambiguity for investigators and subjects. We then provide a brief outline and summary of the major changes proposed in the ANPRM.

Finally, we critically examine two of the ANPRM's specific proposals: (1) improvements to informed consent and (2) the implementation of a new data security and information protection framework. We argue the ANPRM does little more than tinker with the existing approach to informed consent that is, as most agree, far more successful at protecting institutions than educating potential research subjects, and propose an alternative approach to designing informed consent forms that places them in the context of a consent process. With regard to data security, we argue that the ANPRM's proposal to incorporate the standards set forth in the Health Insurance Portability and Accountability Act of 1996 (HIPAA) into these regulations to enhance privacy protections is flawed because the HIPAA rules are intended to control the *distribution* of private information, which is not a significant risk in the research context where privacy concerns are most relevant during the information *collection* process. We argue that the institutional review board (IRB) is in the best position to assess whether that process will be conducted in a manner that protects the privacy interests of research subjects.

1.1 Regulatory Background of Human Subjects Protections in the United States

A framework for protecting human subjects that emphasized informed consent and the creation of IRBs existed in the United States as early as the 1960s (Surgeon General, PHS 1966; Beecher 1970; Barber et al. 1973). However, it was not until 1974 that formal regulations for human subjects protections were promulgated under the statutory authority of the National Research Act (Porter and Koski 2008). The National Research Act, which was passed in response to a series of well-publicized and egregious research abuses during the first two-thirds of the twentieth century, also established the National Commission for the Protection of Human Subjects of Biomedical and Behavioral Research.

Over the next four years the Commission developed one of the seminal documents for the field of research ethics, titled "Ethical Principles and Guidelines for the Protection of Human Subjects of Research," and more commonly known as the *Belmont Report* (National Commission 1979). This short, elegant document, published in 1979, identified respect for persons, beneficence, and justice as three basic ethical principles that should underlie the conduct of biomedical and behavioral research involving human subjects in the United States. Furthermore the *Belmont Report* explained how those principles were to be applied in research practice by, respectively, (1) obtaining informed consent, (2) minimizing risks and ensuring a generally favorable risk–benefit ratio, and (3) selecting subjects fairly (National Commission 1979). The *Belmont Report* was intended to establish a framework for drafting future regulations and guidance for the protection of human research subjects (McCarthy 2008).

The effort to improve the system for human subjects research implementation and oversight has been ongoing since the system was first established. During the first decade after they were crafted, the human subjects regulations were amended and expanded several times. Under the purview of DHHS, they were revised to incorporate the guidelines outlined in the *Belmont Report*, clarify and add specificity to review requirements, and include special protections for certain categories of research subjects considered "vulnerable," such as children (ACHRE 1995). In 1991, fourteen additional federal agencies and departments adopted the basic regulations (subpart A of 45 CFR 46) as the "Common Rule," in an effort to develop uniform and consistent policies for human subjects research across federal funding bodies (ACHRE 1995).

Today the Common Rule governs research conducted or supported by the eighteen federal departments and agencies that have adopted it. In a nutshell, the Common Rule requires that federally funded researchers obtain documented informed consent from research subjects; outlines requirements for IRB membership, function, operations, and recordkeeping; and delineates specific criteria for different levels of IRB review.

The limits of this regulatory system have been addressed by the US General Accounting Office, the Inspector General, the Institute of Medicine, and a number of national bioethics advisory bodies, among others (ANPRM 2011). The IRB system has been described as inefficient, overburdened, lacking expertise, obstructionist to research, and underfunded (Gunsalus et al. 2006; AAUP 2006). However, as mentioned above, the 2011 ANPRM is the first attempt to substantially revise the Common Rule since 1991.

In addition to these long-standing problems, the authors of the ANPRM acknowledge that the research world has evolved over the last four decades and that criticism about the waning applicability of these regulations to current research conditions is widespread. Contributing to this altered environment are technological and scientific advances such as new medical devices, genomics, the Internet, mobile technologies, and stem cell research—all of which have revolutionized how and by whom research is conducted. The types of settings in which research is conducted have also changed dramatically, as community hospitals, outpatient clinics, secondary schools, and practitioners' offices join the traditional research settings of academic medical centers and universities. Federal research budgets and private investments in research have increased exponentially during this period. The expansion of multi-site and international research further complicates the application of an oversight system designed with single-site research in mind (ANPRM 2011, 44513).

The self-professed goal of the ANPRM therefore is to "modernize" the regulations governing federally funded human subjects research so as to increase protections for subjects "while facilitating valuable research and reducing burden, delay, and ambiguity for investigators" (ANPRM 2011, 44513).

1.2 Provisions of the ANPRM

The ANPRM outlines seven areas of concern with the current regulations as applied to twenty-first century research:

1. Current regulations do not adequately calibrate the review process to the level of risk posed by the research. The result is that IRBs spend an inordinate amount of time reviewing minimal risk research, and consequently have less time and fewer resources to devote to higher risk research.

2. The review by multiple IRBs of multi-site research projects is inefficient, overly bureaucratic, and may actually weaken protections for human subjects by diverting valuable resources from reviews of others studies.

3. Current requirements and practices for obtaining informed consent result in lengthy, complex forms that provide inadequate information for, and protections of, potential subjects.

4. Increasing use of genetic material and health data has created a significant swath of research in which the only risk is the inappropriate release of confidential information; a regulatory framework focused mainly on physical, and to a lesser extent, psychosocial risks, is ill-equipped to protect individuals from these new "informational" risks.

5. Current regulations do not provide an adequate mechanism for monitoring and evaluating the system for protecting human research subjects.

6. Current regulations do not protect all research subjects, but only those who participate in research funded by certain federal agencies.

7. Within the current US research infrastructure, multiple, inconsistent regulatory systems can apply to a single study, making compliance complicated and overly burdensome (ANPRM 2011, 44513–14).

The ANPRM presents the following proposals for revising the regulations to address these concerns:

1. *Revised review framework to improve calibration of the review process to the risk of the research.* The ANPRM proposes a revised framework for the research review system to address what many consider the inefficiencies of IRBs that spend too much time and too many resources on reviewing "minimal risk" research and not enough reviewing riskier studies. Under current regulations, a risk is considered "minimal" when "the probability and magnitude of harm or discomfort anticipated in the research are not greater in and of themselves than those ordinarily encountered in daily life or during the performance of routine physical or psychological examinations or tests" (45 CFR 46.102(i), 2011). The regulations refer to a list of categories of minimal risk research that may be reviewed by the IRB through an expedited review procedure. Expedited review is accomplished by an individual appointee of the IRB chair rather than by a fully convened IRB. Procedures that typically are considered no more than minimal risk include collection of blood or saliva, moderate exercise, medical record chart reviews, quality of life questionnaires, and focus groups. The ANPRM's proposals are intended to better calibrate protection procedures to the level of risk inherent in a particular research project than does this current approach. For example, social and behavioral research that is conducted through surveys and interviews mostly presents only informational risks deriving from the inappropriate release of sensitive information that could harm study subjects. Nevertheless, currently many of these studies are subjected to full IRB review (ANPRM 2011, 44515). Under the revised framework, mandatory data security and information protection standards, based on the HIPAA Privacy Rule, would be established to protect identifiable information collected in research. Pre-established procedures for protecting research data would adequately minimize informational risks, and obviate the need for IRB review of the measures taken to protect private information, according to the ANPRM authors. This strategy would in fact eliminate the need for IRBs to review research that poses informational risks only. Critics of the current reliance on IRBs for this protection

argue that IRB members are not necessarily experts on data protection. (ANPRM 2011, 44516) Moreover there is no evidence that IRBs actually protect subjects from informational risks. Mandating the application of pre-established data security and information protection standards calibrated to the level of identifiability of the information collected would adequately minimize informational risks without the involvement of the IRB. Accordingly the ANPRM proposes that only research that involves non-informational risks such as potential physical or psychological harm would be subject to IRB oversight and review. Under the ANPRM framework, research involving greater than minimal risk would still require full IRB review. Expedited review categories would be broadened to include more research activities and would carry with them the presumption that studies involving only the activities listed in the expedited review categories constitute minimal risk research, unless special circumstances are presented that justify closer scrutiny. This represents a change from the current expedited review framework, which requires an IRB determination that the study as a whole is minimal risk even if all of the activities included in the study are on the published list of activities eligible for expedited review. In addition the ANPRM would eliminate continuing review of expedited research, which would further release IRB resources for greater risk research (ANPRM 2011, 44515). Furthermore the ANPRM would remove the concept of "exempt" research from the regulations and redefine the activities that are currently considered "exempt" as "excused" research. According to the Common Rule, there are certain categories of research involving human subjects that may be declared exempt from further review by the IRB, including research involving educational tests, surveys, interviews, and observation of public behavior if the subjects are already public figures or cannot be individually identified; research involving existing, publicly available data; and demonstration projects (45 CFR 46.101(b), 2011). The ANPRM proposes to redefine such activities as "excused" research on the grounds that such activities would still be subject to the mandatory data security and information protection standards mentioned above, and to consent requirements in some cases. The categories of "excused" (formerly "exempt") activities would be broadened to reflect the new framework that excuses all research posing only informational risks from IRB review. These revisions would excuse from IRB review all survey research and research involving identifiable biospecimens and other data (ANPRM 2011, 44515). As the volume of research has grown, IRBs' workloads have increased dramatically. Given the tendency of IRBs to err on the side of caution when evaluating potential risks, IRBs spend more time reviewing minimal risk research than is appropriate. According to the ANPRM authors, this revised framework will significantly reduce this burden by narrowing the range of studies subject to full IRB review (ANPRM 2011, 44516).

2. Increased use of single IRB of record for multisite research. Although not required by the regulations, the current norm for research conducted at multiple locations is to undergo local IRB review at each individual research site. To eliminate the redundancies, inconsistencies, and delays that often result, the ANPRM proposes a requirement that all domestic sites in a multisite study rely upon a single IRB of record for institutional compliance with IRB review requirements contained in the regulations. Local institutions would still be obligated to protect human subjects in accord with the regulations, and could conduct internal ethics reviews outside the regulatory process, at their discretion (ANPRM 2011, 44521-22).

3. Revised requirements for informed consent documentation. Regarding informed consent, the ANPRM considers several revisions to the current process. First, it proposes revising the content requirements for informed consent forms to clarify what information is necessary for inclusion, to restrict inclusion of inappropriate information and institutional boilerplate, to limit the length, and to prescribe how the information is presented within consent documents. Second, the ANPRM seeks input on how to clarify the criteria for the waiver of consent and the waiver of documentation of consent provisions to lessen confusion around and perceived inconsistency in the current regulations. Finally, the ANPRM explains that the Common Rule permits investigators to use general language in consent forms to describe and ask for permission for future research using biospecimens and other data, while HIPAA requires that such authorizations be study specific. The ANPRM solicits input about how to harmonize these conflicting requirements (ANPRM 2011, 44522-23).

4. Implementation of mandatory data security standards. As discussed above, informational risks are dependent on the identifiability of health data. "Identifiability" is a concept that has changed significantly in recent years, thanks to advances in genetics and technologies that increasingly allow the identification of an individual even from so-called de-identified data. For example, researchers have demonstrated that analysis of public genetic genealogy databases, in combination with other publicly available data, can be used to identify individuals (Gymrek et al. 2013).

Indeed complete de-identification of biospecimens is increasingly difficult due to these advances (ANPRM 2011, 44524). The authors of the ANPRM therefore propose categorizing all research involving the primary collection, storage, and secondary analysis of biospecimens as research involving identifiable information—in other words, as human subjects research. As a consequence all research using biospecimens would for the first time require informed consent. Again, the ANPRM looks to HIPAA as a model for providing more effective protection for identifiable health information collected for research. Not only will this strategy create greater harmony between the HIPAA Privacy Rule requirements and the Common Rule, the ANPRM authors contend, it will broaden the scope of data requiring privacy protection (ANPRM 2011, 44525). The ANPRM proposes the application of HIPAA-like data security and information protection standards to all prospective collections of data and biospecimens. The current Common Rule definition of identifiability is narrower than that established under HIPAA. Private information is considered identifiable under the Common Rule if the identity of the subject "is or may readily be ascertained by the investigator..." (45 CFR 46.102(f)(2), 2011). Under HIPAA, eighteen specified identifiers must be removed from the data for it to be considered "unidentifiable." Therefore research data that are not considered identifiable under the Common Rule may be considered identifiable under the HIPAA standards, and would require protection if the HIPAA standards are applied to research. To address the concern that these standards may be overly protective to the extent that they inhibit research, the ANPRM authors would also apply to research data the "limited data set" rules found in the HIPAA law. These rules allow research on data that has been stripped of direct identifiers but that may retain certain other identifying elements, so long as the terms of use are defined in a data use agreement (ANPRM 2011, 44525).

5. Changes to adverse event reporting system. Current regulations regarding how to report safety data are criticized as inconsistent and unclear. For example, the Common Rule requires investigators to report "unanticipated problems" while the FDA requires investigators to report certain "adverse events." The relationship between, and respective definitions of, these terms are unclear and confusing. Moreover the data that are reported under these requirements are stored in different locations, making it impossible to compile and analyze study safety data from multiple sources. Accordingly the ANPRM proposes the following changes to this system: (1) harmonization across all agencies of terminology, scope of data to be reported, and timing of reports, and (2) the establishment of a single website for the electronic reporting of all adverse events and unanticipated problems (ANPRM 2011, 44527).

6. *Extended application of federal human subjects research regulations.* The ANPRM proposes the extended application of the Common Rule to all studies involving human subjects conducted at US institutions that receive any federal funding from a Common Rule agency. Currently domestic institutions have the discretion to apply the Common Rule regulations to research not strictly covered by it that is conducted at their site, such as research funded by a non–Common Rule adopting agency. This change would mandate that further application (ANPRM 2011, 44528).

7. *Harmonization of regulatory guidance.* The ANPRM does not propose a change to accomplish greater harmonization of guidance issued by Common Rule agencies; it merely seeks input on the desirability and appropriateness of uniformity in this area (ANPRM 2011, 44528).

In the following chapters the authors will explore in greater detail and depth some of the issues raised by the ANPRM provisions summarized above. We conclude this introductory chapter with a few critical comments about the ANPRM, from our perspective as representatives of a research ethics education organization.

1.3 PRIM&R's Comments

Public Responsibility in Medicine and Research (PRIM&R) is a nonprofit educational organization committed to advancing the highest ethical standards in the conduct of biomedical and social science/behavioral research. It accomplishes this mission through education, membership services, professional certification, and public policy initiatives. PRIM&R's comments submitted in response to the ANPRM emphasized the impact of its proposals on the appropriate protection of human subjects in research.

Echoing those comments, we note here three major blind spots in the general direction and approach taken by the authors of the ANPRM, and then critically examine two of its specific proposals: (1) improvements to informed consent and (2) the implementation of a new data security and information protection framework.

First, we disagree with provisions in the ANPRM that would require IRBs to justify any oversight or review procedures that would exceed the standards established by the revised rules. IRBs should never be required to report or justify additional measures they adopt to augment protection of human subjects. Federal regulations are considered *minimum* standards for protection, and in our view, to exceed those standards should be encouraged and supported even if it will increase administrative burden and delay the research (Rachlin 2011). Efficiency itself is not a moral imperative or an ethical value, and we believe that human subjects protections should never be compromised by a desire for increased efficiency.

Second, we flag the failure of the ANPRM to emphasize the need and value of robust education for IRB members, chairs, and investigators as a way to enhance protections and efficiency—given that so much of the inefficiency that is criticized in the human research protection system can be traced to inadequate knowledge about how to apply and interpret the current regulations.

Third, we are concerned about the ANPRM's failure to address the vital role that investigators, institutions, and sponsors play in the human subjects regulation system (Rachlin 2011). The rules include and apply to *all* stakeholders in human subjects research. It is the institution and sponsor who are responsible for protecting the safety and welfare of research subjects, and it is the investigator who is responsible for designing ethical studies and implementing an effective informed consent process. These essential responsibilities fade from mind if the regulations speak only to IRBs, as the ANPRM seems to.

1.4 Informed Consent

The ANPRM's overall approach to improving the informed consent process is disappointing. Its almost exclusive focus on consent forms rather than processes is a significant failure to address the most crucial aspect of ethical human subjects research, and in the end, this amounts to little more than tinkering with an approach to informed consent that many agree is hopelessly broken. We argue that improving the informed consent process so that it adequately protects and respects research subjects requires, in part, recalling the original purpose of documentation, namely to memorialize what transpired during the informed consent process. The documentation should not serve as the primary method of informing potential subjects of the risks, benefits, and alternatives to enrolling in a research project.

We agree with the authors of the ANPRM that the forms currently used for informed consent in research have become too long, complicated, and "legalistic." And the more they become so, the less useful they are to potential subjects as sources of information. Indeed today's informed consent forms seem to be designed primarily to provide legal protection for institutions, sponsors, and investigators. They also tend to include every piece of information that pertains to the study, regardless of how useful it might be to a potential subject's decision about whether to participate.

In response, we offer a three-pronged proposal for improving the informed consent process by improving informed consent documents. We propose, first, a shift in the terminology for referring to the documents that contain subject information, from "informed consent forms/documents" to "educational material for potential subjects." We believe this would immediately change understanding of the *purpose* of these materials. Asking subjects to sign long consent "documents" further perpetuates the understanding that these materials have primarily legal implications rather than informational ones. Furthermore, when they are conceptualized as "educational materials for potential subjects," it becomes even clearer that they should be written in language prospective subjects can understand.

This terminology change also underscores the idea that it is not necessary to include in one document *every* piece of information that is potentially useful to a subject. We propose that the information that is in the *primary* educational materials (which replaces the consent document) be instead pared down to the following six provisions, where relevant:

1. A clear statement that "You are being asked to be in a research project, which means the primary purpose is not to treat you, but to gain new knowledge about. . . ."

2. A description of research procedures that a subject would not encounter if she were solely a patient receiving standard treatment.

3. A single list of expected side effects (not "risks") and benefits associated with participating in the study, regardless of which study drug or intervention may cause each (rather than multiple lists of repeated side effects and benefits for each drug).[1]

4. A statement that risks and potential benefits are inherent in all research, with an explanation that risks are bad things that are not expected to happen but that *could* happen. This provision should also include a list of any risks or potential benefits that are unique to the particular study.

5. A statement that the decision to enroll is entirely voluntary and that all standard treatments will still be available if the individual chooses not to enroll in research.

6. A statement that "You are free to withdraw from the study at any time for any reason, even though, in some cases, the actual process of withdrawal must be gradual to prevent harm."

Second, we suggest that potential subjects also be provided with an information booklet that includes all of the other information that is relevant to potential and current subjects, namely "boilerplate" provisions found in every document an institution uses for research permissions, such as the rights of all research subjects to privacy; whom to call with questions or concerns; how research injury is dealt with; the non-waiver of rights; the purpose and agreed-upon societal benefits of research with human subjects (e.g., that this research may help others in the future who suffer from the condition in question); and the risks inherent in all research (e.g., worsening of disease). The rationale for including these in a separate, secondary information document is that they are not matters to which a subject "consents"; nevertheless, all potential and current subjects should be aware of all research risks and protections that are offered to all research subjects.

The third prong of our proposal emphasizes that actual consent occurs during a conversation in which the researcher and the potential subject discuss the study and the information in the educational materials. The potential subject "consents" to participate by orally affirming to the person with whom she is having the consent conversation what she has agreed to. The *documentation* of consent would then be accomplished by the subject's signing a separate brief form that accompanies the educational materials provided, and that indicates that the subject has read and, more important, *discussed* those materials and, having done so, agrees to participate in the research.

1.6 Privacy Provisions of the ANPRM

The ANPRM, as discussed above, would rely on the HIPAA definition of identifiable data and related privacy rules for the protection of research subjects' privacy. The rationale for this proposal is that mandating uniform data security and information protection standards provides greater consistency among multiple regulatory systems. Moreover the risk of inappropriate disclosure of confidential information is basically the same across research proposals. If the only risk of the research is informational in nature, the same procedures will provide adequate protection regardless of other study characteristics. Accordingly the application of uniform standards would reduce the need for IRB review of such risks and the procedures for minimizing them.

While we agree that informational risks are fairly consistent across most studies, and that general standards may be useful for preventing the inappropriate disclosure or re-identification of confidential data, we are opposed to this strategy. We believe there is a stark distinction to be made between research and medical information, and therefore the HIPAA standards, which may provide appropriate protections for medical records, do not provide an appropriate framework for the protection of confidential "research data."

The HIPAA rules are intended to control the release of private medical information to entities such as insurers, law enforcement officers, and other physicians to ensure consistent and informed care for patients. Medical records are created when patients interact with health care professionals. They contain test results, drug information, and medical histories that are regularly distributed to these third parties and are therefore appropriately protected under the HIPAA provisions. Research records, on the contrary, mostly contain data in which no one but researchers would have any interest. Since there is no need to release such data to third parties, there is less risk of inadvertent disclosure of private information. We are in fact aware of no instances of unauthorized release of research data. Therefore the need to de-identify data to the extent possible is not as critical for research data as it is for medical data. Limiting researchers' access to data that have not been stripped of eighteen specific identifiers, or reconstituted in *limited data sets,* amounts to *overprotection* in the research context and will inhibit the conduct of research—results that the ANPRM intends to avoid. Thus the complex and cumbersome system established by HIPAA is neither appropriate nor necessary for protecting research data.

We propose an alternative system for protecting research data. For this proposal, any data collected in the context of an IRB-approved research project would automatically constitute *research* data and be stored separately from medical or other clinical records in accordance with generally applicable standards as proposed by the ANPRM. However, we note that appeal to such preexisting standards for maintaining and storing confidential data is not sufficient for protecting privacy during the *collection* of that data. Collecting data usually involves an interaction with research subjects and thus raises questions about when, where, and how sensitive information is obtained from them. In our view, an IRB is the most appropriate entity to assess whether the proposed data collection procedures will adequately protect subjects' privacy. Once data have been collected, however, questions about appropriate methods for maintaining, moving, sharing, or destroying the data are matters that need not concern the IRB, assuming that there are other effective and enforced privacy mechanisms in place.

We are also opposed to a system that would require consent or "data use agreements" for sharing "unidentified" data, as proposed in the ANPRM and as required under HIPAA. The risk that individuals could be identified and harmed from the *research* use of "unidentified" data is so minimal that the application of these additional requirements would constitute a misapplication of protection. We recommend an alternative system that would allow primary researchers (i.e., those who collect the data for research) to share unidentified research data, including stored biospecimens, with other bona fide researchers (i.e., secondary researchers) without subject consent on the ground that this sharing of information would require no additional interaction with subjects. Furthermore a definition of what constitutes "unidentified" data need not be as stringent as the HIPAA definition of "de-identified" data. We suggest that data be considered adequately *unidentified* if secondary researchers cannot identify the person from whom the data were derived without taking additional steps.

Finally, we believe that a strong enforcement system based on preestablished privacy standards would strengthen protections for research subjects. Human subjects protection rules should make it a crime to intentionally release identifiable research data, or re-identify de-identified research data, without subject consent unless it is absolutely necessary for the protection of the subject. In addition to criminal sanctions, violators should be made ineligible for future federal funding.

These rules could make existing data and specimens available for research without additional review because there would be no additional interaction with human subjects. Moreover the potential for unauthorized release of identified research data would be deterred by strong sanctions. Thus we believe this system provides stronger protections for subjects and better facilitates the use of collected data for research.

1.7 Conclusion

The following chapters will present in-depth explorations of how to regulate risk and protect vulnerable subjects, innovative proposals for redefining the role of the IRB, and critical analyses of privacy and consent in the age of biobanking and genetic research. If the ANPRM does not directly result in new human subjects research regulations, it has at least inspired a renewed examination and discussion of how to effectively protect research subjects without inhibiting the advancement of science, an outcome that we can all support.[2]

Notes

1. PRIM&R's submitted comments did not discuss whether expected or potential benefits should be included in either the primary educational materials or any other consent-related documentation. Thus the inclusion of expected and potential benefits in the educational documents should be understood as our addition, and not a reflection of PRIM&R's official comments.

2. We would like to thank the following members of PRIM&R's 2011 Board of Directors and Public Policy Committee for participating in the discussions that led to PRIM&R's official comments on the ANPRM and, ultimately, to this chapter: A. Cornelius Baker, Joseph J. Byrne, Alexander Capron, David Borasky, Susan S. Fish, George Gasparis, Cynthia A. Gómez, Moira Keane, Paula Knudson, Susan Z. Kornetsky, Robert J. Levine, Charles R. McCarthy, Judy Norsigian, P. Pearl O'Rourke, Ada Sue Selwitz, Barbara Stanley, Walter L. Straus, Jeremy M. Sugarman, and Hugh Tilson. We owe a special debt of gratitude to Executive Director Joan Rachlin and to Public Policy Committee Chair and Board member Leonard Glantz for their wise leadership during the comment development process, and for encouraging us to make this work our own.

References

American Association of University Professors (AAUP). 2006. *Research on Human Subjects*. Washington, DC: Academic Freedom and the Institutional Review Board.

Barber, Bernard, John J. Lally, Julia Loughlin Makarushka, and Daniel Sullivan. 1973. *Research on Human Subjects: Problems of Social Control in Medical Experimentation*. New York: Russell Sage.

Beecher, Henry K. 1970. *Research and the Individual: Human Studies*. Boston: Little, Brown.

Department of Energy. Office of Health, Safety and Security. 1995. Advisory Committee on Human Radiation Experiments: Final Report (ACHRE), ch. 14. http://www.hss.doe.gov/healthsafety/ohre/roadmap/achre/chap14.html.

Department of Health and Human Services (DHHS). 2011. Advance Notice of Proposed Rulemaking. Human subjects research protections: Enhancing protections for research subjects and reducing burden, delay, and ambiguity for investigators. *Federal Register* 76 (143): 44512–31.

Gunsalus, C. K., M. Edward, Bruner, Nicholas C., Burbules, Leon Dash, Matthew Finkin, Joseph P. Goldberg, William T. Greenough, Gregory A. Miller, and Michael G. Pratt. 2006. The Illinois White Paper: Improving the system for protecting human subjects: Counteracting IRB "Mission Creep." The Center for Advanced Study, Urbana Champagne. www.gunsalus.net/IllinoisWhitePaperMissionCreep.pdf.

Gymrek, Melissa, Amy L. McGuire, David Golan, Eran Halperin, and Yaniv Erlich. 2013. Identifying personal genomes by surname inference. Science 339 (6117): 321–24. http://www.sciencemag.org/content/339/6117/321.

McCarthy, Charles R. 2008. The origins and policies that govern institutional review boards. In Ezekiel J. Emanuel, Christine Grady, Robert A. Crouch, Reidar K. Lie, Franklin G. Miller, and David Wendler, eds., *The Oxford Textbook of Clinical Research Ethics*. Oxford: Oxford University Press, 541–51.

National Commission for the Protection of Human Subjects of Biomedical and Behavioral Research. 1979. *The Belmont Report: Ethical Principles and Guidelines for the Protection of Human Subjects of Research*. Washington, DC: GPO.

Porter, John P., and Greg Koski. 2008. Regulations for the protection of humans in research in the United States. In Ezekiel J. Emanuel, Christine Grady, Robert A. Crouch, Reidar K. Lie, Franklin G. Miller, and David Wendler, eds., *The Oxford Textbook of Clinical Research Ethics*. Oxford: Oxford University Press, 157.

Rachlin, Joan. 2011. Public responsibility in medicine and research. *PRIM&R Comments on ANPRM*. https://www.primr.org/uploadedFiles/PRIMR_Site_Home/Public_Policy/Recently_Files_Comments/PRIMR_ANPRM_comments_10.26.11.pdf.

Surgeon General, Public Health Service (PHS) to the Heads of the Institutions Conducting Research with Public Health Service Grants.1966. Clinical research and investigation involving human beings. ACHRE No. HHS-090794-A. PHSCC, Washington, DC.

I
Regulation of Risk

Introduction to Part I—Regulation of Risk

Nir Eyal

Participation in some studies is medically far safer than in the studies that defined research ethics and inspired its regulatory framework. Consider post-approval drug follow-up; observational studies that use publicly available data; many surveys; secondary studies of stored tissue. These studies do not test unapproved biomedical substances on any person. Do they require the protections suitable for paradigm clinical studies? Or can their regulation be lighter?

On the face of it, Rosamond Rhodes's and Ana Iltis's contributions to this volume present opposing approaches to this question. Rhodes laments the red tape of so much research review, and proposes a new category of research, which she calls "*de minimis* risk." Research falling in this rubric involves less risk than what we already categorize as "minimal risk." One example is secondary studies on stored tissue. Normally they pose absolutely no physical risk to the body. The regulation of such studies, Rhodes argues, ought to be dramatically relaxed. Rarely should they require informed consent or independent review—except for brief initial review to confirm that they are *de minimis* risk. Recognizing that some studies are *de minimis* risk would also highlight the rationale behind the already relaxed regulation of "minimal risk" and "exempt" studies. The point of the light regulation of all is that research regulation is necessary only inasmuch as risks are substantial.

One proposal within the 2011 ANPRM is to eliminate continuing review of minimal risk research (as determined by brief initial review). Iltis criticizes this proposal. Her position might initially seem diametrically opposed to Rhodes's position on *de minimis* risk research. Iltis accuses the ANPRM proposal of several fallacious assumptions, namely that there are (virtually) no errors in the initial classification of studies as minimal risk; that a study's risks cannot increase over time; that the value of a study cannot decrease in its course, thus altering its risk to value ratio;

that potential participants' perceptions of these matters are unimportant or insensitive to whether active oversight continues; and finally, that when a study, even a low-risk study, fails to recruit enough participants for its successful completion, it remains permissible to pursue.

On the face of it, Rhodes's and Iltis's contributions are at opposite ends of a logical spectrum regarding minimal risk study regulation and oversight. While Rhodes supports deregulation and lighter oversight for these studies, Iltis supports persisting, active oversight for all studies. However, for the most part, both Rhodes and Iltis could agree that *if* a study were *known* to be and expected to remain very minimal risk, *then* much of the need for oversight would vanish. The difference between their conclusions may stem primarily (though not entirely) from the fact that Rhodes speaks at the level of objective obligations and Iltis, at the level of subjective or epistemic ones. Rhodes supports light regulation for objectively safe experiments and Iltis, heavy regulation for experiments that initially seem objectively safe but that may turn out to be objectively unsafe.

Consider, as an analogy, a pill that would cure patient Joe of his mild disease with no side effects, but that his physician erroneously takes to be unsafe because that pill often kills patients. What the physician fails at the time to appreciate (and any colleague would also fail to appreciate given the state of medical knowledge) is that the active ingredient that kills patients works through interaction with a certain enzyme, which Joe happens to lack. Therefore, objectively, Joe would be cured safely if he took the pill.

What should we say, then: ought Joe's physician to prescribe the pill to Joe? There is a sense in which the physician ought to prescribe it—because it would cure Joe safely; and a sense in which the physician ought *not* to prescribe it—because according to physicians' best knowledge at the time, the pill may well kill Joe. Both senses matter. One sense is objective: the pill is objectively safe and helpful, and should be prescribed. Another sense is subjective or epistemic: contemporaneous evidence suggests that the pill is unsafe, so (in that evidence-dependent sense) it should *not* be prescribed.

Applying the analogy to minimal risk research, Rhodes and Iltis might be talking about different things, rather than engaging each other's positions. Rhodes might be focused exclusively on objectively *de minimis* risk research and Iltis, on research that initially, based on the evidence available at the time, seems safe, but that might still turn out to be risky.

To identify the appropriate level of regulation and oversight for (objectively/subjectively) very low-risk research would have both practical and philosophical importance. Coming years are expected to see a rise in post-approval drug research, observational research on electronic health records, and other (seemingly) physically low-risk studies.

In addition identifying the appropriate level of regulation and oversight for very low-risk studies may help research ethicists explore a surprisingly neglected question: What is the exact goal or purpose of human subject research regulation and oversight, in general?

Let me clarify the question. Obviously research participants usually *should* be offered protections against very dangerous or very disrespectful studies, even when these studies would have otherwise advanced scientific, medical, and public health knowledge, and the public's health. What is the reason that often we should forgo these opportunities to promote knowledge and health?

The main justifications to date assume that in the pursuit of collective goals such as knowledge and population health it remains morally wrong to subject identified individuals, even volunteers, to high medical risk from active intervention in their bodies. But any justification founded on this assumption seems moot in the case of minimal risk studies. They do not subject anyone to high medical risk. That makes minimal risk studies good test cases for the view that what research regulation and oversight are responding to is in part altogether different concerns. Take concerns about the sheer invasion or intervention in someone's body without her consent, or about the use of her "own" body to profit without sharing benefits with her. These concerns may arise about low-risk research as well, for example, about unauthorized studies on donated body tissue and patient information, and about studies of safe and approved substances that do not share financial profits with those whose bodies were used in the investigation. Do we want to insist that even in these minimal risk studies, and assuming that they were bound to remain minimal risk, intense regulation and review remain necessary? If they are *un*necessary, that may suggest that non–risk-related ethical concerns about reciprocity, autonomy, and so forth, are more imagined than real.

This way whether regulation and oversight are needed for low-risk studies is a clue to identifying the exact problem for which research regulation and oversight are appropriate policy responses. If intuitively there is no problem with a minimal risk study that is performed without benefit sharing and without informed consent, then reciprocity and autonomy might lack the general value that many (bio)ethicists have assigned them. The ethics of minimal risk research could thus shed light on the general point of research ethics and on the best ways to conduct, regulate, and oversee high-risk medical investigations as well.

2

De minimis Risk: A Suggestion for a New Category of Research Risk

Rosamond Rhodes[1]

A sign posted on the New Jersey Turnpike declares: "Inspired. Absolute. Infallible." Those declarations refer to the Bible, but it struck me that a number of people who work with research regulation and oversight have a similar attitude toward the Common Rule. I see this and other twentieth-century statements of research ethics as impressive first tries at formulating groundbreaking and complex rules for governing human subjects research. But I also find it hard to imagine that the authors of such could, on their first try, have adequately foreseen the future developments of technology and advances in scientific approaches to understanding the world so as to perfectly formulate the ideal and eternal rules for governing human subjects research. Yet the posture of the Common Rule's many defenders suggests that they regard the current rules as "Inspired. Absolute. Infallible." In this climate of commitment to the perfection of the Common Rule, I am skeptical of whether the Department of Health and Human Services' 2011 ANPRM (DHHS 2011) will actually achieve its goal of meaningful reform.

Many critics have noted that current research regulations and institutional review board (IRB) policies impede research and limit or even discourage learning from clinical practice (Emanuel and Menikoff 2011; Emanuel et al. 2004; Fost and Levine 2007; Resnick 2005). I join their ranks, taking issue with the effects of the rules and their institutional implementation.

For this discussion I will focus my criticism specifically on policies related to informed consent and privacy protection that scientists find especially burdensome, time-consuming, and costly (Kulynych and Korn 2002; IDS 2009). Informed consent is an important consideration in the ethical design of human subjects research, particularly in clinical trials of novel interventions that are likely to involve significant burdens and risks. Starting with the Nuremberg Code's pronouncement that informed consent is "absolutely essential" (Nuremberg Military Tribunals 1949–1953), research ethics codes, declarations, and other documents that set standards for human subjects research have maintained a similarly strict requirement for informed consent.

In some circumstances, however, there may be strong and overriding reasons for proceeding with studies without informed consent. Many people, such as infants, profoundly mentally retarded individuals, the unconscious, and the demented cannot provide informed consent. Often surrogate consent may be sufficient for enrolling subjects in a study, and sometimes, for example, in emergency situations, studies may ethically proceed without consent. In such circumstances we can rely upon presumed prior consent, a well-accepted concept from political philosophy, to explain why informed consent may not be necessary. When a choice is eminently reasonable, the kind of choice that no rational person could reasonably refuse to endorse, we presume that the individual involved is such a rational and reasonable person, and proceed *as if* the individual involved had actually made the choice.[2] When the risks involved in a study are miniscule or the harms are not significant and only short-lived, the anticipated benefits to the individual or society can justify participation based on hypothetical presumed prior consent, as the current regulations sometimes allow.

The problem with today's informed consent requirements is that for some projects that pose only negligible risks to participants, it is essentially impossible to meet existing regulatory requirements for informed consent. Some scientific studies such as public health surveillance (PHS, monitoring the health of a community), quality assurance (QA, systematic documentation and analysis of hospital activities), and quality improvement (QI, formal analysis of performance) are categorized as activities that are exempt from compliance with the informed consent requirement, and they are not counted as "research." Yet what counts as research and what does not is hard to discern because its defining characteristics are not conceptually clear. Some activities that employ new computer technologies to learn from large data sets cannot be undertaken without running afoul of informed consent requirements, for example (Angrist 2010; Fost and Kudsk 2004).

In response to these problems, rather than offering modifications to the existing framework, I will identify a critical oversight in the regulations and offer a solution that could make them more coherent. First, however, I will explain two problems that arise because of the current regulations. The recommendation that I offer has implications for several areas that the proposed reforms aim to address: currently exempt activities, informed consent requirements, using leftover clinical samples, survey research, and minimizing information risks.

2.1 One Problem: Confusion and Inconsistency

Although PHS, QI, and QA studies provide important social benefits, the criteria for drawing a line between what counts as research and what does not are vague. The Common Rule defines "research" as "a systematic investigation, including research development, testing and evaluation, designed to develop or contribute to generalizable knowledge" (45 CFR 46.102(d)). Yet all scientific studies are systematic and designed to produce knowledge, and all knowledge is generalizable, regardless of whether it comes from activities that are identified as "research" or PHS, QI, or QA.

Data garnered from PHS are analyzed, and the conclusions that follow from the analysis are the knowledge that supports interventions to contain infection, improve health and clinical outcomes, and prevent further spread of diseases. Similarly QA data provide the knowledge that guides hospitals to assure the quality of their care. The knowledge generated from QA data allows institutions to detect and rectify practices that put people at risk, including deviations from standard operating procedures and unforeseen results of new cost containment measures. And data from QI activities can lead to knowledge that is used to alter practice so as to achieve the highest quality care at the most reasonable cost. Analysis of QI data provides the knowledge base that allows institutions to compare the quality and efficiency of their performance to national databases, to implement programs that improve patient outcomes, and to avoid errors (Cohen et al. 2008). Even when a QI activity is initially intended to apply to a single setting, whatever is learned can surely be applied in other similar settings.

It is therefore not surprising that institutions and public health agencies are confused about what to call their studies (Kofke and Rie 2003; Kass et al. 2003). The controversy over whether Peter J. Pronovost's famous checklist study should have been counted as research or QI is a case in point (Baily 2008; Miller and Emanuel 2008; Flanagan, Philpott, and Strosberg 2011; Pronovost et al. 2006; Pritchard 2008; Gawande 2007). Dr. Pronovost and his institution determined that his standard of care interventions were QI; therefore IRB review and obtaining informed consent from each ICU patient involved in the study were not required. If instead they had determined that the study was research, the IRB would have had to review it and the investigators would have had to obtain informed consent from each involved patient. As a QI activity, every patient could have been included in the study. As research, patients or surrogates could have withheld consent, thereby excluding relevant data, introducing possible data bias, and potentially skewing the findings. The point is that numerous experts disagreed about whether the Pronovost study was QI or research and who the study subjects actually were. There is no ethically or scientifically significant distinction between QI and research in that both activities are theory-driven, hypothesis-based, and both involve systematic collection of data, analysis, and drawing actionable conclusions that count as knowledge.

Even though most PHS, QA, and QI activities are appropriately overseen by an agency or institutional committee, as exempt activities there is no regulatory framework that requires their review and oversight. The current regulations create informed consent obstacles that sometimes amount to unreasonable burdens, particularly when the risks involved are negligible. At the same time, by exempting PHS, QA, and QI from all regulatory requirements, regulations may do too little to assure participants and the public that these activities are well designed and involve only reasonable risks. As typically occurs, review and oversight by an agency or internal committee should be required for all of these activities. Institutional review brings what may otherwise be concealed into the light; it provides extra sets of eyes to assess the appropriateness of what is proposed, and it assigns responsibility for the project to both the individual scientist and the institution.

Often there is no significant difference between scientific activities called "research" and those given other names. Rather, there is only a stipulation framed in uninformative terms. In contrast, the most ethically significant difference between studies is the likelihood and seriousness of risk to which human subjects are exposed and the importance and likelihood of the expected benefits. As such, the regulatory focus should be directed toward the assessment of participants' exposure to risk in relation to anticipated benefits, rather than to deciding whether or not a study is "designed to develop or contribute to generalizable knowledge" and should be considered "research."

2.2 Another Problem: Genome and Microbiome Research

The advent of genetic biobanks (that physically or electronically store human DNA), sample banks (that store samples of human tissue or products), human microbiome research (that investigates the bacteria, viruses, and fungi that live on us and in us and interact with the human genome), and new computer technologies has allowed scientists to conduct new kinds of investigations and share data across the globe. These developments have also exacerbated some problems in research ethics and created new difficulties.

Many biobanks and sample banks obtain consent from sample donors. When samples are collected, neither researchers nor donors can know the full extent of their future use in research projects. Although donors can give blanket consent for their samples' future research use, they cannot provide meaningful "informed" consent to any specific future studies because they have no information about those studies. When blanket consent is obtained, biobanks and sample banks are unable to conform with several of the General Requirements for informed consent enumerated in the Common Rule, such as providing "an explanation of the purposes of the research and the expected duration of the subject's participation," "a description of any benefits to the subject or to others," and "the approximate number of subjects involved in the study" (45 CFR 46.116(a)–(b)). Although the Common Rule already permits IRBs to waive requirements for informed consent when "[t]he research involves no more than minimal risk to the subjects" and when "[t]he research could not practicably be carried out without the waiver or alteration," IRBs may be reluctant to grant waivers, particularly for studies involving genetic material (45 CFR 46.116(c)–(d)).

To avoid the informed consent problem, some centers resort to anonymizing samples (Clayton 2005). This makes it nearly impossible (or at least unlikely) to re-identify the sample donors, thereby protecting donor privacy, whether donors are concerned about it or not. Although anonymizing allows investigators to use the materials without obtaining informed consent, it also means that investigators are unable to match samples with the donors' medical records or contact donors again when doing so would enhance research aims. Such measures obliterate the associated phenotype information, and thereby severely diminish the samples' scientific value.

Recent genomic and microbiome research, far more than prior clinical trials, requires broad participation to produce meaningful findings. For example, some studies focus on determining whether all human beings share a single identifiable "core" microbiome (Shade and Handelsman 2011), while others aim at determining how the microbiome is affected by individual genotypes and environmental exposures, or whether changes in the microbiome over time cause, or predict, human disease

(Turnbaugh et al. 2007). For large-scale studies of how the human microbiome evolves over time, many samples will come from fecal specimens or from skin, nose, mouth, and vaginal swabs of healthy individuals. In studies to determine whether the microbiome is predictive of particular illnesses, it will be necessary to collect samples from some individuals with the disease condition and compare them with samples from "normal" individuals. At the same time most of the sample collection associated with microbiome and biobank genetic studies are likely to involve only minute physical risks, the kind of risks involved in, say, having a cheek swab. In most cases the physical risks of future sample use are so small compared with the risks of everyday life that they should be considered *de minimis*. Although some authors have cautioned about risks to privacy in biobank research, institutional policies and security measures to safeguard confidentiality have been established to minimize breaches in confidentiality. Thus the likelihood of social or psychological risk is also vanishingly small and can be forestalled with measures that do not inhibit research.

The explicit policy of the NIH Human Microbiome Project (HMP) is that "pre-publication metagenomic and associated data should be released to the scientific community as quickly as possible" (http://nihroadmap.nih.gov/hmp/datareleaseguidelines.asp). To this end, the HMP includes a number of member organizations and resource repositories such as the Biodefense and Emerging Infections Research Resources Repository (BEI) and American Type Culture Collection (ATCC). These organizations and resource repositories connect to a centralized data and metadata repository referred to as the Data Analysis and Coordination Center (DACC). The DACC allows for rapid information sharing among researchers who are working on projects that may be either intimately or tangentially connected. Open sharing of data has allowed scientists to build on each other's work and facilitated the remarkably rapid advance in learning about the human microbiome.

2.3 Recommendation for a New Category of Research Risk

In light of these considerations, it strikes me that the difference between studies that involve negligible risks and those that involve some everyday risk should be recognized and those that involve the least risk should be treated differently from the rest. Therefore I suggest creating a new category of research risk, *de minimis* risk. Existing US federal regulations and some IRB guidance documents refer to three categories of research risk: (1) minimal risk, (2) a minor increase over minimal risk, and (3) more than a minor increase over minimal risk. According to 45 CFR 46.102(i), "[m]inimal risk means that the probability and magnitude of harm or discomfort anticipated in the research are not greater in and of themselves than those ordinarily encountered in daily life or during the performance of routine physical or psychological examinations or tests." For example, a study involving only a blood draw would count as minimal risk because the risks of the procedure are no greater than the risks associated with a routine physical examination.

The term "*de minimis* risk" would indicate an even lesser degree of risk. This new subcategory of minimal risk would apply to studies involving only negligible physical, social, or psychological risk where nothing inherently dangerous, such as using an identifiable leftover blood sample, is done to the body. Obtaining informed consent should *not* be an absolute requirement for studies that involve only *de minimis* risk. This recommendation would make permission to proceed with a study without informed consent the default position for studies that involve only *de minimis* risk; oral or blanket agreement should still be obtained when investigators and/or reviewers determine that obtaining it is feasible and the burdens involved would be reasonable. For example, obtaining a cheek swab involves only a *de minimis* risk. In most circumstances, explaining what is being done and allowing the person to volunteer or opt out of providing the sample is entirely feasible because the person is present and eliciting agreement entails no significant burdens. In that the future uses of the sample will not be known, agreement would be something less than "informed consent." Yet the deviations from the requirements of 45 CFR 46.116 would be accepted.

When it is feasible and when the effort involved in explaining and allowing for opting-out is reasonable, investigators should obtain agreement for something like a cheek swab. In a time-sensitive study that involves obtaining cheek swabs from unconscious trauma patients the default position of not requiring informed consent or even agreement would apply because the risks involved are *de minimis*.

This recommendation reflects the requirement of balancing risks and benefits. The Nuremberg Code (Nuremberg Military Tribunals 1949–1953), the original 1964 version of the Declaration of Helsinki (World Medical Association 2008), and the Common Rule all explicitly endorse a view that research risks should be balanced against the societal benefits that the project promises. Nevertheless, implementation of the current rules often seems to ignore the importance of adopting a balanced approach. Instead, those who oversee research often focus narrowly on protecting research participants from *any* risks, regardless of how unlikely, fleeting, or trivial the anticipated harm. When the physical and other risks involved are negligible and unlikely, and the study promises to provide a societal benefit, a reasonable assessment should conclude that the balance tips toward promoting scientific advance. Policies that consider only the risks, and deliberately ignore the possible social benefits that research could provide, express a distorted view of what ethics entails and therefore produce regulations that are ethically flawed.

The category of *de minimis* risk would apply to a number of kinds of research and play a role in policy governing the conduct of such studies.

2.3.1 Exempted Research

The Common Rule, 45 CFR 46.101(b), already implicitly employs a standard similar to the *de minimis* risk standard when it exempts several kinds of studies from the regulations. It exempts educational research, food evaluation, research involving existing data or specimens when they are publicly available, and research involving existing data when they cannot be identified or linked to the subjects. These studies all involve only *de minimis* risk. My proposal would include all of these already exempt studies under the new *de minimis* risk research category, thereby making the reason for the exemption explicit. A clear demarcation of which studies may proceed without informed consent would constrain the paternalistic inclinations of oversight agents and also legitimize other research goals such as advancing the social good and providing a benefit to other patients.

2.3.2 Biobank and Sample Bank Studies

Even when the process of sample collection involves more than *de minimis* risk, subsequent use of samples in biobank and sample bank studies involves only *de minimis* risk of physical harm. The only foreseeable harms related to using already collected samples involve possible social and psychological harms from allowing legal proceedings, insurers, family members, employers, or others to violate confidentiality constraints and gain access to biobank materials. NIH Certificates of Confidentiality have been developed to address that need, although some have argued that these Certificates provide imperfect protection (Beskow et al. 2008; Hermos and Spiro 2009). To the extent that people are still at risk, a more effective mechanism for protecting samples from legal proceedings and other illegitimate access may be in order. When microbiome biobanks and sample banks are safeguarded from use in criminal investigations, immigration proceedings, insurance markets, and the like, and from confidentiality violations that could involve sharing personal information with family members, schools, or employers, studies using these samples will involve only *de minimis* risk. Directly responding to concerns about safeguarding biobank confidentiality with stronger legal protections would be a coherent and effective way of dealing with the problem. It would also be a far better alternative than having investigators sacrifice the value of samples by anonymizing them, and a more transparent and honest approach than redescribing biobank and sample bank studies with such obfuscating language as "human nonsubject research" (Brothers and Clayton 2010).

Furthermore, to directly address the problems associated with obtaining informed consent, regulatory requirements should be adjusted to incorporate an exemption from informed consent for biobank and sample bank studies, in some respects the polar opposite of what the ANPRM proposes (DHHS 2011, 44515). This can most easily be accomplished by classifying further research uses of collected samples as *de minimis* risk research. This should be the case even for studies using de-identified samples that are linked to medical records (as opposed to anonymized samples that can no longer be linked to a specific human source). Because the physical risks involved in using these samples are only *de minimis*, and because recontacting sample donors to obtain study-specific informed consent is costly, burdensome, sometimes unwelcome, and may not be feasible, informed consent for subsequent studies should not be required.

2.3.3 Research on Populations
Public health studies, as well as QI and QA studies that do not involve direct interference with participants' bodies (e.g., sampling effluent from a community), should be considered *de minimis* risk. Because no physical risk is involved and because the confidentiality risk is vanishingly small, informed consent should not be required whenever general participation is needed and when obtaining agreement from individuals is unreasonably difficult or not feasible.

2.3.4 Discarded Biological Samples
In the course of clinical care, biological samples are routinely collected for analysis. Material that remains after its clinical purpose has been accomplished is often discarded. Some otherwise discarded samples will be valuable in various lines of research. The risks involved in using these

samples are only *de minimis*, because nothing additional is done to the body of the sample donor. Because it is feasible to allow patients to opt-out of the future research use of their samples at the point when samples are collected, and because providing the opportunity to opt-out would make the process transparent and more acceptable to patients, institutions should adopt an opt-out policy for the research use of remaining biological samples. Such a practice, which is already in place at many institutions, would allow the use of remaining de-identified samples linked to medical records from non-refusing patients in research without their informed consent.

2.3.5 Patients without Decisional Capacity

In some states and in some institutions, surrogate consent for research with patients who lack decisional capacity is restricted or not accepted, often because the state's surrogacy law does not extend to research (Gong et al. 2010). This is a problem because 45 CFR 46.116 only explicitly allows "the subject's legally authorized representative" to provide informed consent for research when a patient cannot consent. Yet the value of collecting samples from people who cannot consent could be significant in some studies. Because of the negligible risks of harm, and the importance of advancing the social good, the involvement of patients without decisional capacity should be allowed for studies that involve only *de minimis* risk without surrogate informed consent, but with surrogate agreement when feasible.

2.3.6 Surveys

IRBs often grant survey studies exemption from informed consent requirements because participants can easily refuse to participate, omit answers to questions, and discontinue their participation at any point. In addition, because surveys do not involve physical risks greater than a paper cut, they should be classified as *de minimis* risk and, as a rule, be exempt from informed consent requirements.

2.4 Conclusion

This discussion demonstrates that informed consent should not be considered an absolute requirement for the ethical conduct of human subjects research. Instead, we need a more nuanced and contextual approach to determining when and which information about a study should be provided to the participants. The level of risks and harms involved in participation, as well as the burdens, costs, and feasibility of providing the information and obtaining consent, all have to be considered. Different circumstances will require different standards. For clinical trials of new interventions that involve significant risks and burdens, robust informed consent from the participant should continue to be the standard. For clinical trials with participants who lack decisional capacity, surrogate informed consent for research should be accepted just as it is for clinical procedures. In some studies that involve only *de minimis* risk, agreement based on less than full information will be adequate. And there will be some circumstances where no consent is required at all.

This proposal for establishing *de minimis* risk as a new subcategory of research risk has several advantages. It puts the focus of research ethics where it belongs: on an assessment of risks and benefits. Furthermore it avoids the confusion engendered by relying on a stipulative, incoherent and intention-based definition of "research" that leaves public health agencies and institutions with irresolvable dilemmas. A *de minimis* risk category also reduces unreasonable obstacles that inhibit studies that should be encouraged. It clearly identifies significant reasons that explain why consent is not required and demarcates a broad range of studies that do not require consent.

Allowing studies to proceed under the category of *de minimis* risk would strike a reasonable balance between advancing biomedical science and societal health, and the importance of respecting persons. Studies that fit this category would be exempt from informed consent requirements because the risks involved are truly *de minimis*. In substance, this approach is compatible with recent conclusions of an Institute of Medicine Report that recommends relaxing informed consent requirements for studies that are not clinical trials (2009). Establishing this new subcategory of risk, however, would not be granting blanket exemption from obtaining participants' agreement or blanket consent. The importance of each study, the feasibility of obtaining agreement, and the risks to the participants should still be assessed and balanced. When agreement or blanket consent can be obtained with reasonable effort, investigators should be required to obtain it even when the studies involve only *de minimis* risk.

Skeptics may fear that too much in this proposal is left to the imprecise assessment of what is reasonable and feasible. They may feel more comfortable with a bright line definition and uncomfortable with leaving decisions to judgment. I offer several points in response to such concerns. The Common Rule's existing standard for determining when study risks are minimal uses a comparison to the risks of everyday life. This comparison also requires judgment. To add precision, perhaps the privacy risks of *de minimis* risk studies can be compared with the everyday privacy risks of using a store credit card or posting on Facebook. Such a comparison would tell us that most people consider such privacy disclosures low priority compared to the benefits. Biobanks and sample banks already employ far more privacy protections than other everyday exposures that the public considers reasonable.

Similarly, employing a definition also requires judgment. The Pronovost study saga illustrates the pitfalls of using a conceptually incoherent definition as the standard for drawing lines. Although the *de minimis* risk standard relies on judgment, tying the judgment to the overall risks and benefits and feasibility is a coherent and relevant standard for making the assessment. Perhaps the imprecision of judgments as to reasonableness and feasibility cannot be avoided, perhaps others can offer additional useful conceptual benchmarks for refining and guiding the assessment, and perhaps this problem, along with other matters of judgment, will have to be left to IRBs and other institutional groups that bear oversight responsibility.

Notes

1. This chapter derives from the "Human Microbiome and the Social Fabric" working group. The work was funded by the NIH National Human Genome Research Institute (NHGRI) Human Microbiome Project.

2. This chapter draws on two previously published papers, Rhodes (2005) and Rhodes et al. (2011). Here I follow John Rawls (1993), who states that it is "rational" to accept the positions that reason tells us will further basic human goals such as avoiding pain and disability and preserving life. It is "reasonable" to commit oneself to abide by those commitments so long as we can expect others to do so as well. I also follow T. M. Scanlon's negative formulation of the principle (1998).

References

Angrist, Misha. 2010. Urge overkill: Protecting deidentified human subjects at what price? *American Journal of Bioethics* 10 (9): 17–18. doi:10.1080/15265161.2010.494217.

Baily, Mary A. 2008. Harming through protection. *New England Journal of Medicine* 358 (8): 768–69. doi:10.1056/NEJMp0800372.

Beskow, Laura M., Lauren Dame, and E. Jane Costello. 2008. Certificates of confidentiality and the compelled disclosure of research data. *Science* 322 (5904): 1054–55. doi:10.1126/science.1164100.

Brothers, Kyle B., and Ellen W. Clayton. 2010. Human non-subjects research: Privacy and compliance. *American Journal of Bioethics* 10 (9): 15–17. doi:10.10 80/15265161.2010.492891.

Clayton, Ellen W. 2005. Informed consent and biobanks. *Journal of Law, Medicine and Ethics* 33 (1): 15–21. doi:10.1111/j.1748-720X.2005.tb00206.x.

Cohen, Alan B., Joseph D. Restuccia, Michael Shwartz, Jennifer E. Drake, Ray Kang, Peter Kralovec, Sally K. Holmes, Frances Margolin, and Deborah Bohr. 2008. A survey of hospital quality improvement activities. *Medical Care Research and Review* 65 (5): 571–95. doi:10.1177/1077558708318285.

Emanuel, Ezekiel J., Anne Wood, Alan Fleischman, Angela Bowen, Kenneth A. Getz, Christine Grady, Carol Levine, et al. 2004. Oversight of human participants research: Identifying problems to evaluate reform proposals. *Annals of Internal Medicine* 141 (4): 282–91.

Emanuel, Ezekiel J., and Jerry Menikoff. 2011. Reforming the regulations governing research with human subjects. *New England Journal of Medicine* 365 (12): 1–6. doi:10.1056/NEJMsb1106942.

Fost, Norman, and Robert J. Levine. 2007. The dysregulation of human subjects research. *Journal of the American Medical Association* 298 (18): 2196–98. doi:10.1001/jama.298.18.2196.

Flanagan, Brigid M., Sean Philpott, and Martin A. Strosberg. 2011. Protecting participants of clinical trials conducted in the intensive care unit. *Journal of Intensive Care Medicine* 26 (4): 237–49. doi:10.1177/0885066610390867.

Gawande, Atul. 2007. A lifesaving checklist. *New York Times*, December 30.

Gong, Michelle N., Gary Winkel, Rosamond Rhodes, Lynne D. Richardson, and Jeffrey H. Silverstein. 2010. Surrogate consent for research involving adults with impaired decision making: Survey of institutional review board practices. *Critical Care Medicine* 38 (11): 2146–54. doi:10.1097/CCM.0b013e3181f26fe6.

Hermos, John A., and Avron Spiro. 2009. Certificates should be retired. *Science* 323 (5919): 1288–99. doi:10.1126/science.323.5919.1288c.

Infectious Diseases Society of America (IDS). 2009. Grinding to a halt: The effects of the increasing regulatory burden on research and quality improvement efforts. *Clinical Infectious Diseases* 49 (3): 328–35. doi:10.1086/605454.

Institute of Medicine. 2009. *Beyond the Privacy Rule: Enhancing Privacy, Improving Health through Research*. Washington, DC: National Academies Press.

Kass, Nancy, Peter J. Pronovost, Jeremy Sugarman, Christine A. Goeschel, Lisa H. Lubomski, and Ruth Faden. 2003. Controversy and quality improvement: Lingering questions about ethics, oversight, and patient safety research. *Joint Commission Journal on Quality and Patient Safety* 34 (6): 349–53.

Kofke, W. Andrew, and Michael A. Rie. 2003. Research ethics and law of healthcare system quality improvement: The conflict of cost containment and quality. *Critical Care Medicine* 31 (3): S143–52.

Kulynych, Jennifer, and David Korn. 2002. The effect of the new federal medical-privacy rule on research. *New England Journal of Medicine* 346 (3): 201–204.

Miller, Franklin G., and Ezekiel J. Emanuel. 2008. Quality-improvement research and informed consent. *New England Journal of Medicine* 358: 765–67. doi:10.1056/NEJMp0800136.

Nuremberg Military Tribunals. 1949–1953. *Trials of War Criminals before the Nuremberg Military Tribunals under Control Council Law No. 10*. Nuremberg, October 1946–April 1949. Washington, DC: GPO.

Pritchard, Ivor A. 2008. Letter to Dr. Peter Provonost regarding indwelling catheter procedures. US Department of Health and Human Services, Office for Human Research Protections. July 30. http://www.hhs.gov/ohrp/policy/Correspondence/pronovost20080730letter.html.

Pronovost, Peter, Dale Needham, Sean Berenholtz, David Sinopoli, Haitao Chu, Sara Cosgrove, Bryan Sexton, et al. 2006. An intervention to decrease catheter-related bloodstream infections in the ICU. *New England Journal of Medicine* 355: 2725–32. doi:10.1056/NEJMoa061115.

Resnick, David B. 2005. Eliminating the daily life risks standard from the definition of minimal risk. *Journal of Medical Ethics* 31: 35–38. doi:10.1136/jme.2004.010470.

Rawls, John. 1993. *Political Liberalism*. New York: Columbia University Press.

Rhodes, Rosamond. 2005. Rethinking research ethics. *American Journal of Bioethics* 5 (1): 7–28. doi:10.1080/15265160590900678.

Rhodes, Rosamond, Jody Azzouni, Stefan B. Baumrin, Keith Benkov, Martin J. Blaser, Barbara Brenner, Joseph W. Dauben, et al. 2011. De minimis risk: A proposal for a new category of research risk. *American Journal of Bioethics* 11 (11): 1–7. doi:10.1080/15265161.2011.615588.

Scanlon, Thomas M. 1998. *What We Owe to Each Other*. Cambridge: Harvard University Press.

Shade, Ashley, and Jo Handelsman. 2011. Beyond the Venn diagram: The hunt for a core microbiome. *Environmental Microbiology* 14 (1): 4–12. doi:10.1111/j.1462-2920.2011.02585.x.

Turnbaugh, Peter J., Ruth E. Ley, Micah Hamady, Claire M. Fraser-Liggett, Rob Knight, and Jeffrey I. Gordon. 2007. The human microbiome project. *Nature* 449: 804–10. doi:10.1038/nature06244.

World Medical Association. 2008. *Declaration of Helsinki: Ethical Principles for Medical Research Involving Human Subjects*. World Medical Association website. http://www.wma.net/e/policy/b3.htm.

3
Risk Level, Research Oversight, and Decrements in Participant Protections

Ana S. Iltis

Momentum has been building to revisit the federal regulations governing human research since the National Bioethics Advisory Commission's 2001 report on research oversight (NBAC 2001). The Department of Health and Human Services' 2011 ANPRM (Advance Notice of Proposed Rulemaking) is a step in this process of revising the regulations. Several sections of the ANPRM focus on measuring and minimizing research risks and calibrating the scope of oversight to studies' risk levels. This chapter focuses on one risk-related proposal, the proposal to eliminate continuing review of minimal risk research that has undergone expedited review. It examines the goals of the ANPRM, defends a particular interpretation of those goals, and assesses the proposal to eliminate continuing review of previously expedited minimal risk protocols in light of those goals. For this proposal to be consistent with the ANPRM's goals and the goals of human research regulation more generally, three false assumptions would have to be true. The proposal should be abandoned. Instead, current oversight procedures should be made more efficient.

Such efficiency should be pursued even if the Common Rule remains unchanged.

3.1 Goals: ANPRM and the Regulation of Human Research in the United States

As Davis and Hurley explain in chapter 1, the ANPRM proposes numerous changes for the oversight and regulation of human research. One way to evaluate proposed changes is to evaluate whether they contribute to or are compatible with the ANPRM's overall goals. Changes that are incompatible with the goals of the ANPRM (and those goals are appropriate, as I assume) should be abandoned.

The ANPRM targets three areas for improvement: "This ANPRM seeks comment on how to better protect human subjects who are involved in research, while facilitating valuable research and reducing burden, delay, and ambiguity for investigators" (DHHS 2011, 44512). The ANPRM's goals must in turn be compatible with the goals of regulating research because the ANPRM proposes changes to the Common Rule to make it more effective but does not propose changing the purpose of regulating and overseeing research.

There are two main reasons for regulating research. First, to protect human subjects as suggested by the title of the Common Rule, "Protection of Human Subjects." Subject protection can be understood broadly as ensuring (or increasing the likelihood) that all studies meet the six substantive criteria for the ethical conduct of research: social or scientific value, scientific validity, fair subject selection, favorable risk–benefit ratio, informed consent, and respect for potential and enrolled subjects (Emanuel et al. 2000). The regulatory requirement for independent review (Emanuel et al. 2000) provides assurance that these substantive requirements are met (Joffe 2012). The second reason to regulate research is to "compensate for structural asymmetries that compromise the market in [the research] domain" (London 2012, 932). Without oversight, serious coordination problems could emerge, creating incentives that would threaten "continued social support for the research enterprise" (London 2012, 932). Oversight and independent review can foster and maintain trust and confidence in the system, facilitating rather than stifling research (London 2012).

It is in light of this background regarding the goals of research regulation and oversight that we must interpret the ANPRM's goals. These goals appear straightforward, yet there are at least six plausible interpretations. As demonstrated below, the first five are problematic and we should adopt the sixth.

1. The ANPRM's goals are lexically ordered so that one is the most important and every proposed change must advance that goal. The first and second goals must be advanced for a change that advances the third goal to be acceptable. This interpretation would have various permutations depending on the ordering of the goals. Nothing in the ANPRM supports the claim that one goal *must* be achieved to justify changes that promote other goals. For example, if one recognizes the goal of increasing protection of subjects as the primary goal, no other changes would be allowed unless the subjects would end up *better* protected even if those changes

allowed for equal protections and decreased burdens on investigators. Such a requirement would limit the possibility of progress on other goals unnecessarily. Interpretation 1 should be rejected.

2. Every change must advance all three goals. This is unnecessary and would virtually eliminate the possibility of improvement because few changes could accomplish all three goals. It should be rejected.

3. Proposed changes that result in overall better protection are to be pursued even if they involve decrements in the protection of some subjects. Changes that result in overall fewer burdens for investigators are acceptable even if they result in increased burdens, delays, or ambiguities for some investigators. Changes that obstruct or discourage some research are acceptable if they facilitate other areas of research more, yielding overall more research. Interpretation 3 introduces inappropriate trade-offs between individual subjects. Human research involves trade-offs between subjects and society. Regulations are meant to protect *all* subjects. To reduce the protection of some—the assurance that the research in which they participate meets those standards—by shifting protection resources to others is problematic. Subject protection is not a zero-sum game nor are IRB resources fixed;[1] resource shifting is not essential to providing adequate protection. All subjects deserve the same assurance that studies in which they participate meet the requirements for the ethical conduct of research.

4. Proposed changes that lead to significant gains in one area may (or should) be pursued even if they result in setbacks in other areas as long as the gains outweigh the setbacks. Interpretation 4 allows for trade-offs among the three areas targeted for improvement. Increased protection may justify increased burdens, delays, or ambiguities for investigators or procedures that may obstruct research. More research at a faster pace or fewer burdens, delays, or ambiguities for investigators may justify decreased protections. But investigator burdens and subject protection may not be commensurate as this interpretation assumes.[2] Moreover the utilitarian calculus of more results in less time and for less money contrasts sharply with a system meant to protect the safety, rights, and interests of *each* subject. Nevertheless, additional protections should be justified before they are implemented. Adequate protection may not require every imaginable protection.

5. Proposed changes that advance one goal and do not set back other goals are acceptable. Interpretation 5 treats all areas targeted for improvement as equally important. To be compatible with the ANPRM's

goals, a practice would have to advance at least one of the three goals and not set back another area. We would be prohibited from rectifying deficiencies in subject protection if doing so imposed any additional burdens, delays, or ambiguities on investigators or made some research less likely to be done. This is odd given that the overall purpose of the system is to protect human subjects. Some adherents to the research imperative would argue that we ought to pursue more research at a faster pace to alleviate human suffering even if we have to sacrifice subject protection. For example, as Lord Sainsbury, Science Minister in Great Britain, said of stem cell research: "The important benefits which can come from this research outweigh any other considerations" (quoted in Callahan 2003, 57; see Gallagher and Harlow 2000). Daniel Callahan (2003), and before him Hans Jonas (1969), argued against the research imperative—not against the importance of research, but against the view that the pursuit of research was more important than adherence to moral rules. Callahan worried that the research imperative could lead "scientists and others to see ethical scruples and precautionary principles simply as obstacles to overcome" (2003, 133).

6. Proposed changes that decrease burdens, delays, or ambiguities for investigators or that facilitate valuable research are permissible if they increase protection of subjects or maintain the current level of protection. Maintaining at least the current level of protections is a necessary side constraint.

Interpretation 6 prioritizes subject protections. Changes must either increase protections or advance another goal without decreasing subject protections. Decreasing protections is contrary to the purpose of regulating research, which the title of the Common Rule indicates is not to "make research happen" or "obstruct research" but to protect subjects. To protect subjects is to ensure that the requirements for the ethical conduct of research are met. The sixth interpretation is appropriate. This is not to say that we may not eliminate oversight practices but rather that we must maintain the assurance that studies meet the requirements for the ethical conduct of research. Eliminating oversight practices would be permissible if it did not compromise the assurance that the requirements for the ethical conduct of research were met.

When we adopt interpretation 6, five types of outcomes are compatible with the ANPRM's goals:

a. Increased protections.

b. Decreased burdens, delays, or ambiguities for investigators and increased protections.

c. Decreased burdens, delays, or ambiguities for investigators and no change in level of protections.

d. Greater facilitation of research and increased protections.

e. Greater facilitation of research and no change in the level of protections.

3.2 Evaluating the Proposed Elimination of Continuing Review for Previously Expedited Minimal Risk Studies

The ANPRM proposes that "[c]ontinuing review would be eliminated for all minimal risk studies that undergo expedited review, unless the reviewer explicitly justifies why continuing review would enhance protection of research subjects." (DHHS 2011, 44515). The ANPRM also proposes to expand the range of studies that would qualify for expedited review (44516). For this proposal to be compatible with the ANPRM's goals, it would have to result in one of the five outcomes above. There is no reason to believe that the proposal would increase the protection of subjects. It could lead to resource shifting that increases protection of some by decreasing protection of others but jeopardizing protection of some subjects for the benefit of others is incompatible with the goals of regulating human research and the ANPRM. It does not meet outcomes a, b, or d. Insofar as eliminating continuing review does not add protections, to be compatible with the goals of the ANPRM it would have to advance at least one of the other goals and avoid decrements in protection.

Does the proposal avoid decrements in subject protections? At least three assumptions would have to be true if we are to believe that eliminating continuing review of expedited studies would not jeopardize the assurance that studies meet the criteria for the ethical conduct of research at their inception and throughout the course of the study. These assumptions are false.

The first assumption is that errors in classifying studies as minimal risk and eligible for expedited review are nonexistent or negligible. Currently, upon continuing review, we may identify errors made during previous reviews. If we remove that opportunity, errors in initial classification that underestimate study risks are likely to go unnoticed. Other errors not detected on initial expedited review also are less likely to be noticed later, such as mistakes or omissions in an informed consent document. The new system would decrease protection; that is, it would decrease the assurance we have that studies meet the criteria for the ethical conduct of research.

The second assumption that must be true is that risks are static (or always decrease) and study value is static (or always increases). Ethical research requires that a study's potential benefits be reasonable relative to the anticipated risks, its risks be minimized, and it have social and scientific value and validity (45 CFR 46.111(a) (2005); Emanuel et al. 2000). If a study is deemed minimal risk and approved using expedited review, it might never be reviewed again. Investigators might not note new risks and notify IRBs unless prompted, as they are by the continuing review process, to revisit and document risks. Protocols might not be updated and new information might not be disclosed to subjects. Although one might think that merely requiring investigators to report this information would be sufficient, such an approach would rely too heavily on investigators to remember the reporting requirement. In other areas this has been deemed insufficient. For example, many of us are required to notify various offices about changes in our conflicts of interest. Although we should notify them at the time of a change, we are asked to complete new reporting forms yearly at least in part because people are likely to forget to report changes.

To maintain the current level of protections while eliminating continuing review, the risks associated with all studies that are deemed minimal risk and allowed to undergo expedited review would have to be static (or would decrease) over time. Imagine that a study is judged minimal risk and eligible for expedited review because it involves a medication for which no IND is required and no other source of significant risk is present (OHRP 1998).[3] During the trial, another study indicates possible additional risks of the drug not previously detected in people with particular risk factors and recommends that doses for those people be reevaluated. The continuing review process can trigger consideration of new risk information by reviewers and investigators.[4] Such a trigger is missing in a system lacking continuing review.

Similarly we would have to assume that a study's value remains the same (or increases) over time. Even a minimal risk study should be discontinued if its value decreases so that its value no longer is reasonable relative to its risks (45 CFR 46.111 (2005); Emanuel et al. 2000). Imagine that the USPHS/Tuskegee syphilis study had been a well-designed study in which no deception was used, informed consent was obtained, subjects were selected fairly, and so on. At its inception, it was primarily an observational study aimed at understanding the course of untreated syphilis, for which no effective treatment was available.[5] The risks associated with having syphilis and being in an observational study at that time were minimal—there was no effective treatment and the risk of observation itself was low. As penicillin became available and was known to cure syphilis, the risk of being in an observational study increased, and the value of understanding the natural course of untreated syphilis decreased. What one could describe as a minimal risk study at its inception (assuming the many unethical aspects of the study had been avoided), over time involved more than minimal risk. What one could describe at its inception as a study that might provide useful information (assuming the study were well designed and executed), over time could not offer scientifically and socially valuable information because it concerned the natural course of a disease that could be cured fairly easily.[6] The risks and social and scientific value of what starts off as a minimal risk study may change over time.

Even if studies and the risk–benefit ratio remain unchanged, studies reviewed once and never subject to continuing review may continue for decades without changes in the protocol or consent document. Yet perceptions of the information potential subjects ought to or must receive change over time. Consider the debate over the use of stored human biological materials for research, particularly genetic research.[7] Specimens collected at one time for research purposes may have been collected for a particular type of research. Over time new technology and advances in our understanding of genetics have led to an interest in using these specimens for new types of research. Although there would be no further interaction with subjects, insofar as they were identifiable, new research on those stored specimens constitutes human research. There has been much debate about the extent to which those stored samples may be used for studies beyond the kinds of research described to subjects as part of the informed consent process in part because views have changed about what kinds of information people must have as part of giving informed consent (e.g., see Kapp 2008; Clayton et al. 1995). Studies that involve only the collection of minimal amounts of blood may be approved through expedited procedures (category 2) and considered minimal risk (OHRP 1998). When submitting these kinds of studies for continuing review, investigators and IRBs can acknowledge changes in the information that should be shared or the scope of permissions solicited from subjects. Failure to submit studies to continuing review eliminates the systematic opportunity to acknowledge such changes.

The third assumption is that it is permissible to continue studies experiencing slow recruitment and unlikely to be completed. On continuing review, investigators provide a recruitment update. If recruitment is slow,

IRBs may ask for improvement plans because one requirement for ethical research is scientific value and validity (Emanuel et al. 2000). If slow enrollment continues and it is implausible that the sample size will be sufficient, the IRB may close the study because participants should not be exposed to research risks or burdens, however minimal, if the study is unlikely to be valid. Research risks and burdens must be reasonable relative to the potential benefits.[8] Eliminating continuing review eliminates the opportunity to identify poor enrollment and demand improvement or close studies. Alternatively, one could assume that investigators conducting minimal risk expedited studies always meet their enrollment goals.

These assumptions are false. Eliminating continuing review of previously expedited minimal risk studies would decrease the protection of human subjects; it would jeopardize the assurance we have that studies meet the requirements for the ethical conduct of research at their inception and throughout the course of the study. Thus the ANPRM's proposal should be abandoned. The current model of continuing review may not be the only way to ensure that studies continue to meet the criteria for the ethical conduct of research, but some mechanism for providing ongoing assurance is necessary.

3.3 Responding to Criticisms of Research Oversight Practices

Preserving continuing review of expedited studies helps ensure that studies initially approved continue to meet the requirements for the ethical conduct of research. This protects not only individuals but the integrity of the system and trust in the research enterprise (London 2012). There is, however, significant room for improvement in our system, including in how continuing review is conducted.

There has been much criticism of the oversight system,[9] and the ANPRM attempts to respond to some of these concerns. However, it is important to distinguish between (1) noting burdens, delays, and practices that obstruct or slow down research caused by IRBs working inefficiently or instituting restrictions not necessary for the ethical conduct of research and (2) claiming that research oversight necessarily is inefficient or unnecessary because we would have the same protections and assurances without oversight, or that oversight is inappropriate because it is more important to advance research than to protect subjects. If IRBs are inefficient and annoying, then we need to establish standards for IRBs, or determine how to accomplish oversight goals differently. We should not presume that without oversight all studies will meet the criteria for the ethical conduct of research. We should not ask subjects to participate in studies that may at some point not satisfy the conditions for the ethical conduct of research.

Other than the criticism that research oversight should be abandoned because it is antithetical to academic freedom (which assumes that academic freedom is more important than the goals of research oversight; see Hamburger 2005; Thomson et al. 2006), criticism of IRBs should be seen as calls to improve. Emanuel et al. (2004) identified a number of problems and suggestions. Others also have recommended areas for reform or improvement. The focus here is not outlining a performance improvement plan for research oversight, but it is useful to understand the kinds of changes that could support the ANPRM's goals:

- Ensuring adequate resources to support oversight (Emanuel et al. 2004; Steinbrook 2002).
- Improving education for investigators on research design and conduct (Emanuel et al. 2004; Joffe 2012; Steinbrook 2002).
- Educating IRB members and professionalizing IRB work (Emanuel et al. 2004; Steinbrook 2002) so that effective and efficient research oversight is appreciated and emphasized (Joffe 2012).
- Establishing standards for assessing IRBs (Emanuel et al. 2004), evaluating them (Joffe 2012; Coleman and Bouesseau 2008), and perhaps accrediting IRBs (Steinbrook 2002).

Insofar as risks or value of research may change, research oversight is a process that involves fallible human beings, and studies sometimes cannot meet their recruitment goals, continuing review plays a role in ensuring that approved studies continue to meet criteria for the ethical conduct of research and should not be eliminated even for previously expedited minimal risk studies. Improving how research oversight bodies function is different from eliminating them. One-time review is inconsistent with the goals of human research regulation and the ANPRM because it jeopardizes the assurance that research will meet the criteria for the ethical conduct of research.

Notes

1. This is not to suggest that resources are unlimited. However, there are numerous decisions that affect IRB resources. For example, institutions decide how much to charge sponsors for using their IRBs and doing research on site, institutions decide how much money to allocate to research oversight, and institutions

decide how many employees it will require to provide IRB service and for how long. Thus the resources dedicated to subject protection are not fixed.

2. An additional concern is that proportionality judgments require judgments about which protections warrant additional burdens. Would saving one life out of 100,000 justify additional requirements that add $50 to the cost of enrolling each subject? There is no single scale on which we can measure proportionality; such judgments involve assigning value to different outcomes to compare them.

3. Such a study would be eligible for expedited review under category 1 in the guidelines set forth by DHHS (1998).

Clinical studies of drugs and medical devices only when condition a or b is met.

a. Research on drugs for which an investigational new drug application (21 CFR part 312) is not required. (Note: Research on marketed drugs that significantly increases the risks or decreases the acceptability of the risks associated with the use of the product is not eligible for expedited review.)

b. Research on medical devices for which (i) an investigational device exemption application (21 CFR part 812) is not required, or (ii) the medical device is cleared/approved for marketing and the medical device is being used in accordance with its cleared/approved labeling.

4. Whether we should expect reviewers to find this information or know it is part of a larger discussion about the expertise and expectations of reviewers, important issues that have not received sufficient attention (see Joffe 2012). Although IRBs often rely on investigators to note the significance of new information, continuing review can serve as a trigger for investigators. Obligating investigators to answer specific questions and provide specific information may help them provide the relevant information to IRBs. Given what we know about how long it takes to translate research findings to practice (AHRQ 2001; Lenfant 2003), it is unreasonable to think that investigators necessarily will recognize the need to change their study, notify subjects, or contact the IRB without explicit prompts.

5. For further discussion of arsenic therapy used to treat syphilis, see Jones (1993, 45–47). I say "primarily" because some participants were offered some interventions, which compromised the scientific integrity of the study as a study of "Untreated Syphilis in the Negro Male," as it was described in the medical literature (e.g., see Shafer, Usilton, and Gleeson 1954).

6. I thank Nancy M. P. King for discussing this example with me.

7. In addition to debates over the use of stored samples originally collected for research, there has been extensive discussion and litigation over research using samples originally collected for clinical purposes, such as research on stored newborn blood spots (see Taylor and Wilfond 2004; Tarini et al. 2010; Botkin 2005; Kharaboyan et al. 2004; *Beleno v. Tex. Dep't of State Health Servs.*, No. SA-09-CA-188-FB (W.D. Tex. 2009); *Bearder v. Minn.*, No. 27-CV-09–5615 (Minn. Dist. Ct. 2009)). I thank Nancy M. P. King for discussing this example with me.

8. One exception might be in studies offering subjects a prospect of benefit that exceeds the research risks and burdens.

9. Several categories stand out (see Joffe 2012): variability of IRB judgments (Hirshon et al. 2002; Stair et al. 2001; McWilliams et al. 2003; Stark et al. 2010), redundancy (Burman et al. 2001; Emanuel et al. 2004); mission creep and infringements on academic freedom (Gunsalus et al. 2006; White 2007; Thomson et al. 2006; Hamburger 2005); investigator, sponsor, and institutional costs (Stewart et al. 2010; Silberman and Kahn 2011; Humphreys et al. 2003; Sugarman et al. 2005; Wagner et al. 2003); impeding valuable research and costing lives (Whitney and Schneider 2011); and complicating informed consent documents to the detriment of potential subjects (Burman et al. 2001; Schneider 2010).

References

Agency for Healthcare Research and Quality. 2001. *Translating Research into Practice (TRIP)-II: Fact Sheet.* http://www.ahrq.gov/research/trip2fac.htm.

Botkin, Jeffrey R. 2005. Research for newborn screening: Developing a national framework. *Pediatrics* 116 (4): 862–71.

Burman, William, Randall Reves, David Cohn, and Robert Schooley. 2001. Breaking the camel's back: Multicenter clinical trials and local institutional review boards. *Annals of Internal Medicine* 134 (2): 152–57.

Callahan, Daniel. 2003. *What Price Better Health?* Berkeley: University of California Press.

Clayton, Ellen W., Karen K. Steinberg, Muin J. Khoury, Elizabeth Thomson, Lori Andrews, Jo Ellis Kahn Mary, Loretta Kopelman, and Joan O. Weiss. 1995. Informed consent for genetic research on stored tissue samples. *Journal of the American Medical Association* 274 (22): 1786–92.

Coleman, Carl, and Marie-Charlotte Bouesseau. 2008. How do we know that research ethics committees are really working? The neglected role of outcomes assessment in research ethics review. *BMC Medical Ethics* 9 (1): 6.

Department of Health and Human Services (DHHS). 2011. Advance Notice of Proposed Rulemaking. Human subjects research protections: Enhancing protections for research subjects and reducing burden, delay, and ambiguity for investigators. *Federal Register* 76 (143): 44512–31.

Department of Health and Human Services. Office for Human Research Protections (OHRP). 1998. Categories of research that may be reviewed by the institutional review board through an expedited review procedure. *Federal Register* 63 (216): 60364–67.

Emanuel, Ezekiel J., David Wendler, and Christine Grady. 2000. What makes clinical research ethical? *Journal of the American Medical Association* 283 (20): 2701–11.

Emanuel, Ezekiel J., Anne Wood, Alan Fleischman, Angela Bowen, Kenneth Getz, Christine Grady, Carol Levine, et al. 2004. Oversight of human participants research: Identifying problems to evaluate reform proposals. *Annals of Internal Medicine* 141 (4): 282–91.

Gallagher, Ian, and Michael Harlow. 2000. Health chiefs? Yes to human clones. *International Express*, August 1–7, p. 10.

Gunsalus, C. K., M. Edward. Bruner, Nicholas C. Burbules, Leon Dash, Matthew Finkin, Joseph P. Goldberg, William T. Greenough, Gregory A. Miller, and Michael G. Pratt. 2006. The Illinois White Paper. Improving the system for protecting human subjects: Counteracting IRB "mission creep." The Center for Advanced Study, Urbana Champaign. www.gunsalus.net/IllinoisWhitePaperMissionCreep.pdf.

Hamburger, Philip. 2005. The new censorship: Institutional review boards. Working paper 95. Public Law and Legal Theory, University of Chicago. http://www.law.uchicago.edu/files/files/95-ph-censorship.pdf.

Hirshon, Jon M., Scott Krugman, Michael Witting, Jon Furuno, Rhona Limcangco, Andre Perisse, and Elizabeth Rasch. 2002. Variability in institutional review board assessment of minimal-risk research. *Academic Emergency Medicine* 9 (12): 1417–20.

Humphreys, Keith, Jodie Trafton, and Todd H. Wagner. 2003. The cost of institutional review board procedures in multicenter observational research. *Annals of Internal Medicine* 139 (1): 77.

Joffe, Steven F. 2012. Revolution or reform in human subjects research oversight. *Journal of Law, Medicine & Ethics* 40 (4): 922–29.

Jonas, Hans. 1969. Philosophical reflections on experimenting with human subjects. *Daedalus* 98 (2): 219–47.

Jones, James H. [1981] 1993. *Bad Blood*. New York: Free Press.

Kapp, Marshall B. 2008. Biobanking human biological materials: Issues surrounding the collection of samples for use in future research. *International Journal of Pharmaceutical Medicine* 22 (2): 75–84.

Kharaboyan, Linda, Denise Avard, and Bartha M. Knoppers. 2004. Storing newborn blood spots: Modern controversies. *Journal of Law, Medicine and Ethics* 32 (4): 741–48.

Lenfant, Claude. 2003. Shattuck Lecture. Clinical research to clinical practice — Lost in translation? *New England Journal of Medicine* 349: 868–74.

London, Alex J. 2012. A non-paternalistic model of research ethics and oversight: Assessing the benefits of prospective review. *Journal of Law, Medicine and Ethics* 40 (4): 930–44.

McWilliams, Rita, Julie Hoover-Fong, Ada Hamosh, Suzanne Beck, Terri Beaty, and Garry Cutting. 2003. Problematic variation in local institutional review of a multicenter genetic epidemiology study. *Journal of the American Medical Association* 290 (3): 360–66.

National Bioethics Advisory Commission. 2001. *Ethical and Policy Issues in Research Involving Human Subjects*. Bethesda: NBAC.

Schneider, Carl E. 2010. The hydra. *Hastings Center Report* 40 (4): 9–11.

Shafer, J. K., Lida Usilton, and Geraldine Gleeson. 1954. Untreated syphilis in the male negro. *Public Health Reports* 69 (7): 684–90.

Silberman, George, and Katherine L. Kahn. 2011. Burdens on research imposed by institutional review boards: The state of the evidence and its implications for regulatory reform. *Milbank Quarterly* 89 (4): 599–627.

Stair, Thomas O., Caitlin R. Reed, Michael S. Radeos, Greg Koski, and Carlos A. Camargo. 2001. Variation in institutional review board responses to a standard protocol for a multicenter clinical trial. *Academic Emergency Medicine* 8 (6): 6–10.

Stark, Ann R., Jon E. Tyson, and Patricia L. Hibberd. 2010. Variation among institutional review boards in evaluating the design of a multicenter randomized trial. *Journal of Perinatology* 30 (3): 163–69.

Steinbrook, Robert. 2002. Improving protection of research subjects. *New England Journal of Medicine* 346 (18): 1425–30.

Stewart, David J., Simon N. Whitney, and Razelle Kurzrock. 2010. Equipoise lost: Ethics, costs, and the regulation of cancer clinical research. *Journal of Clinical Oncology* 28 (17): 2925–35.

Sugarman, Jeremy, Kenneth Getz, Jeanne L. Speckman, Margaret M. Byrne, Jason Gerson, and Ezekiel J. Emanuel. 2005. The cost of institutional review boards in academic medical centers. *New England Journal of Medicine* 352 (17): 1825–27.

Tarini, Beth A., Aaron Goldenberg, Dianne Singer, Sarah J. Clark, Amy Butchart, and Matthew Mason Davis. 2010. Not without my permission: Parents' willingness to permit use of newborn screening samples for research. *Public Health Genomics* 13 (3): 125–30.

Taylor, Holly A., and Benjamin S. Wilfond. 2004. Ethical issues in newborn screening research: Lessons from the Wisconsin cystic fibrosis trial. *Journal of Pediatrics* 145: 292–96.

Thomson, Judith J., Catherine Elgin, David Hyman, Philip Rubin, and Jonathan Knight. 2006. Research on human subjects: Academic freedom and the institutional review board. *Academe* 92 (5): 95–100.

Wagner, Todd H., Aman Bhandari, Gary L. Chadwick, and Daniel K. Nelson. 2003. The cost of operating institutional review boards (IRBs). *Academic Medicine* 78 (6): 638–44.

White, Ronald. 2007. Institutional review board mission creep: The Common Rule, social science, and the nanny state. *Independent Review* 11 (4): 547–64.

Whitney, Simon, and Carl Schneider. 2011. A method to estimate the cost in lives of ethics board review of biomedical research. *Journal of Internal Medicine* 269: 392–406.

II
Protection of Vulnerable Populations

Introduction to Part II—Protection of Vulnerable Populations

Patrick Taylor

The future of research on so-called vulnerable populations depends on what makes them distinct and also on vulnerabilities shared with all other research participants. Like all research participants, members of vulnerable populations are personally vulnerable to misunderstanding and mistakenly assessing procedures, risks, and benefits; deception; being over-influenced by financial incentives, therapeutic hope, pressure, and the desire to please; and, in an interventional study, the interplay among their current health, their nonresearch clinical care, and the intervention. Regulations respond by generally requiring consent—although to a very broad range of risks—and relying on IRB review to police the clarity, comprehensiveness, and procurement of consent, limit financial compensation, and implement a vaguely stated outer limit on exposure to risks in relation to direct benefits. The fundamental challenges to that construct illustrated by this volume therefore affect vulnerable population research as well. Critiques based on IRB variability, third-party assessment superseding personal acceptance of even minimal risk (a formula tellingly inverted when risk is declined), and comparing employment rights, perhaps collectively bargained, to name three examples, each provoke thought here too.

But vulnerable populations are also each defined through some differentiating characteristic that cuts across race, religion, and most categories that law treats as suspect. The characteristic limits the range of possible choices open to population members and their freedom to exercise unconstrained choice. It thus makes them vulnerable to exploitation for others' benefit and exposure to extraordinary risks. For example, prisoners are isolated, without rights, dignity, or sympathies, and dependent on guards whose personal disdain may shape their uses of government's almost absolute power. Regulations governing prisoner research thus confine permitted studies to those that have population relevance or direct personal relevance, and IRBs must include a specialist. Under the regulations, another vulnerable population—children—are considered competent to, at best, add their assent to a parent's research consent, unless state laws specifically empower minor consent in parallel nonresearch contexts; respect for persons embeds battery's simple protection to *refuse* a touch, without the rationality or experience that would conceptually empower an autonomous "yes." Regulations limit the degree of risk even parents can consent to, on a sliding scale dependent on research purpose and personal or group benefit. Similarly pregnant women and embryo or fetus are likely differentially benefited or placed at risk by study procedures. A woman's choice is complicated by the interests of father and embryo or fetus and pregnancy stage, and is made more difficult if the woman is stressed physically, emotionally, or circumstantially. Neonates, infants within the first 30 days of life, are completely vulnerable, and biologically unique, making risk and benefit inferences from non-neonate data additionally uncertain. Here too, complex regulations prescribe what risks may be accepted, for what research purpose, for whose benefit, and with what parental consent. Thus the existing set of vulnerable population regulations are really siblings in a family of regulations, with overlapping features and common parentage in the root regulations applicable to human subjects research more generally, but variations not wholly explained by their differences in interest.

The works in part II include two challenges and one defense of existing regulations. Their procedural posture should not be confused, however, with the aim or force of their critiques, or in the strength of their normative arguments for future regulation.

Parasidis, a challenger, faults the regulations for their non-inclusion of soldiers in the military, whose obligation to obey assertedly has been exploited to expose them to unjustifiable risks by leadership that has been historically noncompliant with basic conditions of research regulation. Combining examples with an implicit appeal to justice, Parasidis argues that soldiers' altruism should not be the basis for, in effect, trivializing their autonomy through military authority of questionable beneficence. One might question whether such a problem could be wholly resolved by substitution of one set of regulations for another, and whether regulations that limited research purpose to addressing conditions soldiers as a group might face, or relative risk, would be much of a barrier given the examples Parasidis cites and soldiers' nonresearch risks. But those questions, while significant, are less important than his compelling reminder that regulations should address evident abuses, and his implicit expansion of justice—the most narrowly construed of the Belmont principles—to questions greater than the proportionality of research benefits to the selection of research participants.

Next, Braddock connects the fairly recent development of community engagement with the regulatory absence of a voice for pediatric participants other than individual, protocol-specific assent where that occurs. The argument is less that principle compels the engagement of pediatric populations than that wise practice will choose it. But in casting such engagement as "partnership" and giving it wide topical scope, Braddock demands a degree of respect and visibility for children's views that may prove tectonic, for assent, as currently justified, is hardly a partnership model in the sensitivities and mental range it attributes to children. Considered as a critique of vulnerable population regulations, this chapter is therefore, perhaps unintentionally, quite radical: unlike existing regulations, which protect through *restricting* the arena for personal choice, future regulations should consider expanding the range and influence of participant choice, from a limited yes/no to here's-how and this-would-be-better.

Finally, Obasogie's target is a report of the Institute of Medicine that recommended relaxing regulatory restrictions on research on prisoners in light of the different approach contemporaneous academic ethics would assertedly employ to evaluate the question today. The essence of Obasogie's critique is that a theoretical conditional subjunctive grounded in reflective self-examination by a discipline is not an adequate substitute for a policy recommendation grounded in fresh factual inquiry. Whether prisoners are vulnerable and, if so, to what are empirical questions. Whether and how to protect is inescapably normative, but it is also inescapably empirical. Both normative and empirical aspects ask more than conceptual redefinition. Of course, there should be room for a discipline, just like a conscientious appellant, to confess error, if error—or some Precambrian primitiveness now happily overcome—is a just description of original recommendations. But if Obasogie is right, the impulse to confess error might better apply to the report than existing regulations. Obasogie also faults the IOM for ignoring market conditions that could foster prisoner vulnerability—scarcity of participants amid great demand given large revenue opportunities. But one is left wondering, more broadly, about the cultural effect of such a force, and in particular how to keep not just vulnerable populations, but ourselves and our own evaluative stances, free from its potential influence as we co-create the future of human subject regulation.

4

Classifying Military Personnel as a Vulnerable Population

Efthimios Parasidis

One of the primary goals of the Common Rule is to ensure that protocols governing human subjects research provide adequate protections for vulnerable populations. The 2011 ANPRM underscores the importance of adopting additional safeguards for vulnerable populations, yet does not include military personnel in its definition of "vulnerable." This omission fails to account for decades of unethical research on service members and the coercive nature of the relationship between senior and subordinate in the military. DHHS should amend the Common Rule to explicitly classify military personnel as a vulnerable population.

The Common Rule grants additional safeguards to populations that are "likely to be vulnerable to coercion or undue influence" so as "to protect the rights and welfare of these subjects" (45 CFR 46.111(b)). Given the dynamics of military hierarchy and the legal requirements set forth by the Uniform Code of Military Justice (10 USC 47), there can be no question that military personnel are a class of individuals that is vulnerable to coercion and undue influence. Military command structure, mandatory use of investigational medical products, informed consent waivers, and the problem of mixed agency (i.e., circumstances where a military physician has an obligation to someone other than the patient, such as a commanding officer) are factors that support this characterization.

The impact of current protocols governing military research is exacerbated when one considers socioeconomic demographics of the military and the fact that federal law precludes civil remedies against the military, even in instances where military actors have intentionally violated legal protections governing human subjects research (Parasidis 2012a, 726–28). In this chapter, in addition to arguing that the Common Rule should explicitly classify military personnel as a vulnerable population, I suggest additional safeguards that should be incorporated into the Common Rule as a new regulatory subpart.

4.1 Emergence of Military Personnel as a Vulnerable Population

For over a century the US military has conducted and sponsored cutting-edge medical and technological research, and many of the resulting products have revolutionized daily life for both military and civilian populations. Although regulatory guidelines mandate that military physicians and researchers obtain voluntary and informed consent prior to experimentation on human subjects, these protocols have not been followed faithfully. Moreover, in a number of instances, military research and military medicine have coalesced. Some experimental products have been characterized as "pre-treatments," while others have been tested both in the lab and on the battlefield.

The latter, often referred to as "field testing," is noteworthy because, when a medical product is field-tested, regulatory guidelines provide soldiers with far less protection than otherwise would be available had the soldiers received the identical product in the context of a clinical trial. Within the context of field-testing, the US Department of Defense (DoD) has sought and obtained informed consent waivers by arguing that national security interests require that soldiers not be permitted to opt out of "treatment" with investigational products.

Reviewing the military's actions informs an analysis of why military personnel should be classified as a vulnerable population for purposes of human subjects research. My discussion in this section focuses on three areas: (1) studies related to atomic, biological, and chemical warfare; (2) experimental use of medical products as prophylaxis against anticipated biowarfare; and (3) the development of biomedical enhancements for service members.

4.1.1 Studies Related to Atomic, Biological, and Chemical Warfare

Beginning in the mid-twentieth century, the US military focused its research on experiments related to atomic, biological, and chemical (ABC) warfare. The ABC experiments reflected contemporary national security priorities and included both offensive and defensive endeavors. Three examples include studies related to mustard gas, atomic weapons, and psychotropic drugs. Since these examples have been detailed elsewhere (Parasidis 2012a, 729–57), I will provide a brief overview that highlights facts that are particularly relevant to my analysis.

The military's mustard gas research, which was conducted primarily in the 1940s, involved thousands of soldiers in studies that included "race-based" experiments and "man-break" tests. The race-based experiments sought to determine whether people with darker skin tone were less susceptible to mustard gas. During the man-break tests, military researchers locked soldiers into gas chambers and inundated the chambers with mustard gas until the point that the men became incapacitated (Smith 2008, 517–18).

Officers working on the mustard gas experiments recruited soldiers under false pretenses—when the soldiers would report for duty, officers would order the soldiers into gas chambers. A Naval Research Laboratory report noted that, for soldiers who "did not cooperate fully," an "explanatory talk, and, if necessary, a slight verbal dressing down ha[d] always prove[d] successful" (Moreno 2000, 48). Commanding officers threatened soldiers with sanctions that included immediate court martial and forty years in prison. During the experiments, soldiers were exposed to gas levels that were equivalent to those reported on World War I battlefields. The tests caused significant injuries that included blindness, severe burns, internal and external bleeding, cancer, asthma, and psychological disorders.

For decades, the US government refused to acknowledge the existence of the studies or provide injured service members with compensation or long-term health care. It was not until 1991—nearly five decades after the first studies began—that the government officially admitted to the use of soldiers in research. The government also admitted that it did not fully disclose safety risks or obtain informed consent from the research participants, and that the service members may have suffered adverse health effects as a result of their participation in the studies (IOM 1993, v–vii).

Contemporaneous with the mustard gas experiments, and for decades thereafter, the US military conducted radiation experiments on American soldiers and civilians. In addition to testing the destructive capabilities of nuclear weapons, military researchers examined the effects of nuclear warfare on humans, animals, and the environment. While the military publicly denied any potential harm to humans, plants, or animals, internal documents indicate that government officials had determined that there existed a causal relationship between radiation exposure and serious adverse health effects (Human Radiation Experiments Report 1996, 6–14). During the experiments, and despite the health and environmental hazards, the Commissioner of the US Atomic Energy Commission privately asserted that "[w]e must not let anything interfere with this series of tests—nothing" (Ball 1986, 41). In the 1990s the government acknowledged that hundreds of thousands of American service members had been involved in at least 1,400 radiation projects over a thirty-year period during and after World War II (Schroeter 1996, 151).

Along with the mustard gas and radiation experiments, the US military engaged in decades of classified research, beginning in the 1940s and continuing through the 1970s, to ascertain whether psychotropic drugs could be used as chemical weapons or interrogation-facilitating agents (Amoroso and Wenger 2003, 570; Price 2007, 8–9). During the early stages of the research, the US military recruited Nazi scientists who had studied and participated in torture and brainwashing. Several of the Germans had been recently identified as war criminals, and the US falsified documents to conceal their true identities (Gimbel 1990, 441–42). The military later justified its actions by arguing that national security interests far outweighed any ethical concerns.

The psychotropic drugs were given to service members and civilians without their knowledge or consent. Studies were conducted in military facilities and university medical centers, and many human subjects experienced serious adverse side effects (Price 2007, 9–11). Internally, the military justified the secret testing on "'unwitting, nonvolunteer' Americans" by arguing that national security interests permit "a more tolerant interpretation of moral-ethical values" (*United States v. Stanley*, 483 US 669, 686–89, 1989; J. Brennan dissenting).

4.1.2 Experimental Use of Medical Products as Prophylactic Treatments

Since at least the 1990s the US military has required that service members subject themselves to both investigational and off-label use of medical products (Nightingale, Prasher, and Simonson 2007, 1047), both of which involve utilization of a medical product for an indication that has not earned FDA approval. In instances where off-label or investigational use is required pursuant to DoD protocols, 10 USC 1107 sets forth notice and consent procedures that must be followed. The statute allows for an informed consent waiver in instances where the President determines that national security interests justify force-wide nonconsensual use for off-label or investigational products.

Nonconsensual use of off-label or investigational medical products raises a number of serious concerns. While physicians may prescribe drugs for off-label indications, the decision to do so must be based on an evaluation of a patient's particular health and risk factors, and should only occur where medical data reflect meaningful evidence that the potential benefits are likely to outweigh the known or expected risks, and the patient provides informed consent to the treatment. In a number of instances the military has made off-label and investigational use of medical products compulsory for service members as a whole, and has not sought to obtain informed consent or provide adequate risk disclosures to individual soldiers (Parasidis 2012a, 741–50). For purposes of this chapter, I explore three examples—pyridostigmine bromide (PB), the botulinum toxoid (BT) vaccine, and the anthrax vaccine.

Details of DoD's efforts to mandate investigational use of PB and the BT vaccine are found in *Doe v. Sullivan*, 938 F.2d 1370 (DC Cir. 1991). After petitioning the FDA to establish a new rule that waives informed consent requirements for investigational use of medical products in times of existing or anticipated combat activities, the DoD sought and obtained permission from the FDA to use PB and the BT vaccine pursuant to the new regulation. Fearing use of chemical weapons during the Gulf War, the military decided to administer PB and the BT vaccine to all soldiers. At the time, the FDA was evaluating the safety and efficacy of both products as pretreatments for chemical warfare.

In its informed consent waiver request to the FDA, the DoD argued that it would not be feasible to obtain informed consent because a soldier's "personal preference" does not supersede the military's view that the drug and vaccine would contribute to the "safety of other personnel in a soldier's unit and the accomplishment of the combat mission." The DoD also argued that "obtaining informed consent in the heat of imminent or ongoing combat would not be practicable" (Ibid.).

The FDA granted the DoD's requests, but the decision was not without controversy. The DoD claims that it trusted that the FDA had granted permission to use the investigational drug without informed consent because the FDA believed that the drug was deemed to be safe. The FDA, on the other hand, claims that it granted the waiver because it believed that the DoD determined that military necessity required an informed consent waiver.

Regardless of the reason why the FDA granted the waiver, as a condition of the FDA's permission to use the investigational medical products without informed consent, the DoD agreed to (1) provide information on PB to all service members; (2) collect, review, and make reports of adverse events related to PB; (3) label PB as an investigational product that was solely for "military use and evaluation"; (4) ensure that each dose of the BT vaccine was recorded in each service member's medical record; and (5) maintain adequate records related to the receipt, shipment, and disposition of the BT vaccine. The DoD failed to comply with each of these requirements (FDA 1999, 188–89).

Following the use of PB and the BT vaccine during the Gulf War, veterans began suffering from serious health problems that include cognitive difficulties, chronic headaches, widespread pain, skin rashes, respiratory and gastrointestinal problems, and other chronic abnormalities. Gulf War veterans have been diagnosed with amyotrophic lateral sclerosis at a much higher rate than that of the general population or veteran populations from other wars, and children of Gulf War veterans are born with birth defects at an alarming rate. Commonly referred to as Gulf War illness, these health problems affect over 175,000 veterans, which amounts to more than 25 percent of the fighting force during the war. PB is included in the list of factors that are most likely to be a contributing factor to Gulf War illness (Gulf War Illness Report 2008, 1–10).

The military's off-label use of vaccines continued after the Gulf War. In 1998, the DoD implemented the Anthrax Vaccine Immunization Program (AVIP), which requires the anthrax vaccine for all service members who are deemed by the DoD to be at risk for anthrax exposure. Although the vaccine had earned FDA approval to protect against cutaneous anthrax, the military sought to use the vaccine as a pretreatment for inhalation anthrax, which constituted an off-label use.

In 2003, as outlined in the case of *Rempfer v. Sharfstein*, 583 F.3d 860 (DC Cir. 2009), six service members filed a lawsuit seeking to enjoin the military from continuing AVIP because the military did not obtain informed consent prior to the force-wide off-label inoculations, nor did the DoD obtain a waiver for the informed consent requirements. Thus, the service members argued, the DoD failed to comply with 10 USC §1107. A federal court agreed, and issued a preliminary injunction that halted AVIP. Days later, the FDA approved the anthrax vaccine "independent of the route of exposure," which captured the indication of inhalation anthrax. The court then vacated the FDA's decision on procedural grounds because the agency did not follow regulatory guidelines governing approval of the vaccine for the new indication.

While *Rempfer* was not the first case to challenge AVIP, it was the first time a court held against the DoD. Prior to the *Rempfer* decision, a number of military courts rejected arguments identical to those raised by the *Rempfer* plaintiffs. The military courts focused on the fact that AVIP constituted a military order, and that the soldiers who refused the vaccine must be punished for violating an order. Importantly, military courts systematically denied soldiers the ability to introduce evidence of the vaccine's risks, arguing that the risks were not relevant to the question of whether a soldier disobeyed an order (Parasidis 2012a, 744–45).

Shortly after the *Rempfer* decision, Congress stepped in to aid the DoD by enacting the Project BioShield Act of 2004, which grants the FDA the ability to permit population-level off-label or investigational use of medical products during a declared emergency (Nightingale, Prasher, and Simonson 2007, 1046). In turn, the FDA used its newfound power to grant the DoD the ability to continue using the anthrax vaccine, a move that trumped the court order. During the time that the DoD was permitted to continue with AVIP pursuant to the emergency order, the FDA again approved the vaccine regardless of the route of exposure. Although service members once again challenged the FDA's decision, a federal court dismissed the lawsuit because it found that the FDA had not acted arbitrarily or capriciously in approving the new indication during its second review. Since March 1998, over 2,300,000 service members have received the anthrax vaccine. For a number of service members, however, the administration of the vaccine is not reflected in the official medical records maintained by the military (Parasidis 2012a, 746).

Reports have highlighted the DoD's failure to adequately monitor health concerns related to AVIP. Despite being required to implement medical monitoring and report vaccine-related adverse events, the DoD has failed to keep adequate medical records and has actively discouraged reporting of adverse events. The DoD's acts and omissions have resulted in "[p]reposterously low adverse report rates" and a sparse medical record from which to conduct meaningful risk–benefit evaluation. Rather than using medical monitoring as a way to better understand the risk–benefit profile of the vaccine and promote the health of service members, DoD personnel viewed the reporting of adverse events as a "politically sensitive" issue and sought "to avoid it" (Anthrax Vaccine Congressional Report 2000, 1–3, 34–38).

4.1.3 Development of Biomedical Enhancements for Service Members
The fundamental goal of military training is to enhance service members—to make them smarter, stronger, and more able fighters. Increasingly, enhancement techniques have sought to leverage innovative medical products and technologies. Much of the military's contemporary research program is coordinated by the US Defense Advanced Research Projects Agency (DARPA). According to DARPA, its mission is to "create strategic surprise for US adversaries by maintaining the technological superiority of the US military" (DARPA 2012). Current research sponsored by DARPA and the DoD aims to ensure that soldiers have "no physical, physiological, or cognitive limitations" (Annas and Annas 2009, 286).

As the director of DARPA explains, the agency's goal is to exploit "the life sciences to make the individual warfighter stronger, more alert, more endurant, and better able to heal" (Moreno 2006, 11).

DARPA's "Persistence in Combat" program aims to create soldiers who are "unstoppable because pain, wounds, and bleeding are kept under their control" (Annas and Annas 2009, 286). This program includes research directed at developing a vaccine that will block intense pain within seconds, use of photobiomodulation to accelerate wound healing, and the creation of a chemical cascade to stop bleeding within minutes (Annas and Annas 2009). The agency's Metabolic Dominance program seeks to create a "'nutraceutical,' a pill with nutritional value that would vastly improve soldiers' endurance" (Moreno 2006, 121). DARPA's vision is "to enable superior physical and physiological performance by controlling energy metabolism on demand. An example is continuous peak physical performance and cognitive function for 3 to 5 days, 24 hours per day, without the need for calories" (Moreno 2006).

Coupled with these programs, "the security establishment's interest and investment in neuroscience, neuropharmacology . . . and related areas [are] extensive and growing" (Moreno 2006, 4). Under the Augmented Cognition program, DARPA seeks to "develop the technologies needed to measure and track a subject's cognitive state in real-time" (51). Another goal is to create brain-to-computer interfaces, whereby soldiers can communicate by thought alone. This includes systems that can relay messages, such as images and sounds, between human brains and machines, or even from human to human. Service members can receive commands via electrodes implanted in their brains, or be wired directly into the equipment they control (Hoag 2003, 796–98). Through implanted electrodes, DARPA is researching whether neurostimulation can improve impaired cognitive performance and reduce the effects of sleep deprivation on soldiers. As one DARPA official explains, "DARPA is about trying to do those things, which are thought to be impossible, and finding ways to make them happen" (Moreno 2006, 12, 127).

4.2 Contemplating Additional Safeguards for Military Personnel

Given the extensive research conducted and/or sponsored by the military and the military's emphasis on biomedical enhancements, a reevaluation of human subjects protocols for military personnel is both timely and prudent. Should DHHS amend the Common Rule to classify military personnel as a vulnerable population, any IRB that approves research on military populations would need to condition the research on implementation of safeguards that are specifically tailored to "protect the rights and welfare" of the research participants. The adoption of additional safeguards serves to acknowledge the fact that military personnel are subject to undue influence or coercion that is likely to disrupt fundamental principles governing protections for human subjects research. As it does for pregnant women, human fetuses, neonates, children, and prisoners, DHHS should incorporate additional safeguards for military personnel into the Common Rule via a new regulatory subpart. The safeguards should, at a minimum, address current limitations of military IRBs and the lack of adequate measures to ensure the confidentiality of research-related decisions of military personnel. My recommendations in this chapter focus on these two areas.

By way of analogy, given the long history of egregious research on prisoners, the Common Rule requires IRBs that consider prisoner research to include a prisoner or prisoner representative on the IRB. In chapter 6, Osagie Obasogie highlights the reasons underlying the additional safeguards for prisoners and the concerns raised by biomedical research in the prisoner context. The parallels between prisoner research and research on military personnel are striking, and an analysis of the two populations, placed in the context of the respective concerns, is revealing.

For military personnel, amendments to the Common Rule could include a requirement that each IRB must have one or two active-duty or retired service members or service member representatives, and/or that each IRB include a civilian human subjects research specialist. Inclusion of these additional members would help bring new perspectives to the IRB deliberation process that may not be present under existing guidelines. An amended Common Rule could also specify the parameters surrounding a military IRB's decision to approve a protocol. Such parameters could include assurances that any approved research must not include risks that are not commensurate with nonmilitary populations, that researchers will take appropriate steps to ensure that a soldier's decision to participate in the research will not adversely impact the soldier's conditions of service or career, and that follow-up examination and medical care will be provided for all participants. Analogous protocols apply to research that utilizes prisoners as human subjects.

In instances where research earns IRB approval, the Common Rule should require that approval be predicated on use of independent consent monitors. Consent monitors are a helpful way of assessing decision-making capacity and evidence of subject's preferences and interest in participating in the research (Silverman 2011, 6). Consent monitors can also serve to track whether military personnel understand the distinction between research and clinical care, and help ensure that military personnel are not subject to undue coercion by physicians or researchers. While current DoD guidelines permit use of consent monitors or an ombudsman, neither is required (DoD 2011, 23–24). Given the long history of egregious conduct, use of independent consent monitors would provide military personnel with a tangible change in military medical practice and research.

Coupled with use of independent consent monitors, maintaining the confidentiality of the medical decisions and medical records of military personnel is imperative. As documented, the military has threatened and taken severe punitive measure against soldiers who have refused to participate in research or have refused medical products that were not FDA-approved for the use intended by the DoD. In addition, military commanders have characterized both situations as routine aspects of military training. This view dates back at least as far as the radiation experiments and is still offered as a reason why informed consent should not be universally required (Amoroso and Wenger 2003, 569).

Treating military personnel as on-call human subjects flies in the face of medical ethics and disrupts important notions of trust and respect that underlie the special relationship between superior and subordinate (Annas 2011, 632). As explained in the DoD's influential treatise, *Military Medical Ethics*, a "person or soldier cannot truly be regarded as a voluntary participant in research unless he or she is fully informed that he or she is participating in research activities, and made aware of the risks and benefits this research may entail" (Amoroso and Wenger 2003, 570). This notion mirrors the perspective of the National Commission, which argues that "informed consent requires conditions free of coercion and undue influence" and that "[u]njustifiable pressures usually occur when persons in positions of authority or commanding influence—especially where possible sanctions are involved—urge a course of action for a subject" (National Commission 1979).

Each service member should be afforded an opportunity to determine if they wish to participate in biomedical research or be administered a medical product that has not earned FDA approval for the intended use. The decision-making process should consist of a confidential discussion between a service member and a military physician, during which the service member should be provided with information related to all known or expected risks, any anticipated therapeutic benefits, treatment options in the event of an adverse event, and the ability to opt out of the use at any time. Use of consent monitors is likely to help achieve these goals. Maintaining the confidentiality of the process and the soldier's decision is integral to ensuring that the potential for retaliation for nonparticipation is minimized. Stiff penalties for retaliatory actions would further serve to incentivize superior officers against punishing service members who elect not to participate in experimental studies or ingest medical products for investigational or off-label purposes.

As a twenty-two-year veteran and officer in the US Army Medical Material Development Activity explains, individual consultation with service members would not impose an undue burden on the military: "As the largest training organization in the United States, perhaps in the world, DoD clearly has the capacity and resources to provide adequate information to each service member before he or she takes or uses an investigational product" (FDA 1999, 54, 182). A failure to do so could prove detrimental to future military efforts. For example, forced use of unapproved medical products has resulted in the loss of experienced service members. Notably, these service members did not have a negative opinion of vaccines in general but rather expressed concern over the off-label use of the anthrax vaccine (GAO 2002, 3–17).

The DoD has long argued that military necessity must trump a soldier's ability to decide whether he or she will submit to medical treatment deemed necessary by the armed forces. While this position is persuasive in instances where a failure to submit to treatment may place the military mission or others at risk, an exception should be made for investigational or off-label use of medical products. The FDA review process is not a rubber stamp, but rather a detailed analysis that considers anticipated risks and benefits in an effort to determine if a medical product is likely to be safe and effective for its intended use. Notably, 92 percent of products that enter clinical trials fail to earn FDA approval (*Nature Medicine* Editorial 2010, 347). Furthermore a study in the *Journal of the American Medical Association* found that of 160 commonly prescribed medicines, 73 percent of off-label uses "had little to no scientific support" (Psaty and Ray 2008, 1949). These statistics are significant when one considers that military populations may not opt out of treatments that the DoD deems are necessary for combat. The link between PB and Gulf War Syndrome should serve as a reminder of the serious adverse health effects that could result from mandatory use of experimental medical products. The DoD should not be permitted to mandate force-wide administration of a medical product absent FDA approval for the intended use.

4.3 Conclusion

The motto of the American military physician is "to conserve the fighting force," yet the last decade has seen a notable shift in emphasis to enhancing the fighting force through novel applications of biomedical enhancements. The nefarious conduct of military officials during the course of the mustard gas, radiation, and psychotropic drug experiments provides ample evidence of the "lies and half-truths" that the DoD has utilized in the name of national security. Indeed the Army Inspector General has acknowledged the "inadequacy of the Army's institutional memory" regarding research on service members (Moreno 2000, 254). When one considers socioeconomic dimensions of the armed forces, this history of neglect has served to further societal inequalities. As a judge on the Sixth Circuit and former Commander in Chief of the Ohio National Guard explains, "in a democracy we have far more to fear from the lack of military accountability than from the lack of military discipline or aggressiveness" (*Jaffee v. United States*, 663 F.2d 1226, 1267 (3d Cir. 1981)).

Despite the Supreme Court's deference to military judgment, the Court has also indicated that service members are entitled to constitutional protections as Americans (*Chappell v. Wallace*, 462 US 296, 304 (1983)). At the individual level, each service member should maintain patient autonomy and the right to refuse investigational or off-label products without fear of punitive repercussions. In the aggregate, the law should serve to instill a sense of confidence in service members that those with power will be held accountable for actions that violate individual rights. Patient autonomy and human dignity ought not be extinguished because one elects to serve their country and defend American freedoms.

Amending the Common Rule to classify military personnel as a vulnerable population not only will provide service members with additional safeguards, it will engage a national dialogue related to justice and beneficence in military medicine and research. While an amended Common Rule is not a panacea for addressing past wrongs or ensuring that future wrongs will be avoided, it does serve as an intelligent step toward harmonizing national security interests with fundamental principles of research ethics.

Note

Portions of this chapter were previously published in Parasidis (2012a, b).

References

Amoroso, Paul J., and Lynn L. Wenger. 2003. The human volunteer in military biomedical research. In Thomas E. Beam and Linette R. Sparacino, eds., *Military Medical Ethics*. Washington, DC: Borden Institute, 563–660.

Annas, Catherine L., and George J. Annas. 2009. Enhancing the fighting force: Medical research on American soldiers. *Journal of Contemporary Health Law and Policy* 25 (2): 283–308.

Annas, George J. 2011. American vertigo: "Dual use," prison physicians, research, and Guantanamo. *Case Western Reserve Journal of International Law* 43 (3): 631–50.

Anthrax Vaccine Congressional Report. 2000. The Department of Defense anthrax vaccine immunization program: Unproven force protection. *HR Report* 106-556.

Ball, Howard. 1986. Downwind from the bomb. *New York Times Magazine*, February 9, pp. 32–42.

DARPA. 2012. DARPA: Our work. Defense Advanced Research Projects Agency, Washington, DC. http://www.darpa.mil/our_work/.

Department of Defense (DoD). 2011. Protection of human subjects and adherence to ethical standards in DoD-supported research. Instruction No. 3216.02, November 8. http://www.dtic.mil/whs/directives/corres/pdf/321602p.pdf.

Doe v. Sullivan, 938 F.2d 1370 (DC Cir. 1991)

Food and Drug Administration (FDA). 1999. Protection of human subjects: Informed consent, exception from general requirements. Interim Final Rule. 64 *Federal Register* 192, 54, 188.

Gimbel, John. 1990. German scientists, United States Denazification policy, and the "Paperclip Conspiracy." *International History Review* 12 (3): 441–65.

Government Accountability Office (GAO). 2002. Anthrax vaccine: GAO's survey of guard and reserve pilots and aircrew. September. http://www.gao.gov/new.items/d02445.pdf.

Hoag, Hannah. 2003. Remote control. *Nature* 423 (6942): 796–98. doi:10.1038/423796a.

Human Radiation Experiments Report. 1996. *Final Report of the Advisory Committee on Human Radiation Experiments*. New York: Oxford University Press.

Institute of Medicine (IOM). 1993. *Veterans at Risk: The Health Effects of Mustard Gas and Lewisite*. Washington, DC: National Academies, Institute of Medicine.

Jaffee v. United States, 663 F.2d 1226, 1267 (3d Cir. 1981)

Moreno, Jonathan D. 2000. *Undue Risk*: Routledge.

Moreno, Jonathan D. 2006. *Mind Wars*. New York: Dana Press.

National Commission for the Protection of Human Subjects of Biomedical and Behavioral Research. 1979. *The Belmont Report: Ethical Principles and Guidelines for the Protection of Human Subjects of Research*. Washington, DC: GPO

Nature Medicine Editorial. 2010. Mechanism matters. *Nature Medicine* 16 (1): 347. doi:10.1038/nm0410-347.

Nightingale, Stuart L., Joanna M. Prasher, and Stewart Simonson. 2007. Emergency Use Authorization (EUA) to enable use of needed products in civilian and military emergencies, United States. *Emerging Infectious Diseases* 13 (7): 1046–51.

Parasidis, Efthimios. 2012a. Justice and beneficence in military medicine and research. *Ohio State Law Journal* 73 (4): 723–93.

Parasidis, Efthimios. 2012b. Human enhancement and experimental research in the military. *Connecticut Law Review* 44: 1117.

Price, David H. 2007. Buying a piece of anthropology. *Anthropology Today* 23 (3): 8–13. doi:10.1111/j.1467-8322.2007.00510.x.

Psaty, Bruce M., and Wayne Ray. 2008. FDA guidance on off-label promotion and the state of the literature from sponsors. *Journal of the American Medical Association* 299 (16): 1949–51. doi:10.1001/jama.299.16.1949.

Rempfer v. Sharfstein, 583 F.3d 860 (DC Cir. 2009)

Research Advisory Committee on Gulf War Veterans' Illnesses (Gulf War Illness Report). 2008. *Gulf War Illness and the Health of Gulf War Veterans: Scientific Findings and Recommendations*. Washington, DC: GPO. http://www.va.gov/RAC-GWVI/docs/Committee_Documents/GWIandHealthofGWVeterans_RAC-GWVIReport_2008.pdf.

Schroeter, Leonard W. 1996. Human experimentation, the Hanford Nuclear Site, and judgment at Nuremberg. *Gonzaga Law Review* 31 (2): 147–262.

Silverman, Henry. 2011. Protecting vulnerable research subjects in critical care trials: Enhancing the informed consent process and recommendations for safeguards. *Annals of Intensive Care* 1 (8): 1–7. doi:10.1186/2110-5820-1-8.

Smith, Susan L. 2008. Mustard gas and American race-based human experimentation in World War II. *Journal of Law, Medicine and Ethics* 36 (3): 517–21. doi:10.1111/j.1748-720X.2008.299.x.

5
Children as Research Partners in Community Pediatrics

Adam Braddock

A major goal of community pediatrics as a field of medicine is to identify and reduce the social, economic, and other environmental causes of poor child health (AAP 2005). Research in community pediatrics has blossomed in the wake of the discovery of social determinants of health (Greenberg 2003). Obesity, asthma, and environmental exposure to lead and other toxins are examples of child health problems that are impacted by social and economic disparities, and approaches to their evaluation and treatment may benefit from community-focused research. As community pediatrics research has gained prominence, community consultation and participation have been emphasized as ways of ensuring ethical and appropriate research (Duggan et al. 2005; AAP Committee on Native American Child Health and Committee on Community Health Services 2004). Involving community members in the research process can have many benefits for communities as well as for the research itself. Community participation can demonstrate respect for communities, improve the relevance of research to the communities most affected by poor health outcomes, elicit ideas for community health interventions, and enhance the skills and capacities of community participants (Buchanan, Miller, and Wallerstein 2007; Israel et al. 2010).

This chapter provides a framework for thinking about community research partnerships with children. I begin by briefly reviewing the federal regulations governing research with children. I define community research partnerships and show that there are practical, developmental, and moral reasons to encourage research partnerships with children, and that the status of children and adolescents as a "vulnerable population" provides additional support for community research partnerships. I then turn to age considerations, how to define communities in research partnerships, and the form and content of potential research partnerships with children. I conclude with some recommendations for institutional review boards (IRBs) regarding research partnerships with children; much could be done to promote this important form of research.

5.1 Children and the Common Rule

The Federal Policy for the Protection of Human Subjects ("Common Rule") identifies children and adolescents as a "vulnerable population" and regulates research with this group under subpart D, "Additional Protections for Children Involved as Subjects in Research" (45 CFR 46). Subpart D has not been adopted by all federal agencies, but where it has, it applies to research subjects who have not reached the legal age of consent in the jurisdiction where the research is conducted (45 CFR 46.402). The regulations classify pediatric research according to the level of risk and the prospect of direct benefit for study participants. "Minimal risk" research is defined as research in which "the probability and magnitude of harm or discomfort anticipated in the research are not greater in and of themselves than those ordinarily encountered in daily life or during the performance of routine physical or psychological examinations or tests" (45 CFR 46.102). Research that poses minimal risks may be approved without prospect of direct benefit for children in the study (45 CFR 46.404). For "minor increase over minimal risk" research, studies that do not provide the prospect of direct benefit may be approved for pediatric subjects if they are likely to provide generalizable knowledge of the subject's condition or disorder that is vital to understand or ameliorate it (45 CFR 46.406). This section permits a somewhat higher level of risk for studies that focus on a subject's medical condition without prospect of direct benefit. For research involving the prospect of direct benefit to participants, some studies may be approved that present "greater than minimal" risk (45 CFR 46.405). The regulations also provide a mechanism for federal panel review of research that would not be approved under the criteria above (45 CFR 46.407), and set out requirements for obtaining child assent and parental permission for research participation (45 CFR 46.408).

The aim of these regulations is to ensure adequate protections for pediatric research subjects by classifying research according to the level of risk and benefit. These requirements are more stringent than the regulations governing competent adults in the Common Rule, which do not specify the degree of risk acceptable for research other than requiring that risks are "minimized" and "reasonable in relation to anticipated benefits" to the individual subjects and/or society (45 CFR 46.111).

Despite the aim of the federal regulations to provide adequate protections to research subjects, the increasing importance of community research in medicine has revealed the limitations of current regulations in evaluating research concerning communities. A weakness of traditional research ethics is its focus on risks and benefits to individual research participants, ignoring the significant community risks and benefits that occur in research involving identifiable communities (Wallwork 2008). Research partnerships with communities add an additional layer of complexity by presenting risks and benefits related to the partnership process itself.

The following discussion of community partnerships will demonstrate the complexities of incorporating community perspectives into the research process. However, the discussion will also highlight the potential rewards of community collaboration and the need for researchers and research institutions to adapt to the emergence of community-engaged research in pediatrics and other fields.

5.2 Defining Community Participation

Community partnerships in research can range from passive consultation to enlistment of community members in leadership and decision-making roles. The idea of community participation has been formalized as community-based participatory research (CBPR), which is defined by the Agency for Healthcare Research and Quality as "a collaborative research approach that is designed to ensure and establish structures for participation by communities affected by the issues being studied, representatives of organizations, and researchers in all aspects of the research process to improve health and well-being through taking action, including social change" (Viswanathan et al. 2004). CBPR represents a commitment to meaningful involvement of community members in the research process, including selection of study topics, study design, participant recruitment, data collection, data analysis, and dissemination of research findings.

In practice, the role of community members in CBPR is often more narrowly focused on the strengths and abilities that researchers believe community members bring to the research effort. For example, community members with knowledge of neighborhood demographics might assist in participant recruitment. Community members that know which issues are most important to the community might aid in the selection and framing of the research topic. Many CBPR advocates view the ultimate goal as projects in which community members have an equitable role in all phases of research (Israel et al. 1998).

Children have traditionally been passive beneficiaries of community participation in research. Because children are developing cognitively and may be unable to provide informed consent, their opinions, values, and perspectives have been underrepresented in community pediatrics research. Even among manuscripts described as "CBPR with youth," only 15 percent of studies actually involved youth as partners in the research process (Jacquez, Vaughn, and Wagner 2013). Excluding young people's perspectives might make sense for research targeting very young children and research in which child input is impractical or irrelevant to the study. However, many pediatric community-based studies might benefit from research partnerships with children.

5.3 The Case for Children as Research Partners

There are practical, developmental, and moral reasons to encourage partnerships with children in community pediatrics research.

5.3.1 Practical Reasons

Research that includes children as partners may improve the quality of research results. Participatory research with adults has been advanced as a way of increasing the likelihood of research success (Israel et al. 1998). Meaningful partnerships with children will foster trust between the community and researchers and increase researcher accountability to the community. These factors might improve research quality by providing greater access to community members and by reducing participant withdrawal. In addition partnerships with children might improve the relevance and validity of research data by providing an opportunity for young people to convey knowledge of their own lives and experiences (Jacquez, Vaughn, and Wagner 2013). Young people's perspectives on issues such as school bullying and violence, mental health, and substance abuse can contribute to the research product and ensure that results reflect the concerns and opinions of the population studied.

5.3.2 Developmental Reasons

Children may have more sophisticated cognitive skills than previously thought (Kellet 2010). For example, some children have capacities greater than expected for age because of their experiences with chronic illness (Kodish 2005). Community psychologists have recognized the potential for children to contribute to the research process and have started teaching research skills to children (Langhout and Thomas 2010). A study in Ghana, Malawi, and South Africa involved youth ages 10 to 18 interviewing their peers about how problems with transportation and mobility affect their access to education, health care, and other services (Porter et al. 2010). In another study, an 11-year-old girl created a research narrative about her difficult experiences traveling with her wheelchair-dependent father (Kellet 2010). Some psychologists have found productive ways of engaging even younger children in the research process (Clark 2010). While adolescents are obvious candidates for research partnerships, these projects suggest that younger children also have the developmental maturity to take on an active role in the research process if researchers provide sufficient support.

5.3.3 Moral Reasons

There are several moral reasons for promoting children as research partners. Children are important members of their communities and have responsibilities in rituals, traditions, and other activities that may relate to the community research topic. Partnership in research is a way of acknowledging these roles and respecting the place of children and adolescents within the network of relationships and institutions that make up a community. Moreover research may have long-term effects that disproportionately impact children in the community. For example, genetic research could result in discrimination or societal stigma that affects future employment. Involving children in the research process may uncover or highlight unintended long-term effects and encourage the development of adequate research protections against harms arising from research. These benefits of child participation mirror some of the benefits of adult participation in community research, which include revealing community concerns, interests, and potential harms that researchers would not know if the community were not consulted (Weijer and Emanuel 2000).

Active participation in community research also has educational value for children. Fostering children's moral development has been advanced as a justification for nonbeneficial pediatric research (Bartholome 1976). Participatory research may have more educational value than traditional research because it teaches the values of equality, empowerment, and community solidarity through the research process. Indeed participatory research has been used to foster citizenship and political involvement in children through art (Montero 2009). Beyond fostering moral development, participatory research will teach children about the research process and the importance of scientific knowledge for the welfare of society.

Finally, research partnerships permit children to have a say in matters that affect their lives, which is one of the principles of the United Nations Convention on the Rights of the Child (UNCRC 1989). Taken to its extreme, this principle overstates the ability of children to consider the risks and benefits of important decisions and usurps the role of parents in guiding and protecting children. However, the need to protect children from potential harm and exploitation is consistent with the developmentally appropriate participation of children in the research process.

5.3.4 Vulnerability and Research Partnerships with Children

Understanding the reasons that children are a vulnerable population can also support research partnerships. Ken Kipnis describes vulnerability as "a certain precariousness in the condition of the subject: a state of being laid open or especially exposed to something injurious or otherwise undesirable, a potential avenue of attack" (Kipnis 2003, 108–109). Based on this definition, Kipnis identifies seven vulnerabilities of children as research subjects. His vulnerabilities include "incapacitational" vulnerability—lack of capacity to deliberate and decide about research participation; "juridic" vulnerability—lack of authority as a result of legal subordination; "deferential" vulnerability—patterns of deference as a result of social pressure; and "social" vulnerability—belonging to a group whose rights and interests have been socially disvalued (Kipnis 2003, 110). Children are vulnerable not only because of their inability to provide informed consent, but also because of social circumstances that leave them open to exploitation.

Incapacitational vulnerability holds for children who lack the developmental maturity to make decisions about research participation and are therefore vulnerable to exploitation by researchers. DeBruin (2004) recognizes that the remedy for this type of vulnerability is "paternalistic protections" designed to limit the degree of risk subjects are exposed to in a research study. These added protections are reflected in the federal regulations governing research involving children as subjects, which limit the research that is permitted without prospect of direct benefit to research subjects.

However, the remedy for vulnerability related to context or circumstance—such as juridic, deferential, and social vulnerabilities—is not paternalistic protections. These forms of vulnerability stem from marginalization, lack of authority, or other socially mediated factors, and are remedied by empowerment of research subjects:

Paternalistic protections, premised on the assumption that the vulnerable are incapable of protecting themselves, only serve to further demean such persons, and cannot be justified as remedies for these types of vulnerability. Instead, the research context should be designed to address the special risks of unjust treatment by, for example, using participatory research to empower such vulnerable participants to use their abilities to protect themselves. (DeBruin 2004, 77)

Research partnerships can therefore reduce these contextual types of vulnerability in children by providing a means of empowerment. Participation in the research process provides a safeguard against exploitation of children without further limiting their access as research subjects. This principle of reducing vulnerability through community-based participatory research has also been advocated for other vulnerable populations, including prisoners and individuals in developing countries (Perez and Treadwell 2009; Justo 2004).

5.3.5 Risks of Partnership with Children

While research partnerships with children are supported by many practical, developmental, and moral considerations, these partnerships do present unique risks to participants because of the nature of the collaborative process. For example, partnerships risk disruption to the community and inappropriate research roles for children. Disruptions to the community may result from conflict among community members during the research process, especially concerning sensitive topics like sexuality (Ross et al. 2010a). Research partnerships might generate stress or animosity among children and parents when community members disagree about an important issue. Research partnerships also risk giving children unwarranted influence over the research process. If children are given unreasonable tasks, asked their opinions on research questions designed for adults, or otherwise involved in a study in a developmentally inappropriate manner, research partnerships could produce unhelpful results or even harm children.

While the possibility of these harms should be considered in decisions regarding the permissibility of research partnerships, these risks seem relatively small. Research partnerships may be more likely to result in improvements in community dialogue than community disruption. The risk of developmentally inappropriate roles for children can be mitigated by careful attention to the content of research partnerships and the developmental status of children involved in research partnerships. It is hard to see how these or other partnership risks would qualify as greater than minimal risk under the federal regulations. However, there may be other risks—for example, individual and community risks related to research outcomes—that determine the permissibility of research projects apart from risks associated specifically with the partnership process (Ross 2010).

5.4 Forming Research Partnerships with Children

5.4.1 Assent as a Guide for Age Considerations in Research Partnerships

The concept of assent has informed discussions of child involvement in research and clinical decision-making (Kon 2006). "Assent" can be defined as a child's affirmative agreement to participate, and child assent with parental permission is a way of adapting the consent process to the pediatric population.

The discussion of assent in pediatrics provides an example of how pediatricians have formalized the relationship between age, maturity, and involvement in clinical or research decisions. While subpart D of the human subjects research regulations states only that IRBs should consider whether children in a particular study have the capacity to assent (45 CFR 46.408), pediatricians have developed more detailed recommendations regarding child assent. In American Academy of Pediatrics (AAP) clinical guidelines, examples of children as young as 8 are given to demonstrate when child assent is required for care, and informed consent is considered possible starting at 14 years of age (AAP Committee on Bioethics 1995). In AAP research guidelines, child assent in research is considered necessary starting at age 7 (AAP Committee on Drugs 1995a, b). The ages in these guidelines are similar to the ages of children described earlier in research partnerships with community psychologists and suggest some parallels in the maturity required for assent and participation in the research process. Depending on the research study and the skills required, some 7- and 8-year-old children are likely capable of collaborating with researchers during the research process.

While assent is a useful guide for age considerations in research partnerships, assent and participation in the research process require different skills. For example, a research project that involves children as data gatherers might require interpersonal and communication skills different from the cognitive skills involved in assent. Because the content of research partnerships will depend on the research project, it is difficult to provide age cutoffs or guidelines for participation in research partnerships. Consideration of both the content of the partnership and the developmental level of children will determine whether involvement is appropriate.

5.4.2 Defining the Community

Defining the community and how the community will be represented are important considerations in community-based research. Ross et al. (2010) use the concept of a structured group to define community engagement in research. A group might be defined by ethnic, socioeconomic, cultural, geographic, or medical factors. Once a group has been identified, appropriate representation and participation of the group must be determined. This determination is made through the group's structure, which requires identifying leadership and organization within the group. Structure is critical to community engagement because it provides a way to represent the interests, goals, and beliefs of community members during the research process. When researchers approach a group, it may already have a useful structure. If group structure is not in place then researchers may facilitate its development by appealing to a community-based organization (CBO) or prompting community members to organize on their own (Ross et al. 2010).

In pediatrics this concept of community as a structured group can be used with some modifications. For pre-adolescent children, the community should generally be understood as containing both parents and children. For example, a researcher wishing to study diet patterns among Hispanic elementary school students might engage children and their parents through school-based activities and a neighborhood Hispanic association. Similar principles apply in understanding a community of younger children with a chronic disease such as diabetes; these children can be understood as part of a community that includes other children with this disease and their parents. However, a group of adolescents (e.g., HIV-positive adolescents) may be understood as its own community. There may be important reasons for considering adolescent communities apart from parents, especially for sensitive topics like sexually transmitted infections, contraception, or drug use. The aim is identification of the proper scope of the community in question, and then determining how members of the community will participate or be represented in the research partnership.

5.4.3 Examples of Research Partnerships with Children

Adult community research partnerships have involved collaboration in all phases of the research process, including (1) selection of research topic, (2) study design, (3) participant recruitment, (4) data collection, (5) data analysis, and (6) dissemination of research findings. Partnerships with children are possible in these six phases as well. An example of a community health project that engaged youth in several stages of the research process is a study that involved adolescents in a community assessment of adolescent substance abuse (Brazg et al. 2011). This study used Photovoice, which is a method of research in which participants take photographs as a way of identifying and representing community concerns. In this study adolescents from an upper-middle-income community in Washington state took photographs answering the question, "In your community, what influences local adolescents' decisions to use or not to use alcohol and other drugs?" (Brazg et al. 2011, 504). Adolescent participants were involved not only in taking the photographs (data collection) but also in coding and photograph selection (data analysis) and dissemination of findings through a public presentation and exhibit. The authors felt that the study increased dialogue between adolescents and adult community members about adolescent substance abuse, enhanced data for inclusion in a community assessment report regarding adolescent substance abuse, and provided the community with a tangible product for discussions and actions around this issue (Brazg et al. 2011).

Another example of research partnerships with children is a study aimed at developing an online curriculum for youth with disabilities transitioning to postsecondary education (Rosen-Reynoso et al. 2010). In this study youth were involved in all stages of research in an iterative process of curricular development that included many revisions based on youth feedback. Youth (many with disabilities or special health care needs) were involved as research partners in several different groups in the study: the participatory research team, a youth advisory board, community-based organizations, and focus groups. The result was an online curriculum called OPT4College that covers postsecondary education options, college applications, financial aid, and medical and educational transition steps for individuals with disabilities or special health care needs. The researchers began testing the effectiveness of the curriculum with youth serving roles in participant recruitment and interviewing (Rosen-Reynoso et al. 2010).

These examples illustrate the variety of participatory roles that children and adolescents can have in community research. Forming research partnerships with children requires several critical considerations, including how the community will be defined and represented, the age and developmental level of children that will participate, and the content of participation. However, many of these questions are similar to the questions addressed by researchers in adult community-based participatory research, and the proliferation of participatory studies involving adults suggests that these challenges can be overcome.

5.5 Research Partnerships and IRBs

The 2011 ANPRM (DHHS 2011) details several proposed changes to the federal regulations governing human subjects research. None of the revisions refer to subpart D or otherwise apply specifically to the pediatric population. Current federal regulations permit many research partnerships with children and revision of the regulations in light of these partnerships is likely unnecessary. However, I offer the following recommendations to IRBs to further promote the development of research partnerships with children:
1. Include IRB members with expertise in evaluating pediatric community-based participatory research.
2. Include children in pediatric IRB review of community-based participatory research.

Including IRB members with expertise in pediatric community-based participatory research would help ensure that pediatric IRBs have the knowledge to assess this form of research. IRBs without adequate knowledge of CBPR may be less likely to provide appropriate review and may fail to permit worthy research because it does not fit into the traditional research paradigm. Moreover the presence of pediatric IRB members with expertise in CBPR could signal to others in the research enterprise the importance of this form of research. Including children in IRB review of pediatric CBPR would extend the principles of community partnership with children to the IRB review process itself, where children and adolescents could provide their own perspectives regarding review of research protocols. The process of partnership with children in IRB review would reinforce the commitment to respecting and empowering the voices of children in the research process.

Following these recommendations would provide some support for community research partnerships with children and encourage understanding among researchers and research institutions of the challenges, goals, and benefits of these research partnerships. Community research partnerships can be promoted by making IRBs more comfortable reviewing these studies and researchers more aware of the possibilities for collaboration with children.

5.6 Conclusion

Skeptics of community research partnerships with children will argue that these partnerships overestimate the abilities of children to participate in a sophisticated research process. Some research may indeed be too sophisticated for children to have a partnership role, but many other studies will provide opportunities for meaningful partnership. While children are not little adults, they possess many skills that are relevant to community research. If clinical and research assent are possible for children as young as 8 years old, children are likely to have thoughts and feelings about the research process and deserve respect for their developing autonomy and role in the community. Questions will arise about when children's views should be incorporated into the research process, but the same issues are present with participatory research involving adults.

Community pediatrics research should strive to engage children in the research process. If they provide sufficient protections, research partnerships can help researchers achieve their scientific goals while respecting the valuable perspectives of young people.

References

American Academy of Pediatrics (AAP) Committee on Drugs. 1995a. Guidelines for the ethical conduct of studies to evaluate drugs in pediatric populations. *Pediatrics* 95 (2): 286–94.

American Academy of Pediatrics (AAP) Committee on Bioethics. 1995b. Informed consent, parental permission, and assent in pediatric practice. *Pediatrics* 95 (2): 314–17.

American Academy of Pediatrics (AAP) Committee on Native American Child Health and Committee on Community Health Services. 2004. Ethical considerations in research with socially identifiable populations. *Pediatrics* 113 (1): 148–51.

American Academy of Pediatrics (AAP). 2005. The pediatrician's role in community pediatrics. *Pediatrics* 115 (4): 1092–94.

Bartholome, William G. 1976. Parents, children, and the moral benefits of research. *Hastings Center Report* 6 (6): 44–45. doi:10.2307/3561149.

Brazg, Tracy, Betty Bekemeier, Clarence Spigner, and Colleen E. Huebner. 2011. Our community in focus: The use of Photovoice for youth-driven substance abuse assessment and health promotion. *Health Promotion Practice* 12 (4): 502–11. doi:10.1177/1524839909358659.

Buchanan, David R., Franklin G. Miller, and Nina Wallerstein. 2007. Ethical issues in community-based participatory research: Balancing rigorous research with community participation in community intervention studies. *Progress in Community Health Partnerships* 1 (2): 153–60. doi:10.1353/cpr.2007.0006.

Clark, Alison. 2010. Young children as protagonists and the role of participatory, visual methods in engaging multiple perspectives. *American Journal of Community Psychology* 46 (1–2): 115–23. doi:10.1007/s10464-010-9332-y.

DeBruin, Debra A. 2004. Looking beyond the limitations of "vulnerability": Reforming safeguards in research. *American Journal of Bioethics* 4 (3): 76–78. doi:10.1080/15265160490497579.

Department of Health and Human Services (DHHS). 2011. Advance Notice of Proposed Rulemaking. Human subjects research protections: Enhancing protections for research subjects and reducing burden, delay, and ambiguity for investigators. *Federal Register* 76 (143): 44512–31.

Duggan, Anne, James Jarvis, D. Christian Derauf, C. Andrew Aligne, and Jeffrey Kaczorowski. 2005. The essential role of research in community pediatrics. *Pediatrics* 115 (4 suppl):1195–1201. doi:10.1542/peds.2004-2825T.

Greenberg, Robert E. 2003. Community pediatrics research. *Pediatrics* 112 (3): 766–69.

Israel, Barbara A., Amy J. Schulz, Edith A. Parker, and Adam B. Becker. 1998. Review of community-based research: Assessing partnership approaches to improve public health. *Annual Review of Public Health* 19 (1): 173–202.

Israel, Barbara A., Chris M. Coombie, Rebecca R. Cheezum, Amy J. Schulz, Robert J. McGranaghan, Richard Lichtenstein, Angela G. Reyes, Jaye Clement, and Akosua Burris. 2010. Community-based participatory research: A capacity-building approach for policy advocacy aimed at eliminating health disparities. *American Journal of Public Health* 100 (11): 2094–2102. doi:10.2105/AJPH.2009.170506.

Jacquez, Farrah, Lisa M. Vaughn, and Erin Wagner. 2013. Youth as partners, participants or passive recipients: A review of children and adolescents in community-based participatory research (CBPR). *American Journal of Community Psychology* 51 (June): 176–89. doi:10.1007/s10464-012-9533-7.

Justo, Luis. 2004. Participatory research: A way to reduce vulnerability. *American Journal of Bioethics* 4 (3): 67–68.

Kellet, Mary. 2010. Small shoes, big steps! Empowering children as active researchers. *American Journal of Community Psychology* 46 (1–2): 195–203.

Kipnis, Kenneth. 2003. Seven vulnerabilities in the pediatrics research subject. *Theoretical Medicine and Bioethics* 24 (2): 107–20.

Kodish, Eric. 2005. Ethics and research with children: An introduction. In Eric Kodish, ed., *Ethics and Research with Children: A Case-Based Approach*. New York: Oxford University Press, 3–25.

Kon, Alexander A. 2006. Assent in pediatric research. *Pediatrics* 117 (5): 1806–10.

Langhout, Regina D., and Elizabeth Thomas. 2010. Imagining participatory action research in collaboration with children: An introduction. *American Journal of Community Psychology* 46 (1–2): 60–66. doi:10.1007/s10464-010-9321-1.

Montero, Maritza. 2009. Community action and research as citizenship construction. *American Journal of Community Psychology* 43 (1–2): 149–61.

Perez, Leda, and Henrie M. Treadwell. 2009. Determining what we stand for will guide what we do: Community priorities, ethical research paradigms, and research with vulnerable populations. *American Journal of Public Health* 99 (2): 201–204. doi: 10.2105/AJPH.2008.125617.

Porter, Gina, Kate Hampshire, Michael Bourdillon, Elsbeth Robson, Alister Munthali, Albert Abane, and Mac Mashiri. 2010. Children as research collaborators: Issues and reflections from a mobility study in sub-Saharan Africa. *American Journal of Community Psychology* 46 (1–2): 215–27. doi:10.1007/s10464-010-9317-x.

Rosen-Reynoso, Myra, Matthew Kusminsky, Stelios Gragoudas, Heather Putney, Morgan K. Crossman, James Sinclair, and Jadine Yarde. 2010. Youth-based participatory research: Lessons learned from a transition research study. *Pediatrics* 126 (3 suppl):S177–82.

Ross, Lainie F. 2010. 360 Degrees of human subjects protections in community-engaged research. *Science Translational Medicine* 2 (45): cm23. doi:10.1126/scitranslmed.3001162.

Ross, Lainie F., Allan Loup, Robert M. Nelson, Jeffrey R. Botkin, Rhonda Kost, George R. Smith, Jr., and Sarah Gehlert. 2010. Human subjects protections in community-engaged research: A research ethics framework. *Journal of Empirical Research on Human Research Ethics* 5 (1): 5–17. doi:10.1525/jer.2010.5.1.5.

UNCRC. 1989. Declaration of the Rights of the Child. UN Committee on the Rights of the Child, Geneva.

Viswanathan, Meera, Alice Ammerman, Eugenia Eng, Gerald Gartlehner, Kathleen N. Lohr, Derek Griffith, Scott Rhodes, et al. 2004. *Community-Based Participatory Research: Assessing the Evidence*. Rockville, MD: Agency for Healthcare Research and Quality.

Wallwork, Ernest. 2008. Ethical analysis of research partnerships with communities. *Kennedy Institute Journal of Ethics* 18 (1): 57–85.

Weijer, Charles, and Ezekiel J. Emanuel. 2000. Protecting communities in biomedical research. *Science* 289 (5482): 1142–44. doi:10.1126/science.289.5482.1142.

6

Back to the Future? Examining the Institute of Medicine's Recommendations to Loosen Restrictions on Using Prisoners as Human Subjects[1]

Osagie K. Obasogie

The chapters in this volume generally use the 2011 Advance Notice of Proposed Rulemaking (ANPRM) as a starting point to discuss the changing landscape of human subjects research regulation. This chapter, however, discusses an issue that is not explored in depth in the ANPRM yet is part of bioethicists' broader conversations about rethinking existing rules: human subjects research with prisoners. A key example of this effort can be seen in the Institute of Medicine's (IOM) 2006 recommendations to DHHS to loosen federal restrictions (45 CFR 46.300 et seq.) regarding the use of prisoners as human subjects in biomedical, epidemiological, and behavioral research (IOM 2006). Supporters of these recommendations point to the growing need for more clinical trial participants, improved institutional oversight, greater penetration of ethical values into research norms since the current restrictions were implemented in the 1970s, and prisoners' right to be included in biomedical and behavioral research. Critics tend to highlight past abuses and their likelihood to repeat themselves.

While at odds, this conversation's high stakes have led both sides to largely focus on the possible outcomes of this proposed shift rather than to look more carefully at how normative claims emanating from ethics discourses are being leveraged to recommend substantial changes to regulatory policy. Although it would be an overstatement to say that the prison research debate has been wholly consequentialist in nature, the current framing nonetheless takes the recommendations largely at face value without examining how the IOM reasoned to its recommendations. This raises a central question: What methods, approaches, and assumptions did the IOM rely upon in recommending that current restrictions should be loosened? Was the IOM's approach to research ethics—in terms of the methods used, the social contexts it identified as relevant to the issue, and the normative paradigms chosen to inform its decision-making—robust enough to justify overturning thirty years of regulatory precedent?

I argue that it was not. Biomedical and research ethics offer many contributions for thinking through the proper relationship between doctors and patients as well as the government's role in protecting human subjects in scientific research. While ethics certainly has a place in policy discussions, I argue that it is not in and of itself a sufficient basis from which to develop public policy. This is where the IOM Committee's report misses the mark. The IOM Committee largely treats its report as a scholarly exercise in ethics that should be adopted as regulatory policy rather than embracing its role as an independent government advisor that can provide the necessary bridgework to bring ethical inquiries into public policy-making in a robust and credible manner. This shortcoming is evident in at least three ways. First, from a methodological standpoint, the IOM Committee did not undertake a serious empirical assessment (i.e., collecting primary data) of modern prison conditions and instead based its updated ethical framework on a literature review of scholarly papers. Second, in terms of having an appropriate context from which to understand the ethics of prison research, the IOM Committee situated its ethical inquiries into prisoners' vulnerability by looking only at prisons' shifting demographics (racial disparities, health inequalities, etc.) without examining how shifting market conditions may lead researchers to treat vulnerable human subjects in a less-than-virtuous manner. Last, the IOM Committee did not meaningfully acknowledge other substantive sources that inform normative commitments to human subject protection outside of research ethics or biomedical ethics—namely human rights. Taken together, these methodological, contextual, and substantive critiques suggest that the IOM's recommendations leave too much to be desired to meaningfully inform regulatory policy. Each of these limitations will be discussed below.

6.1 The Institute of Medicine's Recommendations on Prison Research

6.1.1 Background
In 2004 the DHHS Office for Human Research Protections commissioned the IOM to "review the ethics regarding research involving prisoners" (IOM 2006). In particular, the IOM was charged with "examining whether the conclusions reached in 1976 by the National Commission for the Protection of Human Subjects of Biomedical and Behavioral Research

(Commission) remain appropriate today" (IOM 2006). The 1976 Commission was convened following the revelation of significant abuses in scientific research as a way to improve government oversight and human subject protection. To the extent that it is widely acknowledged that the 1976 Commission's report was the basis for current federal regulation of human subjects research, and that the agency commissioning the report (DHHS) is the regulatory body that oversees and enforces these regulations, the IOM report has been seen largely as a serious attempt to rethink current restrictions on using prisoners in human subjects research.

The IOM report is the most recent chapter in a much longer conversation on using prisoners as human subjects (Hornblum 1998). Prisoners' participation in biomedical and behavioral research was common in the United States throughout most of the twentieth century. Today we largely associate unethical practices such as coercion and not obtaining subjects' consent with Nazi medicine's ghastly horrors. But these practices were far from unique to the Holocaust; ethical lapses led popular drugs such as Retin-A to be developed literally on prisoners' backs before being mainstreamed into many Americans' drug cabinets. Indeed the questionable practices that ultimately led to the dramatic postwar increase in using prisoners as human subjects predated the Nuremberg trials by nearly half a century.

Despite the horrific stories that came out of the Nuremberg trials and other narratives detailing Nazi research practices, medical researchers in the United States continued to go about their business without giving much thought to the Nuremberg Code or other emerging ethical principles (Hornblum 1998). American exceptionalism and the increasing profit motive stemming from rapidly expanding research industries clouded opportunities for self-reflection, leading to inmates' continued exposure to dangerous research. This included radioactive blood tests, live cancer cell injections, and even behavioral and mind control experiments. It was not uncommon for inmates to be either purposely given a disease or kept from safer alternatives in order to test experimental drugs or procedures. This quickly became standard fare: according to some reports, 90 percent of all new pharmaceuticals were tested on prisoners until the 1970s (Urbina 2006).

Sensibilities began to shift in the 1970s with a number of revelations regarding the unethical treatment of vulnerable communities—both prisoners and nonprisoners. The growing criticism of human subjects research among the general population was ushered in by a number of events, but none so striking as the uncovering of the Tuskegee experiment in which rural Black men with syphilis were deliberately left untreated so that researchers could study the course of their disease. However, public exposure of what was happening within prisons also played a key role. For example, it was during this period that the Holmesburg Prison experiments became public; an array of studies coordinated in large part by the University of Pennsylvania used prisoners to explore everything from shampoo and deodorants to dioxin and chemical warfare materials. It was not uncommon for prisoners to suffer significantly during these experiments (Urbina 2006). Major pharmaceutical companies were involved, such as Dow Chemical and RJ Reynolds, not to mention the United States Army (Hornblum 1998).

With these revelations came the National Commission for the Protection of Human Subjects of Biomedical and Behavioral Research. This commission was created by the National Research Act, Pub. L. 93–348, 88 Stat. 342 (1974), to "develop ethical guidelines for the conduct of research involving human subjects and to make recommendations for the application of such guidelines to research conducted or supported by [what is now DHHS]" (1976 Commission). The Commission based its 1976 recommendations on an examination of "the conditions under which [prison] research is conducted, and the possible grounds for continuation, restriction or termination of such research" (1976 Commission). To do this, "members and staff made site visits to four prisons and two research facilities outside prisons that use prisoners, in order to obtain first-hand information on the conduct of biomedical research and the operation of behavioral programs in these settings" (1976 Commission). These visits included interviews with prisoners who had participated in research while incarcerated, as well as with nonparticipants. For the Commission, the task of developing ethical practices was as much of an empirical investigation as a principled one. These site visits provided a grounded assessment for what the Commission considered to be the key ethical considerations regarding prisoners' human subject participation: "(1) whether prisoners bear a fair share of the burdens and receive a fair share of the benefits of research; and (2) whether prisoners are, in the words of the Nuremberg Code, 'so situated as to be able to exercise free power of choice'—that is, whether prisoners can give truly voluntary consent to participate in research" (1976 Commission). By explicitly referencing the Nuremburg Code, the Commission implied that the abuses conducted by American physicians and researchers raised concerns similar to those raised by scientists put on trial after World War II. To the extent that the American research industry did not see itself in this manner, drawing upon the Nuremburg Code to ground recommendations for American physicians' behavior was a profound paradigm shift. To be sure, the Commission noted, "it is within the context of a concern to implement these principles that the Commission has deliberated the question of use of prisoners as research subjects" (Commission 1976).

This sensibility led the Commission to take a protectionist approach in providing recommendations regarding prisoners' participation in biomedical and behavioral research. In applying the basic ethical principles of justice ("that persons and groups be treated fairly") and respect for persons ("that the autonomy of persons be promoted and protected"), the Commission rejected other interpretations and favored the protection of prisoners from abuse and exploitation:

When persons seem regularly to engage in activities which, were they stronger or in better circumstances, they would avoid, respect dictates that they be protected against those forces that appear to compel their choices. (Commission 1976)

While the Commission's definitions of "justice" and "respect for persons" as motivating ethical principles may seem vague, they nonetheless gave substance to its protectionist approach that led to important recommendations. For example, the Belmont Report—developed in the 1970s in the wake of public outcry over abuses with research subjects—proposed ethical principles that informed new rules in the Code of Federal Regulations that strengthened all human subject protections. Additional subparts were added to provide specific protections for research involving vulnerable subjects. Subpart C reflects many of the recommendations put forth by the 1976 Commission. It permits research with prisoners only when it falls within one of four categories:

1. studying the possible causes, effects, and processes of incarceration and/or criminal behavior;

2. studying prisons as institutional structures or prisoners as incarcerated persons;

3. research on conditions that particularly affect prisoners as a class; or

4. research developed to improve subjects' health and well-being.

The general standard that governs subpart C is one of "minimal risk," or that the potential harm to research subjects should not exceed what one might encounter in daily life or routine medical examination. Under these regulations (which only apply to research funded or conducted by DHHS, the Social Security Administration, the Central Intelligence Agency, or voluntarily compliant institutions), "the default position is that no such research [with prisoners] should occur, and the four or five categories of research allowed under the regulations are essentially exceptions to that general rule" (IOM 2006).

6.1.2 The 2006 IOM Report and Its "Evolved" Ethical Framework for Evaluating Prison Research

The IOM's 2006 report, *Ethical Considerations for Research Involving Prisoners*, was commissioned by DHHS, and the Committee's charge "was to explore whether the conclusions reached in 1976 . . . remain appropriate today" (IOM 2006). Weighing in at 265 pages, the report takes what appears to be an exhaustive look at all of the issues involved. Concluding that current restrictions should be loosened while boosting overall oversight, the IOM makes five major recommendations:

1. Expand the definition of "prisoner."

2. Ensure universal, consistent ethical protection.

3. Shift from a category-based to a risk–benefit approach to research review.

4. Update the framework to include collaborative responsibility (e.g., developing research in collaboration with prisoners and prison staff).

5. Enhance oversight of research involving prisoners.

The first and last two recommendations are largely uncontroversial if not unequivocally beneficial in and of themselves. The third recommendation—shifting from prisoners' almost categorical exclusion from research to a more permissive risk–benefit analysis—is where the ethical road meets the legal rubber. This recommendation will be the focus of the rest of this chapter.

As discussed earlier, current regulations (informed by the 1976 Commission's ethical framework and findings) prioritize justice—defined here as whether prisoners are treated fairly and whether they bear a fair share of the research benefits and burdens—and respect for persons, which questions whether prisoners have enough personal autonomy to give voluntary consent. In short, the 1976 Commission felt that prison was no place to conduct widespread scientific research. The 2006 IOM Committee begins by creating "an updated ethical framework" based on its conclusion that "ideas about justice and respect for persons have evolved over the past three decades" (IOM 2006). Put differently, the 2006 Committee sidesteps the threshold issue concerning prison conditions presented by the 1976 Commission and instead asks whether ideas about ethical principles have changed. Its first evolutionary update is to "[question] the myopia caused by ... a narrow focus" (IOM 2006) on informed consent. After reviewing a handful of articles, the Committee notes, "more attention needs to be paid to risks and risk–benefit analysis rather than the formalities of an informed consent document" (IOM 2006). This shapes the major recommendation to stop thinking of prisoners as a category of individuals who, by default, should not be human subjects. Instead, the Committee recommends looking at each research proposal on a case-by-case basis to assess its potential risks and benefits. The Committee's second evolutionary update is to expand "justice" from its original meaning in 1976 to now include collaborative responsibility, whereby prisoners are able to give input on research design.

This shift from a substantive approach to justice and respect for persons (emphasizing protection, fairness, and burden-sharing) to a more procedural mechanism (emphasizing representation, along with the noncategorical risk–benefit analysis) constitutes the IOM Committee's "evolved" or "updated" ethical framework. The Committee believes that prisoners' participation should no longer be highly restricted simply because they are prisoners, which runs directly against the 1976 Commission's concern with prisoners as a category of human subjects to the extent "that the status of being a prisoner makes possible the perpetration of certain systemic injustices" (Commission 1976). The 2006 IOM Committee suggests changing regulatory policies to cut in a different, more permissive direction: the benefits and risks of research should be weighed independently before a decision is made.

6.2 Beyond Consequences: A Critique of the Institute of Medicine's Recommendations

The IOM's updated ethical framework and recommendations have not been discussed widely. While perspectives have been mixed, the existing discourse has been largely consequentialist in nature; namely the focus has been on the potential outcomes that this shift might produce. There has not been a robust scholarly critique of the *reasoning* and *methodology* behind the IOM's proposed ethical stance on prisoners' participation as human subjects. This section fills this gap.

The IOM's updated ethical framework leads to a series of important questions. How did the IOM Committee come to its decision? What were the Committee's reasons for supplanting the 1976 Commission's ethical framework? How do they justify recommending a substantial departure from thirty years of regulatory policies regarding prisoners' participation as human subjects? Are the reasons and ethical principles behind these justifications persuasive? Are there any limitations with the logic behind the IOM Committee's new ethical framework?

The IOM report is certainly laudable in attempting to provide better oversight for prisoners' participation as human subjects and reviewing whether the ethical commitments made three decades ago still serve prisoners' best interest. Yet there are at least three key critiques of the committee's approach—spanning its methods, context, and substance—that raise serious questions about the IOM's more permissive ethical framework.

6.2.1 Methodological Critique

How we come to a particular decision is often as important as the decision itself. Thus critiquing the methods behind the IOM's report involves investigating the data, assumptions, conclusions, and arguments that inform the ethical choices that are made. The first methodological issue stems from the fact that the Committee "visited one prison and one prison medical facility to discuss experimentation with current prisoners and peer educators" (IOM 2006). This rather cursory firsthand look at the modern conditions of prison life is a stark contrast to the more in-depth examination made by the 1976 Commission, which based its recommendations on conditions observed during four site visits made to different types of prisons across the country. The 1976 Commission based its assessment on an empirical investigation into prisoners' lived conditions and developed an ethical framework of protectionism that evolved out of its grounded assessment that basic ethical norms of justice and respect for persons would be difficult to achieve in a prison setting. Not only did the IOM Committee not replicate the methodological rigor behind this approach, it also did not fully engage the conditional nature of the 1976 Commission's sense of when these restrictions should be lifted: "should coercions be lessened and more equitable systems for the sharing of burdens and benefits be devised, respect for persons and concern for justice would suggest that prisoners not be deprived of the opportunity to participate in research."

This first critique concerning the Institute of Medicine's cursory assessment of modern prison life is tied to a second methodological critique. Rather than engaging in an empirical understanding of prison conditions and how this may affect prisoners' participation in scientific research, the IOM relies heavily on shifting academic perspectives to form its ethical framework. What is remarkable, however, is that the IOM Committee bases this new framework—which drives its policy recommendation to loosen restrictions—not on a substantial shift in the literature documenting prison experiences but rather on what it calls an evolution in the ethics literature:

> Ideas about justice and respect for persons have evolved over the past three decades. To construct a comprehensive ethical framework for thinking about research in prisons, [we explore] recent research ethics scholarship. Changes in the way these principles have been conceptualized have influenced the shape of our recommendations. (IOM 2006)

Put another way, the committee bases its recommendations largely on a literature review. While there is certainly a place for assessing academic perspectives as part of the process of reviewing the adequacy of current regulations, prisons are profoundly unique environments whose every nuance and empirical reality must be brought into the policy-making process. There is a strong argument that the focus of the Committee's ethical reasoning—that "ideas about justice and respect for persons have evolved over the past three decades"—misses the point. The question is not simply whether academics, clinical practitioners, and other medical professionals have changed their minds but, more important, whether the conditions giving rise to the 1976 Commission's ethical framework—such as coercion and lack of privacy—have been substantively addressed. The IOM Committee does not fully address this threshold question.

6.2.2 Contextual Critique

The IOM report uses past abuses with research in prisons as the main basis from which to situate its recommendations. This means that this history functions as the primary contextual backdrop that informs the IOM's understanding of the situation, the risks, and dangers involved, and the sensitive ethical terrain that needs to be navigated. This history provides a context that informs every aspect of the report, perhaps as a way to demonstrate a commitment to not allowing the past to become present. This is evident in different ways. The most explicit example is the report's second chapter, where the Committee discusses current prison demographics, health issues, and research environment in relation to the past. This chapter provides a veritable laundry list of all the conditions that complicate the idea of conducting ethical research in prison environments, and how these conditions have worsened in just about every conceivable way. Health care is abysmal, the incarcerated population has exploded and prisons are overcrowded, racial minorities are disproportionately represented, the number of incarcerated women has increased significantly, and prisoners are routinely exposed to violence.

But are changing prison demographics the only relevant context from which to think through the ethical challenges presented by using incarcerated people in scientific research? What is remarkable about the IOM's conceptualization of prisoners' vulnerability is that it is framed as a function of "what happens in prisons" rather than the commercial forces that, in some instances, can lead researchers to seek prisoners in the first place. Put differently, the IOM Committee understands the potential for abuse stemming only from prison conditions, not the *market conditions* that can make prisons attractive places for research entities to find cheap and plentiful human subjects and perhaps not uphold the highest ethical standards.

For example, existing shortages of human subjects can intersect with research interests in a manner that may exacerbate prison research abuses. It is estimated that as much as $5 million (not to mention countless opportunities to improve patients' lives) is lost each day a new medication's approval stalls, and 80 percent of all drugs tested on humans never receive FDA approval, partly as a result of this shortage (Evans, Smith, and Willen 2005). While the pharmaceutical industry did not play a formal role in IOM's recommendations, it would not be implausible to think that the well-documented inadequate supply of human subjects, their high demand, and the strong financial incentives to resolve this imbalance may have influenced the overall sensibility in research and professional communities to relax current restrictions. Timothy Wiegand notes:

Currently, there is a significant demand for pharmaceutical testing. From 1995 to 2005, the contract research industry, grown out of the increasing need for subject recruitment for clinical trials, has grown from a 1 billion to a 7 billion dollar per year industry. Along with increasing testing needs has come high profile cases of drug toxicity, and these cases have created increased public awareness about the need for study and surveillance of drug toxicity. For example, it has been suggested that increased testing of Vioxx would have prevented the delay in discovering its cardiovascular toxicity. (2007, 37)

It is surprising that the IOM report does not acknowledge how profit motives and market dynamics can play as significant of a role as prison conditions in giving rise to potentially abusive research environments. The search for new blockbuster drugs is a powerful motivator for corporations seeking to maintain their profitability. Sectors of the research industry immediately recognized how loosened regulations concerning prisoners' participation in scientific research might dramatically improve their bottom lines, as noted in this pharmaceutical newsletter:

> The pharmaceutical industry, who said it was not involved in the [IOM] panel's decision, will be thrilled at the news, as it continues to struggle to recruit enough suitable patients for clinical trials. Patient recruitment is now consuming thirty per cent of clinical trial time—more time than any other clinical trial activity—and almost half of all trial delays result from patient recruitment problems. These delays are costing drug companies over half a million dollars for specialty products and more than 8m [euro] for blockbuster brands in lost sales and are also causing the cost of running clinical trials to skyrocket. Meanwhile, the 2.3m-strong US prison population remains an untapped resource for patients who are perfect for clinical trials. (Barnes 2006)

The crucial role that human subjects play in the profitability of research efforts draws attention to the pressures that can lead to vulnerable populations' questionable treatment by researchers. This highlights the extent to which the conditions that shape human subjects abuse are not simply those that come from the living conditions of participants but also those that shape the financial interests of the industries conducting the research. While there has been conversation about the changes needed in prison environments before such research can be truly ethical, there needs to be more thought about the changes that need to occur within the research industry before they are once again given greater access to prison populations.

6.2.3 Substantive Critique

This leads to the third critique: isolating the ethical questions surrounding the use of prisoners as human subjects from broader normative paradigms directly relevant to prisoners' daily lives—most important, human rights—may obscure the full impact of the IOM's recommendations. The methodological critique concerned itself with how the IOM Committee came to its recommendations and the contextual critique examined which set of conditions the Committee acknowledged as relevant to its deliberations. This substantive critique deals with how the Committee engages the substance of its ethical deliberations with other normative paradigms relevant to the treatment of human subjects. Notably, the IOM's failure to meaningfully engage with established human rights norms and standards—such as those laid out in the Universal Declaration of Human Rights—is troubling. To be sure, the IOM report discusses the ways in which prison settings complicate traditional notions of informed consent and noncoercion. But it is one thing to discuss these complications as merely a matter of research ethics. It is quite another to engage them as a matter of human rights.

Although the IOM might resist this type of dual engagement with both ethics and human rights as being too far afield from its mandate and area of expertise, such responses to this critique fail to acknowledge the interconnected nature of biomedical ethics and human rights. Bioethicist Arthur Caplan has noted, "bioethics was born from the ashes of the Holocaust" (Annas 2005, 161). Similarly human rights took on a new importance during this period. George Annas notes that ethics and human rights "have a natural symbiosis . . . [that] can be most closely discerned in crimes against humanity that have historically involved physicians, such as torture, imprisonment, execution, and lethal human experimentation" (Annas 2005, xiv). This passage draws attention to the unique role prisoners have played in the development of ethics and international human rights. While they are often considered to be two distinct fields, a growing number of scholars are realizing that "human rights and medical ethics are complementary, and the use of the two together maximizes the protection available to the vulnerable patient" (Peel 2005, 173).

The connections between bioethics and human rights is far from coincidental; vesting internationally agreed-upon rights in every person and creating ethical standards for research involving human subjects were and continue to be seen as two sides of the same coin shielding humanity from reliving its darkest moments. Biomedical ethics—and in particular, research ethics—are most legitimate when subjects' human rights are secure. It makes little sense for ethical inquiries to isolate themselves from human rights. Continuing to do so can lead to situations where research ethics can be misused to exacerbate human rights violations; subjects living in conditions where basic human rights are not upheld might agree to participate in studies that they otherwise might not—a subtle but important form of coercive leverage.

Is it possible to conduct ethical research with prisoners in a way that is consistent with various human rights norms? This is an important empirical and legal question that is beyond this chapter's narrow focus on a substantive deficit within IOM's chosen ethical framework. But without this deeper analysis and integrated framework that substantively brings both ethics and human rights considerations directly into its policy deliberations, the IOM's recommendation to loosen current restrictions might have the unintended effects of exposing prisoners to additional health risks and exacerbating ongoing human rights violations.

6.3 Conclusion

To date, the recommendations put forth by the 2006 IOM report have not led to any changes in the regulations governing human subjects research with prisoners, although changes to subpart C are still possible. Before DHHS moves forward with any further consideration of the IOM report, the methodological, contextual, and substantive limitations raised by this chapter should be taken seriously. As biomedical and research ethics are sought to inform increasing areas of regulatory policy, what is important is that there be a broad recognition that ethical inquiries are not, in and of themselves, a source of public policy. While their contributions are invaluable, too much is at stake when such policy recommendations are not methodologically robust, do not acknowledge the rich and overlapping contexts that inform the issue, and isolate one set of moral principles without a substantive engagement with other relevant norms. Regrettably, in these and other failures, the IOM's report may very well come to stand for the proposition of how *not* to infuse ethics into regulatory policy.

Note

1. This chapter is excerpted from my work that previously appeared in the *Stanford Journal of Civil Rights and Civil Liberties* as: Prisoners as human subjects: A closer look at the Institute of Medicine's recommendations to loosen restrictions on using prisoners in scientific research, *Stanford Journal of Civil Rights and Civil Liberties* 6 (2010): 41.

References

Annas, George J. 2005. *American Bioethics: Crossing Human Rights and Health Law Boundaries*. Oxford: Oxford University Press.

Barnes, Kirsty. 2006. Prisoners may be used to fill clinical trial patient shortage. Outsourcing-Pharma.com. August 17. http://www.outsourcing-pharma.com/Clinical-Development/Prisoners-May-be-used-to-fill-clinical-trial-patient-shortage.

Evans, David, Michael Smith, and Liz Willen. 2005. Big pharma's shameful secret. *Bloomberg Markets*. (December): 36–62. http://www.journalism.columbia.edu/system/documents/523/original/2006_Evans_Big_Pharma_s_Shameful_Secret_MAG.pdf.

Hornblum, Allen M. 1998. *Acres of Skin: Human Experiments at Holmesburg Prison*. New York: Routledge.

Institute of Medicine (IOM). 2006. Ethical considerations for revisions to the Department of Health and Human Services Regulations for protection of prisoners involved in research. *Ethical Considerations for Research Involving Prisoners.* July 12. http://www.iom.edu/Reports/2006/Ethical-Considerations-for-Research-Involving-Prisoners.aspx.

National Commission for the Protection of Human Subjects of Biomedical and Behavioral Research (Commission). 1976. *Report and Recommendations: Research Involving Prisoners.* http://videocast.nih.gov/pdf/ohrp_research_involving_prisoners.pdf.

Peel, Michael. 2005. Human rights and medical ethics. *Journal of the Royal Society of Medicine* 98 (4): 171–73.

Urbina, Ian. 2006. Panel suggests using inmates in drug trials. *New York Times.* August 13. http://www.nytimes.com/2006/08/13/us/13inmates.html.

III

Redefining the Participant–Researcher Relationship and the Role of IRBs

Introduction to Part III
Redefining the Participant–Researcher Relationship and the Role of IRBs

I. Glenn Cohen

Does the existing US regulatory framework applicable to human subjects research work? If it didn't, how would we know? Even if it has its flaws, how would we determine if there is a better path forward, lest the perfect becomes the enemy of the good?

Consider the case of the QWERTY keyboard. The story goes (though there has been contestation of the history, to be sure) that in the case of typewriters, the QWERTY key layout was less efficient than the Dvorak Simplified Keyboard (DSK). QWERTY beat out the DSK and other systems because "the mechanical arms tend[ed] to jam less with the QWERTY keyboard than the alternatives," but that "arm-jamming problem was minimized in later developments of the typewriter and, in fact, totally eliminated with the innovation of the ball-point typewriter," and yet users "continued to favor QWERTY over the more obviously superior DSK" because of path dependence (Marciano and Khalil 2012, 76).

Is the US human subjects research regulatory framework the QWERTY keyboard of the bioethics world? It made sense at one time, but now there are much better alternatives? How hard would it be to change to a different system? Each of the chapters in this section address this and related questions in different ways.

McDonald et al. explain how "[t]he dual challenge presented is to both know and show how far the current system of human research protection achieves its stated ends." They argue that it "[i]t is essential to move from a compliance paradigm to a concordance model that centers on results or outcomes for participants and thus treats compliance as a means to an end," and that "[e]ffects on participants" (their touchstone) "can only be gauged by taking a participant-centered perspective." They describe how the ANPRM makes some movements in the right direction, but how far the current regulatory system is from achieving this ideal.

Stark evaluates the existing paradigm using ethnographic methods such as firsthand observations and audio recordings of a year's worth of IRB meetings, as well as interviews with a national sample of IRB members and chairs. She shows that contrary to the assumptions of the framework's positivistic architecture—whereby rules are announced and administered consistently across IRBs—most IRBs actually use "local precedents" as a heuristic tool. The dominant mode of reasoning is thus not an application of the top-down principle to new cases but instead "sideways" analogical reasoning from prior cases and resolutions of the IRB. Many law readers will be struck by how similar this approach is to common law reasoning of trials courts, but there is a problem with *that* analogy: in the court systems there is a higher court or courts available to correct errant interpretations and choose between conflicting rules of "local precedents"—for example, the US Supreme Court's role in resolving long-standing "circuit splits" between the numerous US Courts of Appeals. There is no "Supreme Court of IRBs" to play a similar function in research ethics, nor has the Office for Human Research Protections (OHRP) been able to effectively "legislate" answers to the disagreements that crop up in effective and timely ways. Stark examines several different paradigm shifts that might correct the problems posed by the use of "local precedents" without completely reconfiguring the existing regulatory framework applicable to human subjects research.

Persad examines that framework from the perspective of deliberative democracy theory and considers how commitment to participatory inclusion models would alter matters, drawing analogies from the incorporation of these approaches in other US agencies and federal schemes. Applying participatory inclusion to a specific issue faced in research ethics review—the current public benefits exemption to IRB review—Persad demonstrates how participatory inclusion models might offer an improvement over the status quo.

Capron sets his sight on the way in which informed consent has become a sacred cow in research ethics. His chapter shows that a "large gap has opened between informed consent as an object of veneration and its actual role as a governing concept in research with human subjects," and examines how different governance paradigms might bridge that gap and do for research ethics what informed consent alone cannot.

Shah, by contrast, sees the problem and need for revision as to the "who" and not just the "what" of research ethics regulation. For her, the problem is the failure to put adequate responsibilities on investigators and sponsors, and she would impose duties on these parties to ensure the scientific validity of research, determine that the risk to participants is justified by the benefit to them or to society and that the risks have been minimized, protect and respect participants during research, and plan in advance for how to address their ethical obligations more generally.

Taken together, these chapters evince the empirically driven, creative, regulatory re-imagining that is exactly what we need in research ethics. One area that demands further thought, though, is the political economy of revising US regulatory standards. The long-gestation and ultimate (at the moment) stalling of the ANPRM suggests that there are powerful forces preventing reform. How would industry and researchers themselves react to this? Like the QWERTY keyboard, are there entrenched users who would resist any move toward these new paradigms, or are there glide paths toward disruptive innovation, or at least incentive-based programs or "nudges" that might be tried? How can experimentation *in* regulatory frameworks for experimentation be done in a way that we can pilot new approaches, evaluate them, and scale up appropriately?

References

Marciano, A., and E. L. Khalil. 2012. Optimization, path dependence and the law: Can judges promote efficiency? *International Review of Law and Economics* 32: 72–82.

7
Toward Human Research Protection That Is Evidence Based and Participant Centered

Michael McDonald, Susan Cox, and Anne Townsend

The 2011 ANPRM (DHHS 2011) offered an outstanding vantage point to consider the potential effectiveness of the changes proposed to the Common Rule, as well as the fundamental effectiveness of the human research protection (HRP) systems that have developed in the United States and countries with parallel systems.

The US regime for HRP affects directly or indirectly provisions in other countries. *The Belmont Report* (National Commission 1979) was widely influential in the establishment of HRP governance structures around the world (Brody 1998; McDonald 2009). Thus, in Canada, significant research funding comes from US agencies subject to the Common Rule. This has led to the establishment of specialized research ethics boards (REBs) compliant with the Common Rule. (REBs are the Canadian equivalent of US institutional review boards, IRBs.) Effects are also felt through the International Conference on Harmonization Good Clinical Practice (ICH-GCP) rules (International Conference on Harmonization 1997).[1] The United States has further made significant efforts to export its brand of HRP to developing countries.

7.1 Fundamental Question

The fundamental question we raise in this chapter is whether HRP systems following the US model actually do what they claim: protect participants without needlessly impeding socially beneficial research as measured by standards such as the 1978 *Belmont Report* from the US National Commission for the Protection of Human Subjects of Biomedical and Behavioral Research (US Department of Health and Human Services 1978).[2]

Critics note that this question can only be answered by examining *evidence* of participant protection. In a major report on the Canadian system of HRP, McDonald and colleagues called for independent, evidence-based assessment of protection measures based on solid research and judicious experimentation (McDonald et al. 2000). In 2004 Emanuel and colleagues in the Consortium to Examine Clinical Research noted, "The current system does not systematically assess performance or outcomes" (Emanuel et al. 2004). In a 2005 analysis of interviews with members of REBs across Canada undertaken in the late 1990s Beagan and McDonald concluded, "It is paradoxical that those in the health professions base their practice on evidence-based standards except in the case of ethical review" (Beagan and McDonald 2005).

The dual challenge presented is to both know and show how far the current system of human research protection achieves its stated ends. The important 2002 Institute of Medicine document, *Responsible Research: A Systems Approach to Protecting Research Participants*, reports the following: "The lack of empirical data on the performance of protection programs, the absence of defined measurable outcomes or other criteria for their on-going evaluation, and the scant knowledge of approaches and methods by which programs have been improved have hindered efforts to initiate QI (quality improvement) measures" (Institute of Medicine 2002). One might also wonder whether HRP is used more for risk management by research institutions and sponsors rather than for genuine protection of research participants (Stark 2012).

Recent European commentators concur. Coleman and Bouësseau identify an "exclusive focus on structure and process" in assessing UK research ethics committees (RECs) that is "incapable of answering the bottom-line question: whether REC review actually protects the rights and interests of research participants and their communities. . . ."(2008). In discussing audit processes for UK RECs, Davies says, "Although such [an] audit is essential to demonstrate 'due process' and can assure a consistent, accountable process, it does not make any statement on the outcome of RECs' deliberations in terms of research safety or acceptability. So we do not know whether RECs are inconsistently right or wrong" (Coleman 2004; Davies, Wells, and Czarkowski 2011).

7.2 Evidence-Based HRP

The question of human research protection effectiveness is a major, if not the major, question in Common Rule reform particularly, and in HRP system design more generally. Current systems of HRP in the United States and elsewhere are based on a compliance paradigm. Beyond asking whether there is compliance with regulations, it is essential to ascertain what actually results. It is essential to move from a compliance paradigm to a concordance model that centers on results or outcomes for participants and thus treats compliance as a means to an end. Effects on participants can only be gauged by taking a participant-centered perspective.

In a recent paper McDonald and Cox suggest evidence-based research on HRP that should be deployed or translated into action/practice and generate feedback for more research (McDonald and Cox 2009). They call for a five-step process: (1) asking for information, (2) acquiring information, (3) appraising information, (4) applying results, and (5) auditing the process, which, if used iteratively, would lead to improved HRP.

Others advocate an evidence-based approach in key areas: consent (Sugarman et al. 1999; Katz and Fox 2004; Nelson and Merz 2002), therapeutic misconception (Applebaum, Roth, and Lidz 1982; Sankar 2004), the role of research workers (Kaufert, Kaufert, and Labine 2009), researcher–research participant relationships (Morris and Balmer 2006), recruitment of research participants (Townsend et al. 2011), and the impact of sharing research results with participant communities (Bombard, Cox, and Semaka 2011). The literature includes nuanced reflections on the methodological and ethical challenges of conducting research on the ethics of research (Cox and McDonald 2007; Cox et al. 2009; Owen et al. 2009).

7.3 Our Research: The Centering Project

Our study conducted over the last six years—*Centering the Human Subject in Health Research: Understanding the Meaning and Experience of Research Participation*—addresses two key parts of the effectiveness question: (1) how subjects experience research participation and (2) how these experiences are interpreted by researchers and research ethics committee members. Our findings are directly relevant to particular changes proposed in the 2011 ANPRM (e.g., risk, systematic gathering of data on adverse events, and research that is exempt from review) and, more important, to developing an evidence-based system of protection, shifting from a culture that focuses on compliance to one that centers on protections that are meaningful from the perspective of participants.

Our three-phase project comprised: (1) an extensive literature review and interviews with a diverse group of health research participants about their experiences as well as with REB/IRB members, researchers, research workers, policy makers, and specialists in research ethics about their understanding of research subjects' experiences; (2) four case studies of independent research projects (a clinical trial, chronic illness study, genetic disorder study, and a health study involving aboriginal people) in which we reviewed project documents (e.g., ethics review applications, interviewed research participants, research team members, and REB members); (3) knowledge translation and exchange.[3]

7.4 Relevant Findings from the Centering Project

We present two themes from our research to illustrate how an evidence-based and participant-centered approach could be useful for the Common Rule revision process specifically as well as HRP generally: (1) participants' experiences of risk as "impact" and (2) the benefits and burdens of research participation. In these and other themes we found both similarities and dissimilarities between the perspectives of those conducting and regulating research and the perspectives of participants.

7.4.1 Risks: "'Impact' Is a Better Word Than 'Risk'"

Proposed Common Rule revisions around risk focus on (1) whether full review by the IRB is required, and (2) whether whole areas of research are so risk free as to be exempt from IRB review. Absent from leading documents (Emanuel and Menikoff 2011; 76 Fed. Reg. 44,512) is a discussion of how participants think about risk. By contrast, we suggest a participant-centered view of risk. This requires understanding how participants experience risks in research rather than making ex ante judgments about potential degrees of risk (Townsend and Cox 2014). Thus the question of whether IRBs are estimating risk correctly cannot be dealt with properly unless it includes the effects of research on participants as perceived by those participants.

We found that participants often identified risks that were not anticipated by researchers or the REB. A good example comes from our chronic illness case study, which was based on a health survey about the impact of chronic illness on parenting. One researcher stated, "We didn't think that there was any risk from . . . the survey, other than the time that they committed" (Researcher 704). Yet participants saw the matter differently. One described how exhausted she felt after completing the survey because her efforts to give accurate answers made her "mentally tired." She explained how normally she would "sugarcoat" her symptoms, and not admit to others, or herself, how she really felt. Completing the survey forced her to face up to her illness and how her life had changed (HS715).

Another participant (HS709) noted that "[t]he hardest part of filling it in was that I couldn't be this super-mom that I used to be before I got

[sick] and so that affected my attitude as far as I just wanted that back. . . ." A third participant (HS714) spoke very movingly about how completing the questionnaire made her think about how much more fatigued she felt and how much she hurt. She said, "[W]hen I finished the whole survey . . . I cried. I had a couple cups of tea. And I don't do that . . . my rule is I don't have pity parties, it's just the way my life is now, I move on from that. But I was very sad when I finished the survey."

Some participants conveyed unexpected resiliencies and strengths allowing them to cope with memories of previous ability when reminded in a questionnaire of their present infirmity. For example, they accepted "being upset" by reflecting on their illness and lives in order to contribute to research: "I guess my belief is deeper than whatever I'm going through personally" (HS709). While regulations are framed in terms of *risk*, the research participants, researchers, and REB members we interviewed used the language of *impacts*. One research participant (HS710) said *impact* is "a *much* more appropriate term for this form of survey" because "it really depends on where the individual person is in the . . . process of illness." She added, "[T]he ethics board has to be aware that there are going to be people in situations of more emotional vulnerability."

While both research participants and REB members talked about "risks" as "impacts," our participants described impacts in experiential terms (e.g., the unexpected emotional impact of completing a questionnaire on chronic illness) as opposed to REB members and researchers who described impacts more in terms of compliance (e.g., whether responding to such a questionnaire was minimal risk or not). However, we would argue that the point of the latter activity (minimal risk classification or not) is to determine prospective impacts on participants; hence there is much to be learned by understanding participants' experiences, be they described as *risks* or *impacts*. The examples cited here have implications for IRB and researcher assessments of potential risk and for various safeguards and mitigating strategies (e.g., in the consent process and through offering support services such as counseling). What we are proposing then for human research protection is something akin to patient-centered and evidence-based medicine, namely a focus on participant experiences grounded in systematic research.

In regard to the proposed revisions of the Common Rule pertaining to risk, there are two underlying problems. First, the collection of data called for in section VI of the ANPRM revolves around regularizing adverse event reporting. While this is a worthwhile endeavor, it neglects the need for data on how participants experience adverse and other events in research and fails to consider life contexts. While adverse data collection may in some sense appear more "objective" (morbidity and mortality information), human research protection is about the protection of people whose "subjective" experiences are paramount.

Second, the proposed revisions are marked with what appear to be ex ante attempts to determine what types of research are low or even no risk to ground the categories of expedited review and excluded studies according to their methodology (e.g., social sciences and behavioral research; see 76 Fed. Reg. at 44518–19). How can one be sure that it is the methodology used that determines the potential harm to participants? Our data show that even apparently low-risk survey studies can have high impact on participants. A better approach would be to gather contextualized data on how participants experience research to develop an evidence-based grounding for categorizing risks.

7.4.2 Participants' Experiences of Benefits and Burdens: "A Soul Destroying Test"

Subjects candidly discussed impacts of participation in terms of benefits and burdens of participation (Townsend and Cox 2013). In some cases these were not well understood or anticipated by researchers or ethics committees. One participant (HS204) described being in a study of menopausal symptoms. In a three-month study period, she was required to adhere to a drug regime and provide a daily journal of the frequency, duration, and intensity of hot flashes. However, her previous coping strategy for dealing with hot flashes was through inattention, that is, to deliberately ignore these experiences. This strategy was undermined by the research design. Thus a potential impact was missed because it was thought that recording data is an objective experience with no significant effect on the participant. This oversight also calls into question research validity through the failure to account for a confounding factor.

Some burdens involved trial tests that were exhausting and challenging for participants and could serve as a reminder of their progressive deterioration. A participant described doing a test that required complicated addition said, "I used to be a scientist and when you can't add numbers together, that's . . . a soul destroying test" (HS 921). Yet the same participant questioned an occasion when the test was not done because the apparent failure to follow the protocol could, in his view, undermine research validity for the experimental medication he was taking. He therefore did not want his personal discomfort to interfere with the research.

At a more mundane level we found that the cumulative effects of relatively trivial burdens led to dissatisfaction and even alienation, particularly for debilitated individuals. One clinical trial participant (HS201) described more frequent visits to the research center than originally outlined due in part to cancellations and physician unavailability. Ignoring these matters made a difference to participants and even elicited the feeling that a bargain was not being kept. Some participants felt that this showed a lack of concern and respect. Hence it is necessary to move beyond objective prediction of the consequences of participation (e.g., a delayed appointment) to understanding the significance these effects will likely have for participants in the context of their relational setting (e.g., a feeling of disrespect).

7.5 Implications

We offered brief profiles from our research from two areas—risks–benefits and burdens—to illustrate the centrality of participant experiences to the HRP enterprise. They show ways in which viewing participants' diverse experiences through the lens of qualitative research can contribute important evidence and radically reshape ethical review and governance by re-framing existing issues, identifying new issues, displaying divergent ethical priorities, re-evaluating the implications of research participation, and restructuring researcher–participant relationships.

Participant accounts of their research experiences should inform current and future proposals for research. First, they would alert the IRB or researcher to potential impacts and experiences of participants that might otherwise have escaped notice. Such accounts also offer insight into how participants respond to such impacts. Second, they would help prospective participants make better-informed decisions about which studies to participate in and what to anticipate as their involvement in the research progresses.

7.5.1 Beyond Compliance

Rigorous assessment of the experiences of human subjects would help address the question of whether prescribed requirements and processes effectively achieve the intended objectives of providing human research protection. This in turn would provide a sounder approach to determining if the current system is, as some critics allege, overprotective or, as others contend, either underprotective or appropriately protective (McDonald 2001). It would also assist researchers and IRBs who may base their decisions on "best guesses" rather than evidence.

The findings presented above provide insights into how participants in a wide range of health research reported their experiences. They are relevant to multiple levels of HRP, including the level of individual research projects and various governance levels. They strongly suggest the need to track what happens to participants following ethics review and use the results to improve policy and practice.

Current HRP systems fail to do this in any systematic way. Reliance is instead placed on adventitious anecdotes, complaints, and highly formalized adverse event reports. Thus current systems are reactive and passive. Even processes aimed at past performance (e.g., audit and accreditation) focus on compliance with rules and regulations rather than actual effects on participants and other key stakeholders. Imagine, if you will, that health care were provided in a similar way—gauging its success by how often patients complained and how well health care providers followed established medical protocols, but never looked at morbidity/mortality or at patient satisfaction.

This raises fundamental issues around respect for research participants and ensuring they have a meaningful part in the HRP system (Cox et al. 2011). The current system of making decisions on people's behalf without listening to them reminds us of the saying arising from the disability rights movement, "Nothing about us without us," that is often quoted in health policy documents as a mantra for patient engagement and the importance of listening to the voice of patients as partners (Boote, Baird, and Sutton 2011; Charlton 1998; Health Council of Canada 2011; Staniszewska et al. 2011; Nierse et al. 2012). We argue that this shift in health policy toward treating patients as partners should be replicated in research policy by treating participants also as partners.

In general terms, we would advance the following argument:

1. Policies, regulations, ethics review, and consent forms do not in themselves provide human research protection.

2. Participants and the populations from which subjects are drawn deserve reasonable assurance that they are protected in research.

3. Reasonable assurance of protection requires good evidence.

4. The experiences of research participants form the most crucial part of such evidence.

5. There is a general failure to gather evidence about the experiences of participants.

6. Hence it is ethically essential to seek such evidence and act upon it.

Systemically there is a need to develop effective mechanisms to gather, assess, and utilize evidence of the effects of research participation on subjects' lives. Such mechanisms include research, monitoring, auditing, and quality assurance and quality improvement measures such as survey tools to systematically gather input from participants, researchers, and IRB/REB members.[4]

7.5.2 Recommendations for Practice and Policy

Our findings and our empirically driven approach should be important to those who compose the regulatory triangle—regulators, the regulated, and those who are supposed to benefit from regulation, particularly research participants. While the ANPRM calls for collection of adverse events data on "hot spots of research risk" (Emanuel and Menikoff 2004, 1148), there are no recommendations for systematically gathering data on participants' experiences and using these data to shape regulations.

We envision a two-stage evidence-based and participant-centered process: (1) the pursuit and use of best evidence about the impact of potential changes in the Common Rule on participants and (2) asking IRBs and researchers to take a much more evidence-based approach that focuses on participant perspectives and concerns. Furthermore such evidence should be shared with prospective participants in research enabling them to make more informed decisions about research participation.[5]

The discussion of issues 11 and 12 (expedited review), along with 10 (minimal risk), in the ANPRM suggests that risk is associated with the "kind of study" the research is. But it may also be associated with the competence of the researchers and the context of the study. The same consideration applies to issues 17 and 18 with respect to types of study exempt from review (e.g., social and behavioral research). Issues of risk are likely multifactorial. Moreover risk is unlikely to be static over time or with different individuals. Thus an individual may be more vulnerable at one time and much less susceptible to adverse impacts at other times. For example, we found that participants in the survey study who had been diagnosed with the chronic illness after they had children were much more affected by answering the questionnaire than those who had lived with their chronic illness for a time before becoming parents. For the former, the contrast of before and after was starker than for the latter. In sum, evidence-based research would help provide IRBs, researchers, and policy makers with usable indicators of relevant factors. Hence we reject the frequently advanced argument that some kinds of social science research (e.g., surveys) should be exempt from ethics review due to their inherently harmless nature.

7.6 Limitations

Our examples range from the mundane to the unusual. Some may be surprising and others not. Our point is not to "exceptionalize" the experiences of research participants. Rather, it highlights the need to track and understand their diversity and richness and integrate this into improved systems of protection.

To be sure, the participant-centered approach we advocate faces the "heterogeneity" and "aggregation" problems identified by Meyer in her discussion of the regulation of research risk in chapter 20 of this volume. That is, participants in various contexts will have diverse experiences of given risks (the heterogeneity problem). Hence it will be difficult to come up with generalized rules or processes for categorizing levels of risk (the aggregation problem). However, this is a problem faced in many areas of life, including, for example, medicine, where physicians have to adapt the generalized results of research to particular patients and subpopulations. We suggest that IRBs and researchers face a similar, but nonetheless ethically unavoidable, challenge: adapting their judgments and practices to the special circumstances of individuals and populations involved in their research.

In this chapter we draw mainly on participants' reports of their own experiences. We also interviewed researchers and IRB/REB members on their understanding of research participants' experiences. We examined these in case studies in which we asked the question "Do you see what I see?" of participants, researchers, and IRB/REBs involved in the same study. In some cases we found shared insights, and in others, clear discontinuities. This variability accords with the everyday experience of social life. What is important is how we respond to the very real possibilities of important gaps in shared understanding in these situations.

7.7 Conclusion

We have taken an evidence-based approach to proposed changes to the Common Rule. The main evidence we draw on is from accounts of individuals who have been health research participants. We believe that if human subjects research protection is going to be meaningful, that will be reflected largely in the experience of research participants who are sociologically and ethically "key" informants. We urge using this key to unlock the door of HRP revision. Finally, we hope that the process of reflecting on and implementing changes in the Common Rule improves human research protection in the United States and elsewhere.[6]

Notes

1. The ICH-GCP is part of an international effort to harmonize technical requirements for the registration of pharmaceuticals for human use. It is specifically concerned with ethical and scientific quality standards "for designing, conducting, recording and reporting trials that involve participation of human subjects to ensure that the rights, safety and well-being of the trial subjects are protected." It is also designed to "ensure the credibility of clinical trial data." Most countries adhere to the ICH-GCP since it allows trials conducted by its standards to be recognized in multiple jurisdictions. See http://ichgcp.net/.

2. *The Belmont Report* contained three basic principles that have been highly influential internationally: respect for persons (their autonomy and dignity), beneficence (avoidance of harm and concern for well-being), and justice (in terms of the fair distribution of the benefits and burdens of research).

3. Recorded semi-structured interviews and focus groups were transcribed verbatim. Analysis was conducted in stages using a constant comparative approach involving grounded theory (Charmaz 2006). The data were systematically compared to determine emergent themes and variations. NVivo software-assisted coding.

4. See for example the three survey tools found at http://www.researchethicssurvey.ca/. These were designed by a consortium in which the authors of this paper were involved.

5. A valuable repository of accessible participant narratives can be found at the UK website healthtalkonline.org in the section on clinical trials (http://www.healthtalkonline.org/medical_research/clinical_trials).

6. The Canadian Institutes of Health Research provided its support of this project (Grant MOP 77671). We gratefully acknowledge the participants, researchers, REB members, policy makers, and research ethics scholars who provided data for our project. Finally, we express our gratitude to members of our research team: our co-investigators, Patricia and Joseph Kaufert (University of Manitoba), and our research assistants at the University of British Columbia (Sara Hancock, Darquise Lafrenière, Natasha Damiano Paterson, Nina Preto, Catherine Schuppli, and Kim Taylor) and at the University of Manitoba (Dhiwya Attawar, Lisa Labine, and Toni Morris-Oswald).

References

Applebaum, Paul S., Loren H. Roth, and Charles W. Lidz. 1982. The therapeutic misconception: Informed consent in psychiatric research. *International Journal of Law and Psychiatry* 5: 319–29.

Beagan, Brenda, and Michael McDonald. 2005. Evidence-based practice of ethics review. *Health Law Review* 13 (2–3): 62–68.

Bombard, Yvonne, Susan M. Cox, and Alicia Semaka. 2011. "When they hear what we say": Presenting research to participants and communities. *Journal of Empirical Research on Human Research Ethics* 6 (3): 47–54.

Boote, J., W. Baird, and A. Sutton. 2011. Public involvement in the design and conduct of clinical trials: A review. *International Journal of Interdisciplinary Studies* 5 (11): 91–106.

Brody, Baruch A. 1998. *The Ethics of Biomedical Research: An International Perspective.* New York: Oxford University Press.

Charlton, James I. 1998. *Nothing about Us without Us.* Berkeley: University of California Press.

Charmaz, K. 2006. *Constructing Grounded Theory: A Practical Guide Through Qualitative Analysis.* Thousand Oaks, CA: Sage.

Coleman, C. 2004. Rationalizing risk assessment in human subject research. *Arizona Law Review* 46: 1–50.

Coleman, Carl H., and Marie-Charlotte Bouësseau. 2008. How do we know that research ethics committees are really working? The neglected role of outcomes assessment in research ethics review. *BMC Medical Ethics* 9 (6).

Cox, Susan M., and Michael McDonald. 2007. Research on research ethics: Must the ethics researcher become an ethics cop, consultant or conduit? *Journal of Empirical Research on Human Research Ethics* 2 (1): 94–95.

Cox, Susan M., Kelley Ross, Anne Townsend, and Roberta Woodgate. 2011. From stakeholders to shareholders: Consumer collaborators in health research. *Health Law Review* 19 (3): 63–71.

Cox, Susan M., Anne Townsend, Nina Preto, Roberta Woodgate, and Pam Kolopack. 2009. Ethical challenges and evolving practices in research on health research. *Health Law Review* 17 (2–3): 33–39.

Davies, H., F. Wells, and M. Czarkowski. 2011. Standards for research ethics committees: purpose, problems and the possibilities of other approaches. *Journal of Medical Ethics* 35: 382–83.

Department of Health and Human Services (DHHS). 2011. Advance Notice of Proposed Rulemaking. Human subjects research protections: Enhancing protections for research subjects and reducing burden, delay, and ambiguity for investigators. *Federal Register* 76 (143): 44512–31.

Emanuel, E., Anne Wood, A. Fleischman, A. Bowen, K. Getz, Christine Grady, Carol Levine, D. Hammershmidt, Ruth Faden, Lisa Eckenwiler, C. Muse, and Jeremy Sugarman. 2004. Oversight of human participants research: Identifying problems to evaluate reform proposals. *Annals of Internal Medicine* 141 (4): 282–91.

Emanuel, Ezekiel, and Jerry Menikoff. 2011. Reforming the regulations governing research with human subjects. *New England Journal of Medicine* 365: 1145–50.

Health Council of Canada. 2011. How engaged are Canadians in their primary care? Results from the 2010 Commonwealth Fund in International Health Policy Survey. In *Canadian Health Care Matters, Bulletin 5.* Toronto: Health Council of Canada. http://www.healthcouncilcanada.ca/rpt_det.php?id=148.

International Conference on Harmonization. 1997. *International Conference on Harmonisation of Technical Requirements for the Registration of Pharmaceuti-*

cals for Human Use Good Clinical Practice: Consolidated Guidelines. Ottawa: Minister of Health.

Institute of Medicine. 2002. *Responsible Research: A Systems Approach to Protecting Research Subjects.* Washington, DC: Institute of Medicine.

Katz, A. M., and K. Fox. 2004. *The Process of Informed Consent: What's at Stake.* Boston: Department of Social Medicine, Harvard Medical School.

Kaufert, Patricia, Joseph Kaufert, and Lisa Labine. 2009. Research ethics, interpreters and biomedical research. In U. Ozolin, S. Hale, H. Slater, and L. Stern, eds., *Quality in Interpreting: A Shared Responsibility—Critical Link 5.* New York: Benjamins.

McDonald, M. 2001. Canadian governance of health research involving human subjects: Is anyone minding the store? *Health Law Journal* 9: 1–21.

McDonald, Michael. 2009. From code to policy statement: Creating Canadian policy for ethical research involving humans. *Health Law Review* 17 (2–3).

McDonald, Michael, and Susan M. Cox. 2009. Moving towards evidence-based human participant protection. *Journal of Academic Ethics* 7 (1): 1–16.

McDonald, Michael, Brenda Beagan, Fern Brunger, Bernard Dickens, Jean Joly, T. Douglas Kinsella, Bartha Maria Knoppers, Therese Leroux, Barbara McGillivray, Michael Asch, Delphine Roigt, and Marcelo Victor Otero. 2000. *The Governance of Health Research Involving Human Subjects.* Ottawa: Law Commission of Canada, xxiv, 363.

Morris, Norma, and Brian Balmer. 2006. Volunteer human subjects' understandings of their participation in a biomedical research experiment. *Social Science and Medicine* 62: 998–1008.

National Commission for the Protection of Human Subjects of Biomedical and Behavioral Research. 1979. *The Belmont Report: Ethical Principles and Guidelines for the Protection of Human Subjects of Research.* Washington, DC: GPO.

Nelson, Robert M., and Jon F. Merz. 2002. Voluntariness of consent for research: an empirical and conceptual review. *Medical Care* 40 (9): 69–80.

Nierse, C., K. Schipper, E. van Zadelhoff, J. van de Griendt, and A. Abma. 2012. Collaboration and co-ownership in research: Dynamics and dialogues between patient research partners and professional researchers in a research team. *Health Expectations* 15 (3): 242–54.

Owen, Michael, Claudia Emerson, Pam Kolopack, Nina Preto, Heather Sampson, Anne Townsend, Donald Willison, and Roberta Woodgate. 2009. Informing governance through evidence-based research on REBs: Challenges and opportunities. *Health Law Review* 17 (2–9): 40–46.

Sankar, P. 2004. Communication and miscommunication in informed consent to research. *Medical Anthropology Quarterly* 18 (4): 429–46.

Staniszewska, S., A. Adebajo, B. Barber, P. Beresford, L. Brady, J. Brett, J. Elliott, et al. 2011. Developing the evidence base of patient and public involvement in health and social care research: the case for measuring impact. *International Journal of Consumer Studies* 35 (6): 628–32.

Stark, Laura. 2012. *Behind Closed Doors: IRBs and the Making of Ethical Research*. Chicago: University of Chicago Press.

Sugarman, Jeremy, et al. 1999. Empirical research on informed consent: An annotated bibliography. *Hastings Center Report* 29: S1–42.

Townsend, Anne, Zubin Amarsi, Catherine Backman, Susan M. Cox, and Linda Li. 2011. Communications between volunteers and health researchers during recruitment and informed consent: Qualitative content analysis of email interactions. *Journal of Medical Internet Research* 13 (4): e84. doi: 10.2196/jmir.1752. http://www.jmir.org/2011/4/e84/.

Townsend, Anne, and Susan M. Cox. 2013. Accessing health services through the back door: A qualitative interview study investigating reasons why people participate in health research in Canada. *BMC Medical Ethics* 14 (40). doi:10.1186/1472-6939-14-40. http://www.biomedcentral.com/1472-6939/14/40.

Townsend, Anne, and Susan M. Cox. 2014. "Impact" is a better word than "risk": Participant accounts of taking part in a chronic illness survey. *IRB: Ethics and Human Research*, forthcoming.

8

Outsourcing Ethical Obligations: Should the Revised Common Rule Address the Responsibilities of Investigators and Sponsors?

Seema K. Shah

In a study evaluating the prevention of HIV transmission from mother to child, HIV-infected pregnant women receive antiretroviral treatment (ART) to prevent transmission during childbirth. Each mother's involvement in this study ends with the birth of her child, when her access to the study drugs also ceases. The investigator plans to refer participants who continue to need treatment to the national program for HIV/AIDS treatment and care after delivery. Assuming that the institutional review board (IRB) raises no objections to the investigator's plan, should she consider her ethical obligations to those participants fulfilled? If the investigator were to consult the Common Rule, she would find little to suggest that she has any further ethical issues to address.

In effect, the Common Rule creates a division of moral labor in research. The current regulations provide that investigators have obligations to obtain informed consent from participants and submit their protocols to an IRB for approval. The IRB in turn is responsible for determining whether research is ethical. The Presidential Commission for the Study of Bioethical Issues recently argued that this approach is flawed (DHHS 2011b, 10). The Commission recommended that the Common Rule address investigator responsibilities in order to harmonize different ethical guidelines and "foster a strong sense of professional responsibility" (DHHS 2011b, 10, 73). Yet the 2011 ANPRM does not remedy the problem—it aims to increase investigator discretion without a corresponding increase in responsibility.

The proposed revisions to the Common Rule may exacerbate the problems caused by a lack of a culture of investigator responsibility (Koski 2003, 403, 410). As discussed by Davis and Hurley in chapter 1 of this volume, the ANPRM laudably attempts to decrease delay in conducting research by, among other things, allowing investigators to file a registration form for "exempt" studies and proceed with research prior to obtaining IRB approval, and by expanding the list of minimal risk research subject to expedited review by only one member of the IRB (DHHS 2011a). The ANPRM's sudden grant of increased discretion without acknowledging the corresponding increased ethical responsibility may lead investigators to try to "get away with" conducting research that is ethically suspect, rather than taking their ethical responsibilities seriously.

I propose that the Common Rule should be revised to include the ethical responsibilities of investigators and sponsors, but that these responsibilities need not be accompanied by enforcement mechanisms. In particular, the revised Common Rule should require investigators and sponsors to: ensure the scientific validity of research; determine that the risk to participants is justified by the benefit to them or to society, and that the risks have been minimized; protect and respect participants during research; and plan in advance for how to address their ethical obligations more generally. This change is important because even after obtaining IRB approval and informed consent, investigators and sponsors continue to have important ethical obligations, in part because of the considerable discretion they must exercise in carrying out their responsibilities. My proposal would signal to investigators, sponsors, and the public that ethical obligations of investigators and sponsors cannot be completely outsourced.

8.1 How Do the Regulations and Proposed Revisions Address Investigators and Sponsors?

The federal regulations governing research only explicitly mention investigators and sponsors in terms of their responsibility to obtain informed consent and IRB approval (45 CFR 46.101–24, 2011, subpart A).[1] The Common Rule therefore seems to imply that once investigators obtain IRB approval and informed consent, they have no further ethical responsibilities.

For instance, the regulations clearly assign ethical obligations to investigators to obtain valid informed consent:

[N]o investigator may involve a human being as a subject in research . . . unless [she] has obtained . . . informed consent. . . . An investigator shall seek . . . consent . . . that provide[s] the . . . subject with sufficient opportunity to consider whether or not to participate and that minimize[s] the possibility of coercion or undue influence. (45 CFR 46.116 (2011))

Contrast this language with the language describing risk–benefit evaluation:

[T]he IRB shall determine that . . .: (1) Risks to subjects are minimized: (i) By using procedures which are consistent with sound research design and which do not unnecessarily expose subjects to risk, and (ii) whenever appropriate, by using procedures already being performed on the subjects for diagnostic or treatment purposes. (45 CFR 46.111(a)–(a1) (2011))

With respect to risk–benefit evaluation, investigators are not mentioned, and the implication is that the IRB has primary responsibility for this important task.

With regard to sponsors, the Common Rule merely requires that the sponsoring institution indicate that it complies with the federal regulations and have "[a] statement of principles governing the institution in the discharge of its responsibilities for protecting the rights and welfare of human subjects of research conducted at or sponsored by the institution . . . " (45 CFR 46.103(b1) (2011)). The regulations do not mention sponsors elsewhere except in the section on informed consent (45 CFR 46.116 (2011)) discussing sponsors with respect to waivers of liability.

The ANPRM does not improve upon the existing regulations in this respect and only addresses investigator obligations regarding informed consent. For instance, the ANPRM asks: "Should the regulations require that, for certain types of studies, investigators assess how well potential research subjects comprehend the information provided to them before they are allowed to sign the consent form?" (DHHS 2011a) Similarly, with respect to conflicts of interest, the ANPRM again addresses this issue through consent requirements: "Should investigators be required to disclose in consent forms certain information about the financial relationships they have with study sponsors?" (DHHS 2011a) Significantly, although disclosure may be a part of the solution, conflicts of interest could be addressed in many other ways. For instance, the regulations could instead explain which conflicts are permissible and which are not.

8.2 Why Should the Regulations Address the Ethical Responsibilities of Investigators and Sponsors?

The regulations should be revised to address the ethical obligations of investigators and sponsors because the current regulations overlook certain ethical obligations of investigators and sponsors, and there is reason to believe that the regulations encourage a culture of compliance rather than one of responsibility, as Greg Koski notes in chapter 22 of this volume.

8.2.1 What Ethical Obligations Do the Regulations Overlook?

By addressing investigator and sponsor responsibilities only minimally and primarily focusing on compliance with IRB review, the regulations and proposed revisions fail to recognize that investigators have important ethical responsibilities. In his seminal 1966 article bringing to light several examples of unethical research, Henry Beecher noted the importance of informed consent in protecting against such abuses, but went on to say that "there is the more reliable safeguard provided by the presence of an intelligent, informed, conscientious, compassionate, responsible investigator" (Beecher 1966, 1354–60). Since Beecher's article was published, IRBs have become an increasingly integral part of the research enterprise. Even assuming an IRB could take over some of these obligations for the investigator, an investigator's ethical obligations cannot and should not be fully outsourced for several reasons.

First, IRB review still allows for considerable discretion for investigators. IRB review occurs before a study begins, and then no less than annually, depending on the level of risk (45 CFR 46.109(e) (2011)). IRBs do not directly review the ongoing conduct of research. In fact, IRBs could not effectively police the conduct of the large volume of research they review because they lack capacity to do so (DuBois 2004, 390).

Second, unexpected events often occur in the course of research, including new research findings, disruptive behavior by participants, or changes in the environment of the research institution. If any of these events have implications for participant welfare or study design, an investigator must consider what to do and whether to inform the IRB. Because the IRB must rely on investigators to report adverse events, protocol violations, and lapses in behavior by the parties involved, and there will be a time lag in obtaining the IRB's answer, the investigator will have to recognize her ethical obligations and, in some cases, temporarily address them.

Finally, scholars have argued that some ethical obligations arise from the investigator–participant relationship. Steven Joffe and Frank Miller have argued that investigators have duties to pursue beneficent purposes, minimize the number of participants, minimize risks and burdens, respect participants, satisfy obligations of justice, provide ancillary care, and help participants transition back to care post-trial (Joffe and Miller 2008, 37–38). Applying these duties to the example at the beginning of the chapter suggests that the investigator should give more thought to her ethical obligations. The investigator's plan to refer mothers back to HIV care immediately after delivery seems unlikely to result in a smooth transition. During that hectic time, mothers may simply fail to obtain the treatment that they need. If the investigator planned instead to allow participants to receive study treatment for a few weeks after delivery and then transition to care outside the study, this would be a better way to fulfill her ethical obligations. Yet the Common Rule provides little room or encouragement for ethical reflection of this sort.

As currently controversial duties become increasingly widely accepted and acknowledged, it seems important for the regulations to address them. Yet not only does the Common Rule fail to acknowledge that these duties are relevant to investigators, but its structure also implies investigators or sponsors should not be concerned with these duties.

8.2.2 A Culture of Compliance as a By-product of the Current Regulations

The current regulations' reliance on IRBs has been subject to considerable criticism by scholars and researchers for being overly bureaucratic. (Saleem and Khalid 2011, 19; Heimer and Petty 2010, 605–606, 622; Schmelzer 2006, 80; Keith-Spiegel and Koocher 2004, 343; De Vries, DeBruin, and Goodgame 2004, 352; Azar 2002, 38). There is some evidence to suggest that the view researchers have of the regulations makes it difficult for them to promote ethical behavior. In its report, the Presidential Commission explained that it "heard from a wide range of research professionals that the procedural requirements of human subjects regulations are often viewed as unwelcome bureaucratic obstacles to conducting research. . . . [R]outinized interpretation can create distance between the underlying ethical principles and how they are viewed and implemented by institutional review boards and the research community." In fact the Commission intended its recommendations "to deflect the tilt that some see favoring process over principle" (DHHS 2011b, 9). Regulations that are sufficiently onerous and seen as illegitimate may lead researchers and sponsors to focus on minimal compliance, and not thoughtful application (Azar 2002, 38).

There is also some evidence to suggest that a substantial minority of researchers engage in unethical behavior. One systematic review and meta-analysis of several studies on scientific misconduct found that 1.97 percent of scientists admitted to fabricating, falsifying, or modifying their data or results, and 33.7 percent admitted committing questionable research practices, such as manipulating their data to make it seem more accurate and concealing conflicts of interest (Fanelli 2009, 6). Strikingly, these numbers are likely to be conservative estimates, given that a reputation of honesty and objectivity is highly valued in science (Fanelli 2009, 9). In another study, the authors similarly found troubling reports of scientific misconduct that are likely to be underestimates: 0.3 percent of scientists admitted to ignoring major aspects of human-subject requirements, 1.7 percent engaged in unauthorized use of confidential information in connection with their research, and 6 percent failed to present data that contradicted their research (Martinson, Anderson, and de Vries 2005, 737). Finally, in one study, over 2,000 investigators indicated they observed 201 instances in which misconduct was likely to have occurred over the course of three years (Titus, Wells, and Rhoades 2008, 980). By extrapolating from these figures and comparing them to the number of incidents reported to the Office of Research Integrity, the authors concluded that the vast majority of incidents of misconduct are never reported (Titus, Wells, and Rhoades 2008, 980). Although it is unclear why scientific misconduct persists, fostering a strong sense of ethical responsibility in researchers is clearly an important way to combat such behavior. Yet fostering professional responsibility is something the Common Rule and ANPRM fail to even attempt.

8.3 How Should the Regulations Address Investigators and Sponsors?

I propose that the regulations require that investigators and sponsors ensure that their research is scientifically valid and pursues beneficent purposes, that the risk to participants is justified by the benefit to them or to society, and that the risks have been minimized as far as possible. The revised regulations should further provide that investigators and sponsors have obligations to protect and respect participants throughout the conduct of research. These ethical obligations are widely recognized and relatively uncontroversial (Emanuel, Wendler, and Grady 2000, 2711).

Some ethical obligations are more hotly debated in the ethics literature. Controversies persist about what standard of care should be offered to participants, whether research has be responsive to the health needs and/or priorities of the host communities, and whether researchers have to make research products reasonably available to host communities (Lie et al. 2004, 190; Schüklenk 2004, 194; Wolitz, Emanuel, and Shah 2009, 847; London and Kimmelman 2008, 82; Macklin 2004, 25). To address obligations like these, the revised Common Rule should provide general ethical requirements based on the professional roles of investigators and sponsors. The regulations could state explicitly that they provide a minimal account of the oversight of research and the ethical considerations that IRBs should take into account when reviewing research, but that both investigators and sponsors have critical roles to play in the ethical conduct of research that are not limited to obtaining IRB review or informed consent. Furthermore, since consensus may emerge around other ethical obligations in the future, the revised Common Rule should acknowledge that investigators should plan in advance for the ethical issues that may arise in research.

This proposal is somewhat similar to existing regulations that do address investigators and sponsors. Although the Common Rule applies to all federally funded research, the FDA has separate, though very similar, regulations governing research with human subjects that apply to products regulated by the FDA—drugs, devices, biologics (45 CFR 46 (2011); 21 CFR 50 (2012)). Unlike the Common Rule, FDA regulations state that "[a]n investigator is responsible . . . for protecting the rights, safety, and welfare of subjects under the investigator's care" (21 CFR 312.60 (2012)). FDA regulations also address sponsors, explaining, for instance, that sponsors should select qualified investigators, ensure adequate monitoring, and communicate with the FDA (21 CFR 312.50 (2012)). My proposal similarly includes requirements for protecting participants and monitoring research that could be added to the Common Rule.

Additionally South African research regulations specify that the investigator should be qualified, have studied the primary literature, and be knowledgeable about the risks (MRC 2006). Like my proposal, the South African regulations provide general guidance for investigators and describe the ethical responsibilities that investigators should have in relatively broad strokes.

8.4 Should These Ethical Obligations Be Enforceable?

Although both the South African and FDA regulations address ethical obligations for investigators and sponsors, neither specifies penalties for noncompliance. This seems to be the right approach. Research regulations should not include enforceable ethical obligations of sponsors and investigators for at least two reasons: (1) legal prohibitions that take a "command and control approach" can backfire and (2) enforcement is not necessary because the law can change behavior without threatening penalties for violation.

8.4.1 Reasons against Enforceable Obligations

The regulations *could* include various penalties for noncompliance for the ethical obligations. For example, they could include fines, a halt to the research in question, or prohibitions from engaging in future research.[2] Creating enforceable obligations, however, can lead to a number of problems.

Because reasonable people may disagree on how to appropriately apply even widely accepted ethical requirements and over the content of more controversial ethical obligations, it may be very difficult to give investigators and sponsors adequate notice about what conduct will violate the law. For example, it can be hard to determine when a researcher has done enough to minimize risk. Ethical obligations that are still the subject of considerable debate, such as ancillary care and post-trial access, have especially unclear parameters. Applying coercive measures to researchers who innocently fail to do enough to fulfill a contested obligation seems unfair. To the extent that the law serves a deterrence function, coercive enforcement would either be ineffective or have an undue chilling effect on research if it is not clear in advance which conduct is prohibited.

Moreover coercive penalties that assume the worst about researchers can backfire. Robert Gatter has argued that lawmakers that take a "command-and-control" regulatory approach can "create an environment in which regulatory targets comply with the law only as needed to avoid punishment and otherwise interpret the law to serve their own interests . . ." (Gatter 2003, 362). Or, as Julian Le Grand has eloquently noted, policies can be disastrous when "fashioned on the basis of a belief that people are knaves if the consequence is to suppress their natural altruistic impulses" (Le Grand 1997, 154). In revising the Common Rule, it is critical not to suppress investigators' ethical impulses; this problem can be avoided by harnessing the expressive potential of law.

8.4.2 The Expressive Potential of Law

Amending the Common Rule has the potential to bring about a change in behavior without coercive penalties through law's expressive function. In general, regulations send a message to the people they regulate. Expressive law is a particular type of law that attempts to shape social norms in order to change individual behavior (Feldman 2009, 178–79). Cass Sunstein explains that laws can be created in an "effort to produce adequate social norms. The law might either do the work of such norms, or instead . . . work directly against existing norms and . . . push them in new directions. The latter idea is grounded on the view that law will have moral weight and thus convince people that existing norms are bad and deserve to be replaced by new ones" (Sunstein 1996, 2031). Sunstein further argues that laws have signaling effects that do not depend on the enforcement of the law (Sunstein 1996, 2032–33).

Although scholars have focused on the expressive effects that laws can have by addressing an issue in a particular way, their arguments imply that the reverse is also true. A failure to address certain obligations may further inculcate or reinforce existing beliefs about their importance. Investigators and sponsors may therefore find it easier to think that they bear few ethical obligations outside of obtaining informed consent and IRB review.

There is also empirical support for the proposition that addressing investigator and sponsor obligations could send a powerful signal even without a threat of enforcement. A study of seatbelt laws showed that although laws with primary enforcement had the largest effects on changing behavior, enforcement was not necessary for the law to have powerful effects on behavior (Wittlin 2011, 419). Surprisingly, laws that had indirect enforcement were also effective in changing behavior. (Indirect enforcement occurred when laws required seatbelt use, but police officers were not allowed to pull motorists over for failure to wear a seatbelt; these laws were only enforced on people who were stopped for other traffic violations.) Even a law that provided *no* sanction for violating it was still effective in changing behavior.

Clearly, more may be needed to ensure that research is conducted within a culture of responsibility. Recognizing the ethical obligations of sponsors and investigators within the Common Rule is an important first step to ensure that research is not characterized by a culture of compliance. Cultural change is not easy, so it is unlikely that this one step in isolation will effect change on a large scale. Dan Kahan has argued that given valid skepticism about the way laws are constructed, people are likely to think that the law accurately reflects moral norms if their peers endorse and comply with the law (Kahan 2000, 614). Using the example of cigarette smoking, Kahan notes that gentle nudges, or small changes in the law that are not accompanied by large penalties, are more likely to convince people of the need for new norms (Kahan 2000, 625–26). Thus it may make sense to start with small changes in the existing regulations, as I have proposed here.

Over time, more changes may be needed to better ensure the ethical conduct of research. The current Presidential Commission explained that although regulations are "an indispensable complement to a culture of virtuous investigators," ideally, research would be governed both by "external regulatory checks and internal embodiment of appropriate professional norms" (DHHS 2011b, 71). The Commission also recommended expanding ethics discourse and education for investigators and the need for stricter professional standards (DHHS 2011b, 72). There are data to support this idea and suggest that a professional oath for researchers could be a way to inculcate ethical values into those practicing the profession. Dan Ariely conducted studies designed to test whether professional oaths could lead to increased ethical behavior. MIT students were incentivized to cheat on an exam in order to be paid higher amounts, but this incentive stopped working when they were first asked to sign this statement: "I understand that this study falls under the MIT honor system." Notably, this effect was seen even though MIT does not actually have an honor code (Ariely 2008, 211–14). Thus a professional oath accompanied by better and more regular ethics training for researchers may be a powerful way to change professional norms.

Another, related approach would be to use the power of shaming. Dan Kahan has further argued (with Eric Posner) that shaming those who violate norms can change behavior (Kahan and Posner 1999, 366). When society fails to hold people accountable for violating laws, laws seem less important or easier to ignore (Gatter 2003, 372–73). Perhaps a National Researcher Databank, like the National Practitioner Databank, could be created so there are clear consequences of shaming researchers who disregard their ethical duties. Additionally it may help to have clearer guidance on ethical violations—a "case law" for research ethics developed by agencies familiar with the principles of ethical clinical research.

The overarching goal should be to ensure that the regulations do not undermine the ethical imperative many researchers and institutions feel to protect and respect research participants (Gatter 2003, 392). Explicitly recognizing the ethical responsibilities of investigators and sponsors within the federal regulations is an important initial step in that endeavor.

8.5 Objections

One objection to my argument might be that I mistake the purpose of the regulations. Given that the Common Rule has a form of regulatory history, namely the *Belmont Report*, the regulations may be intended to narrowly address the oversight of research and the role and function of IRBs, leaving more general ethical obligations to be addressed in the *Belmont Report*.

Although the *Belmont Report* is a document that has stood up well over time, it was published in 1979. The field of research ethics has seen many developments since then. International research has grown considerably, and issues not addressed in *Belmont* have since become commonplace in ethical guidelines and regulations, including standard of care, ancillary care, post-trial obligations, obligations to communities, and benefit sharing (NBAC 2001; Nuffield Council 2002; MRC 2006; World Medical Association 2008; CIOMS 2002). Given these developments and the lack of any updates to the *Belmont Report*, the revised regulations need to serve more of an expressive function.

Others might object that my proposal demands too much. If the risk of research is reasonable and participants give their consent, what other ethical obligations could there be? Even if investigators have other obligations, critics may contend investigators should simply design protocols they believe are ethical and let IRBs ensure they have succeeded.

Although IRBs can (paternalistically) make determinations about risks, IRB and participant decisions could never be sufficient protections against unethical research (Miller and Wertheimer 2007, 24). IRBs have a limited window into research and the process itself, leaving important ethical issues to which only researchers can fully attend. As I have argued, these include unexpected issues that arise in the conduct of research and ongoing respect for persons that is morally required throughout research participation (Emanuel, Wendler, and Grady 2000, 2711). Research participants likely have more limited expertise and ability, and it may be unfair to rely on them alone to assess the risk and value of research (Gatter 2003, 399). Researchers and sponsors are uniquely placed to handle many important ethical decisions because of the complexity of research, the rapidity with which things can change, and the specialized scientific expertise that is increasingly necessary to understand work on the frontier of new knowledge.

8.6 Conclusion

The Common Rule is largely concerned with the obligations of IRBs and only minimally addresses the obligations of investigators and sponsors.

These regulations send a message to researchers, sponsors, participants, and the public, whether or not that message is explicitly intended. The current message is that investigators have minimal discretionary ethical obligations once their protocol has been approved and can outsource the bulk of the ethical work to the IRB. It is the IRB, for example, that will determine whether the benefits of the knowledge to be gained justify the risks to the subject. Yet the regulatory approach of requiring compliance with IRBs and informed consent belies the fact that investigators are entrusted with the primary ethical responsibility to make sound ethical decisions on a daily basis as they conduct research.

The existing regulations and proposed revisions ignore the professional obligations of investigators, along with the critical role that sponsors should and do play. The current window for reform of the regulations presents a rare opportunity to take an important first step and send a signal to the public, investigators, participants, and sponsors alike that the ethical conduct of research depends on placing trust in all of the stakeholders involved.

Notes

This research was supported by the Intramural Research Program of the NIH, in the Warren G. Magnussen Clinical Center. The opinions expressed here are the views of the author. They do not represent any position or policy of the US National Institutes of Health, the Public Health Service, or the Department of Health and Human Services. The author would like to thank Alan Wertheimer, Govind Persad, Annette Rid, Holly Lynch, the participants in the 2012 Health Law and Bioethics Roundtable (co-sponsored by University of Maryland Carey Law School's Law and Health Care Program and the Johns Hopkins Berman Institute of Bioethics), and participants in the "The Future of Human Subjects Research Regulation" conference at the Petrie–Flom Center for their helpful comments and suggestions. A longer version of this chapter was published in the *Journal of Law and Medical Ethics* as: Outsourcing ethical obligations: Should the revised common rule address the responsibilities of investigators and sponsors? *Journal of Law and Medical Ethics* 41 (2): 397–410.

1. The Common Rule only mentions investigators in the description of what research is exempt, the definitions of "human subject" and "intervention," the sections on obtaining and documenting informed consent, and the descriptions of who should receive notice from the IRB about its decision. Subpart C does address investigators' responsibilities with regard to fair subject selection in research with prisoners, but it is not part of the Common Rule.

2. Of course, I am considering penalties separate from the existing authority IRBs have to disapprove research.

References

Ariely, Dan. 2008. *Predictably Irrational: The Hidden Forces That Shape Our Decisions.* New York: HarperCollins.

Azar, Beth. 2002. Ethics at the cost of research? *Monitor on Psychology* 33 (2): 38.

Beecher, Henry. 1966. Ethics and clinical research. *New England Journal of Medicine* 274 (24): 1354–60.

Council for International Organizations of Medical Sciences (CIOMS). 2002. *International Ethical Guidelines for Biomedical Research Involving Human Subjects.* Geneva: WHO.

Department of Health and Human Services (DHHS). 2011. Advance Notice of Proposed Rulemaking. Human subjects research protections: Enhancing protections for research subjects and reducing burden, delay, and ambiguity for investigators. *Federal Register* 76 (143): 44512–31.

Department of Health and Human Services. Presidential Commission for the Study of Bioethical Issues. 2011b. *Moral Science: Protecting Participants in Human Subjects Research.* Washington, DC: GPO.

De Vries, Raymond, Debra DeBruin, and Andrew Goodgame. 2004. Ethics review of social, behavioral, and economic research: Where should we go from here? *Ethics and Behavior* 14 (4): 351–68.

DuBois, James M. 2004. Is compliance a professional virtue of researchers? Reflections on promoting the responsible conduct of research. *Ethics and Behavior* 14 (4): 383–95.

Emanuel, Ezekiel, David Wendler, and Christine Grady. 2000. What makes clinical research ethical? *Journal of the American Medical Association* 283 (20): 2701–11.

Feldman, Yuval. 2009. The expressive function of trade secret law: Legality, cost, intrinsic motivation, and consensus. *Journal of Empirical Legal Studies* 6 (1): 177–212.

Gatter, R. 2003. Walking the talk of trust in human subjects research: The challenge of regulating financial conflicts of interest. *Emory Law Journal* 52: 327–401 (2003).

Heimer, Carol A., and JuLeigh Petty. 2010. Bureaucratic ethics: IRBs and the legal regulation of human subjects research. *Annual Review of Law and Social Science* 6: 601–26.

Fanelli, Daniele. 2009. How many scientists fabricate and falsify research? A systematic review and meta-analysis of survey data. *PLoS ONE* 4 (5): e5738.

Joffe, Steven, and Franklin G. Miller. 2008. Bench to bedside: Mapping the moral terrain of clinical research. *Hastings Center Report* 38 (2): 30–38.

Kahan, Dan M. 2000. Gentle nudges vs. hard shoves: Solving the sticky norms problem. *University of Chicago Law Review* 67: 607.

Kahan, Dan M., and Eric A. Posner. 1999. Shaming white-collar criminals: A proposal for reform of the federal sentencing guidelines. *Journal of Law & Economics* 42: 365.

Keith-Spiegel, Patricia, and Gerald P. Koocher. 2004. The IRB paradox: Could the protectors also encourage deceit? *Ethics and Behavior* 15 (4): 339–49.

Koski, Greg. 2003. Human subjects research and conflicts of interest: Research, regulations, and responsibility. Confronting the compliance myth—A reaction to Professor Gatter. *Emory Law Journal* 52: 403.

Le Grand, Julian. 1997. Knights, knaves or pawns? Human behaviour and social policy. *Journal of Social Policy* 26 (2): 149–69.

Lie, R. K., E. Emanuel, C. Grady, and D. Wendler. 2004. The standard of care debate: The Declaration of Helsinki versus the international consensus opinion. *Journal of Medical Ethics* 30: 190–93.

London, Alex J., and Jonathan Kimmelman. 2008. Justice in translation: From bench to bedside in the developing world. *Lancet* 372 (9632): 82–85.

Macklin, Ruth. 2004. *Double Standards in Medical Research in Developing Countries*. Cambridge, UK: Cambridge University Press.

Martinson, Brian C., Melissa S. Anderson, and Raymond de Vries. 2005. Scientists behaving badly. *Nature* 435: 737–38.

McAdams, Richard H. 2000. An attitudinal theory of expressive law. *Oregon Law Review* 79: 339.

Miller, Franklin G., and Alan Wertheimer. 2007. Facing up to paternalism in research ethics. *Hastings Center Report* 37 (3): 24–34.

National Bioethics Advisory Commission (NBAC). 2001. *Ethical and Policy Issues in International Research: Clinical Trials in Developing Countries*. Bethesda: NBAC.

National Commission for the Protection of Human Subjects of Biomedical and Behavioral Research. 1979. *The Belmont Report: Ethical Principles and Guidelines for the Protection of Human Subjects of Research*. Washington, DC: GPO.

Nuffield Council on Bioethics. 2002. *The Ethics of Research Related to Healthcare in Developing Countries*. London.

Rushton, Harry G. 2008. Institutional review board approval—More red tape or a step in the right direction? *Journal of Urology* 180: 804–805.

Saleem, Taimur, and Umair Khalid. 2011. Institutional review boards—A mixed blessing. *International Archives of Medicine* 4: 19.

Schmelzer, Marilee. 2006. Institutional review boards: Friend, not foe. *Gastroenterology Nursing* 29 (1): 80–81.

Schüklenk, U. 2004. The standard of care debate: Against the myth of an "international consensus opinion." *Journal of Medical Ethics* 30 (2): 194–97.

South African Medical Research Council (MRC). 2006. *Guidelines on Ethics for Medical Research: General Principles*. Pretoria: MRC.

Sunstein, Cass. 1996. On the expressive function of law. *University of Pennsylvania Law Review* 144: 2021.

Titus, Sandra L, James A. Wells, and Lawrence J. Rhoades. 2008. Repairing research integrity. *Nature* 453: 980–82.

Wittlin, Maggie. 2011. Buckling under pressure: An empirical test of the expressive effects of law. *Yale Journal on Regulation* 28: 419–68.

Wolitz, Rebecca, Ezekiel Emanuel, and Seema Shah. 2009. Rethinking the responsiveness requirement for international research. *Lancet* 374 (9692): 847–49.

World Medical Association. 2008. *World Medical Association Declaration of Helsinki: Ethical Principles for Medical Research Involving Human Subjects.* Ferney-Voltaire, France: WMA.

9

Subjects, Participants, and Partners: What Are the Implications for Research as the Role of Informed Consent Evolves?

Alexander Morgan Capron

Informed consent has been described as the "ethical cornerstone" (Morin 1998, 185; Pelias and Markward 2000, 837; Malinowski 2003, 169), and a "central tenet of biomedical research" (Rothstein 2005, 91). Indeed it seems safe to say that most researchers, bioethicists, and institutional review board (IRB) members in the United States—and probably around the world—believe that the answer to the question "What makes research involving human subjects ethical?" is "informed consent" (Emanuel, Wendler, and Grady 2000, 2701). In this chapter, I set out to show that a large gap has opened between informed consent as an object of veneration and its actual role as a governing concept in research with human subjects. Our failure to recognize that gap—and to make necessary policy adjustments—should be on the minds of the drafters of any proposal to reframe the federal regulations for research with human beings. Such attention would be particularly fitting because, I argue, the federal rules themselves bear much of the responsibility for the diminishing importance of informed consent in research.

9.1 Have the Exceptions Swallowed the Rule?

9.1.1 From Nuremberg to the Common Rule: The Primacy of Consent
Prior to World War II, the few cases in which Anglo-American courts addressed medical experimentation involved common law actions for battery or malpractice; not surprisingly, physicians who deviated from accepted medical practices were judged harshly, without regard to the issue of consent (Katz 1972, 526–28). The modern era of research ethics dates to the decision of the Nuremberg Tribunal that passed judgment on the 23 Nazi physicians and administrators in the "Doctors' Trial" from December 1946 to August 1947. In finding 16 guilty, the three American judges at Nuremberg drew a distinction between actions by researchers

that could constitute war crimes and crimes against humanity and those that amounted to "permissible experimentation," a category grounded on the premise that "certain types of medical experiments on human beings, when kept within reasonably well-defined bounds, conform to the ethics of the medical profession generally" and can be justified when they will "yield results for the good of society that are unprocurable by other methods or means of study" (Nuremberg Military Tribunals 1949–1953). The judges then spelled out ten "basic principles [that] must be observed in order to satisfy moral, ethical and legal concepts."

The first of these principles—which collectively came to be known as the Nuremberg Code—begins with the unequivocal declaration, "The voluntary consent of the human subject is absolutely essential." The Nuremberg court elaborated two elements of valid consent in line with existing common law doctrine and the prewar German law (Capron 2008, 614–15): the subject must "have legal capacity to give consent" and "should have sufficient knowledge and comprehension of the elements of the subject matter involved as to enable him to make an understanding and enlightened decision." Given the setting of the Nazi experiments, it is hardly surprising that the court added that the subject must be "able to exercise free power of choice, without the intervention of any element of force, fraud, deceit, duress, over-reaching or other ulterior form of constraint or coercion." Finally, in light of the horrible suffering of many subjects in the Nazi experiments, the tribunal in principle 9 added a new requirement, the right to withdraw consent, which has become an essential part of subsequent regulations: "During the course of the experiment the human subject should be at liberty to bring the experiment to an end if he has reached the physical or mental state where continuation of the experiment seems to him to be impossible."

As a formal matter, the principles articulated by the Nuremberg tribunal continue to govern research. They may have been somewhat diluted in the 1960s by the World Medical Association in the Declaration of Helsinki, originally promulgated in 1964 (World Medical Association 2008), and in the rules issued by Public Health Service and Food and Drug Administration (Curran 1969), but they persist. Indeed the federal regulations appear to be just as devoted to self-determination as the prior judicial decisions. The Common Rule flatly declares, "no investigator may involve a human being as a subject in research . . . unless the investigator has obtained the legally effective informed consent of the subject or the subject's legally authorized representative" (45 CFR 46.116).

Yet the federal regulations have never exhibited the same commitment to the absolute primacy of informed voluntary consent as the Nuremberg Code (Glantz 1992). Moreover the post-Nuremberg documents speak in terms of protecting subjects' "rights and welfare" but are focused on the latter at the expense of the former, especially subjects' right to determine what is or is not in their interests and whether they do or do not wish to be involved in a research protocol.

Besides this inherent equivocation on the importance of informed consent, the Common Rule also contains a second ethical pillar mandated by the National Research Act of 1974—prior review by an IRB—that was absent from the Nuremberg Code or even the original version of the Declaration of Helsinki. While it is true that IRBs spend a great deal of their time reviewing—and often altering—the consent form before they will approve a research project, they also exercise the authority granted them by the exceptions within the Common Rule to let research proceed *without* informed consent. As a result the policy for involving human beings in research has shifted from "thorough-going self-determination," *Natanson v. Kline*, 350 P.2d 1093, 1104 (Kan. 1960), back to an earlier "Don't tell, don't ask" approach—that is, conducting research without full disclosure that subjects are being used or without opportunity for subjects to decline (Menikoff 2006).

If one imagines the set of decisions governed by the choice of research subjects as an "autonomy disk," that once formidable object now resembles a shrinking donut with an ever-growing hole at its center (Capron 2008, 630). From the outside, the donut has been cut back by not allowing willing volunteers to take part in research, typically when an IRB decides it would involve too much risk, a judgment that investigators sometimes doubt the IRB is qualified to make (Brugge 2012). Of greater significance is the enlargement of the donut hole by the numerous exceptions under which research may be undertaken without the consent of its subjects. Ironically, this transformation of the autonomy disk into a donut with a large hole has occurred as a result of the dominant influence of the Common Rule and other federal research regulations in shaping norms regarding human subjects research, including expectations regarding informed consent.

9.1.2 The Cumulative Effect of Exclusions, Exemptions, and Exceptions
One might be tempted to think that individual limitations do not detract from viewing informed consent as a central part of the ideology that since

the *Belmont Report* in 1978 and the research regulations from DHHS in 1981 have attained a "sacramental" status among bioethicists (Parmet 2005, 81). In recent years, however, the exceptions, taken as a whole, have seemed ready to swallow the doctrine.

To start, the Common Rule excludes from the consent requirement (and IRB review) activities that do not "involve" a "human subject" in "research." First, to be involved in research, a person must be personally included in the study or otherwise engaged with an investigator, such as when the person's being or behavior is observed, affected, and/or recorded. Second, the Common Rule is limited to activities with *living* individuals about whom an investigator obtains either "(1) [d]ata through intervention or interaction with the individual, or (2) [i]dentifiable private information" without interacting with the person (45 CFR 46.102). The study of dead people or data and samples derived from them does not qualify. Likewise the collection and examination of information that is already available to an investigator and is not private does not qualify as research with human subjects under the Common Rule. Third, activities—even those carried out by physicians and scientists—are not "research" unless they entail "systematic investigation, including research development, testing and evaluation, designed to develop or contribute to generalizable knowledge" (45 CFR 46.102).

The net result is that many scientific studies are excluded from the requirements for consent and review. But the shrinkage of the "donut" does not stop there because some activities that do qualify as research are exempt from review. Specifically, the Common Rule describes six categories of research with human subjects that need not comply with the federal requirements. One, in particular, exempts medical and health-related research "involving the collection or study of existing data, documents, records, pathological specimens, or diagnostic specimens" from publicly available sources "or if the information is recorded by the investigator in such a manner that subjects cannot be identified, directly or through identifiers linked to the subjects" (45 CFR 46.101(b)(4)).

Research on *identifiable* records and specimen collections may still be carried out without the consent of individual subjects, however, if someone else (i.e., the parent or guardian for a child, or the legally authorized representative of an adult who lacks decision-making capacity) gives permission or if the relevant IRB has waived or altered the requirements for informed consent. A number of grounds for waiving informed consent requirements are recognized in the regulations. For example, under 45 CFR 46.116(c), informed consent rules may be waived for a study approved by a state or local government of a "public benefit or service program." Under the broadest exception, an IRB may decide that it would be "impracticable" to carry out the research without a waiver of consent (45 CFR 46.116(d)). This category was once of particular relevance in studies, typically conducted by behavioral scientists, involving observation or deception, where the subjects would be expected to alter their behavior if they knew what the scientists were studying. But the exception is now widely used in health research, where waivers are granted for studies utilizing closed medical records and specimens collected for other purposes, perhaps many years previously and from a now-dispersed group of people. Informed consent requirements may be waived if the research "could not practicably be carried out without the waiver" provided that the research involves only "minimal risk" and would not adversely affect the subjects' "the rights or welfare"—other, of course, than their right to privacy and right to give or withhold consent, which is what is being waived.

Although the exceptions permitted under 45 CFR 46.116(d) are supposed to be limited to research that imposes no more risk than a subject would encounter in daily living, some other exceptions expose unconsenting subjects to serious or lethal risks. For example, in 1996 the Secretary of DHHS, acting under the authority of 45 CFR 46.101(i), issued a blanket waiver to allow investigators to study new treatments for emergency patients who are temporarily unable to consent (DHHS 1996). Given the life-threatening conditions that characterize such patients, it is not surprising that research conducted under this waiver has led to deaths (Natanson et al. 2008). Likewise, as Efthimios Parasidis suggests in chapter 4 of this volume, the long history of conducting research in the military without consent makes clear that the adage *inter arma enim silent leges* (in times of war, the law stands mute) applies as well in the biomedical realm. Under 10 USC 1107(f), the President may waive the prior consent requirement upon determining that obtaining consent is not feasible, would not be in the interests of national security, or, pursuant to the broader FDA waiver law, 21 USC 355(i)(4), would be contrary to the best interests of the military member.

9.2 Structure and Substance: Why the Slide away from Consent?

9.2.1 Impossibility of Autonomous Authorization

The structural problem with research ethics—that the regulations have created a wide "exit" door from the requirement of informed, voluntary consent—explains *how* consent has come to play a lesser role in research but not *why*. One possible reason has already been mentioned: the review process' orientation toward "protection" of subjects from physical, mental and social risks, not respect for their rights. But even this begs the question: Why would IRBs not conclude that subjects' exercise of informed consent provides the best protection on the ground that individuals should be the judge because they best know their own wants, needs, goals, and values?

Informed consent is an ethical as well as a legal norm when it goes beyond "effective consent" and becomes "autonomous authorization," the term that Ruth Faden and Tom Beauchamp used to signify the situation in which an intentional action, taken largely "with understanding" and "without controlling influence," amounts to an actual authorization by a subject (or patient) of an intervention, not a mere agreement with or acquiescence in a physician's authoritative order (1986, 277–80). Yet it appears that IRBs—among other observers of biomedical research—have come to the conclusion that autonomous authorization is not occurring because very frequently (1) the disclosure of information to subjects is inadequate, (2) subjects do not comprehend what is disclosed, (3) subjects' choices are not voluntary, (4) subjects may be incompetent to make certain choices, and (5) what appears to be "consent" is mere submission or compliance.

Several stratagems have been adopted in response to the "practical disquiet" that has come to characterize ethical thinking about research consent notwithstanding its "theoretical confidence" (Miller and Wertheimer 2011, 201). Responding to evidence on point 1, drafters of regulations and guidelines have specified in detail numerous categories of information that need to be conveyed, and IRBs spend endless hours revising consent forms. Unfortunately, this has not improved point 2; indeed the regulatory scrutiny and IRB attention has resulted in "no detectable improvement in comprehension" (Cohen and Larson 2007, 279). It has instead resulted in longer consent documents, which decreases the likelihood that subjects will read them (Fortun et al. 2008, 628). It also tends to make the documents more complex and elevates the "reading grade-level" required to understand them. Subjects tend to have particular difficulty understanding such key concepts as randomization and placebo controls. In sum, most subjects are "ignorant of [the] basic elements of the research" (Flory and Emanuel 2004, 1593) but are unaware of the problem because they typically overestimate their comprehension, which keeps them from asking questions (Cohen and Larson 2007, 276–77).

Problems 3 and 4 are closely related especially when subjects are drawn from the ranks of patients. The very factors that leave patients feeling they have no real choice about accepting an experimental drug or device—namely the absence of other effective interventions, their inability to afford treatment outside of a research setting, and the resulting depression and anxiety—also create passivity and regression, which can undermine decision-making capacity (Hewlett 1996). The culmination of many of these problems—inadequate transmission of information, miscomprehension, desperation, and temporary incompetence—is the so-called therapeutic misconception, which arises when patient-subjects "conflate the goals and nature of the research and treatment" (Chou and O'Rourke 2012, 146). While an unrealistic appraisal of risks versus benefits in a trial or simple optimism about the outcome does not constitute therapeutic misconception (Horng and Grady 2003), patients who view a clinical trial as their "last hope for improvement" are very prone to misconceiving research as therapy (Kass et al. 1996, 25).

While the stratagems to improve the consent process have thus far proved unavailing, some might say that the only way forward is to admit the problem and insist on conversation between physician-investigators and patient-subjects (Katz 1984). What has happened instead is to implicitly accept that autonomous authorization is usually unattainable but then to permit research to go on nonetheless, either by making ad hoc alterations in the standards for autonomous actions or by simply relying on "legally effective" consent (detailed recitations of risks signed, if not comprehended, by subjects).

9.2.2 The Lure of Utility

A second force cutting away the center of informed consent is the concern in many parts of the research enterprise that progress would come to a stop—or, at the least, be greatly slowed—were informed consent to be the barrier to action that the members of the National Commission and the judges at Nuremberg meant it to be. Today, for many IRBs as well as investigators, the tempo of scientific progress has become "compulsive" (Jonas 1969, 245). Most of the exceptions to informed consent illustrate the felt need to permit the greater good to be served, especially when doing so may also benefit members of a group of which the potential subjects are a part. This rationale is quite explicit in the rules that permit going ahead without consent in cases of experimental interventions for incapacitated emergency patients or in research on service members to develop vaccines and medicines for wartime injuries. This change, which extends to other persons incapable of consenting such as children, treats individuals based on their membership in a group, which was not the orientation of the Nuremberg Code.

The struggle over the proper role for consent is especially acute in what may be the liveliest arena of biomedical research today, namely studies that make use of human biological material and genetic databases, most of it collected as a part of medical care or in research for a specific (now completed) purpose. Not to draw on this vast resource seems very foolish to most researchers, and the Common Rule does indeed give them access, either upon an IRB's finding that obtaining consent would be impracticable (meaning too expensive, slow, and burdensome, and for older samples, often impossible) or because the material they want to use does not carry identifiers linking it to the persons involved. The possibility raised by the ANPRM that all genetic material would henceforth be treated as "identifiable," thereby ending the exclusion of such research from review, has provoked interest in developing new ways of gaining permission to use the material, based either on "opting out" or on one-time "blanket" or "general" consent to store samples and data for future use without the need to obtain consent for particular research projects.

9.2.3 The Evolving Status of Human Beings in Research

The third factor in the hollowing out of informed consent is the change in the perceived status of the human beings on whom research is conducted. The tribunal at Nuremberg regarded the inmates of the Nazi concentration camps as "subjects"—that is, someone under the power of another. The judges therefore articulated the duty of researchers to obtain subjects' voluntary informed consent before involving them in any studies in order to make them agents with the power of self-governance, comparable to the place of citizens in a democracy.

Contrast that view with the one adopted fifty-some years later, when most members of the National Bioethics Advisory Commission accepted the view that the human beings studied by scientists are "participants" in research (2001). I regard it as wishful thinking to suppose that most of the people on whom research is conducted today in the United States are on a par with—that is, are co-equal participants with—the research team and sponsors. Such a co-equal role can occur—for example, when scientists conduct research on themselves (auto-experimentation) or on patients in a long-time relationship with a research team (Fox 1959). But as a general matter, dressing "subjects" up as "participants" may just lessen the felt need to prevent their suffering avoidable harm and violation of rights.

Over the past decade, with the growth of longitudinal research and especially the storage of data and material in "biobanks," the terminology has further evolved to the point where the term "partner" is now sometimes used to describe the research subject (Ziker 2003, 36), particularly the people whose records and samples are made available for future research. As the expectations for consent evolve along with this change in vocabulary and the conceptual alterations that it signals, will participants and regulators come to regard this as a business relationship, in which "caveat emptor" replaces "respect for persons," or will researchers still be expected to honor their deontological duty to disclose all risks, as Shah argues in chapter 8 of this volume?

9.3 What Will Serve the Role That Informed Consent Was Supposed to Play?

The changes in the role of informed consent over the past half-century amount, I believe, to a paradigm shift. When such a shift occurs without notice—we keep venerating informed consent, all the while looking for ways to conduct more and more research without it—the danger is that the various actors are operating on differing assumptions about who is supposed to be doing what for which reasons and consequently, in this case, the functions that informed consent was supposed to play may be left unfulfilled.

9.3.1 Traditional Functions of Informed Consent

Informed consent performs at least three essential functions in the research setting, as a means of respecting individual autonomy, protecting subjects' well-being, and achieving intelligent governance of research (Capron 1974). The first grows out of the familiar bioethics principle of "respect for persons," while the second and third have a more pragmatic, utilitarian cast.

As the first two need no elaboration for present purposes, I turn to the third, "governance," which is the least familiar in part because it is often discussed in terms of autonomy and protection. Governance operates on three levels. The first is the material level, in determining which research projects will go forward. This begins as an expression of individual autonomy as each potential subject decides whether to submit to the protocol. The aggregate effect is that certain research will occur while other research (perhaps with a less appealing risk–benefit ratio or some other drawback) will not. At this level, informed consent is like an automobile ignition that determines whether the engine is on or off. On a second level, informed consent moves beyond being the ignition and acts more like a steering wheel. This is obviously the case in any studies where a subject truly plays the role of a "participant" or "partner" who influences study design or objectives, but it is also true in ordinary circumstances, where subjects can steer the study well or poorly by their conduct—such as their adherence to the protocol—just as can the physicians conducting the study.

The final way that informed consent governs research is through allowing autonomous choices to affect social welfare. This role was captured well by Peter Schuck, writing about informed consent in the context of treatment decisions:

According to neoclassical theory, . . . a transaction increases one's welfare (and indirectly, social welfare) only when it results from one's informed, voluntary choice to engage in the transaction, or when it accurately mimics the choice that one would have made under those ideal conditions. (Schuck 1994, 901)

Thus informed consent regulates not just which projects go forward and how well but also whether individual and group welfare is maximized in the process and in the net outcome (Brody 2001, 1).

9.3.2 Can Diminished Consent (Plus Something Else?) Serve the Needed Functions?

So the basic question is whether it seems reasonable to suppose that the diminished version of informed consent, as constituted in the current rules and structures for biomedical and behavioral research, can be expected to achieve the traditional goals of autonomy, protection, and governance. The answer to this question must be "at the best, imperfectly," since certain aspects of autonomy and governance are inherently linked to individuals exercising their authority over their own participation in research knowingly and voluntarily, and when research that in some way "involves" them can proceed without needing their consent, then of necessity their autonomous authorization is missing.

To the extent that the principal aim of the research ethics apparatus is to protect the welfare of subjects, it may be possible to achieve the protection goal despite diminished or absent consent, but only if those running the apparatus—from the Office for Human Research Protections to the local IRBs—understand the context in which they must exercise their oversight. For example, Miller and Wertheimer have proposed a "fair transaction" model to replace autonomous authorization, which would allow research to proceed even when impediments—like the therapeutic misconception—mean that a potential subject has not chosen to take part in a study with full understanding of what he or she has agreed to do. Whether or not one agrees with Miller and Wertheimer's model, it has the decided virtue of imposing obligations on investigators—and on the IRBs overseeing them—to ascertain the fairness of enrolling subjects in a particular trial according to "criteria for assessing the validity of consent transactions . . . based on fair terms of cooperation for the respective parties that reflect the context of the activity for which consent is given" (2011, 211). Their framework, then, does something that the proponents of the ANPRM do not seem yet to have done, namely to examine the implications of the silent paradigm shift for the various participants in the ethical governance of the research: "If current research oversight is not providing adequate subject protection, the remedy is to improve the safeguards rather than to shift the burden to a consent process that cannot provide the appropriate protection" (2011, 213).

If, as I have argued, we have slid into a post-*Belmont* as well as a post-Nuremberg era, then the people steering the current once-in-a-generation reexamination of the Common Rule should go beyond bureaucratic fiddling and exaltation of the importance of biomedical and behavioral research and search for ways of empowering subjects, investigators, sponsors, IRBs, and perhaps other, newer institutions to realize the goals that autonomous authorization was intended to fulfill. One thing is certain: this sort of enquiry will not occur until we acknowledge how greatly we have upset the old paradigm and either return to the traditional expectations for informed consent or make sure that other actors know that the responsibility for the autonomy, protection, and governance functions now rests with them.

References

Brody, Baruch. 2001. Making informed consent meaningful. *IRB: Ethics and Human Research* 23 (5): 1–5.

Brugge, Doug. 2012. Institutional review boards need to increase their understanding of community-based participatory research: Commentary on a case study in the ethics of mental health research. *Journal of Nervous and Mental Disease* 200 (3): 242. doi:10.1097/NMD.0b013e318247cb05.

Capron, Alexander M. 1974. Informed consent in catastrophic disease research and treatment. *University of Pennsylvania Law Review* 123 (2): 340.

Capron, Alexander M. 2008. Legal and regulatory standards of informed consent in research. In Ezekiel J. Emanuel, Christine C. Grady, Robert A. Crouch, Reidar K. Lie, Franklin G. Miller, and David D. Wendler, eds., *The Oxford Textbook of Clinical Research Ethics*. New York: Oxford University Press, 613–32.

Chou, Pak Hei Benedito, and Norm O'Rourke. 2012. Development and initial validation of the therapeutic misunderstanding scale for use with clinical trials research participants. *Aging and Mental Health* 16 (2): 145–53. doi:10.1080/13607863.2011.602962.

Cohen, Elizabeth, and Elaine Larson. 2007. Improving participant comprehension in the informed consent process. *Journal of Nursing Scholarship* 39 (3): 273–80.

Curran, William. 1969. Governmental regulation of the use of human subjects in medical research: The approach of two federal agencies. *Daedalus* 98 (2): 542–94.

Department of Health and Human Services (DHHS). 1996. Waiver of informed consent requirements in certain emergency research. *Federal Register* 61: 51531–51533.

Emanuel, Ezekiel J., David Wendler, and Christine Grady. 2000. What makes clinical research ethical? *Journal of the American Medical Association* 283 (20): 2701.

Faden, Ruth R., and Tom L. Beauchamp. 1986. *A History and Theory of Informed Consent*. In collaboration with Nancy M. P. King. New York: Oxford University Press.

Flory, James, and Ezekiel Emanuel. 2004. Interventions to improve research Participants understanding in informed consent for research. *Journal of the American Medical Association* 292 (13): 1593–1601.

Fortun, P., J. West, L. Chalkley, A. Shonde, and C. Hawkey. 2008. Recall of informed consent information by healthy volunteers in clinical trials. *QJM* 101 (8): 625–29. doi:10.1093/qjmed/hcn067.

Fox, Renée C. 1959. *Experiment Perilous: Physicians and Patients Facing the Unknown*. New York: Transaction Publishers.

Glantz, Leonard H. 1992. The influence of the Nuremberg Code on U.S. statutes and regulations. In George J. Annas and Michael A. Grodin, eds., *The Nazi Doctors and the Nuremberg Code: Human Rights in Human Experimentation*. New York: Oxford University Press, 183–200.

Hewlett, Sarah. 1996. Consent to clinical research: Adequately voluntary or substantially influenced? *Journal of Medical Ethics* 22: 232. doi:10.1136/jme.22.4.232.

Horng, Sam, and Christine Grady. 2003. Misunderstanding in clinical research: Distinguishing therapeutic misconception, therapeutic misestimation, and therapeutic optimism. *IRB: Ethics and Human Research* 25 (1): 11–16.

Jonas, Hans. 1969. Philosophical reflections on experimenting with human subjects. *Daedalus* 98 (2): 219–47.

Kass, Nancy E., Jeremy Sugarman, Ruth Faden, and Monica Schoch-Spana. 1996. Trust: The fragile foundation of contemporary biomedical research. *Hastings Center Report* 26 (5): 25–29.

Katz, Jay. 1972. *Experimentation with Human Beings: The Authority of the Investigator, Subject, Professions, and State in the Human Experimentation Process.* With the assistance of Alexander M. Capron and Eleanor S. Glass. New York: Russell Sage Foundation.

Katz, Jay. 1984. *The Silent World of Doctor and Patient.* New York: Free Press.

Malinowski, Michael. 2003. Choosing the genetic makeup of children: Our eugenics past–present, and future? *Connecticut Law Review* 36 (1):125–224.

Menikoff, Jerry. 2006. *What the Doctor Didn't Say: The Hidden Truth about Medical Research.* New York: Oxford University Press.

Miller, Franklin G., and Alan Wertheimer. 2011. The fair transaction model of informed consent: An alternative to autonomous authorization. *Kennedy Institute of Ethics Journal* 21 (3): 201–18.

Morin, Karine. 1998. The standard of disclosure in human subject experimentation. *Journal of Legal Medicine* 19 (2): 157–221.

Natanson v. Kline. 1960. 350 P.2d 1093 (Kan.).

Natanson, Charles, Steven J. Kern, Peter Lurie, Steven M. Banks, and Sidney M. Wolfe. 2008. Cell-free hemoglobin-based blood substitutes and risk of myocardial infarction and death: A meta-analysis. *Journal of the American Medical Association* 299 (19): 2304–12. doi:10.1001/jama.299.19.jrv80007.

National Bioethics Advisory Commission. 2001. *Ethical and Policy Issues in Research Involving Human Participants,* vol. 1. Rockville, MD: NBAC.

Nuremberg Military Tribunals. 1949–1953. Vol. 2 of *Trials of War Criminals before the Nuremberg Military Tribunals under Control Council Law No. 10.* Nuremberg, October 1946–April 1949. Washington, DC: GPO. Also available at http://www.loc.gov/rr/frd/Military_Law/pdf/NT_war-criminals_Vol-II.pdf.

Parmet, Wendy. 2005. Informed consent and public health: Are they compatible when it comes to vaccines? *Journal of Health Care Law and Policy* 8: 71.

Pelias, Mary Z., and Nathan J. Markward. 2000. The Human Genome Project and public perception: Truth and consequences. *Emory Law Journal* 49 (3): 837–58.

Rothstein, Mark A. 2005. Expanding the ethical analysis of biobanks. *Journal of Law, Medicine and Ethics* 33 (1): 89–101. doi:10.1111/j.1748-720X.2005.tb00213.x.

Schuck, Peter. 1994. Rethinking informed consent. *Yale Law Journal* 103: 899–959.

World Medical Association. 2008. *Declaration of Helsinki: Ethical Principles for Medical Research Involving Human Subjects.* http://www.wma.net/e/policy/b3.htm.

Ziker, Dana. 2003. Reviving informed consent: Using risk perception in clinical trials. *Duke Law and Technology Review* 2 (1): 1–14.

10

Democratic Deliberation and the Ethical Review of Human Subjects Research

Govind Persad

The Presidential Commission for the Study of Bioethical Issues (PCSBI) recently introduced "[t]he principle of democratic deliberation" (2010; 2012) as part of its reports on the ethics of synthetic biology and of human subjects research. The PCSBI noted that democratic deliberation is "a less familiar principle in bioethics than the principles of beneficence and justice" (2010, 30); indeed no other prominent list of bioethical principles lists anything similar (Veatch 2007). Though new to lists of bioethical principles, democratic deliberation has been employed elsewhere in practical ethics (Gutmann and Thompson 2004, 18–19, 31, 33).

This chapter explains democratic deliberation and considers its implications for ethical review of human subjects research. It argues that democratic deliberation favors the inclusion of research participants' perspectives in ethical review as well as the ethical review of "public benefits" research.

10.1 Democratic Deliberation Explained

Democratic deliberation involves a public exchange of ideas within and across groups of ordinary citizens, experts, and political representatives. Participants should aim to engage actively with one another, and to offer reasons that are acceptable and intelligible to their interlocutors. Decisions should be revisable as new information and new perspectives come into view (DHHS 2010).

The PCSBI emphasized the deliberative character of its own procedures, in particular when engaging with religious and moral concerns about the synthetic biology innovations it was then evaluating (2010, 139). These examples of public involvement far exceed the current requirement in human subjects research that an Institutional Review Board (IRB) include a nonscientific and a lay member (Fost and Levine 2007).

Incorporating democratic deliberation into decision-making can render the resulting decisions both more respectful and more accurate. First, by involving all parties in the decision-making process, democratic deliberation can ensure that the process's outcomes, whatever they are, express participants' values. Amy Gutmann, the PCSBI's current chair, has argued that even when some lose out in democrative deliberation, the outcome is not *imposed* on them, but instead results from something they *authorized* (Gutmann and Thompson 2004, 21–23). Such authorization can differentiate a just from an unjust outcome, even when the content of the two outcomes is identical.

Other legal and political contexts feature democratic deliberation. For example, recent innovations in restorative justice emphasize deliberative engagement between criminals and victims, which makes it possible for both to see the legal resolution as just (Parkinson and Roche 2004, 510). Within the civil law, deliberative engagement helps ensure that contentious processes—such as divorce proceedings and family disputes—respect both prevailing and defeated participants (Menkel-Meadow 2004, 361).

Deliberation can enhance accuracy as well as respectfulness. Each participant in deliberation brings a distinctive positional perspective; an ordinary citizen may have less technical knowledge than an expert but more knowledge about how people are employing technology (Anderson 2003, 57). A well-structured deliberative body can, ideally, know more than even its most knowledgeable individuals, rather than simply knowing as much as its average participant (Gutmann and Thompson 2004, 12).

10.2 Participatory Inclusion: Involving Research Participants in Ethical Review

As we consider how to revise existing human subjects research regulations, consider that a revised Common Rule might incorporate democratic deliberation by drawing on the experience of research participants themselves when reviewing human subjects research proposals. The current regime charges IRBs with protecting research participants, but assigns no member the task of *representing* research participants. While IRBs must "[safeguard] the rights and welfare of human subjects" (45 CFR 44.107(a) (2011)), they are neither required to engage deliberatively with research participants nor to provide a voice for participants in the ethical review process. The lay member on the IRB is not required to learn about, or advocate for, research participants' concerns.

In contrast, professional ethics and policy review boards outside research ethics frequently represent the clients, governments, and professionals they regulate or protect (Porter 1987). These boards exemplify the participatory inclusion of laypeople (Johnson 2009; Agarwal 2008). Numerous legal provisions ensure the participatory inclusion of clients on a variety of committees in the health care context, as shown in table 10.1.

10.2.1 Participatory Inclusion as Democratic Deliberation

How do participatory inclusion statutes advance democratic deliberation? Review boards that are not directly democratic (e.g., the National Park Service's board of directors) often are thought of as democratic because a democratically elected official (the US president) appoints an officer (the secretary of the interior) who in turn appoints the board. In contrast, participatory inclusion aims at more direct legitimacy, by mandating that the board reflect the perspectives of a variety of interests.

Does having a representative group member on an advisory board suffice to drive that group toward democratic deliberation? I'll consider three potential objections: (1) that representing research participants on boards doesn't help protect them and can even hurt their interests, (2) that research participants' interests are best served by a notice-and-comment or survey process rather than a representative member on a board, and (3) that democratic deliberation should have no special solicitude for research participants.

Does Participatory Inclusion Protect Participants?

Rand Rosenblatt worries that a participant representative on an advisory board might provide a veneer of approval without substantively influencing the board's decisions (Rosenblatt 1978). Concerns that procedural protections such as rights of voice and representation are inferior to substantive protections have arisen elsewhere in criminal and civil law (Cassell 2011; MacCoun 2005), and in the development of community advisory boards for clinical research (NIAID 2009). This concern would counsel against representing participants on boards and in favor of instead writing strong participant protections into research regulations. Such a suggestion would parallel the more general argument that an advisory committee can deliberate effectively regardless of its composition, and that considering a committee's output is enough to assess its deliberative efficacy (Walters 2012, 681). But for deliberation to be effective,

Table 10.1

Participants included	Advisory board	Jurisdiction	Source
Benefit recipients	Social Security	Federal	42 USCA 907a(a)(2)(C)
Clients (encouraged)	Adult day care	TN	Tenn. Code Ann. 71-2-410
Consumers	Health care appeals	MA	Mass. Gen. Laws Ann. 6 166
Consumers (2)	Human subjects research	NH	N.H. Rev. Stat. Ann. 171-A:19-a(V)
Consumers (2)	Health care associated infections	CT	Conn. Gen. Stat. Ann. 19a-490n(b)
Consumer member of state board of health	Electronic health information	IA	Ia. Code. Ann. 135.156(2)(a)
Current or former users (>=50%)	In-home supportive services	CA	Cal. Welf. & Inst. Code 12301.3
Deaf (>50%)	Schools for the deaf	KY	Ky. Rev. Stat. 167.037(2)
Disabled and advocates (>50%)	Rehabilitation technology	Federal	29 USCA 764 (D)(ii)
Hearing aid users	Hearing aid fitters' licensure	RI	R.I. Admin. Code 31-5-3.9.2
Mentally ill offenders; relatives	Mentally ill offender task force	CO; AZ	Colo. Rev. Stat. Ann. 18.1-9.104(1)(c)(XIV) (A-C)
Professional clients	Physicians and pharmacists' licensure	SD	S.D. Stat. Ann. 36-4-2.1, 36-11-4.1
Recipients; donors; public	Cord blood stem cell banks	IL; MI	20 Ill. Comp. Stat. 2310/2310-577(d); Mich. Comp. Laws. Ann. 333.2682(4)
Representatives of elderly, needy, or underprivileged	County boards of health	GA	Ga. Code Ann. 31-3-2(a)(6)
Sufferers; family	Mental illness advocacy	Federal	42 CFR 51.22(b)(2)
Sufferers; parents and family	Developmental disability	LA	La. Rev. Stat. Ann. 28-451.3(D)(2)
User advocates	Protection and advocacy service	IN	Ind. Code 12-28-1-6(a)

the deliberative body must "represent a personal, educational, and cultural variety of life experiences" (Estlund 1997, 191). Including research participants in deliberation can help to advance this goal.

Despite his initial worries, Rosenblatt ultimately endorses involving participants in the deliberative process, arguing that doing so can both produce empowering outcomes and itself be empowering:

[I]t is important to remember that the value of consumer participation and agency explanation does not lie solely in the opportunity to secure a different outcome. What Professor Tribe has termed "the right to be heard from, and the right to be told why ... express the elementary idea that to be a person, rather than a thing, is at least to be consulted about what is done with one." Expressed in political terms, this root concept of human dignity highlights the need for a reconstruction of the democratic process, in which consultation over fundamental human needs is not made meaningless by a labyrinthine bureaucracy. By offering unorganized interests the right to participate in programs for their own benefit, the traditions of structural due process also help to encourage its exercise and thereby help to strengthen democratic capacity. (1978, 264)

In the Medicaid context, Rosenblatt therefore endorses "medical care advisory committees," which "include Medicaid recipients and other consumers (as well as providers) in the policy-making process" by giving them "adequate opportunity for meaningful participation in policy development and program administration" (1978, 264).

Survey Representation versus Personal Representation

Including participants' perspectives might be achievable without including participants directly in ethical review: for instance, participants' perspectives could be solicited via a notice-and-comment process analogous to the requirement that administrative agencies solicit and respond to public comments when they engage in rulemaking (Cuellar 2005, 421). For instance, ethics review committees might be required to survey research participants and consider the results when deciding whether to renew or approve protocols.

Representation via surveys, however, may fail to provide participants sufficient voice. To see why, imagine that instead of adding new senators when admitting a new state, new states were instead represented in the Senate through surveys: whenever a bill is proposed in the Senate, new states would be surveyed and the existing senators would be required to attend to the survey results. The new states might complain that (1) senators will not be held accountable for attending to the survey results and (2) minor decision-making will either require a surfeit of referenda or exclusion of those represented by surveys. Similarly a survey of research participants might not be taken seriously by a review board and would be unable to anticipate specific issues that arise in ethical review. In contrast, a participant representative would be on equal footing with other board members and well placed to investigate and deliberate about major and minor issues as they arise. Finally, participatory inclusion approaches do not rule out the use of surveys: the representative, for instance, could survey other participants as part of her review process.

Why Represent Research Participants At All?
What is the normative argument for setting aside special seats for participants? After all, IRB-reviewed research is supported by tax revenue, and benefits many individuals in society who do not participate in research, yet there is no movement to represent these beneficiaries on IRBs.

That participatory inclusion requirements are widespread on boards analogous to ethics review bodies, as table 10.1 indicates, already offers intuitive support for the claim that setting aside seats for participants is justified. But discussions of consociational democracy can provide an additional, more theoretically developed basis for including participants in the ethical review of research. Andreas Føllesdal describes a consociational system as follows:

[C]onsociational democracy . . . . is a non-territorial form of federalism, characterized by cooperation among elites of different segments of a society, often split along religious or ethnic lines. It entails government by grand coalitions, granting autonomy to groups with veto rights over matters important to them. (1998, 202)

Like consociationalism, participant representation constitutes "non-territorial federalism": research participants should be represented in decisions that affect them, even if we do not grant them "veto rights" as the consocialist might (Cuellar 2005, 417). Joshua Cohen and Joel Rogers have similarly suggested that we open up more arenas in democracies for decision-making by bodies of representatives of particular interest groups (1992).

10.2.2 Participatory Inclusion in the Human Subjects Research Context
Many participatory inclusion provisions include clients. Others include people whom institutions evaluate or regulate. Participants are both objects of evaluation and clients: as such, participatory inclusion seems no less appropriate in a research context than in either of the two it melds.

How might research participants' perspectives be better integrated into the ethics review process via participatory inclusion? Laurie Flynn and Ronald Honberg suggest that IRBs reviewing mental health research should "require the inclusion of individuals who have personally experienced severe mental illnesses as consumers or family members," because "consumers and family members, by virtue of their personal experiences, are more likely to focus on those aspects of research designs which may impact (positively or negatively) on the well-being of vulnerable research subjects" (1999, 188). Flynn and Honberg, however, mandate the inclusion of *patients*, rather than *research subjects*. Although research subjects *resemble* patients, subjects and patients are importantly different: for instance, some subjects are healthy volunteers (Keane 2008, 352), and the common good can justify risks to consenting subjects that could not be justified for ordinary patients (Katz 1993, 17).

Additional regulations on IRB composition along the lines Flynn and Honberg suggest, however, may exacerbate concerns that IRBs are overbureaucratized (Fost and Levine 2007, 2196). Regulations on composition that prevent IRBs from achieving a quorum could produce "substitution effects," such as pressures to strip jurisdiction from IRBs, that vitiate their direct effects.

Concerns about overbureaucratization might counsel permitting and encouraging, but not requiring, that research participants be represented in ethical review. This parallels the approach ultimately taken in staffing the boards of the PPACA's health insurance "exchanges." Public comment suggested that board members should have various specific forms of expertise and background. DHHS responded by requiring that "at least one member of the Exchange's board must include one voting member who is a consumer representative," but stopped short of mandating more specific expertise (77 Fed. Reg. 18,301, 18,310).

Representation by advocates rather than fellow participants is also possible, and might help alleviate overbureaucratization concerns by widening the pool of potential representatives or allowing current nonscientific IRB members to serve as advocates. Some nonscientific or unaffiliated members required by current IRB regulations see their roles as including "[r]epresenting . . . human subjects' interests"; "[r]eviewing the research from the point of view of a potential subject"; "[a]cting as the ally or the peer of the research subject," and "[a]cting as a patient advocate and surrogate subject" (Porter 1997, 2 tbl. 1). Nonvoting observers or advisors who explicitly represent research participants' perspectives might augment the phenomenon Porter identifies: Sirotin et al. suggest that "[p]rofessionals who work extensively with prospective research populations could help articulate those perspectives and should be encouraged to formally explore those perspectives, perhaps through focus groups and interviews," and that "IRBs might also work with research subject advocates, who work closely with research participants and seek to represent their perspectives" (2010, 15). Advocates might have expertise that makes them better able to protect participants' interests, may not be vulnerable to conflicts of interest, or might have broader expertise in the conduct of research than individual participants might. These arguments could be counterbalanced, however, by symbolic and practical advantages of having the representative come from the group being represented (Minow 1991, 278–79).

Those revising research ethics regulations should consider more explicitly including research participants' perspectives in review (45 CFR 46.107(f)), which provides that the IRB may "invite individuals with competence in special areas to assist in the review of issues which require expertise beyond or in addition to that available on the IRB," and may already allow the inclusion of participants. The current wording frames the invitees as technical experts, which might seem to exclude participants. But this provision might be understood, or even reworded, to recognize the experiential expertise of research participants—a form of special knowledge that they acquire through experiencing a medical condition and participating in the research enterprise from the participant perspective (Bal, Bijker, and Hendriks 2004, 1340), just as it has been understood to include expert bioethicists (DeRenzo and Wichman 1990, 6). While the current provisions make these experts nonvoting members, the rules could be revised to grant research participant members a voice as voters.

Meanwhile, although 45 CFR 46.111(b) directs the IRB to specially scrutinize the substance of research on vulnerable subjects, it could also justify modifying the review procedure, and thus present an avenue for participant inclusion. Where research proposes to involve vulnerable populations, protecting their interests may counsel democratically including them or their representatives in the deliberations leading up to research approval. The numerous participatory inclusion requirements in statutes regulating mental health, elder care, and disability issues outside of research (reviewed in table 10.1) lend support to such an approach. Indeed IRBs reviewing research on prisoners already are required to include a "prisoner or prisoner representative" under 45 CFR 46.304.

10.3 The Need for Ethical Review of Public Benefits Research

Democratic deliberation also has implications for the exemption of public benefits research—experimental research on the efficacy of programs like Medicare and Medicaid—from IRB review under 45 CFR 46.101(b)(5). The ANPRM suggests expanding the exemption. But deliberative democratic concerns counsel against such expansions. Public benefit research has the potential to force beneficiaries of public programs like Medicaid—who are often socially and economically vulnerable—into research whose intended aims may be contrary to participants' interests. In contrast, ethical review of public benefits research requires those attempting to revise public benefit programs to get the consent of current beneficiaries, which requires that researchers explain the proposed changes and provide an account of why research is justified.

10.3.1 The Public Benefit Exemption
The history of the public benefit exemption suggests that it was initially understood as a procedural change, rather than an exemption from ethical review entirely. Amici curiae in two appellate cases, *C.K. v. New Jersey Dep't of Health & Human Servs.*, 92 F.3d 171 (3d Cir. 1996), and *Beno v. Shalala*, 30 F.3d 1057 (9th Cir. 1994), argued that the public benefits research exemption displaced public benefits research review from IRB oversight, but not from oversight altogether.

Initially, IRBs reviewed public benefits research just as they reviewed other human subjects research, and this practice was upheld in *Crane v. Matthews*, 417 F. Supp. 532 (ND Ga. 1976). *Crane* prompted the public benefits exemption, which removed public benefits research from IRBs' jurisdiction. However, the Ninth Circuit in *Beno* recognized that public benefit research exempt from IRB review is still subject to "an examination of the proposed project's potential danger to participants' physical, mental and emotional well-being," *Beno*, 30 F.3d at 1070. The Third Circuit agreed, stating that "the 'additional layer of review' from which DHHS exempted public benefits experiments was the regulatory requirement of IRB review, not the statutory requirement of review for danger" (*C.K.*, 92 F.3d at 190).

Some have argued for expanding the exemption beyond research on the benefit levels of federal programs like Medicare and Medicaid, thus exempting a wide swath of research on public benefits. Law professor Elmer Abbo argues that quality-improvement research should be exempt from ethical review (Abbo 2007, 579), as does a Hastings Center working group (Baily et al. 2006, S33). The Secretary's Advisory Committee on Human Research Protections (SACHRP) believes "institutions should be able to apply the exemption to public programs supported by state agencies" as well as to federal programs (Office for Human Research Protections 2008).

These arguments have been accompanied by some de facto expansion of the exemption. The DHHS secretary has exempted randomized trials on the quality of care among Medicare beneficiaries (Peikes et al. 2009). Research on the allocation rules for transplantable organs (Egan et al. 2006), and on HIV epidemiology in at-risk communities (Merion et al. 2005), has also been exempted. Most strikingly, research on the prevalence of preterm birth and infant death among participants in the Special Supplemental Nutrition Program for Women, Infants, and Children (WIC) was held exempt. This research involved looking through and analyzing infant death certificates, matching the names on the death certificates to the names of children whose mothers received WIC prenatally, and comparing the death rates of African-American infants and white infants whose mothers were on WIC (Khanani et al. 2010). One can certainly imagine the mothers—had they been asked—refusing permission to have the death certificates coded in this way and matched, as they were, with factors like race and whether the mother smoked tobacco during pregnancy.

10.3.2 Fair Benefits and Public Benefits

Some have already endorsed the ethical review of public benefits research, though without explicitly invoking concerns about democratic deliberation (Harvard Law Review 1995; Rosenbaum 1992, 123–26). Democratic deliberation, I will argue, further favors the ethical review of public benefits research.

Existing advocates have focused on the threat that public benefits research poses to participants' *medical well-being*—that is, the threat that research harms participants. This concern seems to fit into the branch of research ethics that addresses risk–benefit balancing. There is an additional concern, however, that *Beno* and the federal regulations also seem to recognize: the danger that research will use subjects against their will for the benefit of others. This fits more clearly into the branches of research ethics that address informed consent and respect for participants.

In particular, public benefits research potentially stands in tension with the *Belmont Report*'s dictum that research "should not unduly involve persons from groups unlikely to be among the beneficiaries of subsequent applications of the research" (National Commission 1979, 10). This "fair benefits" requirement is echoed in other statements of clinical research ethics, such as CIOMS's requirement that research be "responsive to the health needs and the priorities of the population or community in which it is to be carried out" (2002). Public benefits research frequently involves taking resources away from poor and disadvantaged beneficiaries to see whether these beneficiaries are able to maintain a tolerable standard of living after losing benefits. Therefore the fair benefits requirement may limit public benefits research on economically disadvantaged subjects, particularly when conducted for the benefit of more advantaged individuals who want to minimize the tax burden of supporting entitlement programs rather than for the benefit of other disadvantaged individuals.

Jan Blustein demonstrates this ethical tension in discussing the ethics of the National Job Corps Study, a program evaluation that would fall under the current public benefits exception (Blustein 2005, 824). The study randomized some Job Corps applicants into a control group that did not get to participate in Job Corps (a program that offers educational and vocational training to young adults between 16 and 24 years of age). The study was ostensibly justified on the basis that "random assignment was necessary because it was the only way to provide Congress and the public with credible evidence about the success of the program" (Burghardt et al. 1997). However, participants complained about being treated as guinea pigs and about the study serving the interests of wealthier individuals, but not their own interests (Blustein 2005, 834). As Blustein suggests:

Research is prima facie unjust if some groups disproportionately bear the burdens and others reap the benefits. Yet over the past 30 years, evaluations have been conducted almost exclusively on public programs that benefit low-income and vulnerable populations. Middle-class benefits like Medicare, the home mortgage deduction, and the college Work-Study programs have been largely untouched. To the extent that participants in social program evaluations assume risk or miss out on desired services, this disparity would seem to raise questions of justice. (2005, 838)

In a context—that of federal and state entitlement programs—where there is already a "democracy deficit" and where deliberative involvement with current recipients of entitlements is limited, expanding the public benefits research exemption risks allowing research that fails to adequately represent the interests of participants, and so violates the principle of democratic deliberation.

10.4 Conclusion

How would incorporating a democratic deliberation principle change the ethics of human subjects research? I have argued that it would recommend greater inclusion of participants in the review process, and would counsel against exempting public benefits research from ethical review. This would not give deliberation unlimited scope. Legal institutions, for instance, often are initially constructed through intensive deliberation but later governed by systems of rules that grow out of that initial deliberation (Dryzek 2000, 14). Likewise deliberation might be more important in initial review or the drafting of regulations than in day-to-day enforcement.

Nonetheless, the principle of democratic deliberation supports efforts to make the ethical review of research more publicly accessible. The PC-SBI continued to embrace a principle of democratic deliberation in its recent work on human subjects research ethics (2012). The proposals I suggest give this principle content.

Note

I am grateful to Holly Lynch and to audiences at the Stanford Center for Law and the Biosciences Journal Club and the Petrie–Flom Center at Harvard Law School for their helpful suggestions.

References

Abbo, Elmer D. 2007. Promoting free speech in clinical quality improvement research. *Northwestern University Law Review* 101: 575–92.

Agarwal, Bina. 2008. Toward participatory inclusion: A gender analysis of community forestry in South Asia. In Jorrit de Jong and Gowher Rizvi, eds., *The State of Access*. Washington, DC: Brookings Institution Press, 37–70.

Anderson, Elizabeth. 2003. Sen, ethics, and democracy. *Feminist Economics* 9 (2–3): 239–61.

Baily, Mary Ann, Melissa Bottrell, Joanne Lynn, and Bruce Jennings. 2006. The ethics of using QI methods to improve health care quality and safety. *Hastings Center Report* 36 (4): S1–39.

Bal, Roland, Wiebe Bijker, and Ruud Hendriks. 2004. Democratisation of scientific advice. *British Medical Journal* 29: 1339–41.

Beno v. Shalala, 30 F.3d 1057 (9th Cir. 1994).

Blustein, Jan. 2005. Toward a more public discussion of the ethics of federal social program evaluation. *Journal of Policy Analysis and Management* 24 (4): 824–46.

Burghardt, John, Sheena McConnell, Alicia Meckstroth, and Peter Schochet. 1997. *Implementing Random Assignment: Lessons from the National Job Corps Study*. Princeton: Mathematica Policy Research.

Cassell, Paul G. 2011. Freeing the guilty without protecting the innocent: Some skeptical observations on proposed new "innocence" procedures. *New York Law School Law Review* 56: 1063–96.

C.K. v. New Jersey Dep't of Health & Human Servs., 92 F.3d 171 (3d Cir. 1996).

Cohen, Joshua, and Joel Rogers. 1992. Secondary associations and democratic governance. *Politics and Society* 20 (4): 391–472.

Council for International Organizations of Medical Sciences (CIOMS). 2002. *International Ethical Guidelines for Biomedical Research Involving Human Subjects.* Geneva: WHO.

Crane v. Matthews, 417 F. Supp. 532 (N.D. Ga. 1976).

Cuellar, Mariano-Florentino. 2005. Rethinking regulatory democracy. *Administrative Law Review* 57 (2): 411–500.

Deeds, Bethany Griffin, Marne Castillo, Zephyr Beason, Shayna D. Cunningham, Jonathan M. Ellen, and Ligia Peralta. 2008. An HIV prevention protocol reviewed at 15 national sites: How do ethics committees protect communities? *Journal of Empirical Research on Human Research Ethics* 3 (2): 77–86.

Department of Health and Human Services. Presidential Commission for the Study of Bioethical Issues. 2010. *New Directions: The Ethics of Synthetic Biology and Emerging Technologies.*

Department of Health and Human Services. 2012. *Moral Science: Protecting Participants in Human Subjects Research.* Washington, DC: GPO.

DeRenzo, Evan, and Alison Wichman. 1990. A pilot project: Bioethics consultants as non-voting members of IRBs at the National Institutes of Health. *IRB: Ethics and Human Research* 12: 6–8.

Dryzek, John. 2000. *Deliberative Democracy and Beyond: Liberals, Critics, Contestations.* Oxford: Oxford University Press.

Egan, T. M., S. Murray, R. T. Bustami, et al. 2006. Development of the new lung allocation system in the United States. *American Journal of Transplantation* 6 (5): 1212–27.

Estlund, David. 1997. Beyond fairness and deliberation: The epistemic dimension of democratic authority. In James Bohman and William Rehg, eds., *Deliberative Democracy: Essays on Reason and Politics.* Cambridge: MIT Press, 173–204.

Flynn, Laurie, and Ronald Honberg. 1999. Achieving proper balance in research with decisionally-incapacitated subjects: NAMI's perspectives on the working group's proposal. *Journal of Health Care Law and Policy* 1: 174–92.

Føllesdal, Andreas. 1998. Subsidiarity. *Journal of Political Philosophy* 6 (2): 231–59.

Fost, Norman, and Robert J. Levine. 2007. The dysregulation of human subjects research. *Journal of the American Medical Association* 298 (18): 2196–98.

Gutmann, Amy, and Dennis Thompson. 2004. *Why Deliberative Democracy?* Princeton: Princeton University Press.

Harvard Law Review. 1995. Administrative law—waivers—Ninth Circuit holds statutory waivers for welfare experiments subject to judicial review. — *Beno v. Shalala*, 30 F.3d 1057 (9th Cir. 1994). *Harvard Law Review* 108: 1208–13.

Johnson, Genevieve Fuji. 2009. Deliberative democratic practices in Canada: An analysis of institutional empowerment in three cases. *Canadian Journal of Political Science* 42 (3): 679–703.

Katz, Jay. 1993. Human experimentation and human rights. *Saint Louis University Law Journal* 38: 7–54.

Keane, Moira A. 2008. Institutional review board approaches to the incidental findings problem. *Journal of Law, Medicine and Ethics* 36: 352–55.

Khanani, Intisar, Jon Elam, Rick Hearn, Camille Jones, and Noble Maseru. 2010. The impact of prenatal WIC participation on infant mortality and racial disparities. *American Journal of Public Health* 100 (1): S204–209.

MacCoun, Robert. 2005. Voice, control, and belonging: The double-edged sword of procedural fairness. *Annual Review of Law and Social Science* 1: 171–201.

Menkel-Meadow, Carrie. 2004. The lawyer's role(s) in deliberative democracy. *Nevada Law Journal* 5 (2): 347–69.

Merion, Robert M., Valarie B. Ashby, Robert A. Wolfe, et al. 2005. Deceased-donor characteristics and the survival benefit of kidney transplantation. *Journal of the American Medical Association* 294 (21): 2726–33.

Minow, Martha. 1991. From class actions to Miss Saigon: The concept of representation in the law. *Cleveland State Law Review* 39 (3): 269–300.

National Commission for the Protection of Human Subjects of Biomedical and Behavioral Research. 1979. *The Belmont Report: Ethical Principles and Guidelines for the Protection of Human Subjects of Research*. Washington, DC: GPO.

National Institute of Allergy and Infectious Diseases (NIAID). Division of AIDS. 2009. Recommendations for community involvement in National Institute of Allergy and Infectious Diseases HIV/AIDS clinical trials research. http://www.hvtn.org/community/CAB_Recommendations_Certified.pdf.

Office for Human Research Protections. Secretary's Advisory Committee on Human Research Protections. 2008. SACHRP letter to DHHS Secretary. http://www.hhs.gov/ohrp/sachrp/sachrpletter091808.html.

Parkinson, John, and Declan Roche. 2004. Restorative justice: Deliberative democracy in action? *Australian Journal of Political Science* 39 (3): 505–10.

Peikes, Deborah, Arnold Chen, Jennifer Schore, and Randall Brown. 2009. Effects of care coordination on hospitalization, quality of care, and health care expenditures among Medicare beneficiaries: 15 Randomized trials. *Journal of the American Medical Association* 301 (6): 603–18.

Porter, Joan P. 1987. How unaffiliated/nonscientist members of institutional review boards see their roles. *IRB: Ethics and Human Research* 9 (6): 1–6.

Rosenbaum, Sara. 1992. Mothers and children last: The Oregon Medicaid experiment. *American Journal of Law and Medicine* 18 (1–2): 97–126.

Rosenblatt, Rand. 1978. Health care reform and administrative law: A structural approach. *Yale Law Journal* 88 (2): 243–336.

Sirotin, Nicole, Leslie E. Wolf, Lance M. Pollack, Joseph A. Catania, M. Margaret Dolcini, and Bernard Lo. 2010. IRBs and ethically challenging protocols: Views of IRB chairs about useful resources. *IRB: Ethics and Human Research* 32 (5): 10–19.

Veatch, Robert. 2007. How many principles for bioethics? In Richard E. Ashcroft, Angus Dawson, and Heather Draper, eds., *Principles of Health Care Ethics*. London: Wiley, 43–50.

Walters, Daniel. 2012. The justiciability of fair balance under the Federal Advisory Committee Act: Toward a deliberative process approach. *Michigan Law Review* 110: 677–708.

11
IRBs and the Problem of "Local Precedents"

Laura Stark

In the 2011 ANPRM, OHRP outlined several high-priority problems in the design of human subjects regulations. One of those problems was the lack of a streamlined system for regulating studies that require review at multiple research sites. Here is how OHRP described the problem of multisite research:

> In many cases, a local IRB for each institution does independently review the research protocol, informed consent documents and other materials, sometimes resulting in hundreds of reviews for one study. When any one of these IRBs requires changes to the research protocol that are adopted for the entire study, investigators must resubmit the revised protocol to all of the reviewing IRBs. This process can take many months and can significantly delay the initiation of research projects. Separately, there are reports showing that there can be widely differing outcomes regarding the level of review required from IRB to IRB, even for identical studies. (DHHS 2011)

No doubt, the nearly inexhaustible number of changes that IRBs can request of one study causes logistical problems for investigators and produces unclear benefits for research participants (Gunsalus et al. 2006; Heimer and Petty 2010; Menikoff 2010). But why do IRBs reach different conclusions about the same study and what can be done about it?

This chapter has three goals. First, it introduces the concept of "local precedents" to explain why multisite research presents such a problem. Second, the chapter summarizes my ethnographic research on IRBs to illustrate how local precedents play out in meetings. Third, in light of my empirical findings, the chapter outlines review mechanisms that are configured differently from the local-review system dominant in the United States. I offer three examples of innovative tools that institutions are developing, and I compare their relative merits. The overall goals of the chapter are to encourage a more accurate understanding of why the current review system has been problematic and to encourage constructive reform of a system that both investigators and federal regulators agree is broken.

11.1 What Are "Local Precedents"?

11.1.1 Explaining Differences in Judgment across Boards

As is no doubt familiar to readers, almost all hospitals, universities, and other organizations that support human subjects research have an IRB; even private companies and government agencies have boards. Today most research organizations have at least one IRB or they contract review to a private board. There are currently more than 4,000 boards in the United States alone.

Surveys have reported that when different IRBs are presented with the same standard protocol to review, the boards unfailingly arrive at different judgments about how the protocol needs to be changed before they will approve it (McWilliams et al. 2003). Survey research has fallen short, however, in explaining why this happens. Such research tends to view variable decisions as the product of uneven resources across boards. It suggests that with larger staffs, more time, and better training all boards would arrive at a more "correct" decision about a protocol. Locating the source of uneven decisions in uneven material resources does have some merit. Yet, even if IRBs had equitable material resources—staff, time, and funding—they would not produce wholly consistent decisions.

In my research I found that IRB members rarely deliberated specific protocols by trying to apply abstract rules, such as 45 CFR 46. Instead, they made decisions about a protocol by comparing it to previous cases they decided. As a result local IRBs imprinted the studies they reviewed with their distinctive trove of knowledge and experiences as a group (Stark 2012a).

I call these previous, exemplary cases "local precedents." I use this term to describe the past decisions that guide board members' evaluations of subsequent research. By drawing on local precedents, board members read new protocols as permutations of studies that they have previously debated and settled in order to make decisions that are *locally* consistent over time. IRBs' local precedents tend to be idiosyncratic to each board but reasonably stable within them, which explains how well-supported, fully functioning IRBs can arrive at different decisions about a single protocol.

11.1.2 Thinking in Cases

On the surface it can seem as if IRBs work like juries, but as Carl Coleman (2004) has pointed out, there are striking differences between juries and IRBs (see also Ellison and Munro 2010; Samuel 2009). Both IRBs and juries are groups of individuals that deliberate with the aim of making a final decision. Importantly, however, IRB members work together to decide multiple cases over time, so they develop decision routines that span individual cases.

Unlike juries, IRBs use a particular form of analogical reasoning, one that is site specific. When IRB members and investigators are trained to apply regulations, they are taught to think with a relatively fixed set of well-recognized research scandals: the Nazi doctors' experiments, the Tuskegee syphilis studies, the Milgram obedience-to-authority studies, and the Thalidomide tragedy, for example. These exemplary cases are considered legitimate to take into account when judging protocols. Legal scholars and federal regulators encourage, both implicitly and explicitly, use of these widely shared ethics cases as acceptable heuristic devices: cognitive tools that can boost IRBs' decision-making efficiency. Social psychologists would point out that heuristics enable IRB members to take mental shortcuts in reasoning, specifically, to categorize quickly a protocol as a token of a particular type.

At the same time, IRB members draw analogies to prior cases from within their institutions to judge protocols, not only analogies to classic cases known beyond their institutions' walls. They use these local precedents for the same reason that they use international precedents: to make consistent decisions over time. The side benefit is that precedents, like all heuristic devices, speed their decisions.

There is nothing inherently wrong with using precedents, and indeed some scholars would like IRBs to use more of them (Bean et al. 2010). Precedents are not a problem, however, if a protocol is evaluated at only one site and the study is similar to those the board has evaluated in the past. Alas, this is rarely the case, which is the crux of the problem OHRP outlined in the ANPRM—namely that IRB members commonly use site-specific precedents to evaluate multisite studies. It is possible to see how international precedents might be useful for researchers and funders motivated to move studies forward promptly. Use of local precedents, however, creates conflicting requests for modification across boards and undermines the aims of researchers and funders eager both to begin studies in good time and also to have few site-specific deviations.

Thus IRBs are less akin to juries and more like teams of health care providers. They spend their days considering cases (whether protocols or patients) and making decisions about those cases (whether an IRB recommendation or a diagnosis), often with limited time. Clinicians absorb a stock of cases and appropriate decisions through medical school, residencies, and fellowships. The current debate over evidence-based medicine is precisely about whether clinicians should be allowed to base decisions heavily on their individual experience constituted by an idiosyncratic stock of cases, or whether they should resist context-based judgment (Timmermans and Mauck 2005). The term "judgment" is a more palatable variant of the less democratic-sounding term "discretion," which is indeed what IRB members, like clinicians, have legal authority to use in making their decisions.

My finding that IRB members make decisions based on local precedents also calls into question a common rhetorical claim about human subjects review. According to this view, board members apply fixed regulations to specific protocols with more or less accuracy, resulting in objectively right and wrong decisions. This claim embeds a framework of legal positivism (Kennedy 2004; Koch 1985). By contrast, "reasoning in cases" (Forrester 1996) stems from a pragmatic tradition developed in Anglo-American law and medicine during the late nineteenth century. "If you think that invoking principles will avoid this method of reasoning," historian John Forrester writes with particular reference to case-based decision-making in modern medical ethics, "a skeptic of the relevance of your principles will soon require you to make explicit the exemplar, the prototype, the analogue onto which the invocation of your principles is grafted" (1996). In sum, the way that IRBs work, as I have observed them, resonates more closely with a form of analogical reasoning, or thinking in cases, that is decidedly local not universal.

11.2 Research and Findings

11.2.1 Ethnographic Methods

How do IRBs develop local precedents and with what effect? To answer this question, I attended the monthly or twice-monthly full-board meetings of three IRBs for one year between 2004 and 2005, and audio-recorded most of the meetings. I supplemented these recordings with handwritten field notes and recorded interviews with thirty-four of the boards' members. In the section that follows, I briefly summarize the results of my findings based on this empirical research. More extensive examples from my ethnographic research can be found in Stark (2012a).

11.2.2 Case Study

Through my ethnographic analysis I found that creating local precedents was time-consuming for board members, and they often pursued issues for unpredictable reasons, such as a board member's personal conviction or a research subject's complaint. Once settled, however, boards used these decisions systematically to guide future decisions. In this way, the boards that I observed standardized the types of problems they identified and the changes that they required to protocols, such as the units in which radiation levels should be expressed, how psychological inventories should be described to subjects, and the number of years that a study's approval can be renewed.

For example, after members of one IRB I observed discussed a so-called adverse event in a study that they had previously approved, a psychologist on the board pithily reflected on the board's new position toward subject recruitment: "Sometimes things have to happen before you know what to do in the future" (Feb meeting, transcript location 533). His observation flags the process in which board members used one evaluation as a stock decision to evaluate new protocols. Over the subsequent months, this board member and his IRB colleagues continued to reapply their "new position," which was specifically on when to use opt-out forms, to new protocols that were unlike the exemplar case in terms of the study population, research methods, and level of risk. The board's creation and application of the precedent was done for procedural consistency and had the benefit of once having been justified in the language of ethics. The decision never needed to be justified again. It was fast; it was in some ways satisfying; but it was perhaps inappropriate for the case at hand.

For IRB members, the effects of this local precedent were twofold: first, it allowed board members to make subsequent decisions more quickly without rehearsing settled debates, and, second, it allowed members to defend their decisions on the grounds that they were imposing a consistent local policy. In this instance and many others, board members rarely turned to federal regulations to deliberate a new protocol. They instead identified dimensions of a new study as an example of a problem they had previously decided. With no appeals process in place, IRBs rarely got feedback from investigators on whether they felt board decisions or analogies were appropriate.

The implications were striking. I found that investigators could shape local precedents only in the early stages of review, and that they lost influence over decisions once a local precedent gained inertia with an IRB. It also revealed how IRB members were trained on local boards. In interviews, IRB members told me that experienced board members passed on the substance of prior decisions to new members, who felt they had to gain a sense of at least some of the group's local precedents before they felt competent as reviewers. This process also explains why some IRBs can belabor decisions that others make more quickly. Differences in boards' turnaround times were in part due to whether they had a precedent to apply to a new protocol. Settling contentious questions was time consuming for IRBs. For example, the drawn-out deliberations of an IRB comprised of medical researchers when faced with a qualitative study did not necessarily reflect hostility toward qualitative methods. Instead, protracted deliberations often pointed to a conceptual gap in the precedents that the IRB members could readily call to mind.

In sum, IRB members identified new problems somewhat idiosyncratically. Out of these problems, board members developed remedies to fit the particular instance. But they also used these decisions as prototypes that they applied to subsequent protocols.

11.3 Discussion: Three Review Models to Manage Local Precedents

By understanding how local precedents shape IRB decision-making, it is possible to look to the future of human subjects regulation and ask how we can address the problems caused, in OHRP's words, by "widely differing outcomes regarding the level of review required from IRB to IRB, even for identical studies" (DHHS 2011). Given the unavoidable fact that IRBs have the legal authority to use discretion, it is unlikely that improvements will come from trying to scrub judgment from research review. However, it is possible to harness local precedents and turn them into a productive phenomenon.

Several institutions are developing models that hold on to the advantages of local precedents while minimizing the problems they might cause. To do so, these institutions have either relocated the institutional site of review or created new resources to capture local precedents. These models are not mutually exclusive and, ideally, would work simultaneously. Three models are especially worth considering: study networks, collegial review, and decision repositories.

11.3.1 Study Networks
On this approach, several large, well-funded organizations would review all of the studies that are attached to a common research initiative. For example, the National Institutes of Health has supported networks such as the Central IRB for cancer studies and the HMO Research Network

(HMORN) mechanism (Greene et al. 2010). Other examples include the Multicenter Academic Clinical Research Organization (MACRO) and the Biomedical Research Alliance of New York (BRANY) (Koski et al. 2005). In these cases, hundreds of investigators who are working in one broad area and toward one general goal—but who are doing so at multiple institutions—get reviewed within the same system through "cooperative" or "shared" arrangements (Resnick 2012). Study networks succeed in limiting the problem of local precedents for multisite review because one meta-board essentially settles matters for all institutions and investigators. Ideally, there is only one set of local precedents, that of the study network, to bring to bear on the review process for investigators conducting similar studies at different sites. The added advantage for local boards is that their workloads are substantially reduced.

There are two big limitations to study networks and the promise they hold for managing local precedents: liability and money. Customarily, study networks are not attached to one local institution (as is the case with reciprocal review agreements). Yet, to reap the benefits of networked review—including less local administrative work, fewer conflicts among local precedents, and speedier, consistent decisions—the local review boards must largely defer to the decisions made by the study network. Local boards' liability concerns can undermine these benefits and their concerns are often grounded on the fact that they need to take the local community perspective into account to comply with federal regulations (Klitzman 2012). Indeed the ANPRM recognizes the paradox and ambiguity of asking reviewers to respect the distinctive views of an imagined and undefined local community. Nonetheless, as regulations currently read, community views are essential to incorporate. Since local institutions remain legally accountable for the research their investigators conduct, many are inclined to interpret this requirement strictly, dismantling the advantages of networked review.

Study networks also require substantial funding. Some large-budget funders, such as NIH, are willing to bear the financial burden of administering reviews as part of their interest in seeing results from the studies they sponsor. Many study networks at this point can only be used to review protocols that are well funded in the first place (e.g., that have been funded by a large agency, foundation, or corporation) and whose investigators thereby have access to the study network organized by the funder. Consequently access to study networks is limited in a way that accentuates inequities between institutions that can most easily garner funding and those that cannot. In sum, IRBs are a structural barrier to research that exacerbates differences between resource-rich and resource-poor institutions and investigators.

Independent study networks, which are unattached to research sponsors or local research sites, promise to remedy the problem of access. Compared to traditional institution-based review boards, such boards also have the potential to be more "independent" of financial considerations, a desideratum of a good review process (Macklin 2008). A word of caution is in order, though: network review boards that are unattached to institutions or to one sponsor are less likely to be influenced by financial considerations *only if* the boards are not for profit. Commercial IRBs, such as Western IRB, have received mixed reviews because they (not unlike the FDA, it is worth noting) are paid by the very organizations (i.e., study sponsors) that have an interest in seeing research move ahead posthaste. Similarly study networks, such as BRANY, collect fees to offset the cost of review (Koski et al. 2005). To be sure, university- and hospital-based IRBs are also vulnerable, however gently, to such financial considerations, which can compromise the independence of their review (Macklin 2008). Still, not-for-profit, centrally administered review boards offer the greatest hope for reducing contradictions between local precedents without giving away reviewers' position of relative freedom from financial conflicts of interest.

11.3.2 Collegial Review

"Ethics creep" is often heard as a phrase of derision in research review (Gunsalus et al. 2006; Riordan and Riordan 2009). The demands and mentalities of IRBs have infused the social sciences (not only medicine) and stretched to researchers' preliminary explorations into topics (not only mature research plans). Collegial review takes advantage of ethics creep to minimize use of inappropriate precedents by soliciting input from reviewers who share a field with the investigator.

At universities, collegial review is most common for student projects, and involves local review by members of the (student) researcher's discipline. It is also worth considering the merits of this model beyond student research through a system of review organized around investigators' institutional departments or offices—with all of the political advantages and drawbacks that it implies. The aim of "devolving" review is to move protocol evaluation closer to the people who have expertise in the field in which an investigator is working, and thus to get evaluations from reviewers who know the implications of the proposed methodologies and the populations under study (Stark 2012b). There is little formal documentation on how widespread this model is already (though for a now-dated overview, see Stopp 1985). In addition to review of student protocols, some IRBs authorize department-level subcommittees to complete expedited review for their own investigators, as I found in my own research (Stark 2012a). Other departments intentionally seed IRBs with one of their colleagues to be sure appropriate criteria of evaluation are taken into account in human subjects review (Lederman 2006). Several research universities have independently hit on collegial input and review as a productive model, for example, at Princeton University, University of Chicago, and University of Virginia (Lederman 2007; Dobrin 2012; Silverstein 2012).

The prospect of collegial review raises important questions about the place of personal politics, however. Some have argued that it is not only appropriate but actually desirable for reviewers to assess investigators' quality as researchers (Macklin 2008). It would then stand to reason that review should involve people who have the greatest opportunity to know the reputation of researchers. It is far from clear, however, whether colleagues with limited information—perhaps coming from word of mouth or from outdated opinions—are especially well positioned to judge each others' quality as researchers. My own observations of IRB meetings show that board members already do judge researchers' character and that they do so in ways that few would consider legitimate: by drawing conclusions about the fastidiousness of researchers based on typographical errors in their protocols, for example (Stark 2013). Review by colleagues runs the risk of accentuating *ad hominem* biases in the review process.

There may be a variation of collegial review that avoids department-level dysfunction: namely a more conventional form of peer review. In the United States, the first human subjects review boards developed in tandem with peer review of grant applications (Mandel 1996). This is no accident. Given the similarities between human subjects review and other familiar forums of research review, such as funding panels and editorial boards, it may be worth developing human subjects review into an *external* collegial review mechanism. Universities and hospitals, like presses and funders, would send protocols to researchers outside of their institution who have expertise with a similar methodology or study population. For example, the American Association of University Professors has suggested that professional associations should take the lead on some human subjects review (Thomson et al. 2006). Investigators would have their protocols vetted by other researchers trained in their methodological and disciplinary fields, thus if not curbing the number of local precedents a group creates, then at least promoting the use of precedents appropriate for the research at hand (Irvine 2012).

One of the biggest critiques of IRBs is their lack of breadth—and thus understanding—of research methodologies. Scientists and scholars learn, both formally and tacitly, the appropriate limits of research within their particular disciplinary frameworks. Peer review offers a way to return judgment to researchers' methodological and moral communities.

11.3.3 Decision Repositories

How have different institutions decided similar studies? This is a question that IRB members often ask but can rarely answer. It is a question that board members asked me during the months and years I observed their meetings, and that they ask of each other in national and regional IRB training meetings. A way to provide answers to this question is to create an online repository of approved protocols (appropriately de-identified), an approach that Coleman (2004) and others have advocated.

This approach may be more feasible than others because it does not require that institutions or the federal government fundamentally restructure the review process. There would be no need to fight against the inertia of existing federal policies or against the organization of review at universities and hospitals. Boards would not have to be reimagined; no institutions would have to bear the burden of being an early adopter of a new review mechanism or of interpreting regulations in a new way.

This approach does, however, require the generosity of a few leaders. A repository requires funding, server space, time, and—importantly—the donation of protocols. Researchers are understandably hesitant to share their current research agendas to protect their intellectual property. Completed projects would thus be ideal candidates for posting but would be most quickly outdated. Still, given researchers' critiques of IRBs, it would be a revealing experiment to give investigators the opportunity to participate in creating a solution to the problem they rightly criticize.

Two institutions have already taken the lead to establish decision repositories, but they have done so in very different ways. The Sunnybrook Health Sciences Center in Toronto has created a bank of decisions for the institution with the aim of making more consistent decisions (Bean et al. 2010). The repository is accessible only within the institution, so it can be used to streamline local precedents at one institution over time but cannot be used to resolve local precedents across institutions at one moment in time. Nonetheless, the repository is a fruitful model for imagining how to remedy the problem of local precedents. Decision-making based on local precedent depends on memory, for good and for ill. Without such a record of precedents, IRBs with *low* turnover of members are likely to develop inertia in their decisions, predictably raising a narrow set of problems. Likewise they are apt to become blind—not learning to see other plausible concerns. On the flip side, IRBs with *high* turnover of members are likely to make orthogonal decisions about a protocol over time, for example, when studies come up for annual review. Decision repositories serve as shared memory banks that are open to analysis.

Decision repositories can serve not only IRB members but researchers too. A second model repository is housed in New Zealand where the government has funded a publicly available digital archive of decisions, called The Ethics Application Repository (TEAR) (Tolich and Tumilty 2013). Researchers from any institution, not only in from New Zealand, can post online their IRBs' requested changes and the ultimate decisions of their boards' review, as well as their research materials such as consent documents. As a result researchers can be empowered to do some of the interpretive work for their IRBs. Researchers are in a position, in other words, to teach their IRBs how their studies should be evaluated, to signal to their boards that a research community exists even if the topic or method is new to the reviewers, and to assure IRBs that boards would not be alone in approving a method or topic of research that is unfamiliar to them. Politically, it can also serve as a resource for researchers at institutions with less accommodating IRBs to help them envision how other boards settled similar protocols—and perhaps educate their IRBs (Lederman 2007).

Publicly available IRB decision repositories would helpfully limit local precedents, even if they create what could be seen as a free-rider problem: some people taking advantage of a resource for which others bear the burden. Yet there may be space for appropriate free riders in human subjects review. Decision repositories would allow investigators and IRBs at low-volume and low-resource institutions also to benefit from experiments in human subjects review—unlike creative reconfigurations of boards, such as study networks, which only aid those directly involved with them.

11.4 Conclusion: Local Precedents and the Future of Multisite Studies

My empirical research has led me to doubt that a simple infusion of staff members and funding would erase the variation across IRBs that inconvenience many investigators today, especially those conducting multisite studies. Building on my firsthand observations and audio recordings of the full-board meetings of three IRBs over the course of one year, I found that multisite studies are a problem because IRB members develop site-specific "local precedents" to work more quickly and to make consistent decisions over time. In doing so, different IRBs produce different—but equally legal—requests for modifications based on their different case experience.

Interpretation cannot be eliminated from the application of the law and so local precedents will not go away. They are a function of how board members work and reason as human beings. Local precedents can, however, be managed. The results of my research summarized in this chapter suggest a new explanation for why IRBs reach different decisions, and suggest that reformers should feel tempered optimism about the future of human subjects regulation. With a new understanding of the underlying causes of problems with human subject review, in this case local precedents, it is possible also to imagine new solutions. I have presented three models for review that stakeholders in the process—investigators, participants, board members, and policy makers alike—might consider adopting. These creative efforts suggest there is reason for hope for the future of human subjects review.

Note

I am grateful to Nathan Pauly and Erin Kelly for their expert research assistance, and to Carl Coleman, Lise Dobrin, Rene Lederman, and Martin Tolich for their helpful advice. This chapter has benefited from thoughtful feedback from Holly Lynch and participants in the Petrie–Flom workshop, The Future of Human Subjects Regulation, in May 2012. I am grateful for discussions with participants in two workshops, which helped me refine section 11.4 in particular: first, the National Academy of Sciences Workshop on Proposed Revisions to the Common Rule in Relation to the Behavioral and Social Sciences, held in March 2013, and the Ethics Rupture Invitational Summit, held in October 2012. This chapter substantially develops and applies the concept of "local precedents," which I first defined in chapter 2 of my book, *Behind Closed Doors: IRBs and the Making of Ethical Research* (Stark 2012a).

References

Bean, Sally, Blair Henry, J. Michelle Kinsey, Keitha McMurray, Catherine Parry, and Tiffany Tassopoulos. 2010. Enhancing research ethics decision-making: An REB decision bank. *IRB: Ethics and Human Research* 32 (6): 9–12.

Coleman, Carl. 2004. Rationalizing risk assessment in human subject research. *Arizona Law Review* 46 (1): 1137–87.

Department of Health and Human Services (DHHS). 2011. Advance Notice of Proposed Rulemaking. Human subjects research protections: Enhancing protections for research subjects and reducing burden, delay, and ambiguity for investigators. *Federal Register* 76 (143): 44512–31.

Dobrin, Lise. 2012. From gatekeeping the project to preparing the person: Ethics for emergent methods in "excused," "exempted," or uncovered research. Talk delivered at the invitational summit Ethics Rupture, Fredericton, NB, Canada, October 27.

Ellison, Louise, and Vanessa E. Munro. 2010. Getting to (not) guilty: Examining jurors' deliberative processes in, and beyond, the context of a mock rape trial. *Legal Studies* 30 (1): 74–97.

Forrester, John. 1996. If P, then what? Thinking in cases. *History of the Human Sciences* 9 (3): 1–25.

Greene, Sarah M., Jeffrey Braff, Andrew Nelson, and Robert J. Reid. 2010. The process is the product: A new model for multisite IRB review of data-only studies. *IRB: Ethics and Human Research* 32 (3): 1–6.

Gunsalus, C. Kristina, Edward Bruner, Nicholas Burbules, Leon DeCosta Dash, Matthew W. Finkin, Joseph Goldberg, William Greenough, Gregory Miller, and Michael Gerard Pratt. 2006. The Illinois White Paper. Improving the system for protecting human subjects: Counteracting IRB mission creep. SSRN Working Paper Series, June. http://papers.ssrn.com/sol3/papers.cfm?abstract_id=902995.

Heimer, Carol A., and JuLeigh Petty. 2010. Bureaucratic ethics: IRBs and the legal regulation of human subjects research. *Annual Review of Law and Social Science* 6: 601–26.

Irvine, Janice. 2012. Can't ask, can't tell: How institutional review boards keep sex in the closet. *Contexts* 11 (2): 28–33.

Kennedy, Duncan. 2004. The disenchantment of logically formal legal rationality, or Max Weber's sociology in the genealogy of the contemporary mode of Western legal thought. *Hastings Law Journal* 55 (5): 1031–76.

Klitzman, Robert L. 2012. The myth of community differences as the cause of variations among IRBs. *American Journal of Bioethics* 2 (2): 24–33.

Koch, Charles H. 1985. *Administrative Law and Practice*. Boulder, CO: West.

Koski, Greg, Jessica Aungst, Joel Kupersmith, Kenneth Getz, and David Rimoin. 2005. Cooperative research ethics review boards: A win-win solution? *IRB: Ethics and Human Research* 27 (3): 1–7.

Lederman, Rena. 2006. The perils of working at home: IRB "mission creep" as context and content for an ethnography of disciplinary knowledges. *American Ethnologist* 33 (4): 482–91.

Lederman, Rena. 2007. Educate your IRB: An experiment in cross-disciplinary experimentation. *Anthropology News* 48 (6): 33–34.

Macklin, Ruth. 2008. How independent are IRBs? *IRB: Ethics and Human Research* 30 (3): 15–19.

Mandel, Richard. 1996. *A Half Century of Peer Review, 1946–1996*. Bethesda, MD: Division of Research Grants, National Institutes of Health.

McWilliams, Rita, Julie Hoover-Fong, Ada Hamosh, Suzanne Beck, Terri Beaty, and Garry Cutting. 2003. Problematic variation in local institutional review of a multicenter genetic epidemiology study. *Journal of the American Medical Association* 290 (3): 360–66.

Menikoff, J. 2010. The paradoxical problem with multiple-IRB review. *New England Journal of Medicine* 363 (17): 1591–93.

Resnick, David. 2012. Centralized institutional review boards: Assessing the arguments and evidence. *Journal of Clinical Research Best Practices* 8 (11): 1–13. http://www.firstclinical.com/journal/2012/1211_Centralized.pdf .

Riordan, Diane A., and Michael P. Riordan. 2009. IRB creep: Federal regulations protecting human research subjects and increasing instructors' responsibilities. *Issues in Accounting Education* 24 (1): 31–43.

Samuel, Geoffrey. 2009. Can legal reasoning be demystified? *Legal Studies* 29 (2): 181–210.

Silverstein, Michael. 2012. An epistemological rainbow coalition for ethical peer review in non-clinical research. Talk delivered in session "Compliance in Practice: Creative Engagements with Regulatory Ethics Regimes" at the Annual Meeting of the American Anthropological Association, San Francisco, CA, November 15.

Stark, Laura. 2012a. *Behind Closed Doors: IRBs and the Making of Ethical Research*. Chicago: University of Chicago Press.

Stark, Laura. 2012b. The problem of researcher-trainees in ethics review and what can be done about it. Talk delivered at the invitational summit Ethics Rupture, Fredericton, NB, Canada, October 27.

Stark, Laura. 2013. Reading trust between the lines: "Housekeeping work" and inequality in human-subjects review. *Cambridge Quarterly of Healthcare Ethics* 22 (4): 391–99.

Stopp, G. Harry. 1985. The internal IRB structure: Models in academic settings. *IRB: Ethics and Human Research* 7 (6): 9.

Thomson, Judith J., Catherine Elgin, David A. Hyman, Philip E. Rubin, and Jonathan Knight. 2006. Research on human subjects: Academic freedom and the institutional review board. American Association of University Professors. http://www.aaup.org/report/research-human-subjects-academic-freedom-and-institutional-review-board.

Timmermans, Stefan, and Aaron Mauck. 2005. The promises and pitfalls of evidence-based medicine. *Health Affairs* 24 (1): 18–28.

Tolich, Martin, and Emma Tumilty. 2013. Making ethics review a learning institution: The ethics application repository proof of concept—tear.otago.ac.nz. *Qualitative Sociology*. January 3.

IV
Specimens, Data, and Privacy

Introduction to Part IV—Specimens, Data, and Privacy

Jeffrey Skopek

Biospecimens and associated data from the vast majority of Americans are currently being stored in biobanks and used in medical genomics research, often without the sources' knowledge or consent; for although consent of the source is generally required for human subjects research by federal regulations, researchers can extinguish this requirement for biospecimens and data by de-identifying them. In this way a sample that was donated for use in one type of research may be used in research that breaches the express terms of the donor's consent, and a sample that was extracted in the context of a medical procedure may be used in research without the source's knowledge.

The key question addressed in the following chapters is whether this approach to biospecimens and data is normatively justifiable and pragmatically desirable, and if not, whether the revisions proposed by DHHS are steps in the right direction. These revisions would require consent for *all* research on biospecimens, regardless of de-identification, and require consent for research on data that were collected for research purposes but not for de-identified data that were collected for other purposes. In addition the revisions would allow sources to provide broad consent to future research, rather than the study-specific consent that is currently required.

The central rationale for these proposals is one of pragmatism based on public opinion. DHHS cites numerous studies finding that most Americans think they should have the right to decide whether their biospecimens and data will be used in research, regardless of de-identification, but at the same time, most do not actually want to limit the researchers who will have access to their samples or the diseases that they will study. Thus DHHS reasons that its proposed revisions will not only enhance public trust in biomedical research, but also increase the future availability and research value of stored samples and data.

The debates over these changes, however, have often looked beyond pragmatism to the normative question of whether tissue sources should have a right of control of their tissue and associated data, and if so, on what grounds. There are three primary ways in which arguments for such a right of control are often legally framed.

The first is to characterize the sources as parties entering into a contract with the researchers to whom they donate. On this account the reason that it is objectionable for a researcher to de-identify tissue and data and use them outside the scope of the source's consent is that this constitutes a breach of the parties' agreement. There are, however, challenges to this framing—and not merely those concerning the fact that a true donation, in which the source receives nothing of value in return, is not a contract. The more serious problem arises from the fact that contract law alone will not allow a source to create enforceable use restrictions against researchers who are not party to the contract, and it is highly unlikely, given the nature of biomedical research, that samples will remain solely with their original recipients. This raises the question of whether tissue sources have cognizable interests in their tissue that exist independent of contract.

The second approach answers this question by suggesting that biospecimens and associated data should be seen as special types of personal property on which the source can impose research restrictions—just like one can impose development restrictions on land when selling it. But again, there are legal and normative challenges to this characterization of the interests at stake. Most significant, our law does not allow for the creation of use restrictions on personal property, and there are strong efficiency and fairness justifications for this, grounded in considerations of information costs and dead hand control. In addition the recognition of disassociated rights in biospecimens and data may deter commercial applications by creating uncertainty over legal title, and prevent coordination around socially efficient uses by fragmenting ownership. Thus the core question for this approach is whether a more narrowly tailored property interest can be carved out without doing damage to the foundational architecture of property, such as the "*numerus clausus* principle," which limits property rights to a small number of well-defined types.

The third possibility, and a way of grounding a general right of control outside of property, is to ground the right in principles of tort and the potential harms associated with unconsented research. These could in theory be either privacy- or autonomy-based harms. On the one hand, insofar as de-identification eliminates or significantly reduces the risk of privacy harms—which are not inherent to research use but rather derivative from it—the risk of these harms may not provide a foundation for a general right of control over one's biospecimens and data. Here the decisive question is the instrumental one of whether de-identification is sufficient to guard against privacy harms in light of re-identification techniques. With respect to autonomy-based harms, on the other hand, the instrumental efficacy of de-identification is irrelevant if the harm inheres in the unconsented use itself. Thus the central and difficult question on this account is the normative one of whether the mere unconsented use of tissue and data should—regardless of their identifiability—be understood to violate the source's autonomy. If so, a further question is whether DHHS's shift toward standardized general consent is sufficient to protect this interest.

In conclusion, it's worth highlighting that while each of these three approaches implicates difficult issues of efficiency and justice, these may not be the only values at stake in this debate. More fundamentally this controversy will determine whether ordinary citizens will be able to shape the direction of public sector biomedical research by using their "biocapital" rather than a more limited bundle of resources, such as their money, energy, time, and voice. Thus it is at this core a controversy about the proper rights and capacities of the citizens of liberal legal democracy, the resolution of which entails a choice between what might be seen as competing conceptions of bioconstitutional order.

12

Biospecimen Exceptionalism in the ANPRM

Ellen Wright Clayton

In its ANPRM, OHRP deemed biospecimens to be identifiable per se (DHHS 2011). This conclusion was based on unfounded notions of genetic exceptionalism (Gostin and Hodge 1999) and perceptions of risk that OHRP should explicitly and strongly reject.[1] The realistic likelihood of re-identification is quite small and the risk that harm would ensue in the event of re-identification is smaller still, but OHRP's message that biospecimens are dangerous is clear.

That OHRP perceives biospecimens and genetic information to be particularly risky is inconsistent with its proposal that biospecimens can be used for research without institutional oversight so long as the individuals from whom they are obtained have signed a "standard, brief general consent form" (DHHS 2011, 44519). The content of this form is not spelled out except for the requirement that the patient/participant be given the opportunity to say no to all future research (DHHS 2011, 44519). Although OHRP clearly envisions that people will generally be offered only the opportunity to give or withhold broad consent for future research, they do say that people may also be given choices using check boxes about "what are likely to be a handful of special categories of research with biospecimens . . . given the unique concerns they might raise for a significant segment of the public" (DHHS 2011, 44519–20). Some exceptions to this general framework exist, but the basic notion that a signature on a "standard, brief general consent form" is both necessary and sufficient to avoid IRB review for all research using biospecimens is a significant change, which I will argue risks undermining the public's trust by replacing institutional oversight with, while giving undue weight to, an ill-informed signature on a sweeping form.

12.1 Current Approach to Biospecimens

Under the current Federal Policy for the Protection of Human Subjects, commonly referred to as the Common Rule, 45 CFR 46.101 et seq. (2012), OHRP has repeatedly made it clear that the current regulations do not apply to research conducted with biospecimens that had not initially been collected for research so long as identifiers are removed and are not readily available to the researcher (Office of Human Research Protections 2008). As more fully explained by Evans and Weil et al. (resp., chapters 14 and 17 in this volume), OHRP reasoned that research using de-identified clinical samples does not involve "human subjects" and so is not covered by the current regulations. By contrast, all other research using biospecimens is covered by the Common Rule, including all research using samples that were collected initially for other research purposes as well as all research involving identified clinical samples.

The fact that not all samples are treated the same way has led to heated debates, which have been complicated by the fact the Common Rule and the Health Insurance Portability and Accountability Act (HIPAA) Privacy Rule (45 CFR part 160, and subparts A and E of part 164 (2012)), which sets standards to protect the privacy of most health care transactions, often overlap but are not completely concordant. The two rules, for example, do not approach the issue of de-identification the same way. The Common Rule requires only that "the identity of the subject [not be] readily ascertained by the investigator or associated with the information" (45 CFR 46.102(f) (2012)). The Privacy Rule, by contrast, is much more explicit about when data or samples are sufficiently de-identified to fall outside the requirements of the Rule—either an individual with appropriate expertise has to declare that the risk that data can be re-identified is "very small," or removal of a set of eighteen defined identifiers creates a "safe harbor," so that "there is no reasonable basis to believe that the information can be used to identify an individual" (45 CFR 164.514(b) (2012)). A so-called limited data set, created by the removal of sixteen identifiers, can be used for research without patients' authorization so long as the investigator executes a data use agreement that prohibits the investigator from attempting to re-contact patients and complies with security requirements (45 CFR 164.514(e) (2012)).

12.2 Misjudging the Likelihood and Impact of Identifiability.

The ANPRM cuts through this debate by asserting that biospecimens are identifiable per se, essentially because they contain DNA. Here it is important to be clear about what it takes to identify which individual a particular DNA sample came from. It is, of course, possible to ascertain a person's sex as well as information about some basic characteristics such as eye color, natural hair color, and ancestral origin, but these traits, even when taken together, still apply to very large groups of people. Many women, like me, have blue-gray eyes, blondish hair, and are of Northern European ancestry. Some investigators are attempting to predict some elements of physiognomy from DNA sequence data (Kayser and Schneider 2009), but these efforts, even if wildly successful, are unlikely to link a sequence to a particular person. As has been true for decades, then, the *only* way for the recipient of such data to determine which person a biospecimen came from is to perform genetic analysis that can be matched with an identified sample that has also been subjected to an overlapping genetic analysis or its identified genotypic data.

Concerns, however, have been raised following the publication of articles demonstrating strategies for re-identification. For example, Schadt, Woo, and Hao (2012) demonstrated that it is possible to infer single nucleotide polymorphisms (SNPs) from expression quantitative trait loci (eQTLs), which affect RNA and protein production. The inferred SNPs can then be matched with samples for which SNPs had previously been determined. Their demonstration, albeit elegant, should not be particularly surprising since RNA sequences are derived from DNA.

More recently Gymrek et al. (2013) demonstrated that it was possible to infer the surname of some de-identified DNA sequence records. To accomplish this feat, they developed a software program to extract the short tandem repeats on the Y-chromosome (Y-STRs). They then leveraged publicly accessible genetic genealogy databases that report population statistics about the correlation between Y-STRs and surnames to assign a name to a DNA sequence record. It was claimed that if other data was made available, such as year of birth and state of residence, then an estimated 12 percent of Caucasian males would be expected to be vulnerable. To prove their point, Gymrek and colleagues attempted re-identification on a subset of Utah residents who had made their DNA information publicly available for research. In several instances, the investigators achieved surname inference, and subsequent unique re-identification, with a high degree of confidence. The authors acknowledged that their approach had a significant rate of misidentification and may not be as effective in other populations, especially since people vary in their willingness to make their genetic genealogy information available. They, however, did not point out either the tremendous computational requirements of their approach or, more prosaically, the fact that women cannot be directly identified by this method.

Thus it remains the case that an identified, appropriately genotyped sample is needed to re-identify a biospecimen. At least for the foreseeable future, the risk that a biospecimen from which identifiers have been removed in accordance with HIPAA or even the Common Rule can be re-linked to a particular individual in practical terms seems very low in terms both of probability and especially of adverse consequences.

Where could identified genotypic information from a DNA sample be found? One of the most common sources of such information is the Combined DNA Index System (CODIS) database, which stores the results of DNA analyses conducted by states or other governmental agencies from an array of individuals convicted of, or in some states, simply charged with usually but not always serious crimes and then analyzed for short tandem repeats (STRs) at thirteen sites (National Institute of Justice 2012). CODIS itself contains no identifying information about the individual, only a specimen ID with links to the collecting entity (Federal Bureau of Investigation 2012). Even if these results were available to someone seeking to identify a research biospecimen, they would not be useful in identifying samples that have been used for genome-wide association studies (GWAS) or targeted gene approaches because those approaches do not assay the STR sites. In the future, results in CODIS could conceivably be used to identify biospecimens that had been subjected to whole genome sequencing, which would capture STR sites. Importantly, however, access to CODIS is limited to specifically defined uses by the criminal justice system and strictly controlled by the FBI, as required by the DNA Identification Act of 1994, Pub. L. No. 103–322 (1994) (codified at 42 USC 14132 (2006); (National Institute of Justice 2012).

Another potential identified source of DNA is newborn blood spots, although a number of challenges make them unlikely to be useful for this purpose. States vary widely in how long they keep blood spots. Although some states keep samples for decades, others keep them for no more than a year or two. A few states in recent years have deliberately chosen to retain samples for longer periods, often explicitly to facilitate research (Michigan Department of Community Health 2012), but these choices have often been made after much deliberation and with much transparency about future uses. Newborn screening programs have recently come under scrutiny, in part because some members of the public have objected quite vocally to the government's retention of these spots, particularly over the long term. Highly visible lawsuits reflecting these concerns led Texas and Minnesota in recent years to destroy millions of newborn blood spots, *Beleno v. Lakey,* No. SA-09-CA-188-FB (W.D. Tex., Sept. 17, 2009); *Bearder v. State,* 788 N.W.2d 144 (Minn. Ct. App. 2010); (Wadman 2012). These highly public cases may make other states more reluctant to make blood spots available to others, especially for non-research purposes, in the absence of clearly stated public support.

On a more practical level, state newborn screening programs at present do very little direct genetic analysis. Rather, they primarily assay levels of metabolites, proteins, and hormones. These programs detect a very limited number of mutations in hemoglobin and in the *CFTR* gene. This means that to be useful in identifying another sample, a newborn blood spot would have to undergo further genetic analysis, which may be difficult or impossible if the spot was not stored under the right conditions. This is not to say that newborn blood spots can never be used to identify another sample. One need think only of the case of Anna Lindh, the Swedish Minister of Foreign Affairs, the identity of whose murderer was already suspected and was confirmed in part using a newborn blood spot (Hansson and Björkman 2006), but such cases are rare.

Ironically, the most readily available source of identified genotypes comes from individuals who deposit their results along with their surnames in public genetic genealogy databases. As discussed in more detail above, Gymrek and colleagues were able using these and other public resources as well as cutting edge tools and intensive computational resources to re-identify a number of men.

A larger and more pressing issue at present is why someone would want to try to (re)identify a research biospecimen and what risk such identification would pose to the individual from whom the specimen was obtained. Put another way, if someone already has access to an identified DNA sample, what would they gain by using it to identify another biospecimen? And what harm would result from the re-identification?

12.2.1 Identification of Research Participation

One reason is simply to demonstrate that it is possible to link the two. This was apparently the goal of Homer et al. (2008), who demonstrated that it was possible to show whether an individual was in the case group, the control group, or neither, as well as the more recent work by Schadt, Woo, and Hao (2012) and Gymrek et al. (2013) While a person may be distressed by being identified as having been involved in research, distress alone rarely gives rise to legally compensable damages.

12.2.2 Re-identifying Research Samples to Access and Reveal More Genomic Data about an Individual

A second reason one might seek to re-identify a sample that had been used for research would be to get access to the more extensive genetic analysis that had been done on it. The rapidly decreasing cost of sequencing and SNP arrays, however, means that it would typically be more cost effective to genotype the identified sample one already has in hand rather than try to find a previously analyzed sample. If the match were made using CODIS data, however, the original sample often would no longer exist. In those cases it would likely be more efficient to seek an identified biospecimen among the millions of identified pathological specimens currently maintained in health care institutions and biobanks rather than to try to re-identify a research specimen from which identifiers have been removed.

But even were re-identification being attempted in order to obtain more genomic information about a specific individual, what risk would this pose for the person whose information was identified? As noted above, a person might be distressed to learn that someone had inappropriately obtained access to his or her genetic information, but such dignitary harms by themselves are not likely to be compensable. The real concern from a legal perspective in this and the scenarios immediately following is that the information would be revealed and misused in some way. Yet some legal protection from discrimination in access to employment and health insurance is now available to reduce some risks of harm from the disclosure of genomic information. The Genetic Information Nondiscrimination Act of 2008 (GINA), for example, specifically prohibits employers and health insurers from discriminating against people who have had a "genetic test" or participated in genetic research but who are not symptomatic from any mutations they have (42 USC 300gg-91(d)(16), 2000ff-4 (2012)). The concern expressed by Schadt et al. that GINA would not reach RNA based tests is unfounded since the statute defines "genetic test" as "the analysis of human DNA, RNA, chromosomes, proteins, or metabolites that detects genotypes, mutations, or chromosomal changes" (42 USC 300gg-91(d)(17)(A), 2000ff-7(A) (2012)). For people who are already symptomatic, obtaining information about genetic contributions would typically pose little additional risk of discrimination or other harms beyond that conferred by the disease itself—the fact that a patient, for example, has colon cancer is the major issue, not the factors that contributed to the disease. Nonetheless, the affected individual would receive some protection from the portability provisions of the Health Insurance

Portability and Accountability Act (HIPAA), Pub. L. No. 104–191, 110 Stat. 1936 (1996), and the Patient Protection and Affordable Care Act, Pub. L. No. 111–148, 124 Stat. 119 (March 23, 2010). The Americans with Disability Act (ADA) also applies once affected individuals become significantly impaired, Pub. L. No. 101–336, §2, 104 Stat. 328 (1991), as amended by the Americans with Disabilities Amendments Act, Pub. L. No. 110–325 (2008). These laws are not perfect, but the appropriate response to gaps in their protection is to fill them in.

12.2.3 Re-identifying Research Samples to Access and Reveal Clinical Information about an Individual

Another reason why one might want to identify a research sample is to get access to the clinical information it is associated with. Almost all genetics and genomics research requires some phenotypic information about the individual, which can range from a small number of traits to a much more expansive sampling of the person's medical record. People often express concerns about the privacy of their medical information, which concerns underlie, inter alia, the evolution of medical confidentiality dating back millennia to the more recent passage of HIPAA. Yet in order to assess the risk that someone would attempt to re-identify a de-identified biospecimen so as to access its associated clinical data, one would need to ask how much clinical information about an individual can be obtained through other means. HIPAA, of course, provides some protection for the medical record, but some clinical information can be available outside of the clinical environment and HIPAA's protections, which would decrease the incentive to try to re-identify a sample as a back door to get clinical information. Indeed some of the people who express concern about protecting their information are the ones who share their personal experiences with disease, including their medical information, on social websites. And even were clinical information to be obtained in this manner and revealed, the protections of HIPAA, the Affordable Care Act, and the Americans with Disability Act would still apply.

12.2.4 Re-identifying Research Samples for Purposes of Law Enforcement

Schadt and colleagues raised the specter that law enforcement would genotype crime scene samples in order to make a match with a research sample (Schadt, Woo, and Hao 2012). Several factors make this unlikely. Forensic scientists do not routinely genotype samples. To make a match, they would have to know or at least have a good idea of who the suspect is and where the matching sample or its genotype information is. Unlike CODIS, biospecimens and genotype data are stored in numerous locations, many of which are not easily searchable especially without knowing the name of the individual, and few, if any, of which are centrally indexed. The research sample or the genotype research data would have to be identified, which they often are not.

The more salient point is that it is far more likely that clinical information and clinical samples, and not research samples, will be used for forensic identification. HIPAA explicitly permits disclosure of identified personal health information for law enforcement purposes under a variety of circumstances. When the identity of the suspect is known or even suspected, it would be possible to genotype already existing pathological specimens of the suspect or his or her biological relatives (Greely et al. 2006; Krimsky and Simoncelli 2011). The fact that patients increasingly will undergo multiplex genetic testing as part of their routine medical care means that there will be even less reason to use de-identified research samples for forensic purposes.

12.3 Placing Too Much Weight on a Signature

Especially if one were to assume that OHRP's view of the risk posed by research using biospecimens was correct, the weight that OHRP expects consent to bear is striking. So long as a signature is obtained, OHRP would excuse from IRB review not only all research using de-identified data but also

> ... all secondary research use of identifiable data and biospecimens that have been collected for purposes other than the currently proposed research.... This ... would apply to the secondary use of identifiable data and biospecimens even if such data or biospecimens have not yet been collected at the time of the research proposal, and even if identifiers are retained by the researcher. (DHHS 2011, 44515)

This approach represents a major change from OHRP's interpretation of the current regulations (Office of Human Research Protections 2008), in which protocols using identifiable data and samples require some sort of IRB review and oversight. Excusing all secondary research with data and samples from IRB oversight is all the more remarkable given that OHRP would require only a "standard, brief general consent form"[2] granting unlimited permission for future research uses, which would typically be signed at the time the person seeks clinical care or enters a research protocol. In this section of the ANPRM, OHRP says nothing about ensuring that people understand the implications of what they are agreeing to. Rather, the only requirement is that people be given the opportunity to refuse to permit the biospecimens to be used for research at all. In some cases, OHRP suggests that people may be given the opportunity to decide whether to refuse the use of their specimens and data for certain types of research, but the fact that such tiered consent has gained little traction despite being proposed repeatedly since the 1990s (National Action Plan for Breast Cancer 1998) and is difficult to implement (Weil et al., chapter 14 in this volume) provides little reason to believe that this is a viable strategy. OHRP prefers an opt-in procedure but leaves open the possibility that a written opt-out may suffice in some circumstances. As Rivera also suggests (chapter 16 in this volume), the emphasis is simply on the exercise of choice.

At some level this is not surprising. OHRP cites the growing body of evidence that people just want to be asked (DHHS 2011, 44524), relying in part on *The Immortal Life of Henrietta Lacks* (Skloot 2010), even though the events in that case arose decades before the recognition of the importance of research ethics in this country and the enactment of the Common Rule and in a time of blatant race discrimination. But one has to ask whether people will or even can actually make authentic, informed choices about the uses of their biospecimens and data, or, as suggested by Rivera in this volume, whether they will simply sign these documents the same way they do HIPAA forms and the other blizzard of paper they get whenever they seek health care (McNutt et al. 2008). More general experience suggests that few people read the permissions they sign whenever they download a new piece of software for their computer or their phone or for many other activities of their lives (Milne and Culnan 2004). While such unconsidered signatures are usually legally binding, one might ask whether this practice is ethically or politically sufficient when investigators are asking individuals to permit biospecimens to be used for research that OHRP clearly views as risky, even if the level of its concern is unwarranted. Indeed, one might wonder whether a major reason that OHRP wants signatures on the forms is so people can be "reminded" that they had previously "agreed" to make the biospecimens and data available for research. Realistically, this has so little to do with informed consent or autonomy or respect for persons that it is difficult to know how to characterize what is proposed in the ANPRM. For now, I will use the term "token permission."

OHRP does address the security of biospecimens and data by recommending that the requirements of the HIPAA Security Rule apply to all repositories that hold data and biospecimens. It is worth remembering, however, that in "covered entities" that are subject to all of HIPAA, the HIPAA Privacy Rule permits access to protected information and specimens for a variety of socially important purposes, including law enforcement, research, and public health (US Department of Health and Human Services 2012). Some individuals, however, may find these uses objectionable, and the brief form apparently contemplated by OHRP seems unlikely to inform them of these exceptions to HIPAA so that they can opt out if they desire and if legally permissible.

To some extent, the debate about whether a "standard, brief general consent form" should suffice to excuse research from oversight is surreal because OHRP briefly, but correctly, states that oversight and more complete consent is required if the investigator contemplates returning research results. It is probably a good thing that OHRP did not dive deeply into the question about returning research results given the amount of controversy that surrounds this topic (Clayton 2008; Clayton and McGuire 2012; Fabsitz et al. 2010; Parker 2012; Wolf et al. 2008, 2012), but if recommendations that some results be returned prevail, it will make the "token permission" contemplated here largely irrelevant.

Even if no individual results are going to be returned, the HIPAA security rule, which was implemented primarily to facilitate payment for health care transactions, does not provide adequate protection even when coupled with token permission. The research enterprise, including its use of individuals' data and specimens for the primary goal of creating new knowledge rather than providing immediate benefit to patients and research participants is a social activity that depends on the trust and goodwill of the public and so requires more comprehensive stewardship of these data, including making more explicit professional norms of honoring research participants' privacy and limiting efforts to re-identify individuals from research data derived from them.

Fortunately, even though it appears that OHRP believes that IRB oversight is neither effective nor useful, which is a sad statement, individual investigators and research institutions have already accepted some of the responsibility. Vanderbilt University, for example, created an opt-out biobank of DNA collected from residual blood samples that, while exempt from the Common Rule according to OHRP, has an elaborate system of oversight and accountability including the Institutional Review Board, an Operations Oversight Board, Community and External Ethics Advisory Boards, and the requirement that all investigators execute a Data Use Agreement requiring that users not attempt re-identification (Pulley et al. 2010). Other salutary steps include creating mechanisms for oversight that involve and are accountable to the public and publicly posting generally accessible and understandable descriptions of research projects. Repositories that retain identified samples and information might consider creating mechanisms, similar to those required by HIPAA for clinical data, by which people can track research use of biospecimens and data that pertain to or have been obtained from them.

12.4 Conclusion

In sum, OHRP appears to view biospecimens as intrinsically risky to personal privacy because they contain DNA while requiring no oversight, so long as individuals sign a brief form granting broad consent for research and HIPAA security requirements are met. This formulation both overestimates the risk to personal privacy in an apparent example of biospecimen exceptionalism and undervalues public oversight and accountability in the research enterprise.

Notes

The project described was supported by the National Center for Research Resources, Grant UL1 RR024975–01, and is now at the National Center for Advancing Translational Sciences, Grant 2 UL1 TR000445–06, as well as National Center for Advancing Translational Sciences Grant 1R21HG00612–01. The content is solely the responsibility of the author and does not necessarily represent the official views of the NIH. I would like to thank the members of the conference on The Future of Human Subjects Research Regulation and Lainie Friedman Ross for their helpful comments on earlier versions of this chapter.

1. More recently another federally constituted body, the Presidential Commission for the Study of Bioethical Issues in its report, Privacy and Progress in Whole Genome Sequencing (2012), concluded that whole genome sequence data are identifiable per se. Its justification for this conclusion, while somewhat more defensible, is subject to many of the same criticisms identified below.

2. The Presidential Commission for the Study of Bioethical Issues in its recent report, Privacy and Progress in Whole Genome Sequencing (2012), issued the following strikingly different recommendations for informed consent for the use of the whole sequence data:

Recommendation 3.1 Researchers and clinicians should evaluate and adopt robust and workable consent processes that allow research participants, patients, and others to understand who has access to their whole genome sequences and other data generated in the course of research, clinical, or commercial sequencing, and to know how these data might be used in the future. Consent processes should ascertain participant or patient preferences at the time the samples are obtained.

Recommendation 3.2 The federal Office for Human Research Protections or a designated central organizing federal agency should establish clear and consistent guidelines for informed consent forms for research conducted by those under the purview of the Common Rule that involves whole genome sequencing. Informed consent forms should (1) briefly describe whole genome sequencing and analysis; (2) state how the data will be used in the present study, and state, to the extent feasible, how the data might be used in the future; (3) explain the extent to which the individual will have control over future data use; (4) define benefits, potential risks, and state that there might be unknown future risks; and (5) state what data and information, if any, might be returned to the individual.

References

Americans with Disabilities Act (ADA), Pub. L. No. 101–336, §2, 104 Stat. 328. 1991. As amended by the Americans with Disabilities Amendments Act, Pub. L. No. 110–325 (2008).

Beleno v. Lakey, No. SA-09-CA-188-FB (W.D. Tex. Sept. 17, 2009).

Bearder v. State, 788 N.W.2d 144 (Minn. Ct. App. 2010).

Clayton, E. W. 2008. Incidental findings in genetics research using archived DNA. *Journal of Law, Medicine, and Ethics* 36 (2): 286–91.

Clayton, E. W., and A. L. McGuire. 2012. The legal risks of returning research results. *Genetics in Medicine* 14: 473–77.

Department of Health and Human Services (DHHS). 2011. Advance Notice of Proposed Rulemaking. Human subjects research protections: Enhancing protections for research subjects and reducing burden, delay, and ambiguity for investigators. *Federal Register* 76 (143): 44512.

Department of Health and Human Services. Presidential Commission for the Study of Bioethical Issues. 2012. *Privacy and Progress in Whole Genome Sequencing*. Washington, DC: GPO.

Department of Health and Human Services (DHHS). 2012. Summary of the HIPAA privacy rule, permitted uses and disclosures: (5) Public interest and benefit activities. http://www.hhs.gov/ocr/privacy/hipaa/understanding/summary/index.html.

DNA Identification Act of 1994, Pub. L. No. 103–322 (1994) (codified at 42 USC 14132 (2006).

Fabsitz, R. R., A. L. McGuire, R. R. Sharp, M. Puggal, L. G. Biesecker, L. M. Beskow, E. Bookman, W. Burke, E. G. Burchard, G. Church, E. W. Clayton, J. H. Eckfeldt, C. V. Fernandez, R. Fisher, S. M. Fullerton, S. Gabriel, F. Gachupin, C. James, G. P. Jarvik, R. Kittles, J. R. Leib, C. O'Donnell, P. P. O'Rourke, L. L. Rodriguez, S. D. Schully, A. R. Shuldiner, R. K. Sze, J. V. Thakuria, S. M. Wolf, and G. L. Burke. 2010. Ethical and practical guidelines for reporting genetic research results to study participants: Updated guidelines from a National Heart, Lung, and Blood Institute working group. *Circulation Cardiovascular Genetics* 3 (6): 574–80.

Federal Bureau of Investigation. 2012. Frequently asked questions (FAQs) on the CODIS program and the National DNA index system. http://www.fbi.gov/about-us/lab/codis/codis-and-ndis-fact-sheet.

Federal Policy for the Protection of Human Subjects (45 CFR part 46, "Common Rule"), including selected sections, 45 CFR 46.102(f) (2012), 45 CFR 164.514(b) (2012), 45 CFR 164.514(e) (2012).

Genetic Information Nondiscrimination Act (GINA) of 2008, Pub. L. No. 110-233, 122 Stat. 881, including selected sections 42 USCA 300gg-91(d)(16), 2000ff–4 (2012); 42 USCA 300gg-91(d)(17)(A), 2000ff–7(A) (2012).

Gostin, L. O., and J. G. Hodge. 1999. Genetic privacy and the law: An end to genetics exceptionalism. *Jurimetrics* 40: 21–58.

Greely, Henry T., Daniel P. Riordan, Nanibaa A. Garrison, and Joanna Mountain. 2006. Family ties: The use of DNA offender databases to catch offenders' kin. *Journal of Law, Medicine, and Ethics* 34 (2): 248–62.

Gymrek, M., A. L. McGuire, D. Golan, E. Halperin, and Y. Erlich. 2013. Identifying personal genomes by surname inference. *Science* 339 (6117):321–24. doi: 10.1126/science.1229566.

Hansson, S., and B. Björkman. 2006. Bioethics in Sweden. *Cambridge Quarterly of Healthcare Ethics* 15: 285–94.

Health Insurance Portability and Accountability Act (HIPAA), Pub. L. No. 104-191, 110 Stat. 1936. 1996. HIPAA Privacy Rule, 45 CFR part 160 and subparts A and E of part 164. http://www.hhs.gov/ocr/privacy/hipaa/administrative/privacyrule/index.html.

Homer, N., S. Szelinger, M. Redman, W. Tembe, D. Duggan, J. Muehling, J. V. Pearson, D. A. Stephan, S. F. Nelson, and D. W. Craig. 2008. Resolving individuals contributing trace amounts of DNA to highly complex mixtures using high-density SNP genotyping microarrays. *PLOS Genetics* 4: e1000167.

Kayser, M., and P. Schneider. 2009. DNA-based prediction of human externally visible characteristics in forensics: motivations, scientific challenges, and ethical considerations. *Forensic Science International. Genetics* 3: 154–61.

Krimsky, S., and T. Simoncelli. 2011. *Genetic Justice: DNA Data Banks, Criminal Investigations, and Civil Liberties*. New York: Columbia University Press.

McNutt, L. A., E. Waltermaurer, R. A. Bednarczyk, B. E. Carlson, J. Kotval, J. McCauley, J. C. Campbell, D. E. Ford. 2008. Are we misjudging how well informed consent forms are read? *Journal of Empirical Research in Human Research Ethics* 3 (1): 89–97.

Michigan Department of Community Health. 2012. Michigan BioTrust for Health. http://www.michigan.gov/mdch/0,1607,7-132-2942_4911_4916-209738-,00.html.

Milne, G. R., and M. J. Culnan. 2004. Strategies for reducing online privacy risks: Why consumers read (or don't read) online privacy notices. *Journal of Interactive Marketing* 18 (3): 15–29.

National Action Plan for Breast Cancer. 1998. Model consent forms and related information on tissue banking from routine biopsies. http://bioethics.georgetown.edu/nbac/briefings/jan98/model.pdf.

National Institute of Justice. 2012. DNA evidence: Basics of analyzing. http://www.nij.gov/topics/forensics/evidence/dna/basics/analyzing.htm.

Office of Human Research Protections. 2008. *Guidance on Research Involving Coded Private Information or Biological Specimens.* http://www.hhs.gov/ohrp/policy/cdebiol.html.

Parker, L. S. 2012. Returning individual research results: What role should people's preferences play? *Minnesota Journal of Law, Science, and Technology* 13 (2): 449–84.

Patient Protection and Affordable Care Act (ACA), Pub. L. No. 111–148 (March 23, 2010).

Pulley, J., E. W. Clayton, G. R. Bernard, D. M. Roden, and D. R. Masys. 2010. Principles of human subjects protections applied in an opt-out, de-identified biobank. *Clinical and Translational Science* 3 (1): 42–48.

Schadt, E. E., W. Sangsoon, and H. Ke. 2012. Bayesian method to predict individual SNP genotypes from gene expression data. *Nature Genetics* 5 (44): 603–608.

Skloot, R. 2010. *The Immortal Life of Henrietta Lacks.* New York: Crown Books.

Wadman, M.. 2012. Minnesota starts to destroy blood spots. http://www.nature.com/news/minnesota-starts-to-destroy-stored-blood-spots-1.9971.

Wolf, S. M., B. N. Crock, F. Lawrenz, B. Van Ness, J. P. Kahn, L. M. Beskow, M. K. Cho, et al. 2012. Managing incidental findings and research results in genomic research involving biobanks and archived data sets. *Genetics in Medicine* 14: 361–84.

Wolf, S. M., F. P. Lawrenz, C. A. Nelson, J. P. Kahn, M. K. Cho, E. W. Clayton, J. G. Fletcher, et al. 2008. Managing incidental findings in human subjects research: Analysis and recommendations. *Journal of Law, Medicine and Ethics* 36: 219–48.

13

Biobanking, Consent, and Certificates of Confidentiality: Does the ANPRM Muddy the Water?

Brett A. Williams and Leslie E. Wolf

As Davis and Hurley detail in their chapter, the ANPRM proposes substantial changes to human subjects research regulations, including major proposed changes concerning the use of biospecimens in research. Under the current regulations, much biospecimen research may be conducted without consent. The ANPRM would require written consent for most of this research (DHHS 2011, 44519).

This ANPRM proposal responds to criticisms that the current regulations do not account for scientific advances that present risks in biospecimens research not contemplated when the Common Rule was last amended (McGuire 2008; Wolf 2010). Because the DNA in biospecimens makes them inherently identifiable, the ANPRM argues that consent should be required for such research (DHHS 2011, 44519, 44524).

The recognition of these risks is consistent with recommendations from the National Institutes of Health (NIH) that research projects involving genetics, genomics, or development of biospecimen repositories should consider getting a Certificate of Confidentiality (Certificate) to protect participants (OPRR 1997; NIH 2007). Breach of confidentiality is typically the primary risk in biospecimen research. Ironically, the ANPRM may make it more difficult to provide these protections to research participants. As Ellen Wright Clayton explains in chapter 12 of this volume, the ANPRM contemplates a brief consent form that may be obtained outside a specific research project or repository and even outside the research setting, for example, if biospecimens are collected during clinical care (DHHS 2011, 44519). However, Certificates are only available for research projects and require specific disclosures to research participants (NIH 2003). In this chapter we explore the implications of these potentially conflicting requirements by examining the current regulatory approach to biobanking, the proposed changes under the ANPRM, and the circumstances in which a Certificate of Confidentiality is available. We then propose several approaches to achieve the dual goals of appropriate consent and adequate confidentiality protections. These approaches include technical amendments to either the ANPRM or to the Certificate application process, as well as a more significant change to protect all research data.

13.1 Current Regulatory Approach to Biobanking

Research that involves collecting biological materials by interacting with individuals falls squarely within the human subjects research regulatory framework known as the "Common Rule," which, as Amy Davis and Elisa Hurley describe in chapter 1 of this volume, applies to research conducted or funded by DHHS and other signatory agencies and departments (45 CFR 46). However, as described in more detail below, much biospecimens research may fall within exemptions and exceptions to the Common Rule.

13.1.1 Basic Requirements under the Common Rule

The basic requirements of the Common Rule are covered in great depth throughout this book. Most relevant here is that the regulations specify the information that must be disclosed in the consent document, including a description of the procedures, purposes, expected participant duration of the study, the reasonably foreseeable risks of participation, any benefits to the participants or others from the research, potential alternative procedures or treatments, how confidentiality of identifiable records will be maintained, contact information for questions related to the research, and a statement that participation is voluntary (46.116).

13.1.2 Exceptions to the Consent Requirement

Despite these general provisions of the Common Rule, as Carol Weil et al. also describe in chapter 14 of this volume, much research involving biospecimens may be undertaken without the knowledge or consent of the individuals who donated the materials. When tissue samples are prospectively obtained from living individuals for research purposes, such collection involves "human subjects research" and guidance from the Office for Human Research Protections (OHRP), which oversees the DHHS human subjects research regulations, affirms this position (OHRP 2008). According to that guidance, specimens are considered "individually identifiable" when researchers can link them directly or through coding systems to specific individuals. However, research involving only coded specimens does not involve human subjects if (1) they were not collected for the current research project through an "interaction or intervention with living individuals" and (2) the researchers cannot "readily" identify the donors of the specimens because the investigators do not have access to the key through agreement, IRB approved policies or procedures, or by law (OHRP 2008).

Thus the guidance permits an "honest broker" agreement, where one investigator shares specimens she has already collected with another investigator. Because the second investigator does not obtain the specimens through interaction or intervention with the specimen donors and does not have access to identifiable information, this is not "human subjects research." Similarly investigators who obtain specimens from a central repository that houses biological materials or that collects the materials and ensures that such materials are maintained in conformance with the regulatory requirements, including agreements prohibiting release of identifiable information, are not conducting "human subjects research."

The regulations also contain exemptions from IRB review for certain types of research that would otherwise qualify as "human subjects research." Research involving the collection or study of existing specimens may be exempt if the "information is *recorded* by the investigator in such a manner that subjects cannot be identified, directly or through identifiers linked to the subjects" (45 CFR 46.101(b)(4); italics added). Here the researchers may have access to identifiable private information but can avoid the "human subjects research" regulatory requirements simply by not recording that identifiable information. Importantly, the regulatory language refers to "pathological specimens" or "diagnostic specimens" (§46.101(b)(4)), thus allowing materials collected for clinical purposes to be used for research without consent or any of the other regulatory protections.

As Barbara Evans explains in more detail in chapter 17, even research that does not fall within the exemptions may be conducted without consent if it meets certain criteria. The regulations permit waiver of consent if:

1. the research involves no more than minimal risk to the subjects;
2. the waiver . . . will not adversely affect the [subjects'] rights and welfare;
3. the research could not practicably be carried out without the waiver . . . ; and
4. whenever appropriate, the subjects will be provided with additional pertinent information after participation. (45 CFR 46.116(d)(1)–(4))

Thus a researcher may seek a waiver of consent to use specimens for a purpose not addressed in the original consent. The risks are generally considered minimal because there is no additional physical risk to subjects, the risks to confidentiality are low, and, in many cases, the research could not practicably be carried out without the waiver because a very large number of specimens is needed and/or considerable time has passed since the specimens were collected.

13.2 Advanced Notice of Proposed Rulemaking: Changes to Consent of Biospecimen Collection

As discussed, there are many contexts under the current regulations in which consent for research is not required for biospecimens research. The ANPRM (DHHS 2011) addresses some of the gaps in the current regulations.

The ANPRM's primary change is generally to require written consent for biospecimen research (DHHS 2011, 44515). As Clayton discusses in her chapter, the ANPRM authors conclude that "most individuals want to be able to decide whether their biospecimens are available for research, they often do not desire to have control over which specific researchers use their samples, for which diseases, at which institutions" (44524). The ANPRM would require written consent *regardless* of identifiability for preexisting biospecimens for research, whereas written consent would only be required for identifiable biospecimens if originally collected for *nonresearch* purposes (44519). This proposed change nullifies "the . . . current practice of telling . . . subjects . . . that [their biospecimens] will be used for one purpose, and then after stripping identifiers, allowing it to be used for a new purpose to which the subjects never consented" (44519). Weil et al. provide useful background regarding these changes in their chapter.

To avoid unnecessary restrictions on secondary use of biospecimens (although Suzanne Rivera suggests it fails in this regard in chapter 16 of this volume), the ANPRM suggests use of a "standard, brief general consent form allowing for broad, future research" to meet the new requirements (DHHS 2011, 44519). Rather than project-specific consent, the ANPRM recommends broad consent that "cover[s] all . . . biospecimens to be collected related to a particular set of encounters with an institution (e.g., hospitalization) or . . . collected at anytime by the institution" (44519). Thus the common form would grant consent for all future research, although it would allow subjects to opt out of future research.

Additionally subjects could express preferences using check boxes regarding select research categories to which they may object (e.g., cell line creation or reproductive research) (44519–20).

The ANPRM also responds to the myriad of criticisms about consent forms and IRB review of them and proposes a simplified consent (DHHS 2011, 44522). As Davis and Hurley describe in chapter 1, the ANPRM proposes a number of changes to consent requirements. These recommendations limit IRB oversight over biospecimen research consent forms.

Last, as Davis and Hurley note in their chapter, the ANPRM addresses the informational risks posed by identifiable data, including secondary analyses (DHHS 2011, 44524). As the ANPRM explains, "what constitutes 'identifiable' and 'de-identifiable' data is fluid" and technological advances and increases in available data "may soon allow [individual] identification . . . from data[, particularly DNA,] that is currently de-identified" (44524; Lowrance and Collins 2007). Concluding that IRB review may not be best suited for protecting against informational risks, the ANPRM proposes three requirements to strengthen protections from informational research risks.

First, as Rivera discusses in her chapter, the ANPRM looks to the privacy and security rules of the Health Insurance Portability and Affordability Act (HIPAA) as a model for protecting identifiable information (DHHS 2011, 44526; 45 CFR 160, 164). It would adopt common data security standards, including electronic data encryption and "strong physical safeguards for [paper] information . . . audit trails" and controls that limit who can access to the information (44526). Second, the ANPRM would consider data de-identified or a limited data set "if investigators see the identifiers but do not record them" provided that they follow common data security and information protection standards, eliminating the need for third-party arrangements (44526). Third, the ANPRM proposes "periodic random retrospective audits" to ensure enforcement (44526).

13.3 History and Purpose of Certificates

Certificates authorize researchers to refuse to provide research participants' names and other identifying characteristics in any "Federal, State, or local civil, criminal, administrative, legislative, or other proceeding" (DHHS 2011; 42 USC 241(d)). They were originally adopted in 1970 to protect research participants involved in drug abuse and addiction research, who were at legal risk, including arrest (Federal Drug Abuse Act

1970). Over time, Congress expanded the Certificates' scope to "biomedical, behavioral, clinical, or other research (including research on mental health, including research on the use and effect of alcohol and other psychoactive drugs)" (42 USC 241(d)).

Certificates are intended "to reduce impediments to . . . subject recruitment" (NIH 2003). Certificates permit research participants and investigators to voluntarily disclose identifiable information (NIH 2002a). These nuanced distinctions must be described accurately in the consent form.

13.3.1 Obtaining and Using a Certificate

Certificates are only granted to single, well-defined research projects, although the projects do not have to be federally funded (NIH 2002a). Although federal agencies other than NIH issue Certificates, we focus on NIH because it has taken a leading role in educating researchers about Certificates through its "kiosk" website (NIH 2011). To apply for a Certificate, a researcher must first obtain IRB approval (NIH 2002b). The application must contain the beginning date and expected end date of the research project. The Certificate's protection extends to any research subject while the Certificate is in effect and does not end with the project.

The application must also contain a description of the project's aims and research methods. It must also include information about the study population, their anticipated number, and how they will be recruited. The application must describe how the research participants' identities will be protected, such as through coding strategies, maintaining linking information in locked files, or destroying all identifiers when the study is completed. Additionally the application must include the reasons the investigator needs a Certificate and what sensitive, identifying information the investigator will collect.

Last, the researcher must include the IRB-approved consent form. The consent form must not only explain the Certificate's protections but also caution participants that their participation in the study will not be protected if they or one of their family members voluntarily discloses their participation. The form must detail the situations in which an investigator may choose to voluntarily disclose a subject's identity or participation in the study, such as in situations of suspected child abuse, harm to self or others, or reportable communicable diseases.

13.3.2 Use of Certificates for Biospecimen Research and Repositories

The ANPRM proposals regarding biospecimen research recognize the increasing identifiability of biospecimens due to scientific advances and increasing development of DNA databases. In such research, breach of confidentiality is not only typically the primary risk, but also study participants' main concern (Goddard et al. 2009, 120). The ANPRM's view is consistent with several federal recommendations. The Office for Protection from Research Risks (OPRR) (the predecessor to OHRP) issued a guidance for DHHS-sponsored or -funded human biospecimen repositories recommending that "[a] Certificate . . . should be obtained to protect the confidentiality of repository specimens and data" (OPRR 1997). NIH also recommends that research projects involving genetics, genomics, or the development of biospecimen repositories should consider getting a Certificate (NIH 2007; NCI 2011). Additionally the National Cancer Institute (NCI) suggests that "Certificates . . . should be considered by the biospecimen resource and/or the recipient investigator depending on the level of privacy protection indicated by the study design" (NCI 2011).

NIH has further acknowledged that law enforcement may target repositories to search for DNA matches (NIH 2007). As Clayton explains, law enforcement officers frequently use DNA data, which is stored in the Federal Combined DNA Index System (CODIS) as well as in state databases, as evidence in their investigative work. DNA may also be collected upon arrest under federal law and the law in twenty-five states (e.g., see 42 USC 14135a(a)(1)(A); Kan. Stat. Ann. 21–2511(e)(2); NC Gen. Stat. 15A–266.3A(b)). While NIH encourages sharing of de-identified data, it warns repositories that law enforcement may later request the identifying information connected to any DNA shared (NIH 2007). Thus NIH advocates the use of a Certificate to protect against compelled disclosure of this identifying information (NIH 2007).

NIH also recognizes that emerging technologies have made re-identifying genetic data increasingly easier over time and data that was once considered solidly de-identified can no longer be labeled as such (NIH 2007). Recent studies have shown that a researcher can identify an individual based on only seventy-five nucleotide polymorphisms (SNPs) (McGuire and Gibbs 2006). In another recent study scientists described a statistical method for determining individual genotypes within a mix of DNA samples or data sets containing aggregate SNPs (Homer et al. 2008). While re-identification from an SNP collection requires identified or "reference" samples (Homer et al. 2008), their availability increases with the proliferation of repositories and DNA databases. Although Clayton and Rivera both challenge its position in their chapters, studies like these led NIH to conclude that "[t]echnologies available within the public domain today, and technological advances expected over the next few years, make the identification of specific individuals from raw genotype-phenotype data feasible and increasingly straightforward" (NIH 2007, 6). Thus the need for a Certificate for repositories to protect donors' identities similarly increases.

13.3.3 Disconnect between the ANPRM and the Use of Certificates

While the ANPRM and Certificates seek to protect against informational risks, ironically, the ANPRM's suggested changes may make it more difficult to do so fully. The recommendations make it difficult, if not impossible, for researchers to comply with the Certificate's application requirements, thereby cutting off their studies from a widely recommended protection for such research.

As explained above, a Certificate is available to a "single, well-described" research study. Accordingly a Certificate may not be available to cover the myriad of research projects contemplated by the broad, single consent the ANPRM proposes, especially when specimens are collected during a clinical encounter. Certificates originated to protect study participants, not patients (Brown and Lowenberg 2010; Eiseman et al. 2003, 134). However, given that repositories have received Certificates for broad research goals, perhaps this inconsistency can be resolved.

The problem arising from the ANPRM consent proposals may be more difficult to overcome. (Here we focus on the problems concerning Certificates, leaving the questions about the adequacy of the approach in general to others in this book.) As described, to obtain a Certificate, a researcher must craft a consent form that not only explains the Certificate's protections but also warns participants about the limits of those protections, for example, if they voluntarily disclose their research participation. The consent form must be tailored to the research project's aims and risks so that participants may be fully aware of the need for confidentiality protections and weigh these considerations in deciding about participation. These requirements vary greatly from the ANPRM's consent proposals for a standard, brief consent form that covers all potential future research uses of materials collected. Unless Certificates are mandated for all repositories, the required language is likely not going to be included, and certainly not in the same detail required in the Certificate application. Moreover, even if the standardized consent form included the required Certificate language, doing so may conflict with the ANPRM goals of shortening and simplifying consent. Empirical studies have suggested that NIH-recommended Certificate language can be confusing to participants (Catania et al. 2007). Finally, these consent forms also will not have the requisite IRB approval, creating another barrier to obtaining a Certificate (Wolf, Zandecki, and Lo 2004).

The ANPRM also seeks to move the handling of informational risk related to repository studies outside the IRB process. Although it acknowledges the increasing informational risks relating to data once considered de-identified (DHHS 2011, 44524; Ohm 2010, 1704), the ANPRM suggests that these risks should be regulated through common data security standards, rather than through IRB review. Thus there would be no project-specific IRB evaluation of informational risks and methods to reduce them, as required by the Certificate application process. Additionally, without IRB review, the need for a Certificate may not even surface, which could leave projects vulnerable to compelled disclosure of identifying information (Eiseman et al. 2003; Beskow et al. 2012).

13.4 Recommendations

Overall, the changes proposed by the ANPRM are a step in the right direction. Gaps in the current regulations create informational risks and privacy concerns for biospecimens research. The ANPRM seeks to address these gaps. However, the ANPRM's proposed changes need to be considered in context with other rules and best practices that have been developed to protect human subjects and examined for unintended consequences, such as the conflicts between the ANPRM and the Certificates requirements we have highlighted. A broader review is required to ensure that any regulatory changes have the hoped for effect.

In this particular context, the conflict between the ANPRM and Certificates may be resolved, without sacrificing the ANPRM's beneficial aspects, through changes to the proposed rules. First, the proposed simplified, standardized consent form for biospecimen research could be promulgated as a model consent form, rather than a mandated form. Thus IRB approval of the consent form would still be required—to satisfy the requirements of the Certificate application process—and the form itself could be shorter and more uniform to fulfill the purpose set forth in the ANPRM. This would also allow the IRB to weigh the risks and benefits of recommending a Certificate for the project and approve any necessary Certificate consent language. A model biobanking consent form created under the ANPRM should include optional Certificate language to signal the availability of this Confidentiality protection and help address NIH's requirement that the consent form include Certificate language as part of the application process.

While considering how the Certificate could work within the ANPRM, it would be appropriate to reconsider the recommended Certificate consent language. As the ANPRM states, consent forms have become highly complex and confusing documents (DHHS 2011, 44522), and scholars analyzing Certificate language have echoed this sentiment (Catania et al. 2007). One study found that a majority of consent forms fall in the more difficult, higher grade level readability category, despite IRB's desire and attempts to target lower reading levels (Paasche-Orlow, Taylor, and Brancati 2003). Interestingly, institutions that had compliance issues resulting in OHRP oversight were more likely to have consent forms that met the desired readability level, suggesting a positive role for federal involvement (Paasche-Orlow, Taylor, and Brancati 2003). Using the Flesch–Kincaid Readability scale, which is included in Microsoft Word and was used by Paasche-Orlow, Taylor, and Brancati, we found the current NIH-recommended Certificate language scores at a twelfth-grade reading level—the maximum score, which may underestimate actual reading level—while almost half of American adults read at or below an eighth-grade reading level (Paasche-Orlow, Taylor, and Brancati 2003). Developing standardized, simplified Certificate consent language could ease the tension with the ANPRM, as well as promote human subjects protection goals.

Alternatively, the conflict between the Certificate requirements and the ANPRM may be addressed by changing the Certificate application process. Because the relevant parts of the Certificate application process are not governed by 42 USC 241(d) nor the accompanying regulations, changes to the process itself could avoid some of the requirements of formal rulemaking. Instead, NIH may consider an adjustment to the Certificate application process for biorepositories in light of the ANPRM. This adjustment could include the acceptance of the ANPRM's proposed standardized consent form to fulfill the Certificate application requirement, even without IRB approval.

The justification for an adjustment to the Certificate application process for biorepositories is twofold. First, NIH has identified "[g]enetic studies, including those that collect and store biological samples for future use" as eligible for Certificate protection (NIH 2011). Second, various NIH components have recommended Certificates for biorepositories, as well as publishing best practices for repositories, and most biorepositories operate similarly. Thus a process that is consistent with the ANPRM and facilitates getting a Certificate makes sense for biorepositories, where it may not make sense for studies with widely varying procedures and risks, such as HIV prevention studies or drug abuse studies. Such studies may address "sensitive" topics but can range from anonymous surveys to randomized clinical trials testing medical interventions.

These technical changes might resolve the tension between the ANPRM and the NIH Certificates application process, but a bolder option is also available. While Certificates are an important tool to protect confidentiality of sensitive, identifiable research data, researchers—particularly researchers working with biorepositories—may not be aware of them (Beskow et al. 2012; Wolf et al. 2012). Indeed only about one-quarter of IRB reviews require or recommend Certificates for biobanks, and legal demands for research data may arise unexpectedly and be only tangentially related to the project (Beskow et al. 2012). Perhaps the ANPRM provides the opportunity to substitute the piecemeal approach of the Certificate program for a more comprehensive protection against compelled disclosure for research data. Incorporating Certificate-like protection into the general human subjects protections would ensure that such protections are not overlooked and treat all participants equally with respect to confidentiality. The ethical rationale is simple—research participants share their information to benefit others; both the principles of respect for persons and beneficence suggest that that information should not be available to be used against them. There is legal precedent for protecting research data for entire programs, rather than on a project-by-project basis (e.g., 42 USC 299c-3; 42 USC 242m). While such a move would be controversial and may not be able to be accomplished through the regulatory process alone, it is worth considering.

13.5 Conclusion

The proposals contained in the ANPRM are a step in the right direction and should be encouraged. However, using the example of Certificates for biobanking, we have demonstrated that aspects of the ANPRM may clash with other legal requirements or best practices. There are numerous avenues through which such conflicts may be resolved. Doing so requires looking at the ANPRM in the broader research ethics context to ensure that, in the end, any changes to the regulatory scheme live up to the goal of protecting of human subjects.

Note

The project described was supported in part by Award Number R01HG005087 (PI: Laura Beskow) from the National Human Genome Research Institute

(NHGRI). The content is solely the responsibility of the authors and does not necessarily represent the official views of NHGRI or the National Institutes of Health. This chapter is adapted from Williams and Wolf (2013). We thank the *Journal of Law, Medicine and Ethics* for the permission to adapt the work.

References

Beskow, Laura M., Devon K. Check, Emily E. Namey, Lauren A. Dame, Li Lin, Alexandra Cooper, Kevin P. Weinfurt, and Leslie E. Wolf. 2012. Institutional review boards' use and understanding of Certificates of Confidentiality. *PLoS ONE* 7 (9): e44050. doi:10.1371/journal.pone.0044050.

Brown, Teneille, and Kelly Lowenberg. 2010. Biobanks, privacy, and the subpoena power. *Stanford Journal of Law, Science and Policy* 1: 88–101.

Catania, Joseph, Leslie E. Wolf, Stacey Wertleib, Bernard Lo, and Jeff Henne. 2007. Research participants' perceptions of the Certificate of Confidentiality's assurances and limitations. *Journal of Empirical Research on Human Research Ethics* 2: 53–59.

Department of Health and Human Services (DHHS). 2011. Advance Notice of Proposed Rulemaking. Human subjects research protections: Enhancing protections for research subjects and reducing burden, delay, and ambiguity for investigators. *Federal Register* 76 (143): 44512.

Eiseman, Elisa, Gabrielle Bloom, Jennifer Brower, Noreen Clancy, and Stuart S. Olmstead. 2003. *Case Studies of Human Tissue Repositories: Best Practices for a Biospecimen Resource for the Genomic and Proteomic Era*. Arlington, VA: Rand.

Federal Drug Abuse and Dependence Prevention, Treatment, and Rehabilitation Act. 1970. Part I: Hearings on S. 3562, S. 3246, and S. 2785 before the Special Subcommittee on Alcohol and Narcotics of the Special Committee on Labor and Public Welfare (Federal Drug Abuse Act). 1970. 91st Cong.

Goddard, Katrina A.B, Sabina Smith, Chuhe Chen, Carmit McMullen, and Cheryl Johnson. 2009. Biobank recruitment: Motivations for nonparticipation. *Biopreservation and Biobanking* 7: 119–21.

Homer, Nils, Szabolcs Szelinger, Margot Redman, David Duggan, Waibhav Tembe, Jill Muehling, John V. Pearson, Dietrich A. Stephan, Stanley F. Nelson, and David W. Craig. 2008. Resolving individuals contributing trace amounts of DNA to highly complex mixtures using high-density SNP genotyping microarrays. *PLOS Genetics* 4 (8): e1000167. doi:10.1371/journal.pgen.1000167.

Lowrance, William W., and Francis S. Collins. 2007. Identifiability in genomics research. *Science* 317: 600–602.

McGuire, Amy L. 2008. Identifiability of DNA data: The need for consistent federal policy. *American Journal of Bioethics* 8: 75–76.

McGuire, Amy L., and Richard A. Gibbs. 2006. No longer de-identified. *Science* 312: 370–71.

National Cancer Institute (NCI). 2011. Office of Biorepositories and Biospecimen Research: National Cancer Institute best practices for biospecimen resources.

Accessed December 19, 2012. http://biospecimens.cancer.gov/bestpractices/2011-NCIBestPractices.pdf.

National Institutes of Health (NIH). 2002a. Slide presentation on Certificates of Confidentiality. Accessed December 19, 2012. http://grants.nih.gov/grants/policy/coc/slides_020503/index.htm.

National Institutes of Health (NIH). 2002b. Detailed application instructions for Certificate of Confidentiality: Extramural research projects. Accessed December 19, 2012. http://grants.nih.gov/grants/policy/coc/appl_extramural.htm.

National Institutes of Health (NIH). 2003. Certificates of Confidentiality: Background information. Accessed December 12, 2012. http://grants.nih.gov/grants/policy/coc/background.htm.

National Institutes of Health (NIH). 2007. Policy for sharing of data obtained in NIH supported or conducted genome-wide association studies. Accessed December 19, 2012. http://grants.nih.gov/grants/guide/notice-files/NOT-OD-07-088.html#protection.

National Institutes of Health (NIH). 2011. Frequently asked questions: Certificates of Confidentiality. Accessed December 19, 2012. http://grants.nih.gov/grants/policy/coc/faqs.htm#133.

Office for Human Research Protections (OHRP). 2008. Guidance on research involving coded private information or biological specimens. Accessed December 18, 2012. http://www.hhs.gov/ohrp/policy/cdebiol.html.

Office for Protection from Research Risks (OPRR). 1997. Issues to consider in the research use of stored data or tissues. Accessed December 19, 2012. http://www.hhs.gov/ohrp/policy/reposit.html.

Ohm, Paul. 2010. Broken promises of privacy: Responding to the surprising failure of anonymization. *UCLA Law Review* 57: 1701–77.

Paasche-Orlow, Michael K., Holly A. Taylor, and Frederick L. Brancati. 2003. Readability standards for informed consent forms as compared to actual readability. *New England Journal of Medicine* 348: 721–26.

Williams, Brett A., and Leslie E. Wolf. 2013. Biobanking, consent and certificates of confidentiality: Does the ANPRM muddy the water? *Journal of Law, Medicine & Ethics* 41 (2):440–453.

Wolf, Leslie E. 2010. Advancing research on stored biological materials, reconciling law, ethics, and practice. *Minnesota Journal of Law Science and Technology* 11: 99–156.

Wolf, Leslie E., Lauren A. Dame, Mayank J. Patel, Brett A. Williams, Jeffrey L. Austin, and Laura M. Beskow. 2012. Certificates of Confidentiality: Legal counsels' experiences with and perspectives on legal demands for research data. *Journal of Empirical Research on Human Research Ethics* 7 (4): 1–9.

Wolf, Leslie E., Jolanta Zandecki, and Bernard Lo. 2004. The Certificates of Confidentiality application: A view from the NIH Institutes. *IRB: Ethics and Human Research* 26: 14–18.

14
Mandating Consent for Future Research with Biospecimens: A Call for Enhanced Community Engagement

Carol Weil, Hilary Shutak, Benjamin Fombonne, and Nicole Lockhart

The use of human biological samples, or biospecimens, in medical research has the potential to transform our understanding of health and disease in the age of the genome. Human biological samples are small amounts of human material (e.g., skin, tissue, or blood) that may be removed for clinical reasons (e.g., a diagnostic biopsy or surgery to excise a tumor) or for research purposes. When samples are removed for clinical reasons, remaining tissue that is not needed for diagnosis or any other medical purpose can be donated and stored in biorepositories for future medical research, including genomic studies.

The mapping of the human genome in 2001 represented a watershed moment in medical science, catapulting medical research into the so-called genomic age. The advance of medicine in the genomic age focuses on the origin and progression of disease through the identification of specific genes and the understanding of normal as well as mutated genetic pathways. Biomedical scientists study the causes and effects of genetic variation in individuals, which are multifactorial and complex, including inherited germ-line mutations and spontaneous somatic mutations. Translational researchers develop drugs and diagnostics based on specific gene signatures within cell populations. All these research endeavors require the use and analysis of human biospecimens. By investigating molecular differences in biospecimens collected from multiple individuals with varying diseases, scientists can develop strategies for diagnosing, preventing, and treating medical problems in a more targeted and effective manner.

Policy makers at DHHS recognize the primacy of biospecimens in medical research and the controversial ethical and legal issues implicated by their use. These issues include balancing needs for privacy and consent with the imperatives of investigator access and data sharing. In the ANPRM, DHHS proposed amendments that mandate written informed consent for research involving the use of previously collected human biospecimens (DHHS 2011, 44527). This chapter explores the impact of that potential regulatory change with respect to the ethics and operations of research involving biospecimens. We describe specific shortcomings of the current federal regulations protecting human biospecimens and associated data used in research, explain how proposed changes to consent procedures in the ANPRM could address these limitations while at the same time pose new challenges for health care institutions, and finally, set forth our thesis that enhanced education and collaboration with participant communities would greatly improve implementation of the ANPRM's written consent requirement for secondary uses of biospecimens in research.

14.1 Current Regulatory Framework for Biospecimen Research

Under the current federal regulatory policy protecting human research subjects (45 CFR 46 (2012)), research involving existing biospecimens generally requires informed consent if researchers know, or can readily access, information that would enable them to identify the individuals whose biospecimens are undergoing analysis. This scenario exists because the regulations require either informed consent, or authorized waiver of informed consent, for any research activities involving a defined "human subject." The federal regulations define "human subject" as a live individual about whom an investigator conducting research obtains (1) data through intervention or interaction with the individual, or (2) private information enabling the investigator to readily ascertain the individual's identity (45 CFR 46.102(f) (2012)). In accordance with this definition of "human subject," informed consent is not mandated for research involving previously collected anonymized biospecimens (such that any linkage to a live human being is no longer possible), or for research involving biospecimens that have been de-identified with respect to the researchers (such that the researchers cannot readily ascertain individual identifiers).

In order to further important research without releasing private identifiable information about individuals, researchers distributing biospecimens often dissociate individually identifying information from the biospecimens and replace it with coded information. Questions arise within the current regulatory scheme as to when and to whom private information or coded biospecimens are considered identifiable, and whether research involving coded biospecimens is "human subject" research. The Department's Office for Human Research Protections has issued guidance

(Office of Human Research Protections 2008) that indicates that two conditions must be met in order for research using coded biospecimens to be considered outside the ambit of "human subject" research, and therefore to not require informed consent. First, the biospecimens must be preexisting (i.e., previously collected for a clinical or different research purpose). Second, the research investigator(s) must be unable to readily ascertain the identity of the individuals to whom the coded biospecimens pertain. This second condition is often satisfied by institutional or institutional review board (IRB) policies prohibiting release of the code to investigators and holding investigators to a duty not to seek any identifying information about specimens they receive for research. It can also be satisfied by material transfer and data use agreements between investigators receiving de-identified biospecimens and a biobank or other entity that maintains and protects the confidentiality of identifiable information about the biospecimen donors.

Thus, under current departmental regulations and enforced guidance, secondary research involving the use of coded and de-identified biospecimens stored in biorepositories is not considered to involve human subjects, and consequently does not require informed consent. This common biobanking storage and distribution paradigm is called the "honest broker" model (Dhir et al. 2008) whereby biorepositories retain, but never release to downstream investigators, the link connecting donors to their de-identified biospecimens. The biorepository acts as a trusted intermediary between the institution collecting the biospecimens, which has access to donor identity and medical records, and the downstream institutional or individual researchers, who distribute coded biospecimens and data for research.

14.2 Problems with the Current Regulatory Framework

While the honest broker framework assists institutional biorepositories committed to upholding the informed choices of biospecimen donors, under current human subject rules biospecimens can be de-identified and distributed for research beyond the scope of donor consent. Biospecimens collected for one purpose (e.g., ovarian cancer research) can be coded and distributed to other researchers for unrelated studies, including ones the biospecimen donor might not have supported (e.g., in vitro fertilization research). A notorious example of secondary misuse of biospecimens involves the Havasupai, a small tribe living at the base of the Grand Canyon in Arizona. As noted by Amy Harmon (2010), the Havasupai suffer from an extremely high incidence of diabetes. In 1989 tribal members approached a geneticist at Arizona State University for assistance, and university researchers collected blood samples for diabetes research the following year. But subsequently these biospecimens and associated medical records were used by other researchers for purposes the Havasupai considered offensive. A university investigation uncovered scientific articles indicating that Havasupai blood samples were provided to researchers studying schizophrenia, inbreeding, and theories about the migratory history of the Havasupai, which conflicted with ancestral tribal beliefs. A six-year legal battle ensued, culminating in financial settlement and the return of collected blood samples for burial in accordance with tribal traditions.

Protection of autonomy is too easily sacrificed in a regulatory framework centered on identifiability, in which the duty to obtain consent does not apply to de-identified biospecimens or data. A regulatory framework protecting only identifiable biological material and information creates an ethically indefensible double standard. Moreover research participants do not envision a bright line distinction between identifiable and de-identified biospecimens (Rothstein 2010). De-identification policies that even unintentionally disregard donors' decisions about how their biospecimens may be used, or that preclude re-contact for secondary uses of biospecimens collected without blanket consent, are likely to erode public confidence in the medical research enterprise. The Havasupai research debacle, as well as Texas's destruction of 5.3 million newborn blood spots in settlement of a law suit by parents outraged that researchers were provided de-identified blood spots without parental permission (Waldo 2010), lend testament to the notion that participant trust is diminished by the nonconsensual use of de-identified biospecimens in research (Trinidad et al. 2011). We would expect that recruited individuals will be more likely to participate in research when they believe their preferences are being respected and they can thereby feel engaged and committed to research goals.

Beyond the issue of un-consented use lies the growing problem of implementing effective de-identification strategies for ensuring individual privacy. Recently a number of publications have highlighted previously underappreciated methods for re-identifying various types of genomic data (Gymrek et al. 2013; Schadt, Woo, and Hao 2012; Homer et al. 2008; Malin and Sweeny 2001). Our capability for re-identifying individuals from their de-identified biospecimens or data is likely to expand in the future, due to massive accumulations of data produced as whole genome sequencing and other genotyping technologies become more cost effective and more commonly employed. De-identification cannot guarantee genuine data security in the genomic age and should no longer be the lynchpin for determining whether those who donate their biospecimens for medical research are afforded human subject protection. Indeed for this reason the ANPRM sought public comment on whether all research with biospecimens, and research involving genomic data, should be considered research with identifiable information (DHHS 2011, 44526).

14.3 Rationale for Mandatory Consent for Secondary Uses of Biospecimens in Research

The ANPRM proposed mandatory consent at the time of collection for all future research uses of biospecimens, whether or not the biospecimens would be de-identified. Seeking permission for all future research uses at the time that biospecimens are collected makes logistical sense; the research participant is physically present so there is no tracking required for future re-contact, and the practice is less likely to pose a burden. Moreover obtaining blanket consent for future research uses of biospecimens would avoid the potential misuse of de-identified biospecimens collected for limited purposes, and thus promotes research participant autonomy. In addition the model of broad consent upon collection lends consistency to the biospecimen research enterprise. Research institutions could avoid separate consent policies for secondary research uses of identified versus de-identified material. Contractual arrangements between collecting entities and laboratories, including material transfer agreements for distributing biospecimens, and data use agreements stipulating acceptable data sharing arrangements among entities involved in research analysis, could be streamlined and harmonized.

The public interest is well served by avoiding the need to re-contact biospecimen donors for specific future research studies. Individuals can easily be lost to follow-up, particularly in longitudinal cohorts or large-scale epidemiological studies. Rejecting the use of previously collected biospecimens when donors cannot be located may result in selection bias and inferior, underpowered studies (Bathe and McGuire 2009). Requiring re-contact in order to obtain consent for additional research uses of previously collected biospecimens thus undermines the efficacy of the contributions of all study participants. This can be viewed as an immoral waste of precious resources. Moreover re-contacting former biospecimen donors poses potential added harms. For currently healthy individuals who donated biospecimens as a consequence of needing a biopsy or clinical procedure during a prior illness, re-contact may rekindle unpleasant memories and even provoke severe anxiety or distress. Some individuals, while not traumatized by re-contact, may find it intrusive. Multiple studies indicate that a majority of research participants condone blanket consent if decisions about how their biospecimens will be used in future studies are given to a panel of scientific and ethical experts (Wendler 2006).

Despite the multiple advantages of the blanket consent model, it has been argued that broad consent for future research uses of biospecimens is not truly "informed" consent because research participants cannot obtain a genuine understanding of studies that have not yet been designed or even contemplated (Scott et al. 2012). We believe that broad consent coupled with community engagement can alleviate these concerns and is a better approach than repeated re-contact of participants. In addition, offering "opt out" for specific types of controversial studies (e.g., embryonic stem cell research) circumscribes the scope of broad consent, thereby making it more "informed." Indeed the ANPRM proposed offering individuals the ability to disallow use of their biospecimens for certain purposes (DHHS 2011, 44524).

Alternatively, some biorepositories follow a "tiered consent" model enabling participants to select the types of research for which their biospecimens may be used. Thus, for example, cancer patients might wish their samples to be available for all medical research, or might limit future research uses to the prevention and treatment of cancer. Similarly participants with a rare disease might opt to donate biospecimens for research involving only that condition. Tiered consent has theoretical appeal as a measure promoting autonomy but in practice is problematic. It presents burdensome complications for biorepositories that must ensure distribution for appropriate research uses of samples and data collected under varying arrangements. Furthermore, if researchers discover additional research uses for particular samples that were obtained for limited specified uses, costly efforts may be required to re-contact individuals in order to obtain consent for the additional uses, imperiling important new research and intruding on participant privacy. This not only undermines medical progress, but the autonomy and interests of those who donated their samples for broad future research uses and are hindered from participating in subsequent studies.

Most important, tiered consent can be misleading to participants. Given the nature of scientific research in the era of the mapped genome, with its emphasis on molecular pathways rather than specific organs or diseases, tiered consent options that distinguish between familiar categories are relatively meaningless. Such categories are also difficult for institutional review boards, the entities charged with approving consent forms at research institutions, and biobank managers to interpret when deciding which biospecimens may be utilized for a particular study. NIH-funded researchers are encouraged to share their data, making it increasingly likely that data collected or generated for one specific research project will be used for subsequent studies potentially unrelated to the original research purpose for which the data was collected. The NIH Policy for Sharing of Data in Genome-Wide Association Studies calls for investigators funded by NIH to share appropriately consented de-identified data through a centralized NIH data repository (NIH 2008). Databases such as the NIH Database of Genotypes and Phenotypes (dbGaP) contain genetic information relevant across disease states. While dbGaP does provide for limitations on data sharing linked to consent form language, the database is accessed by both federally funded and for-profit researchers investigating a vast array of conditions. Obtaining broad consent for the use of data generated from research involving biospecimens is thus more transparent than a tiered consent approach because a list of choices for future research could be somewhat disingenuous.

14.4 Challenges of Mandatory General Consent

Certainly operational challenges exist to implementing a system of blanket consent at the time of collection for all future research uses of biospecimens. It is not intuitively clear that a "one-size-fits-all" approach to consent can work with all research participants, from sick patients to healthy altruists. Moreover there is a danger of biased collections if certain populations or communities refuse to donate their biospecimens. Recruiting minority groups into research studies is often difficult (Symonds et al. 2012). If mandatory broad consent were to accentuate existing disparities in minority recruitment, this would be unfortunate as well as unjust. Given the critical role biospecimens play as the first step in the translational research pipeline for development of diagnostics and drugs, introducing such biases during biospecimen collection could perpetuate lasting health disparities.

While blanket consent for biospecimen research may prevent the need for unwanted re-contact and promote efficient use of scarce biospecimen resources, participants deserve richer information about the possible future uses of their biospecimens in research. The challenge we face if we migrate to a mandatory general consent model for secondary research uses of biospecimens is educating prospective participants about the range of potential research uses, the breadth of anticipated data sharing, and the magnitude of genomic research findings that may be generated. The ANPRM, taking into account legitimate concerns about complicated and lengthy research consent forms, advocated for a brief, standardized consent form for biospecimen donation (DHHS 2011, 44515). The envisioned form would cover all biospecimens and data related to a set of encounters with an institution, such as all appointments at a particular clinic for treatment of a single condition, or all visits by an individual to his or her local hospital.

It seems virtually impossible for institutions to comply with the ANPRM proposal for a brief, standardized consent form containing sufficient information to enable informed choice for all participant populations and all types of research. How can a single short form explain the nature and risks of all future genomic and other research activities for any biospecimens collected in the future? Research participants, even those diagnosed with clinical conditions that are the subject of specified research, cannot readily parse the nuances of different study components for which consent might be sought. In a study examining factors associated with enrollment in cancer genetics research (Ford et al. 2006), 1,111 patients diagnosed with colorectal cancer at a gastrointestinal oncology clinic were asked to enroll in a study investigating the role of the *MSH6* gene in familial colorectal cancer. Consent was sought for the following purposes: (1) taking blood for DNA analysis, (2) establishing a cell line from the blood sample for future research uses, (3) reviewing family and medical history, and (4) re-contact about future studies involving first- and second-degree relatives as well as the research participant. These different research activities all involve distinct elements of autonomy and risk—including in the case of the family contacts potential harms to additional family members. Yet, of the 62.2 percent who enrolled in the genetic study, a substantial majority (88 percent) agreed to participate in all study components. In other words, once the decision to donate blood for the study was made, most participants didn't separately evaluate the various distinct aspects of study involvement.

In our view, the consent process for biospecimen donation cannot alone supply the knowledge necessary for informed research participation decisions, especially in genomic studies. It is generally difficult to describe at the outset of a study the range of possible future uses for which biospecimens may be fit. The difficulty is compounded exponentially in today's genomic age, when science and technology are evolving so rapidly. Moreover participants have a wide spectrum of views about what "genetic" research means (Lemke et al. 2010). Consent forms seeking permission to obtain biospecimens for gene sequencing and other genomic research often attempt to define terms like "gene" or "DNA." But a statement that collected specimens may be used for future genetic research studies may indicate to one participant that clinically significant information about inherited disease within his or her family will be generated; to another, it may simply suggest the intention to investigate the genetic basis of disease in general; to yet another, it may signify that cells will be cloned in order to test biomarkers for gene variants. We currently have no commonly shared understanding of what genetic research encompasses.

Consent forms are an inadequate vessel for describing the universe of potential future research uses, as well as potential research findings and their clinical and reproductive consequences for participants, their families, and their communities (Yassin et al. 2012). Consent forms are likewise inadequate for explaining complex and detail-rich research processes, such as the scope of data sharing and the nature of data security procedures. In a Baylor College of Medicine focus group study of patients involved in a gene sequencing study of epilepsy (McGuire et al. 2008), some participants assumed that consent provisions authorizing data sharing applied only to local researchers, while others thought that Baylor investigators could share their data with others without restriction.

Beyond the foregoing limitations, people want and need to know different pieces of information before deciding whether to donate. Some may be concerned about how their information is coded and their data protected; others will want to know whether commercial researchers will have access to their biospecimens for financial profit; still others will wish to understand the nature of any data to be generated and its potential clinical impact on their family or greater ethnic or disease community. And institutional review boards do not necessarily agree with research participants about what is most important to include in biospecimen research consent forms (Beskow et al. 2010).

14.5 Improving the Biospecimen Consent Process via Community Education and Engagement

We believe that community outreach through education and engagement is the key to successful implementation of a broad consent model for secondary research uses of biospecimens, as set forth in the ANPRM.

Ironically, the procedures involved in obtaining informed consent cannot alone accomplish that goal in the context of standardized general consent for future research uses of biospecimens. There is not enough time during the consent process, nor space on the research consent form, to adequately explain the multiple considerations involved in long-term storage of donors' biospecimens, including withdrawal policies, how access decisions are made, and data security procedures such as specimen and data coding. Community education and engagement, in conjunction with a general consent process, can fill the knowledge gaps.

Community advisory boards (CABs), committees of participants that provide a conduit between researchers and enrollees, have emerged as major components of engagement in the biobanking arena for population-based biobanks (McCarty et al. 2008), including banks that collect genetic information (Simon et al. 2011). CABs can help refine consent language and educate investigators about participant concerns with the storage or future uses of their biospecimens. The use of CABs can enhance participant and community protections by encouraging stakeholder involvement in study design and implementation, building mutual responsibility between researcher and participants for the success of the biorepository and its research. Practical difficulties may arise, however, when implementing CABs, including how to define the research community, identifying appropriate stakeholders and representatives to the CAB, determining the issues for which the CAB should be consulted, and translating CAB feedback into useful information (e.g., protocol or consent amendments) (Dickert and Sugarman 2008). CAB operations can also suffer if investigators are not supportive of the CAB's role. Moreover CABs are typically resource limited and are often among the first institutions affected by research budget cutbacks (Strauss et al. 2011).

Despite these noted challenges, CABs can serve a particularly useful function in the genomic age, in de-mystifying genetic research for participants through community outreach and education. Other forms of community consultation such as focus groups and public forums could supplement CABs and educate audiences at all socioeconomic and literacy levels, potentially enhancing recruitment and retention of participants. Ideally these methods of community engagement would promote better science through enrollment of a more diverse and representative population sample.

The public is generally willing to donate their biospecimens and medical data for broad medical research purposes despite increased informational risks in the genomic era. In a national survey, over 90 percent of respondents indicated they would participate in biorepository research (Trinidad et al. 2011). However, due to current limitations in the research participation and consent process, the public lacks complete understanding about what such participation may mean, in terms of the scope of future research, the extent of data sharing, and the potential generation of genetic research results with implications for themselves, their families, and larger community or population groups. If, as proposed in the ANPRM, the human subject protection regulations are revised to require a standardized brief consent form for future research uses of biospecimens, the task of conveying the risks of unwarranted disclosure of information and genetic discrimination, as well as existing legal protections, will become even more difficult.

Knowledge connecting the process of donation to some of the successful narratives of medical research that began with biospecimens (e.g., development of the HER2 diagnostic test for breast cancer) gives people a stake in the outcome of research, making them more willing to donate their own biospecimens. A knowledgeable public thus benefits the research enterprise by engendering feelings of empowerment among prospective participants and diminishing fears of exploitation. Improving the public's scientific literacy supports autonomy and ensures transparency. Community engagement may foster appreciation for the ultimate goals of biobanking, transforming the daunting world of medical research (scientific jargon included) into something comprehensible and meaningful. The consent process falls short by comparison.

Perhaps the most important aspect of community engagement about use of biospecimens in research is that the public can be educated about the evolving nature of informational risks associated with large-scale research databases, including accumulations of genetic and genomic data in publicly funded programs such as the NIH's Database of Genotypes and Phenotypes, the Cancer Genome Atlas Project, and the 1,000 Genomes Project. The offense that might be caused by associating an increased or inherited risk of a stigmatizing disease (depression, alcoholism, etc.) with one's relatives or within an entire community, as the Havasupai experienced with schizophrenia, cannot be overestimated. Concerns about confidentiality are particularly acute for large-scale genetic databases (Godard et al. 2004) where there is greater likelihood of alienating particular groups of people through generation of data linking gene variants to distinct populations. But through community engagement, researchers can explain existing privacy and antidiscrimination laws and empower participants to collaborate with researchers in order to protect community values. In addition participant communities can be educated with positive examples of how data-sharing efforts move genetic research forward by uncovering linkages among gene mutations for multiple conditions, gene expression in individuals, and the symptoms of significant disease.

By engaging the public in an ongoing dialogue about the risks and benefits of biospecimen research, researchers can identify and clarify areas of confusion as well as issues of concern for substantial groups of individuals, and enhance standardized consent forms accordingly. The ANPRM specifically sought guidance about whether standardized consent forms should allow individuals to opt out of specific categories of research known to raise concerns within a significant sector of the public (e.g., investigations of reproductive technologies) (DHHS 2011, 44519–20). Public engagement could assist with identification of such specific research categories, allowing types of research offensive to, or undesired by, certain communities or populations of participants to be deleted from standardized consent forms for specific studies.

14.6 Conclusion

The public generally feels positive about participating in genetic research involving the collection and storage of biospecimens. But in the genomic age, as medical advances are being increasingly linked to targeted molecular research requiring the mining and sharing of vast amounts of data, the research community needs to provide better community education and outreach and promote greater scientific literacy to ensure informed choices about donating biospecimens for research. Community engagement will be particularly helpful if standardized general consent for secondary research uses of biospecimens, as proposed in the ANPRM, becomes the norm and samples are routinely and expectedly collected for broad future medical research. The public needs to understand not only the depth and scope of potential research activities for which their biological specimens may be used, but also the implications of genomic data sharing and the nature and extent of private information that may become accessible. In addition to communicating these risks, community engagement can demonstrate to the public how secondary research involving stored biospecimens promotes efficient use of valuable resources without imposing added physical or psychological risks to individuals. Community engagement may be used to check the pulse of prospective participants on such important issues as the intrusiveness of re-contact, or whether promised disclosure of research findings would induce participants to remain enrolled in longitudinal studies over the course of several years. Additionally public consultation would be useful for making decisions about whether to waive consent for unanticipated future analysis of existing biospecimens and data, including newborn blood spot collections and archives of de-identified samples where re-consent is not an option. Community education and engagement removes the more concerning, less palatable elements of onetime general consent because it offers context to participants donating their biospecimens for broad future research uses. People can choose not to enroll, or can subsequently withdraw if they learn of an objectionable potential use. An engaged community can give feedback to biobank investigators initially and during the course of studies, providing suggestions for further educational and communication efforts, ethical and social policies, and even study design. Educating the public about donating biospecimens for medical research will undoubtedly serve both the investigator community and the participant community in the long run.

Note

The authors wish to acknowledge that this chapter reflects their personal views and not necessarily the opinion of the National Cancer Institute, the National Human Genome Research Institute, the National Institutes of Health, or the US Department of Health and Human Services.

References

Bathe, Oliver F., and Amy L. McGuire. 2009. The ethical use of existing samples for genome research. *Genetics in Medicine* 11 (10): 712–15.

Beskow, Laura, Joelle Friedman, N. Chantelle Hardy, Li Lin, and Kevin P. Weinfurt. 2010. Simplifying informed consent for biorepositories: Stakeholder perspectives. *Genetics in Medicine* 12 (9): 567–72.

Department of Health and Human Services (DHHS). 2011. Advance Notice of Proposed Rulemaking. Human subjects research protections: Enhancing protections for research subjects and reducing burden, delay, and ambiguity for investigators. *Federal Register* 76 (143): 44512–31.

Dhir, Rajiv, A. A. Patel, Sharon Winters, Michelle Bisceglia, Dennis Swanson, Roger Aamodt, and Michael Bechch. 2008. A multidiciplinary approach to honest broker services for tissue banks and clinical data: A pragmatic and practical model. *Cancer* 113: 1705–15.

Dickert, Neal, and Jeremy Sugarman. 2008. Ethical goals of community consultation in research. *Health Policy and Ethics* 95 (7): 1123–27.

Ford, Beth, James S. Evans, Elena M. Stoffel, Judith Balmana, Meredith M. Regan, and Sapna Syngal. 2006. Factors associated with enrollment in cancer genetics research. *Cancer Epidemiology, Biomarkers and Prevention* 15:1355–1359.

Godard, B., J. Marshall, C. Labarge, and B. M. Knoppers. 2004. Strategies for consulting with the community: The cases of four large-scale genetic databases. *Science and Engineering Ethics* 10: 457–77.

Gymrek, Melissa, Amy L. McGuire, David Golan, Eran Halperin, and Yaniv Erlich. 2013. Identifying personal genomes by surname inference. *Science* 18: 321–24.

Harmon, Amy. 2010. Indian tribe wins fight to limit research of Its DNA. *New York Times,* April 21. Accessed October 17, 2012. http://www.nytimes.com/2010/04/22/us/22dna.html?pagewanted=all&_r=0.

Homer, Nils, Szabolcs Szelinger, Margot Redman, David Duggan, Waibhav Tembe, Jill Muehling, John Pearson, Dietrich Stephan, Stanley Nelson, and David Craig. 2008. Resolving individuals contributing trace amounts of DNA to highly complex mixtures using high-density SNP genotyping microarrays. *PLOS Genetics* 4: e1000167. doi:10.1371/journal.pgen.1000167 Accessed August 21, 2013.

Lemke, A. A., W. A. Wolf, J. Hebert-Beine, and M. E. Smith. 2010. Public and biobank participant attitudes toward genetic research participation and data sharing. *Public Health Genomics* 13: 368–77.

Malin, Bradley, and Latanya Sweeny. 2001. Re-Identification of DNA through an automated linkage process. *Proceedings of the American Medical Informatics Association Annual Symposium.* Bethesda, MD: AMIA, 423–27. Accessed October 17, 2012. http://www.ncbi.nlm.nih.gov/pmc/articles/PMC2243547/.

McCarty, Catherine A., Donna Chapman-Stone, Teresa Derfus, Philip Giampietro, and Norman Fost. 2008. Community consultation and commuication for a population-based DNA biobank: The Marshfield Clinic Personalized Medicine Research Project. *American Journal of Medical Genetics* 146A: 3026–33.

McGuire, Amy L., Jennifer A. Hamilton, Rebecca Lunstroth, Laurence B. McMullough, and Alica Goldman. 2008. DNA data sharing: Research participants' perspectives. *Genetics in Medicine* 10 (1): 46–53.

National Cancer Institute. The Cancer Genome Atlas Project. Accessed October 18, 2012. http://cancergenome.nih.gov/.

National Institutes of Health (NIH). Policy for sharing of data obtained in NIH supported or conducted Genome-Wide Association Studies (GWAS). Accessed October 18, 2012. http://gwas.nih.gov/03policy2.html. Last modified August 28, 2008, modification available at http://gwas.nih.gov/pdf/Data%20Sharing%20Policy%20Modifications.pdf.

National Institutes of Health. Database of genotypes and phenotypes. Accessed October 18, 2012. http://www.ncbi.nlm.nih.gov/gap.

1000 Genomes Project. Accessed February 2, 2013. http://www.1000genomes.org/about.

Office of Human Research Protections (OHRP). 2008. Guidance on research involving coded private information or biological specimens. Available at http://www.hhs.gov/ohrp/policy/cdebiol.html.

Rothstein, Mark A. 2010. Is deidentification sufficient to protect health privacy in research? *American Journal of Bioethics* 10 (9): 3–11.

Schadt, Eric E., Sangsoon Woo, and Ke Hao. 2012. Baysian method to predict individual SNP genotypes from gene expression data. *Nature Genetics* 44 (5): 603–608.

Scott, Christopher Thomas, Timothy Caulfield, Emily Borgelt, and Judy Illes. 2012. Personal medicine: The new banking crisis. *Nature Biotechnology* 30 (2): 141–47.

Simon, Christian M., Elizabeth Newbury, and Jamie L'heureux. 2011. Protecting participants, promoting progress: Public perspectives on community advisory boards (CABs) in biobanking. *Journal of Empirical Research on Human Research Ethics* 6 (3): 19–30.

Strauss, Ronald P., Sohini Sengupta, Sandra Crouse Quinn, Jean Goeppinger, Cora Spaulding, Susan M. Kegeles, and Greg Millett. 2011. The role of community advisory boards: Involving communities in the informed consent process. *American Journal of Public Health* 91 (12): 1938–43.

Symonds, R. P., K. Lord, A. J. Mitchell, and D. Raghavan. 2012. Recruitment of ethnic minorities into cancer clinical trials: experience from the front lines. *British Journal of Cancer* 107 (7): 1017–21.

Trinidad, S. B., S. M. Fullerton, E. J. Ludman, G. P. Jarvik, E. B. Larson, and W. Burke. 2011. Research practice and participant preferences: The growing gulf. *Science* 331 (6015): 287–88.

Waldo, Ann. 2010. The Texas newborn blood spot saga has reached a sad—and preventable—conclusion, March 16, 2010. *Genomics Law Report*. Accessed December 20, 2012. http://www.genomicslawreport.com/index.php/2010/03/16/the-texas-newborn-bloodspot-saga-has-reached-a-sad-and-preventable-conclusion/.

Wendler, David. 2006. One-time general consent for research on biological samples. *British Medical Journal* 332 (7540): 544–47.

Yassin, Rihab, Carol Weil, and Nicole Lockhart. 2012. Sharing individual research results with biospecimen contributors: Point. *Cancer Epidemiology, Biomarkers and Prevention* 21: 256. Accessed October 18, 2012. http://cebp.aacrjournals.org/content/21/2/256.

15
Take Another Little Piece of My Heart: Regulating the Research Use of Human Biospecimens

Gail H. Javitt

15.1 Introduction

Access to human biospecimens is essential to the progress of personalized medicine, as it enables researchers to study the influence of genetic variation on human health and disease. Nearly half a billion biospecimens are currently stored in "biobanks" worldwide.

The legal status of and ethical obligations owed to biospecimen contributors is unsettled. The current approach increases barriers to research access but fails adequately to consider the preferences and expectations of contributors.

The ANPRM fails to resolve the legal and ethical challenges associated with research use of biospecimens, and a contemporaneously issued draft guidance from the Food and Drug Administration would further erode protections for biospecimen contributors. An alternative approach presented in this chapter acknowledges the role of biospecimen contributors for legal, ethical, and practical reasons.

15.2 Human Subjects Protection and Biospecimens

As explored in other chapters, the Common Rule evolved in response to physical abuse of vulnerable populations who were unwilling or unwitting research subjects. Biospecimen research presents a different scenario, as it involves minimal physical intervention and a wide range of participants. Biospecimen contributors are sometimes considered "human subjects," but there is no uniform legal approach and courts have been inconsistent in resolving disputes over the research use of biospecimens.

The ANPRM proposes requiring onetime written consent for current and all potential future research uses of human biospecimens (DHHS 2011, 44515). A participant could refuse any future research use or consent prospectively to all uses, but consent to future research uses could not be required as a condition of participation in a current study (DHHS 2011, 44520).

A draft guidance issued jointly by FDA and OHRP in August 2011 would undermine the legal prohibition against including in consent documents "exculpatory language" requiring a subject to waive, or appear to waive, any legal rights (45 CFR 46.116 (2009); 21 CFR 50.20 (2012)). It states that consent documents may include waiver of *any rights* a subject may have with respect to a biospecimen obtained for research purposes. The rationale for this significant interpretive shift is that it has "long been common practice" not to compensate research subjects who agree to provide biospecimens for research purposes even if those biospecimens are later used for commercial purposes (FDA 2011, 2).

15.3 Case Law

Few court decisions address research biospecimen disputes, but they reveal limitations in the current legal and ethical framework and a lack of shared understanding about the role of biospecimen contributors. Inconsistent case law highlights the need for clear and consistent rules.

From a doctrinal perspective, the cases do not distinguish analytically between the dual roles of biospecimen contributors—subject and donor. Informed consent was developed as a means to effectuate the moral principle of autonomy and ensure that the decision to participate was made freely, based on adequate information. It was premised on the view of research participants as inherently vulnerable because the activities in which they would be participating carried a risk of injury and because their relationship with the researcher is one of unequal knowledge and power. In contrast, the human tissue donor has a quasi-contractual relationship with the researcher, and the concept of donation presumes that the donor has an equal position relative to the recipient and therefore the ability to establish the terms of the donation.

Moore v. Regents of the University of California, 793 P.2d 479, 481 (Cal. 1990), involved a patient whose spleen was removed to treat his hairy-cell leukemia. His treating physician then used the excised tumor cells—and tissues subsequently obtained from Moore under false pretenses—to develop a cell line that was then patented by the physician's employer (ibid. at 481–82).

Moore sued for a share of the profits derived from the unauthorized use of his cells, alleging that it constituted "conversion" (tort of interference with right of ownership or possession of property; ibid. at 487). The court denied this claim on the basis that existing laws and precedent did not give Moore any ownership interest in his cells (ibid. at 493). The majority declined to expand the scope of "conversion" because it might have a chilling effect on the conduct of medical research.

The court also rejected arguments grounded in the need to protect patient dignity and autonomy, holding that informed consent could adequately protect these interests (ibid. at 496–97). The court was troubled that the physician withheld information about the cells' value and induced Moore to provide additional samples under false pretenses (ibid. at 496n.41), but considered this a breach of his duty of informed consent. As such, future patients could be protected by requiring informed consent documents to disclose physician financial interests (ibid. at 486, 496–97). Just as patients must be told about physical risks of a procedure, so too they must be informed of economic interests that might cloud the physician's judgment (ibid. at 484–85).

This ruling seems designed to protect the research enterprise while preventing patient deception, but its informed consent analysis is flawed because it does not distinguish between Moore-the-patient and Moore-the-research-subject. Although Moore's physician was aware that the cells might be valuable before the spleen was removed, and therefore had a *potentially* conflicting interest (ibid. at 481), there was no evidence that this knowledge motivated his decision to recommend surgery, or that the surgery was unnecessary. Moore-the-patient was therefore not harmed by lack of knowledge of the financial interest, and would not have been made better off through its disclosure. Indeed, had he known, and changed doctors, he might have been worse off.

Even recognizing that in other circumstances such disclosure could be beneficial, and therefore is a necessary element of consent to medical *treatment*, the court's reasoning nevertheless was insufficient, since it did not recognize the need to protect Moore-the-research-subject. When his cells were collected and used for research, Moore took on a new role, that of research subject. The failure to obtain consent for research was a wrong against Moore-the-research-subject, not Moore-the-patient. By the court's reasoning, had the physician not been Moore's doctor, or had he not had an inkling of the cells' potential research value at the time of surgery, he would have had no obligation to inform Moore of the cells' value. Nor, by this reasoning, did the other defendants have any duty to obtain Moore's consent to use his cells. The court's limited holding therefore does little to protect the interests of the vast majority of tissue sample contributors. Only Judge Most, in dissent, recognized the importance of the silent "third party" to the "biotechnology enterprise" whose contribution of biological materials is essential to its success (ibid. at 516).

Post-*Moore* decisions have similarly failed to properly consider the status of this "third party" (ibid. at 516). *Greenberg v. Miami Children's Hospital*, 264 F. Supp. 2d 1064 (S.D. Fla. 2003), involved a dispute between contributors of human biospecimens for research and the researcher and institution with whom they collaborated in identifying a genetic disease and developing a diagnostic test. Plaintiffs were not informed that the gene would be patented by the researcher's institution and were unhappy that the test was not made freely available. They alleged lack of informed consent, breach of fiduciary duty, unjust enrichment, fraudulent concealment, conversion, and misappropriation of trade secrets (ibid. at 1068). The court dismissed all claims but unjust enrichment. It held that the duty of informed consent did not apply to the researcher because he was not plaintiffs' treating physician (ibid. at 1070). Even if the duty did apply to the researcher, such duty did not include disclosure of financial interests, as plaintiffs were tissue donors, not "objects of human experimentation" (ibid. at 1071).

Greenberg again favored researchers over research participants. Just as *Moore* conflated the contexts of medical treatment and human subject research, which avoided the need to consider the rights of Moore-the-research-subject, *Greenberg* characterized plaintiffs as "donors" rather than subjects and determined that they were not entitled to the protections afforded the latter. However, the informed consent document that the institution required plaintiffs to sign (ibid. at 1069) was clearly provided in a research context, as it was an institutionally required prerequisite to the researcher's undertaking the research. Plaintiffs' signatures reflect that they accepted the status of human subjects, which required the institution to act in a fiduciary role and to ensure that their agreement to participate was given freely and adequately informed (ibid. at 1071). By reinterpreting plaintiffs' status as "donors" after the fact, the court effectively absolved the institution of its human subjects obligations and enabled it to take advantage of the legal status of donation. Although donation agreements are not legally enforceable, donations acquire the legal status of property transfer once a donation is made (Restatement (Third) of Property: Wills and Other Donative Transfers §6.1 cmt. a (2003)). Nothing in the informed consent process alerted plaintiffs to the fact that they were engaging in a legal transaction—property transfer—in which the institution had no fiduciary obligation. Had they been so alerted, they might have attempted to make an independent assessment of their own best interests before agreeing to give the researcher access to their tissues.

As a consequence plaintiffs failed to receive the protective benefits of informed consent to research and were not given the requisite access to information and the ability to negotiate on equal terms that one would expect to accompany donation of property.

This status conflation is echoed in *Washington University v. Catalona* (*Catalona II*), 490 F.3d 667 (8th Cir. 2007), *aff'g* 437 F. Supp. 2d 985 (E.D. Mo. 2006) (*Catalona I*), in which legal status of the contributors of disputed tissue samples was determinative of the legal outcome. Defendant researcher had established a biorepository containing an extensive tissue sample collection, which was funded by and housed at plaintiff's institution (ibid. at 670). Patients were required to sign an informed consent document (ibid. at 671), which generally used the word "donation" to describe participants' provision of samples, and informed participants that their samples might be used by different entities, that they had a right to withdraw from the research and have their samples destroyed, and that they had no claim to the donated tissues or materials or processes derived from them (ibid.).

The researcher sought to take the samples with him to another institution, and obtained release forms from the research participants indicating that they sought transfer of their samples to him (ibid at 672). The institution claimed ownership of the biorepository and specimens (ibid.).

In upholding the lower court's ruling in favor of the institution (ibid. at 673, 667), the appellate court framed the question as follows: "[Do] individuals who make an informed decision to contribute their biological materials voluntarily to a particular research institution for the purpose of medical research retain an ownership interest allowing the individuals to direct or authorize the transfer of such materials to a third party?" (ibid. at 673).

The court held that they do not, finding that the specimens were "inter vivos" gifts from the patients to the institution (ibid. at 673–74). The court found that the patients had donative intent and delivered their property to the donee (the institution), and that the gift was accepted by the donee (ibid. at 674–75). Further the court held that the consent form's right to revoke or destroy the samples did not negate their gift status (ibid. at 675).

Like *Greenberg*, the *Catalona II* decision confuses informed consent with donation. The two documents the court evaluated to assess the tissue contributors' intent were the consent document and the genetics research information brochure (ibid. at 671). These documents were signed by the contributors in the context of a research study in which they were invited to participate as human subjects (ibid. at 674). Although the term "donation" appears in these documents and the participants knew they were transferring their specimens for research purposes, it is unlikely that participants appreciated that they were signing away legal rights by agreeing to be research participants. Construing the term "donation" after the fact as a legal transfer of property under which participants retained no rights to control the use of their tissues takes advantage of their good faith belief that they were human subjects, which they could have reasonably presumed meant that the institution was obligated to act in their best interests.

The court also ignored the troubling issue of "waiver." The consent document contained language under which participants waived any claim to "donated" body tissues and "the right to any new material or process developed through research involving [them]" (ibid. at 671). Such language should, under the Common Rule, have been considered to contravene the prohibition on exculpatory language. By framing the transaction as a donation, the court sidestepped the question of the consent documents' validity (ibid. at 675n.7). The court similarly sidestepped the Common Rule requirement that a participant be allowed to withdraw participation, which logically would require destruction of collected samples. Defendant took the position that it could satisfy participants' request to withdraw by anonymizing the samples while continuing to use them for research (*Catalona I*, 437 F. supp. 2d at 992). While this issue was not addressed on appeal, it is questionable whether post hoc anonymization satisfies the letter or spirit of federal human subjects regulations. Nevertheless, accepting Washington University's interpretation was consonant with the court's conclusion that participants did not retain proprietary interests in their tissues.

Two states, Texas and Minnesota, have faced lawsuits by or on behalf of parents alleging that their children's residual newborn blood spots were stored and used for research without parental consent (Doerr 2010; Drabiak-Syed 2009). In a class action against the Texas Department of Health and Human Services, plaintiffs argued that retention and use of the samples constituted unlawful search and seizure and violated fundamental privacy rights, in contravention of federal and state law. Texas settled the case and agreed to destroy blood samples collected from more than 5 million babies (Doerr 2010). Following the lawsuit, the Texas legislature enacted a law governing the prospective collection of infant blood samples (Tex. Health & Safety Code 33.0021, 33.0111, 33.0112, 33.017 (2009)). The law gives parents the opportunity to ensure that samples taken from their children are destroyed and requires IRB oversight and de-identification of any samples provided to researchers (see ibid.).

Minnesota's newborn screening program was challenged as violating the state's genetic privacy law, *Bearder v. State*, 806 N.W.2d 766 (Minn. 2011). The Minnesota Supreme Court agreed, holding that samples could be retained without parental consent only as long as needed to test them for heritable and congenital disorders, and that any other use, storage, or dissemination required written informed consent from parents or legal guardians (Minnesota Department of Health 2012). Like Texas, the ultimate remedy for unconsented storage was destruction of the residual blood spots (ibid.).

These cases demonstrate the gap in the current regulatory framework between duties owed to research participants from their status as human subjects and those that derive from their status as tissue donors. They also illustrate the lack of agreement among physicians, researchers, and research participants regarding the appropriate conditions under which biospecimens may be collected and used.

15.4 Public Attitudes toward Biobanking

Several studies have attempted to assess public attitudes regarding, and willingness to contribute tissue samples to, biobanks for research. This chapter does not provide a comprehensive review of that literature, much of which reports on research conducted in non-US populations (Melas et al. 2010; Tupasela et al. 2010; Hoeyer 2010; Thornton 2009; Treweek et al. 2009). It also recognizes that much of the research discussed was conducted using hypothetical scenarios, and asking people what they *would* do under certain conditions may not be an accurate measure of how people behave when confronted with real-world circumstances (Bishop 2005). Nevertheless, these studies provide insight into the public's views regarding use of their tissues in research. Examining these viewpoints may aid in understanding the source of the conflicting positions reflected in the above cases and inform the development of policies to avoid such conflicts.

Studies to date support the following with respect to the attitudes of the US population: (1) there is significant public support for the goals of biobank research (Williams et al. 2008; Kaufman, Murphy, et al. 2009); (2) a majority of the public would agree, at least under some conditions, to contribute tissue samples for research (Williams et al. 2008; Kaufman, Murphy-Bollinger, et al. 2009; Kaufman, Murphy, et al. 2009; Lemke, Halverson, and Ross 2012, 1032); (3) there is significant concern about ensuring the privacy of information derived from tissue samples and any associated medical information (Williams et al. 2008); and (4) there is significant public interest in receiving information from research conducted with their tissues if it is relevant to one's health, and in having a choice regarding what information they receive (ibid. at 9; Lemke, Halverson, and Ross 2012, 1033; Kaufman, Murphy, et al. 2009, 334; Murphy et al. 2008, 36–41). For example, a 2007 study by the Genetics and Public Policy Center at Johns Hopkins University assessed public willingness to participate in a hypothetical research study involving biospecimen collection. It explored willingness to participate, privacy concerns, views about informed consent and data sharing, and the impact of modest incentives (Kaufman, Murphy-Bollinger, et al. 2009; Murphy et al. 2009; Murphy et al. 2008, 36–41). The findings showed that a majority of respondents supported the general idea of the study and would likely participate if asked (Murphy et al. 2009, 2131; Kaufman, Murphy-Bollinger, et al. 2009, 645). However, significant concern was expressed, particularly by minority populations, about whether their medical information's privacy would be protected (Murphy et al. 2009, 2131; Kaufman, Murphy-Bollinger, et al. 2009, 645). A sizable minority expressed a preference for separate consent for each project involving their specimens, although participants appreciated the complexities of such an approach. Focus group findings revealed participants' desire for a mutually binding relationship with researchers. The term "contract" arose spontaneously and repeatedly in discussing study participation (Murphy et al. 2009, 2131). Focus group members "viewed a contract as a binding agreement between participants and researchers [not] simply as participants' agreement to participate" (ibid. at 2132). They "thought that a contract might offer participants greater protection than an institutional review board or study oversight committee and provide participants with some level of recourse if researchers strayed from the agreed-upon terms" (ibid.). Participants also identified specific terms they believed should be included in the contract between researchers and participants, such as what samples would be collected, how they would be used, who would have access to study data, what would happen to the samples and data after the study closed, and what would happen if the terms of the contract were breached (ibid.).

The Center concluded that, "the repeated use of 'contract' by focus group participants ... and the overwhelming desire for a contract ... suggested that the public believes that there are or should be reciprocal obligations between researcher and participant," (ibid. at 2133).

The Center also hypothesized that the desire for a contract may reflect a lack of trust in the research enterprise (ibid.), but noted that the importance of trust was similarly observed in a survey conducted by Duke researchers, who found that willingness to participate in biobank research is strongly correlated with the degree of trust that respondents have in researchers (Beskow and Dean 2008).

15.5 Analysis

One of the threshold questions raised by the regulatory oversight of and case law regarding research involving human biospecimens is defining the legal status of those specimens once they have been removed from the human body. There are no easy answers; as one scholar has explained, "the law of the body remains in a state of constant chaos" (Rao 2007).

Under the biospecimens-as-property theory, an individual's body—including biospecimens—is viewed as his or her property such that the unauthorized removal or use of the tissue is theft or trespass (Charo 2006). One concern with recognizing an individual's property right to excised tissue is that it could threaten investigators' access to stored samples and thereby impede scientific advances (ibid. at 1519).

There are other reasons to be leery of the "property" construction, including the effects it could have on public health laws prohibiting the sale and governing the handling of transplantable human organs, and laws governing the disposal of human biological materials (see *Moore*, 793 P.2d at 489). As the court in *Moore* explained, the laws regarding biological materials primarily seek to ensure safe handling of potentially hazardous biological waste, but "the [laws'] practical effect is to limit, drastically, a patient's control over excised cells. . . . [T]he [laws] eliminate[] so many of the rights ordinarily attached to property that one cannot simply assume that what is left amounts to 'property' or 'ownership' . . ." (ibid. at 489, 491–92).

An alternative view is that biospecimens are entitled to protection under an individual's right to privacy. The privacy viewpoint generally accords with findings from surveys of public attitudes regarding the use of human biospecimens, in which participants expressed significant concern about ensuring the privacy of information derived from their tissue samples and any associated medical information included about them (Williams et al. 2008, 8). Some have argued that the privacy framework is ill-suited to biospecimens (Rao 2007, 379).

Whether biospecimens are viewed as property or as protected under an individual's right to privacy, it is clear that many people expect or desire the ability to authorize or deny use of their tissue in research. Indeed public opinion research reveals that many people harbor strong possessive or protective feelings toward their tissue. Such feelings may find their source in religious views on the body (Harmon 2010) or notions of bodily autonomy, that is, the conviction that individuals should retain the power to control the use of their body parts by virtue of the fact that those parts originated in, and once were a part of, them. Even individuals who do not care about the fate of their excised tissues may care about whether the information derived from that tissue could help, or harm, them in the future.

Respect for these interests, regardless of their origins, requires that would-be contributors be asked if they are willing to have their tissue used for research, be informed that once they agree they likely will have no further control over its use, and have an opportunity to negotiate the terms of its use or, failing that, decline to contribute (Vermeulen et al. 2009, 1505; Saunders 2010, 84). Failure to provide such respect can be highly disruptive to research and may lead to the loss of valuable research resources.

The ANPRM correctly recognizes that the duty of informed consent should not turn on a specimen's identifiability. The approach to the research use of biospecimens proposed in the ANPRM would constitute a step forward to the extent it acknowledges that it is necessary to "ask permission" of the contributors of biospecimens, even if such biospecimens are deidentified. However, it arguably falls short in permitting "open-ended" consent, in light of what is known regarding the public's desire to know—and have a more nuanced choice—regarding the use of biospecimens, notwithstanding the logistical difficulties and additional burdens on research that such a system could create (Saha and Hurlbut 2011). The ANPRM also leaves unaddressed the "consent/donation" mismatch, that is, the inherent unsuitability of a consent document to effect what is essentially a contractual (or quasi-contractual) transaction (Maschke 2010, 22).

Most troubling, the FDA/OHRP draft guidance contravenes the bedrock principle of informed consent that subjects may not be asked to waive *any* of their legal rights (see 45 CFR 46.116 (2009); 21 CFR 50.20

(2012)). To do so, the draft guidance relies on the circular logic that because researchers generally have not compensated subjects for commercial use of their biospecimens, subjects are not really giving anything up by relinquishing all legal rights to those biospecimens. But just because researchers generally have not compensated subjects for the commercial use of their biospecimens does not mean that subjects lack such rights as a matter of law. Moreover language can be impermissibly exculpatory even if there is only "appearance" of waiver. A categorical waiver of rights would therefore contravene the prohibition against "exculpatory language."

More fundamental, the consent document is an inappropriate vehicle for effectuating a contractual, or even quasi-contractual, transaction. A consent document's purpose is to inform would-be subjects of the risks and potential benefits to them of research participation. In contrast, a donation agreement is an invitation to engage in a legal transaction under which would-be donors make a gift of themselves to the researcher and institution in perpetuity. Like other tangible gifts that are transferred through donation, the terms of the specimen transfer should be clearly delineated.

To be sure, certain information must be conveyed to subjects and donors because it might influence willingness to participate in research and donate tissue. For example, would-be subjects and prospective donors must be told if research results will be returned to them because such results could be considered a benefit of research participation and could be a factor that a donor considers in deciding whether to make a donation. Similarly would-be subjects and prospective donors need to know about the researcher and institution's financial interests in the research. However, the informed consent document is, first and foremost, a vehicle for risk disclosure, which is a prerequisite to informed consent; it was never intended to serve as the vehicle by which subjects would irrevocably transfer property to researchers and institutions.

The separation of contributor-as-subject and contributor-as-donor could be accomplished by, for example, providing a consent form that outlines the purpose of the research and the risks and benefits of participation and a separate donation agreement that makes clear the terms of the legal transaction and the parties to that transaction. For research not covered by the Common Rule or other federal human subjects regulations, researchers or institutions should nevertheless be required to provide a donation agreement to prospective contributors of tissue. The separate HIPAA authorization that covered entities must obtain from research subjects in addition to informed consent provides precedent for separating the roles of research participant and tissue donor. The HIPAA authorization focuses on privacy, whereas biospecimen contributors may have a broader interest in their specimens than simply protection of personal privacy.

Although requiring separation of research consent from donation agreement may seem like a proposal for adding another step to an already cumbersome process, the additional document is critical to protecting the ethical principles embodied in the requirement for informed consent, acknowledging the tangible and valuable contribution made by specimen donors, and fostering access to biospecimens for research. The success of biobanks "depends upon ongoing public support, participation, and trust in the research endeavor" (Murphy et al. 2008, 41).

Note

Profound appreciation to Katherine Strong Carner for her excellent research assistance in the preparation of this manuscript and to Emily Sherman for her excellent citation checking. Support provided by Award Number RC1RR028876 from the National Center for Research Resources (NCRR). Author's views do not necessarily represent those of the NCRR, NIH, or Sidley Austin. The chapter title comes from Big Brother and the Holding Company, *Piece of My Heart*, on Cheap Thrills (Columbia Records 1968).

References

Beskow, L. M., and E. Dean. 2008. Informed consent for biorepositories: Assessing prospective participants' understanding and opinions. *Cancer Epidemiology, Biomarkers and Prevention* 17: 1440–51.

Bearder v. State, 806 N.W.2d 766 (Minn. 2011).

Bishop, G. F. 2005. *The Illusion of Public Opinion: Fact and Artifact in American Public Opinion Polls*. Lanham, MD.: Rowman and Littlefield.

Charo, R. A. 2006. Body of research—Ownership and use of human tissue. *New England Journal of Medicine* 355: 1517–19.

Code of Federal Regulations (CFR), Title 45, Pt. 46 (2009).

Code of Federal Regulations (CFR), Title 21, Pt. 50 (2012).

Department of Health and Human Services (DHHS). 2011. Advance Notice of Proposed Rulemaking. Human subjects research protections: Enhancing protections for research subjects and reducing burden, delay, and ambiguity for investigators. *Federal Register* 76 (143): 44512–31.

Doerr, A. 2010. Newborn blood spot litigation: 70 days to destroy 5+ million samples. *Genomics Law Report*, February 2. http://www.genomicslawreport.com/index.php/2010/02/02/ newborn-blood-spot-litigation-70-days-to-destroy-5-million-samples.

Drabiak-Syed, K. 2009. Newborn blood spot litigation continues in Minnesota and Texas. *PredictER News*, November 20. http://www.predicter.blogspot.com/2009/11/newborn-blood-spot-litigation-continues.html.

Food and Drug Administration (FDA). 2011. Draft Guidance on Exculpatory Language in Informed Consent. August 19. http://www.fda.gov/downloads/RegulatoryInformation/Guidances/UCM271036.pdf.

Greenberg v. Miami Children's Hospital, 264 F. Supp. 2d 1064 (S.D. Fla. 2003).

Harmon, A. 2010. Indian tribe wins fight to limit research of its DNA. *New York Times*, April 21: A1.

Hoeyer, K. 2010. Donors perceptions of consent to and feedback from biobank research: Time to acknowledge diversity? *Public Health Genomics* 13: 345–52.

Kaufman, D., J. Murphy-Bollinger, J. Scott, and K. Hudson. 2009. Public opinion about the importance of privacy in biobank research. *American Journal of Human Genetics* 85: 643–54.

Kaufman, D., J. Murphy, L. Erby, K. Hudson, and J. Scott. 2009. Veterans' attitudes regarding a database for genomic research. *Genetics in Medicine* 11: 329–37.

Lemke, A. A., C. Halverson, and L. F. Ross 2012. Biobank participation and returning research results: Perspectives from a deliberative engagement in south side Chicago. *American Journal of Medical Genetics* 158A: 1029–37.

Maschke, K. J. 2010. Wanted: Human biospecimens. *Hastings Center Report* 40: 21–23.

Melas, P. A., L. K. Sjöholm, T. Forsner, M. Edhborg, N. Juth, Y. Forsell, and C. Lavebratt. 2010. Examining the public refusal to consent to DNA biobanking: Empirical data from a Swedish population-based study. *Journal of Medical Ethics* 36: 93–98.

Minnesota Department of Health. 2012. Minnesota Department of Health to begin destroying newborn blood spots in order to comply with recent Minnesota Supreme Court ruling, January 31. http://www.health.state.mn.us/news/pressrel/2012/newborn013112.html.

Moore v. Regents of the Univ. of Calif., 793 P.2d 479 (Cal. 1990).

Murphy, J., J. Scott, D. Kaufman, G. Geller, L. LeRoy, and K. Hudson. 2008. Public expectations for return of results from large-cohort genetic research. *American Journal of Bioethics* 8: 36–43.

Murphy, J., J. Scott, D. Kaufman, G. Geller, L. LeRoy, and K. Hudson. 2009. Public perspectives on informed consent for biobanking. *American Journal of Public Health* 99: 2128–34.

Rao, R. 2007. Genes and spleens: Property, contract, or privacy rights in the human body? *Journal of Law, Medicine and Ethics* 35: 371–80.

Restatement (Third) of Property: Wills and Other Donative Transfers §6.1 cmt. a (2003).

Saha, K., and J. B. Hurlbut. 2011. Research ethics: Treat donors as partners in biobank research. *Nature* 478: 312–13.

Saunders, B. 2010. Normative consent and opt-out organ donation. *Journal of Medical Ethics* 36: 84–87.

Tex. Health & Safety Code 33.0021, 33.0111, 33.0112, 33.017 (2009).

Thornton, H. 2009. The UK Biobank Project: Trust and altruism are alive and well: A model for achieving public support for research using personal data. *International Journal of Surgery* 7: 501–02.

Treweek, S., A. Doney, and D. Leiman. 2009. Public attitudes to the storage of blood left over from routine general practice tests and its use in research. *Journal of Health Services Research and Policy* 14: 13–19.

Tupasela, A., S. Sihvo, K. Snell, P. Jallinoja, A. R. Aro, and E. Hemminki . 2010. Attitudes towards biomedical use of tissue sample collections, consent, and biobanks among Finns. *Scandinavian Journal of Health* 38: 46–52.

Vermeulen, E., M. K. Schmidt, N. K. Aaronson, M. Kuenen, M. J. Baas-Vrancken Peeters, H. van der Poel, S. Horenblas, H. Boot, V. J. Verwaal, A. Cats, and F. E. van Leeuwen . 2009. A trial of consent procedures for future research with clinically derived biological samples. *British Journal of Cancer* 101: 1505–12.

Washington University v. Catalona (Catalona II), 490 F.3d 667 (8th Cir. 2007), aff'g 437 F. Supp. 2d 985 (E.D. Mo. 2006) *(Catalona I)*.

Williams, S., J. Scott, J. Murphy, D. Kaufman, R. Borchelt, and K. Hudson. 2008. *The Genetic Town Hall: Public Opinion about Research on Genes, Environment, and Health.* Washington, DC: Genetics and Public Policy Center, Johns Hopkins University. http://www.pewtrusts.org/uploadedFiles/wwwpewtrustsorg/Reports/Genetics_and_Public_Policy/2009PCPTownHalls.pdf.

16

Reconsidering Privacy Protections for Human Research

Suzanne M. Rivera

The ANPRM shines a spotlight on privacy concerns related to human research by suggesting that new, additional protections are warranted to govern the use of existing data and specimens—even when individual identifiers have been removed. This focus on secondary uses of information and biological materials represents a departure from the current regulatory convention of treating de-identified data and specimens as posing little or no risk, on the premise that even highly stigmatizing information would need to be linked (or reasonably linkable) to the original subject in order to result in material harm.

At a time when billions of people routinely and willingly disclose personal information through social media, or in exchange for access to digital applications, the disproportionate concern about use of existing data and specimens requires further consideration. Attitudes about privacy are changing in ways that make some of the proposed new privacy provisions seem quaint and even illogical. Protecting the rights and welfare of research subjects requires consideration of risks in the context of everyday life. An overly cautious restriction on research uses of existing data and specimens is unnecessary and would slow the progress of beneficial research.

16.1 Existing Privacy Paradigms in US Research Regulation

As is detailed in greater depth in the other chapters in this volume, under the current regulations, local IRBs are authorized to permit the re-use of specimens or data without re-consenting the subjects/donors only when it is determined that such use would not pose more than minimal risk. The new privacy provisions of the ANPRM discussed below would undermine the authority of the local IRBs to make these determinations because all secondary uses would be treated as if they were inherently risky.

16.2 Privacy-Related Provisions Contained within the ANPRM Are Misguided

The ANPRM seeks to increase protections against informational risks because, "disclosure of illegal behavior, substance abuse, or chronic illness might jeopardize current or future employment, or cause emotional or social harm" (DHHS 2011, 44516). As the likelihood of harm resulting from the inappropriate use or disclosure of data (including information derived from specimens) is correlated with both the nature of the information and the degree of identifiability, the ANPRM suggests establishment of "mandatory standards for data security and information protection whenever data are collected, generated, stored, or used" (DHHS 2011, 44516). It also calls for additional restrictions, including:

- "general" written consent for research use of biospecimens, even those that have been stripped of identifiers;
- written consent for study of existing data, documents, records, and biospecimens, to include all secondary research use of identifiable data and biospecimens that have been collected for purposes other than the currently proposed research; and
- a prohibition against un-consented re-use of existing de-identified data if they were originally collected for research purposes (un-consented re-use of de-identified data collected for *non-research* purposes would still be permissible). (DHHS 2011, 44516, 44519)

These provisions to address informational risks, though well-intended, are problematic for several reasons. The misguided focus on secondary uses of data and specimens would make it more difficult to conduct important research, with no significant benefit to the people whose de-identified information or biomaterials are used.

16.2.1 Dignitary Harms Overemphasized

The concerns about re-use of de-identified research data or specimens that underlie the privacy provisions in the ANPRM are founded on a belief that there is something inherently wrong or unethical about re-use without consent—even when the researcher does not know to whom the data or specimens belong. This belief flows from a Kantian notion of autonomy that would characterize the use of an individual's personal information without his or her permission (even if de-identified) as a harm to dignity (Shell 2008). Such dignitary harms could be thought to include not only privacy violations but also "group stigmatization due to research findings, inability to control whether one's records will be used for objectionable purposes, and a lack of opportunity to share in profits acquired by data users" (Hoffman and Podgurski 2012, 89).

Although worthy of consideration, this approach disproportionately privileges the principle of respect for persons over other equally important principles for the ethical conduct of research, such as beneficence and justice (National Commission 1979). While respect for persons typically is interpreted to mean that an individual should be able to decide what happens with his or her data or specimens, beneficence suggests that uses of existing data and specimens should be maximized to derive the greatest amount of important knowledge possible. And justice requires a fair distribution of risks and benefits, encouraging broad participation in research across the population in exchange for information that will benefit everyone. In an ideal state, the three principles would achieve a balance, but in practice, they are always in tension with one another. Emphasis of one to the detriment of the other two can lead to undesirable unintended consequences.

16.2.2 General "Blanket" Consent Is Merely Notification

Despite apparent concerns about dignitary harms, the ANPRM proposes a flawed "general consent for future research" (DHHS 2011, 44523) to inform patients that their specimens are broadly available for use (and re-use) by researchers. This model sometimes is referred to as "blanket consent" because it would cover virtually anything a researcher might want to do, now or in the future. It is more of a notification procedure than true informed consent in the sense that individuals are not given sufficient information with which to make an informed decision. Although IRBs currently may waive consent for a given research project when they determine the potential for harm to subjects is low, they must consider the risks and benefits of each study before making the waiver decision. Blanket notices about future use of specimens would cut the need for ethical deliberation out of the process, allowing carte blanche access to all specimens and their associated data for virtually any research purpose—without the benefit of study-specific oversight by an IRB. Ironically, this would protect subjects less than the current paradigm, in which thoughtful review must occur before use of data or specimens can be authorized.

16.2.3 Secondary Use Distinctions Muddy the Waters

Another problem is the false dichotomy established in the ANPRM between data collected for research and data collected for non-research purposes:

a. If the data was originally collected for *non-research* purposes, then, as is currently the rule, written consent would only be required if the researcher obtains information that identifies the subjects. There would accordingly be no change in the current ability of researchers to conduct such research using de-identified data or a limited data set . . . without obtaining consent.
b. If the data was originally collected for *research* purposes, then consent would be required regardless of whether the researcher obtains identifiers. (DHHS 2011, 44519)

This would mean information willingly given by a subject to one researcher and then de-identified cannot be used again by another researcher without consent, but information not willingly given for research can be shared freely once de-identified. This distinction unnecessarily confuses the matter of whether we should be concerned about a violation of autonomy by foregoing consent, or a risk of harm from malevolent uses of the data. If the proposed prohibition against using de-identified data originally collected for research is based on concerns about autonomy, it should also apply to data collected outside of a research setting. And if the proposed prohibition is really based on concerns about informational risks, then the context within which the data were given is irrelevant.

Under the ANPRM proposal, the only way to re-use existing de-identified data originally collected in the context of a research study would be to re-identify it in order to obtain consent for using it in another study. This suggests it would be necessary to obtain signed informed consent documents from subjects whose identifiers were stripped from the data to be studied, which is not just impractical but defies logic. To de-identify a dataset means there is no reasonable way to discern from whom you would have to obtain consent for a secondary use. And if there were a way to re-identify the subjects (which is unlikely and perhaps impossible, see Clayton's discussion in chapter 12 of this book about the difficulty of re-identification), but it is not necessary to do so in order to answer the research question under study, then performing the re-identification solely for purposes of obtaining consent actually increases the risk to subjects by linking their data with identifying information.

16.2.4 HIPAA Standard as Default

As discussed in other chapters of this volume, the default data security provisions proposed in the ANPRM are based on the flawed Health Insurance Portability and Accountability Act (HIPAA) Privacy Rule, "Standards for Privacy of Individually Identifiable Health Information," 45 CFR 164. This rule established national standards for safeguarding "protected health information" (PHI), whether created, used, or shared for treatment or research. It limits the uses and disclosures that may be made of PHI without explicit and specific patient authorization (or waiver of such authorization), and provides a list of 18 data elements that are considered identifiers for purposes of determining whether or not health information is considered linked to an individual. As has been argued by others in this volume, using the HIPAA Privacy Rule as a standard for data security in all human research would be a tremendous mistake.

While a well-intentioned effort to protect patients' health information, the Privacy Rule requires a multitude of burdensome administrative procedures that duplicate existing IRB processes including, for example, the addition of an authorization procedure to the informed consent process already used in research (Kulynych and Korn 2003). Making matters worse, it is not clear that the additional steps required by the Privacy Rule improve patient privacy protection. Some argue that it actually harms patients by misleading them about the extent to which their data are confidential (Sobel 2007). Even the US Department of Health and Human Services Secretary's Advisory Committee on Human Research Protections has recommended that research be exempted from HIPAA Privacy Rule requirements, as originally was proposed when the Privacy Rule was under development (SACHRP 2008).

Application of the HIPAA Privacy Rule across the board would be especially harmful to human research conducted outside the health sciences. Although academic medical centers have found ways to manage their HIPAA obligations in the conduct of biomedical research, the application of these rules to all the other kinds of human research conducted under the Common Rule would not offer sufficient benefits for subjects to justify the additional burdens. Specifically, HIPAA's 18-point standard for identification is much more rigid and rigorous than the Common Rule's "readily ascertainable" standard, 45 CFR 46. If the ANPRM proposal to apply a HIPAA-like security protocol to all research data were adopted, researchers in the social and behavioral sciences, and in other fields like law and the arts, would be held to a privacy standard that was designed to safeguard patients' health information. The risks posed by re-use of existing data about educational techniques, for example, are not equivalent in their sensitivity to re-use of data about medical diagnoses, so the solution for protection need not be equivalent in scope or rigor.

16.3 Changing Social Norms about Self-disclosure and Privacy

The flaws of the ANPRM go beyond the misguided application of one standard for privacy protection (for human subjects) to another (for de-identified data). It also fails to recognize that the very meaning of privacy is changing. At the heart of the proposed new privacy provisions is a set of assumptions about what is (or should be) private.

Everyday life is full of opportunities to disclose information that would otherwise be private, including consumer polls, call-in radio talk shows, and public rallies to support or protest a cause, company, or candidate. This is the standard by which the Common Rule helps us to think about "minimal risk": something you would encounter in everyday life (and for which you do not ordinarily have to sign a consent form to do), 45 CFR 46.116(i).

Further, "everyday life" is an evolving standard. Boundaries between the private and the public are changing, in part due to technologies that enable more ways of sharing information. The Internet has created new avenues for moving formerly private information into a public sphere. Social media platforms (YouTube, Twitter, Facebook, etc.) make it possible for people to express themselves in words, and also to share photos, video, and even medical records (e.g., sonograms), in a virtual public space. Opinions are mixed about whether this is a curse or a blessing, but it would be a mistake to frame new research rules based on an outdated perception of reality.

Though critics assail applications like Facebook for invading users' privacy (McClurg 2011), it is not clear that users view the information they willingly place into a virtual public space as private. Numerous electronic applications ("apps"), available for free or at a price, deliver services and entertainment in exchange for personal information. For example, real-time traffic jams can be sent to your smartphone, but to get this service, your location must be tracked by the provider. The permission for location surveillance is given willingly in exchange for a perceived benefit. Similar apps alert users when ovulation is likely or when prescriptions are due for refills. All this voluntary self-disclosure of personal information (including health information) suggests that perceptions are changing about the nature of privacy itself.

These changing attitudes can be good for health care. Patients derive tangible benefits from sharing their information and by allowing their data to be stored in repositories. One emerging benefit is the advent of so-called personalized medicine, in which an individual's genetic makeup and health history can be taken into account for purposes of optimizing health care options. Although the term "personalized medicine" is used by scientists to describe pharmacogenomic testing to predict individual drug responses, the example most familiar to average consumers is the way your pharmacist can evaluate new prescriptions in light of past prescriptions or known allergies to evaluate the potential for adverse reactions.

Another health benefit to information sharing is the proliferation of online patient communities, which offer both the opportunity for social networking and access to information about treatment alternatives. These virtual spaces are changing the way people communicate and share information about their diseases and diagnoses. The PatientsLikeMe (PLM) online patient community provides a platform for patients who want to share their health information to create collective knowledge about disease, health, and treatments (Frost and Massagli 2008). According to Abril and Cava, these kinds of online health networks are "revolutionizing the way patients share their health information and personal experiences, learn about health conditions, add to the body of scientific data, and socialize with other patients" (2008, 245). These platforms do not merely add value for participants; they indirectly help others by aggregating information that can be mined by researchers for purposes of solving important scientific questions.

None of which is to say that inappropriate uses of private information should not be actionable under the law. Laws like HIPAA and the more recent Genetic Information Nondiscrimination Act of 2008 (GINA) were enacted precisely to address what Korn calls the "pragmatic concern" that misuse of health information could lead to "loss of health insurance, discrimination in employment and social stigmatization" (2000, 964). It is not necessary, via the ANPRM, to layer new restrictions on the use of de-identified data to protect against these concerns.

16.4 Information and Specimens as Property: Who Owns It?

Even if there were agreement that individuals can benefit from disclosing their own information (or donating specimens to a repository), whether for commerce, entertainment, or health care, one objection about secondary uses is that third parties could engage in uses that are objectionable to the donor/discloser and can even make a profit from the use of personal information in which the original owner/discloser does not share. But once individual identifiers are removed, whether from a medical record or a research record, is it still personal information? This is the point at which the ANPRM provisions regarding secondary use of de-identified data or specimens actually stretch our understanding of what a human subject is. By proposing to extend a right to control data or specimens that have been de-identified, the ANPRM would ascribe ownership (and moral status equivalent to a person) to information that has ceased to be personal. But de-identified data (including data derived from specimens) is not personal information anymore because there is no person.

Although people may feel possessive about information that describes them, data (including health information) cannot be owned unless specifically protected, for example, by intellectual property laws (Hall 2010). Correspondingly, in the few well-known legal cases related to property claims over research specimens, as discussed in chapter 15 of this volume by Javitt, the courts did not side with individuals who sought rights to control or profit from use of biological material that had been separated from their bodies, see *Moore v. Regents*; *Washington University v. William Catalona, MD*; and *Greenberg v. Miami Children's Hospital*.

16.5 Potential for Re-identification of De-identified Data

In addition to objections about third-party profiteering, a major concern about the secondary use of research data and specimens is fear that new technologies make (or will soon make) unauthorized re-identification of datasets and specimens possible. For example, Dr. Kathy Hudson of the National Institutes of Health was quoted by Andrew Pollack in a *New York Times* article about the ANPRM on July 24, 2011, as saying, "with modern DNA sequencing, biological specimens are 'inherently identifiable.'"

However, as is argued by Clayton in chapter 12 of this book there is no evidence that unauthorized re-identification by scientific researchers is a significant threat to research subjects' rights or welfare. The entire system of human research protections is based on the idea that researchers bound by the regulations will uphold them. A more reasonable answer to the problem of the hypothetical rogue scientist or malevolent third party is to enforce penalties for violating protocols and regulations, not a shift in the conceptual framework away from confidence in principles of honor and scientific integrity. As stated by the Presidential Commission for the Study of Bioethical Issues, "laws and regulations cannot do all the work necessary to provide sufficient privacy protections. . . . [I]ndividuals who receive such data have professional ethical obligations to protect the data that go beyond the limitations of the legal protections" (2012, 69).

Even if there were motive to try, experts are divided on the extent to which existing technologies and reference repositories make it possible for a researcher to readily ascertain the identity of an individual when the only link is a DNA sample or a de-identified data set. According to El Emam et al. (2006), when the existing heuristics for de-identification are followed, re-identification risks due to record linkage are low. Yakowitz and Barth-Jones similarly assert, "Data properly de-identified under the requirements of HIPAA are quite robust against re-identification attacks" (2011, 4). This means datasets and specimens de-identified per the current regulations would not be re-identifiable to the average scientist.

In contrast, Narayanan and Shmatikov assert that powerful re-identification algorithms render inadequate "the entire privacy protection paradigm based on 'de-identifying' the data" (2010, 26). Similarly Ohm argues that technology has made re-identification so easy that new laws are necessary to "protect all of us from imminent, significant harm" (2010, 1776).

The problem with making decisions about the risks of re-identification based on the findings of Narayanan and Shmatikov or Ohm is that they use as their examples sensational cases in which information technology experts or public policy activists deliberately set out to crack codes in order to uncover vulnerabilities in existing de-identification paradigms. It is noteworthy that these efforts are called "attacks." These examples do not help us to think rationally about research risks. Although a powerful pharmaceutical or insurance company might have the motive and resources to crack a code that an individual scientist would not have the skills or the desire to try, the intent of the Common Rule is to regulate the activities of federally funded researchers, not multinational corporations.

Of course, it is helpful to know where vulnerabilities exist so that they can be addressed. The use of digital media to store and transmit data makes inadvertent breaches possible even when there is no malevolent intent. Bad actors could theoretically buy or hack their way into data repositories that could be used with sophisticated algorithms to re-identify coded data. But, as Tene and Polonetsky assert, "if information that is not ostensibly about individuals comes under full remit of privacy laws based on a possibility of it being linked to an individual at some point in time through some conceivable method, no matter how unlikely to be used, many beneficial uses of data would be severely curtailed" (2012, 66). Rather than restricting the re-use of de-identified research data because of re-identification fears, the more prudent approach would be to reduce the ability to associate data or specimens with an identifiable individual to a reasonably small degree that would allow research to move forward without placing subjects at undue risk.

OHRP already has established that private information or specimens are individually identifiable when they can be linked to specific individuals by the investigator(s) either directly or indirectly through coding systems. Since the regulatory definition of "identifiable" includes the clarification that "the identity of the subject is or may readily be ascertained by the investigator or associated with the information" (45 CFR 46.102(f) (2)), it follows that a mere theoretical possibility of re-identification is not sufficient. The investigator would have to have access to means for re-identification (technology or know-how) and would have to be willing to violate an IRB-approved protocol and—depending on the nature of the data—the HIPAA Privacy Rule.

16.6 Conclusion

Existing regulations govern protection of human research subjects and regulate the use of their data and specimens. In cases where existing data or specimens have been de-identified (meaning researchers cannot readily identify the individuals from whom the data or specimens were obtained) the current rules are less restrictive because the risk to subjects is very small and the potential benefits to society justify the research use.

New rules have been proposed to increase privacy provisions in research because of concerns about informational risks. These new provisions are problematic for several reasons, the most important of which is that they will prevent important and beneficial research.

It is possible to overemphasize individual rights at the expense of group advantage. And it is not clear that privileging autonomy by requiring a "general consent" for future uses of biospecimens, or by prohibiting the un-consented re-use of de-identified data, would protect against the informational risks that are of concern. Disqualifying the use of de-identified data or specimens unless subjects are re-consented is not only illogical but will require collection of more data from more people than is necessary to answer important questions. As Weil et al. argue in chapter 14 of this volume, this is inefficient, a waste of existing resources, and unnecessarily exposes more people to the risk of harm.

Perceptions of privacy are changing in ways that should cause us to question whether our fears about research uses of data are antiquated or irrational. To the extent that vast numbers of people routinely place into the public sphere information that used to be considered personal, these new proposed rules seem out of step. Privacy and data protection are not obsolete concepts, but they must be "balanced against additional societal values such as public health, national security and law enforcement, environmental protection, and economic efficiency" (Tene and Polonetsky 2012, 67).

The use of existing records and specimens for the conduct of research is critical for improving health care and enhancing our understandings of non-biomedical phenomena. Rather than adding new roadblocks to important research that can improve the human condition, we should instead think about de-identified data and discardable specimens as a community asset to be used for the common good. This requires a shift away from protectionism. Instead, we should promote, through responsible stewardship, the importance of "information altruism" (Kohane and Altman 2005).

Self-disclosure is increasing and boundaries between the public and the private are dynamic and contextual. Since people routinely share information about themselves in multiple nonresearch venues, it is not rational to treat data collected or created in a research context differently from information disclosed via other forums. Overregulation imposed solely because of historical imperatives related to prior unethical acts is bad for science and can actually cause unintentional harms to society in the form of opportunity costs.

Note

The author thanks Jessica Berg, Sharona Hoffman, Michael Householder, Michelle McGowan, and Tracy Wilson-Holden for their very helpful input, and Erin Burk for her skilled research assistance.

References

Department of Health and Human Services (DHHS). 2011. Advance Notice of Proposed Rulemaking. Human subjects research protections: Enhancing protections for research subjects and reducing burden, delay, and ambiguity for investigators. *Federal Register* 76 (143): 44512–31.

Department of Health and Human Services. Presidential Commission for the Study of Bioethical Issues. 2012. *Privacy and Progress in Whole Genome Sequencing*. Washington, DC: GPO.

Department of Health and Human Services, Secretary's Advisory Committee on Human Research Protections (SACHRP). 2008. (SACHRP) October 27–28, 2008, meeting presentations. Accessed November 24, 2012. http://www.hhs.gov/ohrp/sachrp/mtgings/mtg10-08/present/carome.html.

El Emam, Khaled, S. Jabbouri, S. Sams, Y. Drouet, and M. Power. 2006. Evaluating common de-identification heuristics for personal health information. *Journal of Medical Internet Research* 8 (4): e28. Accessed November 24, 2012. http://www.jmir.org/2006/4/e28/.

Frost, Jeana, and Michael P. Massagli. 2008. Social uses of personal health information within PatientsLikeMe, an online patient community: What can happen when patients have access to one another's data. *Journal of Medical Internet Research* 10 (3): e15. http://www.jmir.org/2008/3/e15/ Accessed November 24, 2012.

Genetic Information Nondiscrimination Act (GINA) of 2008, Pub. L. No. 110–233, 122 Stat. 881.

Hall, Mark A. 2010. Property, privacy, and the pursuit of interconnected electronic medical records. *Iowa Law Review* 95: 631–63.

Health Insurance Portability and Accountability Act (HIPAA) Privacy Rule, 45 CFR §§160, 164.

Hoffman, Sharona, and Andy Podgurski. 2012. Balancing privacy, autonomy, and scientific needs in electronic health records research. *Southern Methodist University Law Review* 65 (1): 85–144.

Kohane, Isaac, and Russ Altman. 2005. Health-information altruists: A potentially critical resource. *New England Journal of Medicine* 353: 2074–77.

Korn, David. 2000. Medical information privacy and the conduct of biomedical research. *Academic Medicine* 75 (10): 963–68.

Kulynych, Jennifer, and David Korn. 2003. The new HIPAA (Health Insurance Portability and Accountability Act of 1996) Medical Privacy Rule: Help or hinderance for clinical research? *Circulation* 108: 912–14.

McClurg, Andrew J. 2011. Fixing the broken windows of online privacy through private ordering: A Facebook approach. *Wake Forest Law Review Forum*. Accessed April 15, 2012. http://dx.doi.org/10.2139/ssrn.1755170.

National Commission for the Protection of Human Subjects of Biomedical and Behavioral Research. 1979. *The Belmont Report: Ethical Principles and Guidelines for the Protection of Human Subjects of Research*. Washington, DC: GPO.

Narayanan, Arvind, and Vitaly Shmatikov. 2010. Myths and fallacies of "personally identifiable information." *Communications of the ACM* 53 (6): 24–26.

Ohm, Paul. 2010. Broken promises of privacy: Responding to the surprising failure of anonymization. *UCLA Law Review* 57: 1701–77.

Sanchez Abril, Patricia, and Anita Cava. 2008. Health privacy in a techno-social world: A cyber-patient's Bill of Rights. *Northwestern Journal of Technology and Intellectual Property* 6 (3): 244–77.

Shell, Susan M. 2008. Kant's concept of human dignity as a resource for bioethics. In *Human Dignity and Bioethics: Essays Commissioned by the President's Council on Bioethics*. Washington, DC: The President's Council on Bioethics. Accessed November 24, 2012. http://bioethics.georgetown.edu/pcbe/reports/human_dignity/chapter13.html.

Sobel, Richard. 2007. The HIPAA paradox: The privacy rule that's not. *Hastings Center Report* 37 (4): 40–50.

Tene, Omer, and Jules Polonetsky. 2012. Privacy in the age of big data: A time for big decisions. *Stanford Law Review Online* 64: 63–70.

Yakowitz, Jane, and Daniel Barth-Jones. 2011. The illusory privacy problem in *Sorrell v. IMS Health*. Accessed April 15, 2012. http://www.techpolicyinstitute.org/files/the%20illusory%20privacy%20problem%20in%20sorrell1.pdf.

17

In Search of Sound Policy on Nonconsensual Uses of Identifiable Health Data

Barbara J. Evans

Health data and biospecimens are crucial resources for twenty-first century biomedical discovery and health care system improvement (Institute of Medicine 2007, 128–30; Hakimian and Korn 2004, 2500; Institute of Medicine 2010, 1). Health care providers and payers hold large datasets that are potentially valuable as a scientific resource. An estimated 300 million biospecimens were stored in the United States as of 1999, and this inventory was thought to be growing at about 20 million per year (Eiseman and Haga 1999, xvii–xviii). Testing these stored specimens could yield a wealth of additional health-related data including genetic information.

Studies of previously collected data or biospecimens are sometimes called *information-based* research to distinguish them from studies that involve human subjects directly and personally (Institute of Medicine 2009, 7). The Common Rule protects people who participate directly in clinical and behavioral studies but also applies to some categories of purely informational research (National Commission 1978, 56175). The Common Rule's definition of human subject, 45 CFR 46.102(f), includes living individuals about whom an investigator obtains identifiable private information. Even if a person has no direct contact with biomedical researchers, the person may become a human subject if identifiable information flows to an investigator via a health record or biospecimen.

OHRP published guidances in 2004 and 2008 in an attempt to clarify how the Common Rule's informed consent requirements apply to informational research (DHHS 2008). Despite these efforts, the "current requirements for informed consent for future research with pre-existing data and biospecimens are confusing and consume substantial amounts of researchers' and IRBs' time and resources" (DHHS 2011, 44523). The ANPRM explored possible changes to the Common Rule's informed consent framework for informational research, but it was a preliminary, optional step in rulemaking, which is the process federal agencies employ to create or amend their regulations. The ANPRM offered no actual regulatory text for public comment and instead discussed broad directions for reform and sought public input on 74 questions.

The agency received well over a thousand comments, some of them detailed, and more than two years later still had not progressed to the next step of publishing proposed regulations for public comment. Delays are not uncommon in the context of a major rulemaking because initial approaches may lose momentum or need to be adjusted in response to public comments. Whatever the fate of this particular ANPRM, the Common Rule's framework of access to data and biospecimens is a likely target for reforms in coming years.

This chapter explores an important and neglected element of any successful modernization program: reform of the waiver provisions, 45 CFR §46.116(d), of the existing Common Rule. It then turns to a second question: What is the appropriate process for debating and deciding the policies to be embodied in the future Common Rule?

17.1 Nonconsensual Access to Data and Biospecimens for Use in Research

Surveys show that the public has misgivings about any nonconsensual (unconsented) use of patients' private health information, and these concerns are especially intense when identifiable information is involved (Institute of Medicine 2009, 66, 82). The Common Rule requires informed consent as its basic rule but offers a number of pathways for nonconsensual access to data and specimens. These pathways allow researchers to obtain de-identified, coded, and even identifiable data and biospecimens without informed consent.

17.1.1 Research Access under the Existing Common Rule
One access pathway is the exemption, 45 CFR 46.101(b)(4). This exemption allows nonconsensual research use of data and biospecimens that have been de-identified in the sense of having overt identifiers (e.g., names) removed. As Weil et al. discuss in chapter 14 of this volume, OHRP's 2008 guidance offered another important pathway that allows nonconsensual research access to data and biospecimens that have been coded (DHHS 2008). Coding is a process that masks identifying information but stops short of achieving a permanent, irrevocable de-identification (National Bioethics Advisory Commission 1999, 1; FDA 2008, 4–5;

Evans 2009, 318). Overt identifiers that associate a piece of data or a biospecimen with a particular individual are replaced by a code number, but re-identification is theoretically possible using a code key. The use of coded data and biospecimens in research offers various advantages, such as making it possible to update research findings to reflect subsequent clinical observations about the patients whose data and tissues are being studied. Another advantage is that coding preserves the potential to contact those patients in the event researchers discover incidental findings that would have clinical significance in their future medical care (Evans 2009, 317–19). The 2008 guidance allows researchers to use coded data and biospecimens without consent, provided that the researchers receive no access to the code key.

Consent waivers are another major access pathway in informational research. The Common Rule's waiver provisions 45 CFR (46.116(d)) allow IRBs to approve nonconsensual access to data and specimens. As Williams and Wolf explain in chapter 13 of this volume, an IRB must determine that the disclosure of information satisfies several criteria before approving a waiver. Notably, however, these criteria do not explicitly require de-identification or coding (45 CFR 46.116(d)). It would be possible for researchers to obtain identifiable information without consent pursuant to an IRB-approved waiver. In practice, many IRBs would hesitate to conclude that a disclosure of identifiable information meets the criterion that requires minimal risk, but the waiver provisions technically would allow them to do so (Evans 2009, 331).

17.1.2 The ANPRM Approach to Research Access
The ANPRM dedicated significant thought to research that uses de-identified data and biospecimens but scarcely touched on research that uses coded or identifiable health information. In the months leading up to the ANPRM, there had been a lively public debate about the potential to re-identify data and biospecimens shared in de-identified form (Ohm 2010, 1706; Rothstein 2010, 5) although, as Clayton and Rivera note in their chapters, the threat to privacy was at times overstated. The ANPRM proposed to address this problem by adding more stringent consent requirements for studies that use de-identified data and specimens under the exemption (45 CFR 46.101(b)(4) (DHHS 2011, 44518–21, 44527)).

In contrast, the ANPRM merely posed questions about the proper use of consent waivers but proposed no specific reforms (DHHS 2011, 44523–25). This was a serious omission because nonconsensual access to identifiable data and specimens is a pivotal issue in modern biomedicine. De-identified data and specimens have limited scientific utility, and many important scientific, public health, and health care system improvement studies require at least some access to identifiable health information (Evans 2011a, 90–92). As the US Food and Drug Administration noted in a recent report to Congress, "we have come to understand that there may be infrequent occurrences when de-identified datasets may be insufficient to meet the needs of medical product surveillance" (FDA 2011, 11). Epidemiologists also have pointed out that in research "using computer-stored prescription data linked with hospital data . . . it is necessary to have information on identifiers in order to link the data that permits the research to be done" (Weiss 2011, 4–5).

Two areas of difficulty are studies that require longitudinally linked health records and studies that correlate genetic and other diagnostic test results with clinical information. Longitudinal records allow patients' treatments and outcomes to be monitored on an ongoing basis across multiple encounters with the health care system. Linking genetic information from people's biospecimens with clinical data can reveal associations between specific genes and related medical conditions. The US health care system is notoriously fragmented and each individual's health information is widely scattered and stored in many different locations (Hall 2010, 640). Bringing data and biospecimens together to create useful linkages requires at least some access to identifiers to verify whether information received from various locations describes the same person. If data-holders de-identify their data and biospecimens before releasing them to researchers, these resources cannot then be linked back together to form longitudinal health records or specimens annotated with clinical information (Evans 2011a, 93–94).

To add another complication, selection bias (consent bias) is a problem in some research contexts (Institute of Medicine 2009, 209–14). As explained in the chapter by Weil et al., this bias exists when the subset of people who are willing to consent to research are unreflective of the general population scientists are seeking to study. Requiring informed consent may introduce biases that undermine the validity of certain types of scientific study. This problem explains the need for regulatory pathways that allow nonconsensual access to data and biospecimens in situations where the bias would be large enough to make a difference. The waiver provisions of the existing Common Rule purport to address this problem in the following way: they specify that waivers should be approved only when "the research could not practicably be carried out without the waiver" (45 CFR 46.116(d)). Unfortunately, OHRP has done little to clarify what this criterion implies in day-to-day practice.

The ANPRM offered no concrete proposal for improving the Common Rule's waiver criteria and, indeed, talk of amending the regulation seems premature when OHRP has made little effort over the years to clarify the regulation it already has. For example, OHRP could issue guidance instructing IRBs that they would be on safe ground concluding that "the research could not practicably be carried out" without a waiver if the research requires more than 500 health records (or 5,000, or 50,000— the point is to specify a concrete number at which OHRP is prepared to presume that obtaining consent is impracticable; see SACHRP 2008; Evans 2011b, 28). Through guidance, OHRP also could require researchers to make a showing of why it would bias their results to condition access to data on consent: for example, is the study examining a very rare event that might be missed if researchers study a partial data set that includes only consenting individuals (SACHRP 2008; Evans 2011b, 28)? As IRBs struggle with the present lack of clarity, the waiver provisions are criticized both for providing too much and too little data access.

17.2 The Inherent Defect in the Common Rule's Waiver Provisions

Historical factors help explain the modern discontent with the Common Rule's waiver provisions. Before the Common Rule existed, nonconsensual access to data and biospecimens was common in various public health contexts such as reporting of communicable diseases (Amoroso and Middaugh, 2003, 50; Gostin 2008, 4). It apparently also was quite common for researchers to use data and biospecimens without informed consent. In 1974 Congress created a National Commission for the Study of Ethical Problems in Medicine and Biomedicine (National Commission) to help develop the Common Rule, Pub. L. No. 93–348, 88 Stat. 342, 201–202. The National Commission discovered that many investigators surveyed in the 1970s believed consent was unnecessary when a "study was based exclusively upon existing records" (National Commission 1978, 56188).

The Common Rule bears the imprint of customary data-access practices that existed before the regulation came into force (Evans 2011a, 120). Its consent exceptions are historically contingent—in other words, they were shaped by historical accidents and are not necessarily grounded in clear principles that explain why certain uses of data, but not others, warrant nonconsensual access to data and biospecimens. The National

Commission attempted to enunciate such principles in its 1978 report on human subject protections (National Commission 1978, 56181). Unfortunately, as explained below, its recommendations were never properly implemented.

The National Commission incorporated findings of a separate Privacy Protection Study Commission that examined the use of data and biospecimens in research (National Commission 1978, 56181). This privacy study concluded that "medical records can legitimately be used for biomedical or epidemiological research without the individual's explicit authorization," but only if "the importance of the research or statistical purpose for which any use of disclosure is to be made is such as to warrant the risk to the individual from additional exposure of the record or information contained therein." (National Commission 1978, 56181). The National Commission called for an IRB to assure that such conditions are met before approving nonconsensual research uses of existing documents, records, or tissue specimens (National Commission 1978, 56181). The National Commission felt that consent is not needed "if the subjects are not identified or identifiable" (National Commission, 56181). Even in studies "where the subjects are identified, informed consent may be deemed unnecessary" as long as certain criteria are met (National Commission 1978, 56181). One of the recommended criteria was that an IRB should determine that "the importance of the research justifies such invasion of the subjects' privacy" (National Commission 1978, 56179).

The National Commission thus would allow nonconsensual use of identifiable data and biospecimens only when the use could be justified under utilitarian balancing principles. Later commentators have agreed that unconsented uses of data, if they can be justified at all, are justified only when they offer important public benefits (Casarett et al. 2005, 597; Jacobson 2002, 1497–99). The National Bioethics Advisory Commission recognized the need for nonconsensual data use in some circumstances, but only if an IRB determines that "the benefits from the knowledge to be gained from the research study outweigh any dignitary harm associated with not seeking informed consent" (National Bioethics Advisory Commission 2001, 103–104).

Given this wide agreement that nonconsensual access should be allowed only for studies that serve important public purposes, it is surprising that the Common Rule's waiver criteria do not require IRBs to weigh this factor before approving access to data and biospecimens. This omission reflects another accident of history. The waiver provisions (45 CFR 46.116(d)) first appeared in the Common Rule in 1981 (DHHS

1981, 8390). The regulatory record indicates that these provisions were designed for purposes that had nothing to do with health data and biospecimens. Instead, DHHS indicated that waivers were needed in connection with controlled experiments that study how beneficiaries of federal benefit programs, such as Medicare and Medicaid, modify their consumption of health care services in response to various program incentives (DHHS 1981, 8383; Evans 2011a, 122). The waiver provisions thus were never intended for use in approving nonconsensual access to data and biospecimens, and this fact explains why they lack the utilitarian balancing criterion that the National Commission and later bioethicists have recommended.

In the years after 1981 the waiver provisions were pressed into service for approving nonconsensual access to data and biospecimens. Unfortunately, their criteria were never updated to reflect this new application. The Common Rule's waiver criteria are inherently defective as applied to disclosures of identifiable data and biospecimens because they omit a key criterion that the National Commission and later bioethicists felt is crucial to ensure that such disclosures are ethically justified. As a result people whose data and biospecimens are used without consent have no legal assurance that their sacrifice will serve a socially beneficial purpose. Surveys reveal that members of the public are troubled by nonconsensual access to their data and that they care deeply how their data are used (Institute of Medicine 2009, 81–84). The Common Rule's waiver provisions are unworthy of public trust insofar as they allow nonconsensual access without insisting on a publicly beneficial use.

17.3 Directions for Waiver Reform

This defect cannot be repaired merely by inserting a new waiver criterion that requires IRBs to perform utilitarian balancing before approving a consent waiver. Utilitarian balancing is a fine principle, but it is devilishly hard to implement. When DHHS proposed the HIPAA Privacy Rule's waiver provisions a decade ago, the agency attempted to include such a criterion. The draft of the Privacy Rule's waiver provisions would have required IRBs to determine that "the research is of sufficient importance so as to outweigh the intrusion of the privacy of the individual whose information is subject to the disclosure" (DHHS 2000, 82698). This requirement received "a large number" of negative comments that cast grave doubts upon IRBs' competence to administer a utilitarian balancing test (ibid. at 82698). DHHS ultimately removed the nettlesome balancing requirement from the Privacy Rule's waiver provisions (DHHS 2002, 53270). The current HIPAA waiver provisions, like the Common Rule's waiver provisions, do not require IRBs to determine that the proposed research offers benefits commensurate with the burdens it places on nonconsenting individuals (45 CFR 164.512(i), 46.116(d)).

This defect will be difficult but not impossible to address. The US legal system regularly confronts difficult trade-offs between individual and public interests in the context of takings doctrine, which specifies when people's property can be taken without their consent for public uses such as highway construction, industrial development, and land reform. There, too, utilitarian balancing tests have proved difficult to administer and controversial (Evans 2011a, 79–82, 125). Courts and commentators have proposed a number of alternative approaches that may offer ideas for better managing nonconsensual data access. For example, a centralized, national oversight body may be the appropriate institution to decide which types of research offer sufficient public benefit to warrant nonconsensual access to data and biospecimens (Evans 2011a, 126). As local review bodies, IRBs may lack the global perspective required to make this determination. A list of presumptively beneficial data uses could be prepared and OHRP could issue guidance creating a safe harbor for IRBs that grant waivers in connection with the listed types of studies. A related concern is that IRBs, at least as they are constituted under the existing Common Rule, lack basic attributes of independence, legitimacy, and accountability that are necessary when making decisions that burden individual rights. When decisions require delicate trade-offs affecting individual rights, the public expects a level of transparency and independence that IRBs simply do not possess (Evans 2009, 331–32). OHRP could use guidance to create a safe harbor for waiver decisions that voluntarily follow a set of public-regarding procedural norms (Evans 2011b, 28).

Another approach would be to reject utilitarian balancing in favor of natural rights approaches employed in some nineteenth-century takings cases (Claeys 2003, 1577–89). These approaches have considerable resonance with modern, autonomy-based bioethical analysis and emphasize factors such as whether waivers that allow research access to large regionally or nationally scaled data networks offer mutually advantageous exchanges in which each data subject gives something to, but gets potential benefits from, the larger community of other data subjects (Evans 2011a, 127–29). The question is not whether research places *any* burden on the individual, but whether it places disproportionate (unfair) burdens on particular subgroups of individuals. The goal of research oversight would be to ensure strong baseline privacy and data security protections for all data subjects and to discourage data uses that force "some people alone to bear public burdens which, in all fairness and justice, should be borne by the public as a whole." *Armstrong v. United States*, 364 US 40, 49 (1960) (J. Harlan dissenting).

Another valuable insight from takings theory is that it is sometimes easier to enunciate criteria in the negative than in the positive (Evans 2011a, 127). Identifying data uses that *do not* serve a beneficial public purpose may be easier than describing all the data uses that *do*. It may be possible for bioethicists to describe attributes of research that *does not* warrant nonconsensual access to data and biospecimens, even if it will never be possible to specify all the various types of research that may be worthy of consent waivers. For example, ClinicalTrials.gov provides a medium where sponsors of clinical trials are encouraged to disclose information about their planned clinical research projects. There is no similar registry for health informational research that uses data and biospecimens. Perhaps there should be. If such a registry existed, a sponsor's refusal to register an informational research project might be seen as presumptive grounds for waiver denial. If sponsors are unwilling to disclose information about their planned uses of data or biospecimens, this sends a strong signal that the research is aimed at producing private gains rather than public benefits. Research that serves private purposes still would be allowed, but it would be ineligible for consent waivers and would require informed consent. It may be possible for bioethicists to develop a list of "red flags" to guide IRBs on when *not* to approve consent waivers. Such measures could boost the perceived legitimacy of the Common Rule's waiver provisions.

17.4 Need for an Appropriate, Inclusive Process for Establishing Policy

Modernizing the Common Rule's consent framework presents two distinct challenges. The first challenge is to identify sound substantive policy—when should the use of data and biospecimens require informed consent and what additional protections (e.g., data security requirements) should apply to informational research? The second challenge is to ensure an inclusive and legitimate process for debating and deciding policy on these matters. This second challenge is particularly important when stakeholders hold divergent views, as is true in the debate about informed consent and access to data and biospecimens.

The ANPRM presumed that OHRP can amend the Common Rule's informed consent requirements by means of informal rulemaking, the familiar process in which federal agencies publish proposed changes to their regulations, receive written comments from the public, and then develop final, amended regulations that will have the force of law (5 USC 553). Federal agencies often employ informal rulemaking when amending their existing regulations, but it is not an appropriate process if Congress has imposed different requirements in the statute that authorizes an agency to make and amend its regulations. OHRP's legal authority to establish and amend the Common Rule's informed consent requirements comes from an aging statute (42 USC 300v-1), which Congress enacted as part of the National Research Act of 1978 (1978 Act), Pub. L. No. 95–622, 92 Stat. 3412, Title III (1978).

The essence of the challenge DHHS faces today is that it is trying to adapt its regulations for the modern research context using authorities granted by an outdated statute. The 1978 Act imposed special procedures for rulemakings that establish the substantive bioethical requirements of the Common Rule, such as its informed consent provisions. The 1978 Act replaced the earlier National Commission with a new President's Commission for the Study of Ethical Problems in Medicine and Biomedical and Behavioral Research (President's Commission), Pub. L. No. 95–622, 92 Stat. 3412, 301; 42 USC 300v, 300v-1.

Congress delegated the task of developing recommendations concerning the Common Rule's informed consent policies to the President's Commission, rather than to the Secretary of DHHS. When Congress enacted the 1978 Act, Congress already had received and been favorably impressed by the recommendations that the National Commission published in 1978 (National Commission 1978; US Senate 1978, 17). Congress urged the President's Commission to avoid duplicative effort (42 USC 300v-1(a)(2)(3)). The President's Commission endorsed the National Commission's 1978 report, including the recommendations about nonconsensual access to data and biospecimens discussed earlier in this chapter (National Commission 1978, 56181).

Congress placed special constraints on DHHS's authority to establish the Common Rule's informed consent requirements (42 USC 300v-1(b)). This statute requires the Secretary of DHHS either to implement the commission's recommendations or else publish in the Federal Register a formal determination that the recommendations are not appropriate before rejecting them and implementing a different policy. Thus Congress's delegation of rulemaking authority to the Secretary of DHHS was subject to a requirement that the Secretary must relate substantive bioethical provisions of the Common Rule, such as its informed consent policies, to recommendations of the President's Commission. This statute is still in effect today.

The 1978 Act envisioned that the President's Commission would play an ongoing role in developing human subject protection policies. It was to report to the President, Congress, and federal agencies every two years and include a review of the adequacy of the existing regulations and recommend further legislation or rulemaking if needed (42 USC 300v-1(c)). Thus Congress envisioned that the President's Commission would determine when the Common Rule was out of date and recommend appropriate action to address the problem. The Secretary of DHHS's authority is framed in the statute as a power to make rules in response to such recommendations. Unfortunately, the President's Commission no longer exists, and subsequent bioethics advisory bodies have not had the legal status to fill its shoes (Evans 2013, 405–406). The statute does not spell out an alternative pathway for updating the substantive ethical requirements of the Common Rule in its absence.

Congress may have envisioned periodically re-authorizing a President's Commission to guide future policy development. Unfortunately, this plan fell apart late in the 1980s. Congress enacted legislation in 1985 to create a Biomedical Ethics Board that was to "study and report to Congress on a continuing basis on the ethical issues arising from . . . biomedical and behavioral research, including the protection of human subjects of such research," Pub. L. No. 99-158, 99 Stat. 820, 11 (1985). The Board "became politically deadlocked due to abortion politics, its appropriations were frozen, and finally its term expired in 1990" (Poland 1998, 12). As bioethical issues became politically divisive, Congress stopped authorizing bioethics commissions to aid in keeping the Common Rule up to date. This left DHHS with a defective statutory framework that lacks a functioning process for amending key provisions of the regulations, such as the Common Rule's consent provisions.

Without the President's Commission, it is genuinely debatable whether the Secretary of DHHS has legal authority to amend the Common Rule's informed consent provisions (Evans 2013, 403–409). Under the current statute the Secretary's rulemaking authority is triggered by recommendations from a commission that no longer exists. Into this gap the ANPRM presumed that DHHS has authority to update the Common Rule on its own, if there is no President's Commission to recommend that the agency do so. The statute does not clearly grant DHHS this authority (Evans

2013, 403–409). Before the Common Rule's waiver provisions can be fixed, Congress may need to act to clarify DHHS's rulemaking authority.

17.5 Conclusion

There is wide agreement that the Common Rule needs to be modernized for the environment of modern informational research. How to do so is the unanswered question. The search for sound policies on access to data and biospecimens is not just a normative bioethical inquiry. It also requires development of an open, inclusive, and legally sound process for debating and resolving the bioethical questions.

Note

This research was supported by the Greenwall Foundation and the University of Houston Law Foundation.

References

Amoroso, Paul J., and John P. Middaugh. 2003. Research vs. public health practice: When does a study require IRB review? *Preventive Medicine* 36: 250–53.

Casarett, David, Jason Karlawish, Elizabeth Andrews, and Arthur Caplan. 2005. Bioethical issues in pharmacoepidemiologic research. In Brian L. Strom, ed., *Pharmacoepidemiology*, 4th ed. Hoboken, NJ: Wiley, 587–98.

Claeys, Eric R. 2003. Takings, regulations, and natural property rights. *Cornell Law Review* 88: 1549–1671.

Department of Health and Human Services (DHHS). 1981. Final regulations amending basic HHS policy for the protection of human research subjects. *Federal Register* 46 (8): 366.

Department of Health and Human Services (DHHS). 2000. Standards for privacy of individually identifiable health information. *Federal Register* 65 (82): 462.

Department of Health and Human Services (DHHS). 2002. Standards for privacy of individually identifiable health information. *Federal Register* 67 (53): 182.

Department of Health and Human Services (DHHS). 2008. Guidance on Research Involving Coded Private Information or Biological Specimens. http://www.hhs.gov/ohrp/policy/cdebiol.html.

Department of Health and Human Services (DHHS). 2011. Advance Notice of Proposed Rulemaking. Human subjects research protections: Enhancing protections for research subjects and reducing burden, delay, and ambiguity for investigators. *Federal Register* 76 (143): 44512.

Eiseman, Elisa, and Susanne B. Haga. 1999. *Handbook of Human Tissue Resources: A National Resource of Human Tissue Samples*. Santa Monica, CA: RAND Science and Technology Policy Institute.

Evans, Barbara J. 2009. Ethical and privacy issues in pharmacogenomic research. In Howard L. McLeod, C. Lindsay DeVane, Susanne B. Haga, Julie A. Johnson, Daren L. Knoell, Jill M. Kolesar, Joseph D. McInerney, P. David Rogers, and Joseph R. Walker, eds., *Pharmacogenomics: Applications to Patient Care*, 2nd ed. Lenexa, KS: American College of Clinical Pharmacy, 313–38.

Evans, Barbara J. 2011a. Much ado about data ownership. *Harvard Journal of Law and Technology* 25 (1):69–130.

Evans, Barbara J. 2011b. Comments in docket HHS-OPHS-2011-0005; Human subjects research protections: Enhancing protections for research subjects and reducing burden, delay, and ambiguity for investigators. (October 25): 1–36.

Evans, Barbara J. 2013. Why the Common Rule is hard to amend. Symposium: Imagining the Next Quarter Century of Healthcare Law. *Indiana Health Law Review* 10 (2): 363–410.

Food and Drug Administration (FDA). 2008. Guidance for Industry. E15 definitions for genomic biomarkers, pharmacogenomics, pharmacogenetics, genomic data and sample coding categories (ICH, April). http://www.fda.gov/downloads/RegulatoryInformation/Guidances/ucm129296.pdf.

Food and Drug Administration (FDA). 2011. *Report to Congress: The Sentinel Initiative—A National Strategy for Monitoring Medical Product Safety* (August 19). http://www.fda.gov/downloads/Safety/FDAsSentinelInitiative/UCM274548.pdf.

Gostin, Lawrence O. 2008. *Public Health Law*, 2nd ed. Berkeley: University of California Press.

Hakimian, Rina, and David Korn. 2004. Ownership and use of tissue specimens for research. *Journal of the American Medical Association* 292 (20): 2500–2505.

Hall, Mark. 2010. Property, privacy, and the pursuit of interconnected electronic medical records. *Iowa Law Review* 95: 631–63.

Institute of Medicine, Roundtable on Evidence-Based Medicine. 2007. *The Learning Healthcare System: Workshop Summary*. Washington, DC: National Academies Press.

Institute of Medicine, Committee on Health Research and the Privacy of Health Information. 2009. *Beyond the HIPAA Privacy Rule: Enhancing Privacy, Improving Health through Research*. Washington, DC: National Academies Press.

Institute of Medicine, Roundtable on Evidence-Based Medicine. 2010. *Clinical Data as the Basic Staple of Health Learning: Creating and Protecting a Public Good: Workshop Summary*. Washington, DC: National Academies Press.

Jacobson, Peter D. 2002. Medical records and HIPAA: Is it too late to protect privacy? *Minnesota Law Review* 86: 1497–1514.

National Bioethics Advisory Commission. 1999. *Research Involving Human Biological Materials: Ethical Issues and Policy Guidance*, vol. 1. Washington, DC: GPO.

National Bioethics Advisory Commission. 2001. *Ethical and Policy Issues in Research Involving Human Participants*, vol. 1. Washington, DC: GPO.

National Commission for the Protection of Human Subjects of Biomedical and Behavioral Research. 1978. Protection of human subjects: Institutional review boards. National Research Act of 1978 (1978 Act), Pub. L. No. 95–622, 92 Stat. 3412, Title III (1978). *Federal Register* 43 (231): 56–174.

Ohm, Paul. 2010. Broken promises of privacy: Responding to the surprising failure of anonymization. *UCLA Law Review* 57: 1701–77.

Poland, Susan Cartier. 1998. Bioethics commissions: Town meetings with a "blue, blue ribbon." *Kennedy Institute of Ethics Journal* 8 (1): 91–109.

Rothstein, Mark A. 2010. Is deidentification sufficient to protect health privacy in research? *American Journal of Bioethics* 10 (9): 3–11.

Secretary's Advisory Committee on Human Research Protections (SACHRP). 2008. SACHRP Letter to HHS Secretary (January 31). http://www.dhhs.gov/ohrp/sachrp/sachrpletter013108.html.

US Senate. 1978. S. Rep. No. 95–852. President's Commission for the Protection of Human Subjects of Biomedical and Behavioral Research Act of 1978.

Weiss, Stanley H. 2011. Letter dated October 26 from Chair, Joint Policy Committee of the Societies of Epidemiology, to Jerry Menikoff, Director, Office for Human Subject Protections, 4–5. http://www.regulations.gov (referencing document ID: HHS-OPHS-2011–0005–1066).

V
Paradigm Shifts in Research Ethics

Introduction to Part V—Paradigm Shifts in Research Ethics

I. Glenn Cohen

In his novel, *G*, John Berger writes, in what might be thought of as the mantra of our current era, that "never again will a single story be told as though it's the only one" (Berger 1972, 129). In a similar vein, in this part focused on paradigm shifts, each of the chapters seeks to radically reconfigure and reconceive of the US regulatory framework applicable to human subjects research, or in one case, to resist just such a move. Echoing the attitudes of many writing in this section of the book, Greg Koski throws down the gauntlet: "Reform is no longer a reasonable or appropriate goal. As has been said before, we cannot continue to do things essentially the same way, based on the same flawed assumptions and expect to have a different outcome. A complete redesign of the approach, a disruptive transformation, is necessary and long overdue."

In her chapter, Michelle Meyer focuses on several levels of heterogeneity in human subjects research that render the current paradigm problematic. One stems from having a common regulatory framework that governs radically different types of research—from phase I drug trials to anthropological interviewing. Another, and what she suggests to be the deeper problem, is heterogeneity among research participants within a single protocol. These divergences pertain both to a subject's probability of risk versus benefit and to the way in which subjects would *weigh* those risks and benefits in making decisions. Meyer would counsel a radical departure from the existing regulatory framework; for "proposed research involving competent adults, IRBs would continue to prospectively review information disclosure and ensure risk minimization, but they would cede the time-consuming and hopelessly subjective task of risk–benefit analysis to individual prospective participants. Each prospective participant would make an individualized decision about whether participation would be 'reasonable'—not in the abstract, but *for her*."

Zachary Schrag attacks the existing US regulatory framework applicable to human subjects research from a different but very much *simpatico* angle. Schrag is concerned by what might be termed "IRB creep," the way in which IRBs seem to claim jurisdiction over increasing swaths of research. His chapter represents a masterful discussion of how we got from the pre–Belmont Report era of research ethics in the United States to the Belmont Report in 1978 to the current day, and identifies what he sees as some key wrong turns. In particular, he focuses on the extremely wide scope of research that was covered by the statutory and regulatory language, and more specifically, on the problematic notions of "generalizability" and of "subject." Schrag counsels limiting the type of research covered by the framework by restricting regulatory coverage to "biomedical and behavioral research" and redefining subjects as those who could not defend themselves against investigators. More abstractly, he proposes that we reimagine the framework as having at its core the following proposition: "the idea that the right of the people to choose and oversee their government outweighs the personal rights and welfare of public officials to some degree."

Heidi Li Feldman, by contrast, partially parts ways from Schrag and Meyer on what to make of the significance of the heterogeneity of types of research covered by the US regulations. She argues that "whatever the merits of the claim that qualitative research involves fundamentally different epistemologies than quantitative research does, it does not follow that a different way of knowing necessarily, or even probably, changes the ethical threats to human research subjects." The reason, she says, is that the "major ethical threat addressed by the Common Rule is compromise of a human research subject's autonomy" and that threat is common to all of these various forms of research. She grounds this understanding in a thoughtful examination of "The Doctor's Trial" at Nuremberg and examines how "obfuscation of the separateness of persons and the ethical significance of that fact can arise in settings as apparently different as ethnography and biomedical self-experimentation."

Holly Fernandez Lynch suggests that a fruitful starting point for rethinking the US regulatory framework applicable to human subjects research is the set of laws governing the workplace and employment relationships. She notes the ways in which current human subjects research protections are deficient compared to those given to certain American workers, and yet the same rationales that justify various worker protections seem to apply to human subjects. While offering a nuanced recognition of the ways in which workers and subjects may be different, she nonetheless argues for three areas of reform patterned on employment and labor law: relaxing limitations on remuneration for human subjects, providing compensation for injuries sustained during research, and augmenting the "voice" of subjects in governance decisions with some inspiration from labor law.

Finally, Greg Koski, himself the first director of the Office for Human Research Protections, like Schrag, suggests that the current framework is based on a false starting point, in his case the assumption "that left to their own judgment and without constant oversight, scientists will do harm to their human subjects—essentially, we are taking the position that scientists are somehow irresponsible, bad people." Drawing a compelling analogy between the current framework and that which governs the screening done at airports to thwart acts of terrorism, Koski writes that "[i]f either the TSA security system or the 'human subject protection system' were subjected to a thorough, rigorous analysis of their effectiveness as preventive programs, they would almost surely be abandoned on the ground that they are simply not cost effective." He argues instead for a framework that mirrors that of medicine—to assume physicians are caring, well-trained, and care for their patients, and to rely on education, specialty training, professional certification, peer-review, and the potential for malpractice liability or professional censure to do the work.

I want to press the arguments offered by these authors in three directions. First, I want to suggest that there is a significant distributive element to regulatory rethinking along any of the lines they have in mind. Adopting a more research methods-specific regulatory structure will redistribute the regulatory burden in interesting ways. While the through line of many of these chapters is that fields like anthropology and psychology are *over*regulated, it is possible that severing them off from medical experimentation in terms of the oversight framework will cause us to see that the current framework *under*regulates medical research. Another way of putting this point is that adopting fewer transubstantive rules in this area is not the same as reducing regulatory burden, and in some cases that might increase it.

Second, one might suggest that there are at least four forms of heterogeneity at work here. The first is categorical, the heterogeneity of different kinds of research. The second is the heterogeneity as to the size of risks and benefits to various potential research subjects. The third is heterogeneity as to their risk tolerance and weighing of potential benefit and harm. All these are recognized by Meyer, and less directly by others in their chapters. However, to this we might add a fourth form of heterogeneity prompted by some of Feldman's comments in her chapter—heterogeneity as to capacity for authentic autonomous decision making. Instead of, for example, writing consent forms at a low grade school level, perhaps what we need is to scale the consent process to the level of the actual potential participant in the study. Not all subjects understand or misunderstand probabilities to the same extent, so should those differences factor into who we allow to participate and in what contexts? The same might be true as to what kinds of compensation is viewed as undue inducement, if one subscribes to that notion as an ethical problem for research; what may count as undue inducement for those high up on the SES distribution looks quite different from that which counts for those low down. Again, the result would not be a categorical scaling up or scaling down of protections, but instead a participant-specific objection. To be clear, there are serious risks with that kind of approach as well—the cost and training necessary to do participant-specific evaluations, the risk of stereotyping potential participants, the risk that such participant-specific evaluations will introduce selection bias into study designs, that is, risk treating similarly situated people differently, but this seems at least worth discussing.

Finally, each of these authors sketches their preferred paradigm shift for human subjects research as though they had the chance to start over. But, to mix metaphors, writing on a *tabla rasa* is quite different from trying to turn a large ship hurtling toward its destination. There is a huge medico-industrial complex that supports and benefits from the current paradigms in human subjects research that would resist many of these changes. Moreover there is a set of understandably risk-averse governmental officers who do not want to be known as the ones who let "the next Tuskegee" happen. How does one get their buy-in for these kinds of major changes? Are there incremental paths forward toward changing the paradigm, or is that a contradiction in terms? How do politics and paradigms mix?

References

Berger, John. 1972. *G: A Novel*. London: Weidenfeld and Nicolson.

18

What Is This Thing Called Research?

Zachary M. Schrag

Few people believe that IRBs should review every activity conceivably regarded as human subjects research. Some forms of investigation are so unlikely to harm participants that reviewing them is a waste of time and money that could be better spent scrutinizing riskier activities. And, many argue, review boards should not intrude on relationships that our society holds sacred, such as doctor–patient, teacher–student, reader–book, and citizen–government.

Agreeing that not all interactions and investigations should require advance approval is easier than agreeing on where to draw the line. In 1978 Albert Jonsen—a member of the National Commission for the Protection of Human Subjects of Biomedical and Behavioral Research—expressed this problem well when he said of a draft of the Belmont Report that "[t]here is nothing in here that tells us why we are about to make a great big step which we have made from the beginning. Namely, why ought the thing that we are calling research be subject to what we call review?" (National Commission for the Protection of Human Subjects of Biomedical and Behavioral Research 1978a, II–40). Nearly half a century since the first federal requirements for IRB review, that question remains unanswered.

The ANPRM makes only a gesture at this crucial problem, asking, in question 25, if there are "certain fields of study whose usual methods of inquiry were not intended to or should not be covered by the Common Rule . . . because they do not create generalizable knowledge and may be more appropriately covered by ethical codes that differ from the ethical principles embodied in the Common Rule" (DHHS 2011, 44521). But the generalizability of knowledge is only one of several criteria that have been advanced to distinguish research that should and should not be covered by regulations. It is also the least helpful. Limiting IRB jurisdiction to "biomedical and behavioral research" (the language of the federal statute governing IRBs) or to a more limited definition of "subjects" could prove more fruitful.[1]

18.1 Biomedical and Behavioral

Often overlooked in the discussion of the proper scope of the *regulations* governing human subjects research is the fact that they are at least partially based on a statute (42 USC 289) that does not claim to govern all human subjects research but rather "biomedical and behavioral research involving human subjects." Considering congressional intent would yield a narrower understanding of what kind of research should be regulated, and might exclude the work of journalists, historians, and even many social scientists who often interact with people to learn things without imagining themselves to be conducting biomedical and behavioral research.

From 1966 onward, Congress emphasized its concern with "biomedical research" (or "health science") though congresspeople and senators tossed in *behavioral* and *social* just frequently enough to confuse anyone trying to understand the scope of congressional intent. As Congress intensified its interest in 1973, the Department of Health, Education, and Welfare (DHEW) objected to proposed bills as both too narrow and too broad. Too narrow, in that they—unlike DHEW policy—would not cover "certain service programs where it has been determined that the protection of human subjects is needed, such as the hospital improvement programs of the Social and Rehabilitation Service." Too broad, in that a House bill "fails to take into consideration . . . low-risk, high-benefit behavioral research. It applies inflexible standards to every situation in which human subjects are involved in experimentation, both medical and behavioral. It would, in fact, require the participation of physicians in types of behavioral research outside of their purview" Similarly ethicist Robert Veatch noted that the House bill gave the proposed National Commission jurisdiction over "behavioral research," a term that—he argued—could mean either "research in behaviorist psychology" or "any research designed to study human behavior including all social scientific investigation." He warned that "[t]o leave such ambiguity would be a tragedy" (US Congress 1973, 125–27, 240).

Congress ignored the warning. In 1974 it passed the National Research Act that used the terms "biomedical and behavioral research" to define agency and institutional eligibility for training funds, to establish a National Commission for the Protection of Human Subjects of

Biomedical and Behavioral Research, and as part of a requirement that each institution receiving DHEW funds establish an IRB. Yet it left observers guessing about what exactly was meant by "biomedical and behavioral research" (Schrag 2010, 38–40).

Nor was the confusion addressed at the regulatory level, since DHEW issued 45 CFR 46 on May 30, 1974, weeks before the National Research Act was signed into law. The department rejected suggestions that it differentiate "biomedical risks from behavioral risks," and instead wrote regulations "applicable to all Department of Health, Education, and Welfare grants and contracts supporting research, development, and related activities in which human subjects are involved." Thus the scope of the regulation differed from the scope of the statute (DHEW, Office of the Secretary 1974).

The ambiguity of the rules became a matter of legal significance in 1976, when a federal judge found that DHEW Secretary David Mathews had failed to comply with the new regulations when he approved a plan to test the effect of a copayment requirement on Medicaid use. The court noted that the regulations' "language is broad and general, and the provisions themselves do not define the critical terminology—neither 'grants and contracts supporting research, development, and related activities' nor 'human subjects' is defined." The court also rejected the state of Georgia's claim that the regulations should only apply to "biomedical and behavioral research projects involving human subjects which fall under the Public Health Service Act," since only such projects were governed by the new statute. Instead, the court held that "the regulations have been promulgated pursuant to the Secretary's broad rulemaking authority, rather than pursuant to any express terms of a specific statutory mandate," *Crane v. Mathews*, 417 F. supp. 532, 545 (N.D. Ga. 1976).

Two weeks later, Mathews attempted to limit the scope of the regulations, claiming that 45 CFR 46 was designed to apply to "the areas of concern which were addressed in the legislative hearings" leading up to the National Research Act, specifically:

the use of FDA-approved drugs for any unapproved purpose; psycho-surgery and other techniques for behavior control currently being developed in research centers across the nation; use of experimental intrauterine devises; biomedical research in prison systems and the effect of that research on the prison social structure; the Tuskegee Syphilis Study; the development of special procedures for the use of incompetents or prisoners in biomedical research; and experimentation with fetuses, pregnant women, and human in vitro fertilization. (DHEW 1976)

The Georgia state IRB, which had been handed the proposal, was unimpressed by this reasoning. Just nine days after the Secretary's notice appeared, it held that the risks to the Medicaid recipients outweighed the potential benefits of the experiments, and the project ended (Mullen 1976, 260).

Since the failure of these two arguments—Georgia's emphasis on the statute and DHEW's emphasis on the hearings—at the district court level, few participants in the IRB debate have noted the disjuncture between statute and regulations. The ANPRM, for example, uses the term "biomedical and behavioral research" only in its background section, and the rest of the document assumes that DHHS has authority to regulate "social and behavioral research."

Yet those who believe that Congress, rather than the executive branch, holds the legislative power, and that policies should be based on evidence of the sort gathered in the 1973 hearings, may wish that the regulations could be restricted to the language and history of the statute. The same may be true of such textualists as Antonin Scalia who, as a new member of the University of Chicago IRB in the 1970s, wrote that he was "disturbed by the authority I find myself and my colleagues wielding over the most innocuous sorts of intellectual inquiry" (Scalia 1980). In its response to the ANPRM, the American Anthropological Association called for the "delimiting [of] the regulatory object more specifically as 'human experimentation' and/or 'biomedical procedures'" (American Anthropological Association 2011, 1). Though the anthropologists did not cite the statutory language, their proposal would return human subjects regulation to the very areas of concerned identified by Congress and highlighted by Mathews in his interpretation.

18.2 Generalizability

Even as the Medicaid case was being decided using the existing regulations, the National Commission established by Congress in 1974 was considering a wholesale revision of those rules. Since the statute defined neither "research" nor "human subjects," defining those terms was up to the Commission.

The clearest guidance it received from Congress was to ensure that IRBs would not interfere with doctors' daily work. Fearing that the Commission would intrude on "the ordinary practice of medicine," the Association of American Medical Colleges had secured a provision in the final law requiring the Commission to consider "the boundaries between biomedical or behavioral research involving human subjects and the accepted and routine practice of medicine" (US Congress 1973, 204).

In an effort to heed this instruction, the National Commission searched for the proper language. In February 1976 the Commission staff suggested that

> Biomedical and behavioral research involving human subjects refers to a class of activities designed to develop or contribute to generalizable knowledge. By generalizable knowledge, we mean theories, principles, or relationships, or the accumulation of data on which they may be based, that can be corroborated by accepted scientific observation and inferences . . . . By contrast, the practice of medicine or behavioral therapy refers to a class of activities designed solely to enhance the well being of an individual. (National Commission for the Protection of Human Subjects of Biomedical and Behavioral Research 1976, 317–18)

This definition would, the Commissioners hoped, allow doctors to do their work without constantly seeking permission from an IRB (317–23).

The Commission had a harder time deciding what kind of research *should* trigger IRB review. Some emphasized medicine and other therapy. For example, one consultant recommended that

> [b]iomedical or behavioral research involving human subjects should be defined as well-designed and critical investigations of therapeutic techniques with unknown efficacy and/or risks or an attempt to find the etiology of a disease having for its aim the discovery of new facts associated with the 'accepted and routine practice of medicine' with the ultimate goal of providing beneficial effects for human subjects. (Gallant 1976, 13–14)

But in June 1975 the Commissioners decided that they wished to include "social research," though they did not define that term (National Commission for the Protection of Human Subjects of Biomedical and Behavioral Research 1975, 236).

Eventually the Commission included definitions in two key official reports. In its *Report and Recommendations: Institutional Review Boards*, issued on 1 September 1978, the Commission defined "Scientific research" as "a formal investigation designed to develop or contribute to generalizable knowledge" and "human subject" as "a person about whom an investigator (professional or student) conducting scientific research obtains (1) data through intervention or interaction with the person, or (2) identifiable private information." The report also explained that "A research project generally is described in a protocol that sets forth explicit objectives and formal procedures designed to reach those objectives" (National Commission for the Protection of Human Subjects of Biomedical and Behavioral Research 1978b).

Four weeks later, the Commission issued its most famous document, *The Belmont Report: Ethical Principles and Guidelines for the Protection of Human Subjects of Research*. This document defined "research" as "an activity designed to test a hypothesis, permit conclusions to be drawn, and thereby to develop or contribute to generalizable knowledge (expressed, for example, in theories, principles, and statements of relationships). Research is usually described in a formal protocol that sets forth an objective and a set of procedures designed to reach that objective" (National Commission for the Protection of Human Subjects of Biomedical and Behavioral Research 1978c).

The differences are noteworthy. First, Belmont used the terms "subject" or "subjects" more than seventy times without defining them. Second, it offered more qualifiers for "research": an activity would—it seems—need a hypothesis and conclusions to count as research. By contrast, the IRB report notes that "[n]ot all research is intended to provide a definitive test of a hypothesis . . ." (National Commission for the Protection of Human Subjects of Biomedical and Behavioral Research 1978b, 22).

In hindsight, it is surprising that the Commission spent so little time and care on terms that would have such significance. As Tom Beauchamp and Yashar Saghai recently noted, "the criterion of generalizable knowledge, once articulated, did not generate any substantial debate among Commissioners as to its meaning or its ultimate adequacy with regard to various types of learning activities. The notion was not then, and has never since been, carefully analyzed in Commission deliberations, in federal regulations, or in the bioethics literature" (Beauchamp and Saghai 2012, 52).

The significance of these shaky definitions only emerged in the mid-1990s, after federal enforcement efforts led universities and hospitals to become much stricter in their oversight of all forms of research. Searching for a way to avoid review of projects not explicitly exempted by the regulations, regulators and researchers alike seized on the idea of nongeneralizability as a safety valve. Thus, in 1999, a group of federal officials unofficially advised that *research* was that which had "the definite purpose of contributing to generalizable knowledge" and therefore

generally does not include such operational activities as: medical care, quality assurance, quality improvement, certain aspects of public health practice such as routine outbreak investigations and disease monitoring, program evaluation, fiscal or program audits, journalism, history, biography, philosophy, "fact-finding" inquiries such as criminal, civil and congressional investigations, intelligence gathering, and simple data collection or data collection for other purposes. (Shelton 1999, 6)

This is *exaptation*: using a structure for a purpose for which it was not originally designed. What is most striking about this proposal is just how much work the officials hoped a single word—generalizable—could do, and needed to do. It would, they hoped, protect the public health by allowing epidemiologists to track diseases, defend the First Amendment by freeing journalists from IRBs' grasp, defend the nation by allowing unfettered spying, all while letting historians explore the past and philosophers ponder deep truths.

In practice, nongeneralizability proved an uncertain path to freedom. For example, in 2003, OHRP endorsed the idea that a project is generalizable if it is designed to "draw conclusions, *inform policy*, or generalize findings" (Carome 2003; emphasis added). Yet when asked why OHRP chose not to submit the ANPRM (which secured the opinions of hundreds of respondents), another OHRP official explained that "The ANPRM is an administrative procedure to *inform policy*; it is not a systematic investigation and neither is it designed to develop or contribute to generalizable knowledge" (Yoder 2012; emphasis added). In other words, a project that seeks to inform policy either does or does not constitute human subjects research, depending on the whim of regulators. Similarly, as one observer noted of debates about whether quality improvement (QI) projects require IRB review, "Depending on the interpretation of specific words in the research definition—especially 'generalizable'—nearly all QI activities could also be considered research, or only a few" (Baily 2008, 149).

Tom Beauchamp—one of the drafters of the Belmont Report—concurs, noting that because the regulation "does not define any of the several important terms (the key conceptual conditions) used in the definition, such as 'systematic investigation,' 'testing' and 'generalizable knowledge,' . . . these terms can be understood in several ways" (Beauchamp 2011, 384). Contributors to this book agree. Rosamond Rhodes notes that "all knowledge is generalizable," while Michelle Meyer describes the generalizability standard as "necessarily vague."

Nor is nongeneralizability a pleasant route. Having their work declared not to be research exposes historians to both derision and, perhaps, the denial of research funding (Townsend 2011). The Social and Behavioral Science White Paper, a comment on the ANPRM submitted by twenty-two research organizations, finds that distinguishing generalizable from nongeneralizable research "can be a rather insulting task" (American Educational Research Association et al. 2011, 27).

The American Anthropological Association most forcefully denounced the generalizability standard in its comment on the ANPRM, arguing that "[i]f our concern is to identify 'risks' to human research participants, then generalizable/not-generalizable is not a useful diagnostic for distinguishing reviewable from not-reviewable research" (American Anthropological Association 2011). The current regulations, it notes, cannot explain why a harmless question posed to many people deserves more oversight than a devastating question posed to an individual.

The concept of generalizability has helped some teachers and researchers—and a great many doctors—go about their work without having to seek permission. Several leading research universities have deregulated oral history on these grounds, with at least quasi-official sanction. Though critics mock claims of nongeneralizability as indicating a lack of understanding of the regulations (Seligson 2008), such claims can in fact often indicate expertise, just as the knowledge of obscure deductions is the stock in trade of a tax advisor. But generalizability is at best a proxy for other concerns that would be better addressed directly.

18.3 Subjects

If research is to be defined broadly, perhaps "human subjects" could be defined narrowly. The National Commission explored this possibility at its July 1977 meeting, in a discussion that came the closest—though not very close—to a thorough consideration of what kinds of activities merited oversight. The Commissioners pondered cases that most or all of them agreed should not fall under the requirement for IRB review: studies of public documents and anonymous statistics, studies of blood or urine that could not be traced back to its creator, and—though this is less clear—actions within people's scope of employment, such as a change of routine for hospital staff. They wanted to avoid an IRB requirement for research that was not risky, and for research that did not involve the direct interaction with an individual (National Commission for the Protection of Human Subjects of Biomedical and Behavioral Research 1977, 124–60). But they realized that these lines were hard to draw. As Commissioner Robert Cooke posed the riddle, "If you started out in New York harbor to study the flora of New York harbor and you worked back up through the sewage system, back up and back up and finally you get to the source of the e. coli, when does it become human research?" (National Commission for the Protection of Human Subjects of Biomedical and Behavioral Research 1977, 146). Similarly Cooke argued against defining "subject" to mean anyone potentially affected by research "because that would include the world" (143).

Commissioner Albert Jonsen, offered a narrower alternative:

A subject is one who falls within the power of an investigator such as that person's life, health, well-being, reputation, dot, dot, dot, whatever other qualities we consider important can be adversely affected and who cannot, for some reason, defend themselves. (132)

Neither Jonsen's fellow Commissioners nor the staff was enthusiastic about his proposal. Eventually, they settled on a much broader definition of *subject*: "a person about whom an investigator (professional, or student) conducting scientific research obtains (1) data through intervention or interaction with the person, or (2) identifiable private information" (National Commission for the Protection of Human Subjects of Biomedical and Behavioral Research 1978b, xx). The 1981 regulations incorporated this definition with an important change; instead of "person" the regulations specified "living individual," so that research about historical figures or whole communities would not fall under their scope (45 CFR 46.102(f) (1981)).

Like other components of the 1981 regulatory structure, the definition of subject has been modified by federal action. For example, in 1999 the Office for Protection from Research Risks (OPRR) faulted Virginia Commonwealth University for permitting researchers to survey students about their relatives' medical history (Gordon et al. 2011). At the time Robert Levine—who had taken part in crafting the regulatory definition of subject—objected. "Although . . . technically correct, OPRR's interpretation was indeed new," he complained. "In my view, the appropriate action would have been to revise the faulty definition rather than enforce a novel reading of it" (Levine 2001, 162). Some years later, however, he changed his mind about the definition's worth, arguing that "The cause of these controversies is not the definitions themselves. It is the regulatory actions that are contingent on the definitions and their interpretation" and that such "controversies would likely be abated if appropriate additions were made to the list of activities that are exempt from coverage by the regulations . . ." (Levine 2008, 220).[2]

18.4 Conclusion

The history of IRB jurisdiction shows that there are many ways to skin a cat, and that some ways are better than others. Relying on distinctions between generalizable knowledge and nongeneralizable knowledge is the very worst, for in three decades policy makers have proved unable to agree on what this distinction means. A definition of *research* may be helpful in distinguishing medical research from medical therapy, but outside of that realm its value quickly breaks down (Lederman 2007, 312).

Lists of exceptions, or, better yet, lists of triggers, are more precise tools, yet they also lack explicit moral justification. For example, Canada's relatively enlightened 2010 *Tri-Council Policy Statement* declares that art is not research and therefore does not require REB review, but it fails to explain *why* research deserves more scrutiny than art (Interagency Advisory Panel on Research Ethics 2010, article 2.6). Similarly the Common Rule does not govern "educational tests (cognitive, diagnostic, aptitude, achievement), survey procedures, interview procedures, or observation of public behavior" if "the human subjects are elected or appointed public officials or candidates for public office" (45 CFR 46.101(b)(3) (2005)). Implicit in this provision is the idea that the right of the people to choose and oversee their government outweighs the personal rights and welfare of public officials to some degree. But that idea is not articulated in the regulations, nor in the *Federal Register* notice that accompanied the introduction of this provision in 1981.

By contrast, two of the efforts explored here give some sense of the logic behind the distinctions. The first is Secretary Mathews's interpretation in 1976 of 45 CFR 46 as applying only to "the areas of concern which were addressed in the legislative hearings." Though the statement seems to have been written with the relatively base motive of escaping from a lawsuit, it can suggest two more principled approaches. First, that the list of activities requiring review should be based on some empirical evidence, and second, that regulations should be grounded in legislation, rather than in the wishes of unelected executive branch officials or Commission members. Of course, those latter groups can work out the details of legislation, but they should not craft rules that are grossly removed from the concerns of Congress.

Returning the regulations to their statutory basis by restricting them to "biomedical and behavioral research" thus has some attractions. To be sure, any category will have fuzzy boundaries, and fields like health services research will remain a challenge to any regulatory regime (Schauer 2008; National Bioethics Advisory Commission 2000, 6). But we can imagine definitions of "biomedical" based on other regulations, such as those defining "health information," as "any information, whether oral or recorded in any form or medium, that (1) is created or received by a health care provider, health plan, public health authority, employer, life insurer, school or university, or health care clearinghouse; and (2) relates to the past, present, or future physical or mental health or condition of an individual; the provision of health care to an individual; or the past, present, or future payment for the provision of health care to an individual" (45 CFR 160.103 (2012)). Or we could start fresh, defining "biomedical and behavioral research" as "a systematic investigation, including research development, testing and evaluation, designed to develop or contribute to general knowledge about the structure and function of the human mind and body. It does not include research about specific individuals, social groups, or organizations."

The proposals with the most solid ethical grounding are those that define a "subject" in ethical terms. Albert Jonsen touched on real ethical concerns in his July 1977 proposed definition of *subject*: "one who falls within the power of an investigator such as that person's life, health, well-being, reputation, dot, dot, dot, whatever other qualities we consider important can be adversely affected and who cannot, for some reason, defend themselves." The key word here is *power*. What Jonsen understood—and what few before or since have—is that restricting scholars' pursuit of the truth is a dreadful act, which cannot be justified by such minor goals as duplicating existing layers of peer review, or protecting the reputations of universities. Rather, the only justification for IRB review of any activity is to prevent researchers—however well-intentioned—from abusing their power. And when one considers the topics that Congress examined in its hearings, one finds that that legislators were indeed concerned with people who could not defend themselves against investigators, for example, because they were prisoners or because the researchers were lying to them. In 2000 Harold Shapiro—chair of the National Bioethics Advisory Commission—echoed Jonsen's definition when he stated that "the issue that always comes back in my mind . . . is we find ourselves dealing with vulnerable—people who are vulnerable for one reason or another." This definition would not, he suggested apply to much survey research. "You get this anonymous phone call at 6:00 o'clock at night. When you do not want to answer you just hang up the phone. That is easy" (National Bioethics Advisory Commission 2000, 92).

Defining research is not easy, but it is necessary, and we can do better than we have since 1981. In the end, then, my answer to the ANPRM's question 25 is that the Common Rule should be revised not to exclude certain fields as nongeneralizable but to revise the definition of *human subject* to conform with the concerns expressed by Congress when it passed the National Research Act and with the meaning of the term as commonly understood. Mere *interaction* with a person does not make that person a subject.

Notes

1. In a longer version of this paper, I explore efforts to base IRB jurisdiction on the funding received by a project or the risk it imposes, and to limit IRB jurisdiction by establishing exceptions to general rules and by setting triggers for IRB oversight (see Schrag 2012).

2. In this essay, Levine erroneously claims that the 1981 definition of human subject "had not been recommended by the National Commission" (2008, 219). That Levine, who served as a key consultant to the Commission, should make this error suggests the ways in which the Commission failed to coordinate its various reports.

References

American Anthropological Association. 2011. Comments on proposed changes to the Common Rule (76 FR 44512). http://www.regulations.gov/#!documentDetail;D=HHS-OPHS-2011-0005-0608.

American Educational Research Association, Federation of Associations in Behavioral and Brain Sciences Consortium of Social Science Associations, American Political Science Association, et al. 2011. Social and Behavioral Science White Paper on Advanced Notice for Proposed Rulemaking (ANPRM). Felice J. Levine, Richard O. Lempert, and Paula R. Skedsvold, eds. http://www.regulations.gov/#!documentDetail;D=HHS-OPHS-2011-0005-1102.

Baily, Mary Ann. 2008. Quality improvement methods in health care. In ed. Mary Crowley, ed., *From Birth to Death and Bench to Clinic: The Hastings Center Bioethics Briefing Book for Journalists, Policymakers, and Campaigns*. Garrison, NY: Hastings Center, 147–52.

Beauchamp, Tom L. 2011. Viewpoint: Why our conceptions of research and practice may not serve the best interest of patients and subjects. *Journal of Internal Medicine* 269 (April): 383–87.

Beauchamp, Tom L., and Yashar Saghai. 2012. The historical foundations of the research-practice distinction in bioethics. *Theoretical Medicine and Bioethics* 33 (1): 45–56.

Canada. Interagency Advisory Panel on Research Ethics. 2010. Tri-Council Policy Statement: Ethical Conduct for Research Involving Humans. http://www.pre.ethics.gc.ca/eng/policy-politique/initiatives/tcps2-eptc2/Default/.

Carome, Michael. E-mail to Lori Bross. December 1, 2003. http://www.nyu.edu/research/resources-and-support-offices/getting-started-withyourresearch/human-subjects-research/forms-guidance/clarification-on-oral-history/michael-caromes-email.html.

Crane v. Mathews, 417 F. supp. 532, 545 (N.D. Ga. 1976).

Department of Health and Human Services (DHHS). 2011. Advance Notice of Proposed Rulemaking. Human subjects research protections: Enhancing protections for research subjects and reducing burden, delay, and ambiguity for investigators. *Federal Register* 76 (143): 44512.

Department of Health, Education and Welfare (DHEW). 1976. Secretary's interpretation of "subject at risk." *Federal Register* 41 (125): 26572.

Department of Health, Education and Welfare, Office of the Secretary. 1974. Protection of human subjects. *Federal Register* 39 (105): 18914.

Gallant, Donald M. 1976. Response to Commission duties as detailed in PL 93-348, §202(a)(1)(B)(i). In National Commission for the Protection of Human Subjects of Biomedical and Behavioral Research, ed., *Appendix to the Belmont Report*, vol. 2. Washington, DC: GPO.

Gordon, Judith B., Robert J. Levine, Carolyn M. Mazure, Philip E. Rubin, Barry R. Schaller, and John L. Young. 2011. Social contexts influence ethical considerations of research. *American Journal of Bioethics* 11 (5): 24–30.

Lederman, Rena. 2007. Comparative "research": A modest proposal concerning the object of ethics regulation. *Political and Legal Anthropology Review* 30 (2): 305–27.

Levine, Robert J. 2001. Institutional review boards: A crisis in confidence. *Annals of Internal Medicine* 134 (2): 161–63.

Levine, Robert J. 2008. The nature, scope, and justification of clinical research: What is research? Who is a subject? In Ezekiel J. Emanuel, ed., *The Oxford Textbook of Clinical Research Ethics*. Oxford: Oxford University Press, 211–21.

Mullen, Lon. 1976. Human experimentation regulations of HEW bar Georgia Medicaid cutback. *Clearinghouse Review* 10: 259.

National Bioethics Advisory Commission. 2000. Transcript. 39th meeting, April 6, 2000.

National Commission for the Protection of Human Subjects of Biomedical and Behavioral Research. 1975. Transcript. 8th meeting, June 27–28, 1975.

National Commission for the Protection of Human Subjects of Biomedical and Behavioral Research. 1976. Transcript, 15th meeting, February 13–16, 1976.

National Commission for the Protection of Human Subjects of Biomedical and Behavioral Research. 1977. Transcript, 32nd meeting, July 1977.

National Commission for the Protection of Human Subjects of Biomedical and Behavioral Research. 1978a. Transcript, 39th meeting, February 1978.

National Commission for the Protection of Human Subjects of Biomedical and Behavioral Research. 1978b. *Report and Recommendations*. Institutional Review Boards. Washington, DC: GPO.

National Commission for the Protection of Human Subjects of Biomedical and Behavioral Research. 1978c. *The Belmont Report: Ethical Principles and Guidelines for the Protection of Human Subjects of Research*. Washington, DC: GPO.

Scalia, Antonin. 1980. January 24 letter to Ithiel de Sola Pool. Ithiel de Sola Pool Papers, MC 440, Institute Archives and Special Collections, MIT Libraries, Cambridge.

Schauer, Frederick. 2008. A critical guide to vehicles in the park. *New York University Law Review* 83: 1109–34.

Schrag, Zachary M. 2010. *Ethical Imperialism: Institutional Review Boards and the Social Sciences, 1965–2009*. Baltimore: Johns Hopkins University Press.

Schrag, Zachary M. 2012. What is this thing called research? http://papers.ssrn.com/sol3/papers.cfm?abstract_id=2182297.

Seligson, Mitchell A. 2008. Human subjects protection and large-N research: When exempt is non-exempt and research is non-research. *Political Science and Politics* 41 (03): 477–82.

Shelton, James D. 1999. How to interpret the federal policy for the protection of human subjects or "Common Rule" (part A). *IRB, Ethics and Human Research* 21 (6): 6–9.

Townsend, Robert B. 2011. Getting free of the IRB: A call to action for oral history. *AHA Today*. http://blog.historians.org/2011/08/getting-free-of-the-irb-a-call-to-action/.

US Congress. House Committee on Interstate and Foreign Commerce. 1973. Biomedical research ethics and the protection of human research subjects. Hearings before the Subcommittee on Public Health and Environment. Washington, DC: GPO.

Yoder, Freda E. 2012. E-mail message to author. April 27.

19
What's Right about the "Medical Model" in Human Subjects Research Regulation

Heidi Li Feldman

Bioethics experts Paul Weindling and Volker Roelcke suggest that current bioethical thinking may use an incomplete picture of the historical context of the Nuremberg code. Volker Roelcke writes: "rather than being the result of a coercive state, Nazi medicine illustrates how medical researchers and their representative bodies co-operated with and even manipulated a totalitarian state and political system relying on expert opinion, in order to gain resources for the conduct of research without any moral and legal regulation." He states that Nazi doctors "followed the intrinsic logic of their scientific disciplines and used the legally and ethically unrestricted access to human beings created by the context of the political system and the conditions of war" (WHO Bulletin, on the occasion of the 60th anniversary of the Nuremberg Code; see Theiren and Mauron 2007).

19.1 Introduction

A prominent strand of criticism of the current IRB system contends that today's Common Rule—the foundational US regulation for research on human subjects regulation—presupposes a "medical model" for research on human subjects and regulation thereof (Van den Hoonaard 2001, 38; Hoeyer, Dahlager, and Lynöe 2005; Nelson 2004). Critics assert that this makes the IRB system inappropriate, even ethically corrupt, particularly for regulating research in the social and behavioral sciences. These critics warn that IRB review unduly threatens academic freedom, especially for qualitative researchers who employ "inquiry models that take explicit account of alternative epistemologies," epistemologies that do not "focus on objectivity and causal connections, as well as generalizability" (Lincoln 2005, 171).

The tenor of these criticisms is that social and behavioral research does not really pose an ethical threat in the way that biomedical research does. On this view, regulating social and behavioral research serves no meaningful ethical purpose, amounting only to an undue burden on scholarly inquiry. But this line of criticism bites only if the so-called medical model introduces an erroneous conception of the ethical perils posed by research on or with human subjects, whether the research is biomedical, social, or behavioral.

In this chapter I argue that whatever the merits of the claim that qualitative research involves fundamentally different epistemologies than quantitative research does, it does not follow that a different way of knowing necessarily, or even probably, changes the ethical threats to human research subjects. While those threats might be redressed differently depending on the research methods involved, they still demand the attention of researchers and IRB boards. Human subjects deserve protection from ethical violations whatever the method or discipline of the researcher's inquiry.

The major ethical threat addressed by the Common Rule is compromise of a human research subject's autonomy. The Common Rule relies on a number of measures, especially informed consent, to prevent researchers from disenabling or ignoring subjects' capacity for agency or self-determination when it comes to participating in the research project. The relevant conception of autonomy is neither idealized nor utopian. It does not equate autonomy with decision making from an entirely pure standpoint, one completely unadulterated by context or personal traits.

Today's principles emerged from an awareness that a much less rarified conception of autonomy is in play when researchers make humans their subjects. On this conception, the decision to participate in research should be just that: a decision, a relatively conscious, relatively uncoerced choice to involve oneself in an activity not ordinarily encountered in one's daily life, and therefore to encounter risks different in degree and kind than those one would otherwise face. A researcher is not expected to create a Kantian hyperworld for human subjects. After all, researchers themselves do not live in such a world. In addition to IRB oversight, researchers operate under other constraints, for example, whether they have financial support to pursue their work and whether they can obtain sufficiently talented helpers. The Common Rule expects and requires researchers to make good faith efforts to understand the risks and harms their research may pose to potential subjects and to convey that understanding to potential and ongoing subjects. Essentially this means treating the subject as having a certain equality with the researcher: an equality of autonomy when it comes to research.

Such equality demands that as the researcher may decide whether and how to conduct her studies, the subject may also decide whether and how to participate. Researchers do not embark on their work without an opportunity to consider how it may harm themselves. Researchers can choose to abandon their projects. A researcher respects a subject's autonomy, his status as a self-determining agent, by according the subject the same meaningful opportunity to choose to participate and then to continue participating in the enterprise.

I contend that whatever methods a researcher uses, whatever the degree of risk posed by these methods, whatever the kind of possible harms involved, the question of a subject's autonomous participation remains the same. Different methods, different degrees of risk, and different kinds of harms may have to be explained differently in order for somebody to authentically authorize her participation in research. Sensitivity to these differences, however, does not yield the conclusion that social and behavioral research poses only *de minimis* threat to the autonomy of human subjects. As with any human subjects research, the divergence in ends and circumstances between researcher and subject demands careful consideration of when and how the researcher's perspective may obscure his appreciation for the autonomy and authority of the subjects with whom he interacts.

19.2 The Emergence of a Principle of Robust Consent

As is well known, the origins of the Common Rule lie in the Nuremberg Code, itself a product of post–World War II trials that assessed the criminality of research on human subjects performed under the auspices of Adolf Hitler's Third Reich. In these trials neither prosecutors nor defendants concerned themselves with today's categorization of research into biomedical, social, and behavioral. The Nuremberg prosecutors focused on a more relevant distinction: between research and the other conduct at issue in the war trials. Most of the acts for which defendants were prosecuted involved the infliction of pain, injury, and death, as did the research for which some defendants were on trial for conducting. Yet scientists, doctors, and their aides were not prosecuted for torture or murder. They were prosecuted for criminal research on human subjects, done for so-called anthropological purposes (Nuremberg Military Tribunals 1946–1949a, 37).

This research followed a "therapeutic pattern":

> Experiments concerning high altitude, the effect of cold, and the potability of processed sea water have an obvious relation to aeronautical and naval combat and rescue problems. The mustard gas and phosphorous burn experiments, as well as those relating to the healing value of sulfanilamide for wounds, can be related to air-raid and battlefield medical problems. It is well known that malaria, epidemic jaundice, and typhus were among the principal diseases which had to be combated by the German Armed Forces and by German authorities in occupied territories. To some degree, the therapeutic pattern outlined above is undoubtedly a valid one, and explains why the Wehrmacht, and especially the German Air Force, participated in these experiments. (Nuremberg Military Tribunals 1946–1949a, 37)

Furthermore experiments were performed to develop a new branch of science, the science of efficient genocide. The prosecution termed this science "thanatology" (Nuremberg Military Tribunals 1946–1949a, 38). "The thanatological knowledge . . . supplied the techniques for genocide. . . . This policy of mass extermination could not have been so effectively carried out without the active participation of German medical scientists" (38).

The scientists and doctors prosecuted at Nuremberg included prominent professionals, their stature established before the rise of the Third Reich.

> Outstanding men of science, distinguished for their scientific ability in Germany and abroad, are the defendants Rostock and Rose. Both exemplify, in their training and practice alike, the highest traditions of German medicine. Rostock headed the Department of Surgery at the University of Berlin and served as dean of its medical school. Rose studied under the famous surgeon, Enderlen, at Heidelberg and then became a distinguished specialist in the fields of public health and tropical diseases. Handloser and Schroeder are outstanding medical administrators. Both of them made their careers in military medicine and reached the peak of their profession. (Nuremberg Military Tribunals 1946–1949a, 68)

These prominent administrators, scientists, and doctors did not simply engage in thoughtless killing. Along with younger "rising stars," they organized and conducted experiments funded by and in the interests of the Third Reich. The German biomedical research establishment pursued "therapeutic" medical ends, such as an understanding of the effects of chemical warfare and extreme climatological conditions on aviators and others. It also experimented in the service of a social end, the development of thanatology, the efficient elimination of segments of the population deemed undesirable. However difficult to understand it now, this was normal medical and social science in the Third Reich, conducted not by Nazi politicians or military but by accomplished scientists whose training and professional stature predated Hitler's state.

The Nuremberg prosecutors did not concern themselves with whether thanatology was a biomedical science or a social or behavioral one. This is because the prosecution focused on how the human subjects were treated *qua* subjects by those who used them for their research purposes, as those purposes were understood by the researchers themselves. The Nuremberg prosecutors did not rest their case on the distastefulness of the purposes of the researchers or on the epistemological style or value of the research design or even on the pain and suffering experienced by the human subjects. The prosecutors focused on the failure of the researchers to treat those they experimented with as autonomous individuals capable of giving or declining consent to participate. Researchers in the Third Reich era rejected even explicit requests from subjects to discontinue their participation in experiments even if this meant harsher living conditions. Participants themselves drew a distinction between simple confinement and being subjected to experimentation while confined. If the underlying confinement already severely compromised subject autonomy, the refusal to permit exit from experiments completely smothered it.

The prosecution emphasized two features of the experiments performed under Hitler's auspices. First, that doctors, scientists, and medical administrators sought knowledge and understanding when they studied what happened to people they exposed to malaria or plunged into ice cold water for extended periods. Second, that researchers and administrators ignored subjects' objections to participating and efforts to stop participating, even when the subjects understood that a refusal to participate would put them in line for execution or reassignment to wretched working conditions within a concentration camp. Prosecutors concentrated on the meaninglessness of any formal consent given by subjects and the researcher's refusal to respect requests to discontinue participation.

What came out of "The Doctors' Trial" at Nuremberg was an official statement that put meaningful consent at the heart of human research ethics.

> The voluntary consent of the human subject is absolutely essential. This means that the person involved should have legal capacity to give consent; should be so situated as to be able to exercise free power of choice, without the intervention of any element of force, fraud, deceit, duress, over-reaching, or other ulterior form of constraint or coercion; and should have sufficient knowledge and comprehension of the elements of the subject matter involved as to enable him to make an understanding and enlightened decision. This latter element requires that before

the acceptance of an affirmative decision by the experimental subject there should be made known to him the nature, duration, and purpose of the experiment; the method and means by which it is to be conducted; all inconveniences and hazards reasonable to be expected; and the effects upon his health or person which may possibly come from his participation in the experiment. (Nuremberg Military Tribunals 1946–1949b, 181)

Consent does not prevent injury or pain. It does not guarantee the worthiness of the researcher's goals or her field of inquiry. Consent does, however, force notice of the separateness of persons, an ethically important fact closely associated with the exercise of autonomy.

19.3 Separateness of Persons

The separateness of persons signals the differences between different people's ends and the distinctiveness of what goes into each person's flourishing. The separateness of persons does not necessarily mean opposition between their ends. Nor does it imply isolation or lack of relationships with other people. Nor does separateness presuppose any particular power dynamics between different individuals. Separateness is simply a feature of ethical life. Because of separateness, we cannot simply conflate one person's ends or well-being with another's. People may share ends, their well-being may be bound up with one another, and they may be aware of this mutuality and connection. But shared ends are shared by separate persons, and mutual well-being involves the flourishing of separate individuals.

When a person is caught up in the pursuit of his or her own ends, it is psychologically easy for him or her to discount other people's ends, to downplay tension between realizing his or her own ends and respecting others', and to give unwarranted priority to his or her own flourishing. This is a matter of more than simple selfishness. It is a problem of perspective. Our ends constitute a lens through which we see the world, making expedients salient and masking potential obstacles, sometimes to the point of making those potential obstacles invisible. Having a ready supply of human subjects serves a researcher's ends *qua* researcher; devoting time and energy to ensuring subject autonomy, not so much. Fully informed subjects may decline to participate at all, possibly elevating informed consent from an inconvenience to a serious impediment.

The separateness of persons is hard for researchers to keep in mind not because of something inherent in any academic discipline or experimental design, but because of many of the traits that distinguish successful researchers. Consider some of these traits: passionate inquisitiveness, commitment to discovery and learning, ambition, self-directedness, ability to focus. For a person with these qualities, one's own ends loom particularly large. The separateness of others from one's own projects tends to recede from view.

Philosophically, threats to the separateness of persons come from two directions. One is from utilitarianism. Utilitarianism collapses all individuals into one aggregated bearer of a single end, maximization of utility, however utility is then understood (Rawls 1999, 24). The other threat stems, perhaps somewhat surprisingly, from libertarianism. Libertarianism's individualistic focus might suggest that a libertarian would never lose sight of the separateness of others. But libertarianism's individualism is essentially first-personal. It threatens the separateness of others because of its elevation of the significance of one's own self and one's own ends. Libertarianism invites the individual to adopt a perspective from which the separateness of others represents only a problem to be brushed aside, rather than an ethically salient fact to be respected.

When researchers complain that ethical and legal regulation interferes with their academic freedom, they voice a libertarian complaint:

What we are suggesting is that what is being taken out of an individual's hands is the ability to make decisions as an autonomous researcher working within the healthy parameters that the academy previously had established. Instead, in a litigious environment, guidelines are developed that seek to ensure that the institution is not liable to any risk. The individual professor no longer fully decides the research design, who to protect, where to conduct research, or what to ask. The institution determines the answers, and if the individual disagrees, then the research shall not be done. (Tierney and Corwin 2007, 397)

This is the libertarian voice, objecting to state-based regulation. Traditional libertarianism is especially wary of the state, which the libertarian sees as the major threat to individual autonomy. Libertarians traditionally have been less concerned with other sources of threat to individual autonomy and freedom. Thus the libertarian researcher does not focus on the threat to others' autonomy that the researcher and his methods may pose. Without further argument, however, it is difficult to conclude that the only ethically significant threats to individual freedom arising in the research context derive from the state's regulation of researchers, whether direct or through delegation to bodies within a researcher's institution.

19.4 Closeness Can Threaten Separateness: Ethnography and Self-Experimentalism

The problem of losing sight of separateness does not correlate with whether a method calls for intimacy or formality between researcher and subject, or whether it requires physical proximity and interaction or physical distance with no direct interaction. Certainly other people's separateness can go unnoticed when we situate ourselves so far from them that we cannot make them out distinctly. To us they become dots on our own horizon, blending with the context in which we pursue our own ends. But there is another path to effacing the separateness of others. This is the path of closeness, of intimacy. Consider the ethnographer self-consciously devoted to a hermeneutic fusion of horizons with those she goes to observe:

> For ethnographers, the primary data-gathering tool consists of the relationships that we forge with those whose lifeworld we are trying to understand. Few of us start with specific hypotheses that we will later test in any systematic way.

For the immersed ethnographer, the riskiness posed to others by the enterprise of "forging relationships" can seem minimal to nonexistent:

> We cannot inform our subjects of the risks and benefits of cooperating with us for a number of reasons. First, the risks and benefits for subjects are not so different from those of normal interaction with a stranger who will become a close acquaintance, an everyday feature of a lifeworld, and then disappear, after observing intimate moments, exploring deep feelings, and asking embarrassing questions. There is the risk inherent in any fleeting human relationship—the risk of bruised feelings that come from being used, the loss when a fixture in a social world disappears, or the hurt of realizing that however differently it felt in the moment, one was used as a means to an end.

But to the reflective ethnographer, the risks to others posed by relationships formed in the process of research are more serious than suggested at first:

> This risk is magnified by a certain unavoidable deception in every ethnographic investigation, a certain pretense that comes from trying to have both researcher and informant forget that what is going on is not a normal, natural exchange but research—not just everyday life as it naturally occurs but work, a job, a project—"No really, I'm interested in what you have to say, think, feel, and believe for more than my own narrow instrumental academic purposes."

Yet even the reflective ethnographer has difficulty maintaining a working awareness of the risk her research poses to others:

Finally, we cannot define risk because few of us believe that being an ethnographic informant is a risky business. We believe this despite considerable anthropological and sociological evidence to the contrary. (Bosk and de Vries 2004, 253)

This remarkably frank, self-reflective assessment of the practice and point of ethnography highlights how getting too close to somebody else encourages both parties to ignore or forget their separateness. While this happens in ordinary life, it becomes a matter for human research ethics when a researcher goes out of her way to forge the intimate connections, not for private or essentially personal reasons, but for the sake of pursuing knowledge intended to be shared at large. At that juncture the researcher occupies a different relationship to those with whom she is forging intimacy than they are forging with her. It is this research-oriented relationship, I argue, that the researcher must share with the subject if the subject's autonomy is to be preserved.

A similar problem of preserving subject autonomy in the face of intimacy arises in a research setting that may well seem radically different from the ethnographer's: the context of self-experimentation by physicians and other biomedical researchers. In that framework, potentially problematic closeness of subject to researcher (and vice versa) arises because the subject and the researcher are the same person, although each persona may occupy very different facets of that person's makeup. How can a researcher gain sufficient perspective on the aspects of herself not caught up in the research program to know that her decision or agreement to experiment on herself does not stampede the parts of her with projects and ends detached from, and perhaps endangered by, the ends of her research? Just as ethnography calls for a fusion of horizons between the observer and the observed, and therefore a deconstruction of boundaries, a similar deconstruction is demanded when biomedical researchers experiment on themselves.

Some biomedical researchers have recognized this explicitly. Consider David Clyde, a physician and parasitologist who worked on developing a vaccine against resistant malaria in the 1970s (Shiff et al. 2003). Clyde experimented on "prisoner-volunteers" just when concern was mounting over a prisoner's ability to genuinely consent to be a human subject given the coercive atmosphere of prison settings (Altman 1987, 161). Clyde himself did not have this worry, but he did maintain that at least one scientist must go through the experimental process with the prisoners. Clyde specifically wanted to find out "about any side-effects such as lingering taste, nausea, insomnia, which, being subjective, were difficult to elicit by questioning others" (Altman 1987, 161). In other words, Clyde wanted to know about the effects of the vaccine from the inside out, by inhabiting the perspective of the subject as well as that of the researcher. Presumably, Clyde found value in reporting his own subjective experience of malaria despite his reservations about gaining understanding through others' self-reports of their experience of experimental vaccines.

Other biomedical researchers evidence the deconstruction of the subject-researcher boundary by noting that even when they are obviously experimenting on themselves, they do not conceive of themselves as research subjects. Consider Dr. Scott M. Smith, who investigated the use of curare to be used in conjunction with anesthesia (Utah Society of Anesthesiologists 2013). In 1946 Smith wanted to know whether curare eliminated the sensation of pain as well as stilling muscle movement. This required receiving increments of curare and signaling to observers whether he experienced pain or other sensations while under the influence of the drug.

In the hope of getting a clear-cut answer to his questions, Smith decided to take a dose three times larger than he had ever administered to a patient. "It may sound funny," he said, "but I did not think that I was experimenting on myself. I believed the drug was safe because I had used so much of it already [on other people, without their knowledge] and had observed its action. And there was an antidote—neostigmine—available. (Altman 1987, 82)

Thirty years after the experiment, Smith observed that he never considered performing it on somebody else, and that even if it had occurred to him to do so, he "doubt[ed] [he] could have convinced anyone else to participate" (Altman 1987, 82).

Whereas Clyde self-consciously used self-experimentation as a tool for ascertaining "subjective" effects of a drug, Smith's use of himself as a research subject seemed to distract him entirely from the fact that he was self-experimenting. Both men's experiences and their interpretations of them illustrate how self-experimentation closes the gap between researcher and subject. Clyde lost his distrust of subjective self-reporting when he reported to himself; Smith lost his sense of what constituted research on a human subject. Just as the ethnographer relies on a sort of perspectival sleight of hand, so does the biomedical self-experimenter. The illusions relied upon may yield revelations but they can also obscure important aspects of what is actually happening.

Altering one's perspective to achieve closeness to research subjects (yourself or others) may or may not interfere with scholarly value of one's findings. Regardless, such closeness and conflation of perspectives can distort both the researcher's and the subject's perception of the risks and harms associated with the experiment. If people become research subjects without an appropriate appreciation of such risks and harms, they cannot be participating autonomously. To be the author of the decision to participate in a potentially dangerous situation that you would not ordinarily encounter, you need to appreciate that the situation is indeed out of the ordinary and that it might cause you physical, psychic, or economic injury. You must be positioned to see these features.

This is the point of informed consent. Informed consent implements the separateness of persons. The process of obtaining informed consent is a mechanism for communicating information, fostering understanding, and provoking the subject to consider the methods, risk level, and type of potential harms to which she may expose herself should she choose to participate. Informed consent is not an end in itself. It is a tool for highlighting the subject's separateness from the researcher even when both are embodied in the same person, and then using that separateness as a way to confer a perspective on the research and the subject's role in it such that the subject has a meaningful opportunity to authorize her participation.

19.5 Conclusion

Nazi-sanctioned research gave rise to the Nuremberg Code's lexical prioritization of subject autonomy over other ends and values. One major threat to subject autonomy, obfuscation of the separateness of persons and the ethical significance of that fact, can arise in settings as apparently different as ethnography and biomedical self-experimentation. The central aim of IRB regulation is to preserve subject autonomy whatever the research settings.

It is not entirely clear what critics of today's Common Rule mean by a "medical model" or its influence on current regulation of human subjects research. If by "medical model," critics simply mean an approach to human subject research that gives the subject autonomy priority over other interests and values, their beef is not with anything peculiar to medical research or to biomedical experimentation. Their beef might be with giving subject autonomy that lexical priority. If so, they need to make the case that some other end or value trumps subject autonomy or at least should be weighed against it as a possible reason for permitting researchers to experiment on human subjects without providing them as full and meaningful an opportunity as possible to authorize their own participation.

IRB regulation based on the protection of autonomy via informed consent procedures is not totalitarian nor intolerant of variety in research methods and fields of study. Indeed IRB regulation treats social, behavioral, and scientific research with equal gravity. When one person examines another for the purpose of scholarship and public knowledge, the possibility of encroaching upon the subject's autonomy does not vary according to the disciplinary categories that may be relevant for other purposes. IRB review based on the Common Rule focuses on safeguarding autonomy in context. IRBs consider the specifics of protocols from different disciplines. To the extent that different methods or fields vary in how they may interfere with subject autonomy, the Common Rule allows researchers to tailor their informed consent procedures to those specifics.

Perhaps those who charge that the "medical model" is irrelevant to social and behavioral research have a slightly different concern. Perhaps they believe that the major ethical problem arising from human subject research is the infliction, or risk of infliction, of *physical* injury. The current Common Rule does not directly protect against this specific problem. It does attempt a certain kind of protection for subjects, but not direct protection from physical harm. Current regulation aims to create a situation where subjects can meaningfully decide for themselves which risks of whatever harms to undertake. The need to regulate for this purpose arises whenever research poses a significant degree of risk of injury, whether physical, emotional, or financial, whether tangible or intangible. Injuries and risks are not exclusive to medical research. An accidental dissemination of personal data collected in a survey may lead to emotional and financial injuries more extreme than some nontrivial physical ones. Interviews with those who have lived through years of civil war or been subject to war crimes may cause intense psychological discomfort or mental anguish. The point of making autonomy central to human subjects research regulation is to ensure that potential subjects understand such risks, and then choose for themselves whether to participate in research. The significance of autonomy does not vary according to the type of possible injury, although risks of different kinds of injury may require different techniques for ensuring autonomous participation in human subjects research.

References

Altman, Lawrence K. 1987. *Who Goes First? The Story of Self-experimentation in Medicine*. New York: Random House.

Bosk, Charles L., and Raymond G. de Vries. 2004. Bureaucracies of mass deception: Institutional review boards and the ethics of ethnographic research. *An-*

nals of the American Academy of Political and Social Science 595 (1): 249–63. doi:10.1177/0002716204266913.

Hoeyer, Klaus, Lisa Dahlager, and Niels Lynöe. 2005. Conflicting notions of research ethics: The mutually challenging traditions of social scientists and medical researchers. *Social Science and Medicine* 61 (8): 1741–49. doi:10.1016/j.socscimed.2005.03.026.

Lincoln, Yvonna S. 2005. Institutional review boards and methodological conservatism: The challenge to and from phenomenological paradigms. In Norman K. Denzin and Yvonna S. Lincoln, eds., *The SAGE Handbook of Qualitative Research*. Thousand Oaks, CA: Sage , 165–81.

Nelson, Cary. 2004. The brave new world of research surveillance. *Qualitative Inquiry* 10 (2): 207–18. doi:10.1177/1077800403259701.

Nuremberg Military Tribunals. 1949–1953a. *Trials of War Criminals before the Nuremberg Military Tribunals under Control Council Law No. 10*, vol. 1. Nuremberg, October 1946–April 1949. Washington, DC: GPO. http://www.loc.gov/rr/frd/Military_Law/pdf/NT_war-criminals_Vol-I.pdf.

Nuremberg Military Tribunals. 1949–1953b. *Trials of War Criminals before the Nuremberg Military Tribunals under Control Council Law No. 10*, vol. 2. Nuremberg, October 1946–April 1949. Washington, DC: GPO. http://www.loc.gov/rr/frd/Military_Law/pdf/NT_war-criminals_Vol-II.pdf.

Rawls, John. 1999. *A Theory of Justice*. Cambridge: Belknap Press of Harvard University Press.

Shiff, Clive, Louis Molyneux, Peter Trigg, and Anatoli Kondrachine. 2003. David Francis Clyde, 1995–2002. *Bulletin of the World Health Organization* 81 (2): 149.

Theiren, Michel, and Alexandre Mauron. 2007. Nuremberg Code turns 60. *Bulletin of the World Health Organization* 85 (8): 573.

Tierney, William G., and Zoé B. Corwin. 2007. The tensions between academic freedom and institutional review boards. *Qualitative Inquiry* 13 (3): 388–98. doi:10.1177/1077800406297655.

Utah Society of Anesthesiologists. 2013. About USA. Utah Society of Anesthesiologists website. Accessed January 14. http://www.usahq.org/history-of-the-usa.

Van den Hoonaard, Will C. 2001. Is research-ethics review a moral panic? *Canadian Review of Sociology and Anthropology. La Revue Canadienne de Sociologie et d'Anthropologie* 38 (1): 19–36. doi:10.1111/j.1755-618X.2001.tb00601.x.

20

Three Challenges for Risk-Based (Research) Regulation: Heterogeneity among Regulated Activities, Regulator Bias, and Stakeholder Heterogeneity

Michelle N. Meyer

As Davis and Hurley explain in their chapter, the ANPRM outlined seven areas of "concern" about, and proposed changes to, the Common Rule. A brief commentary by the ANPRM's architects suggests, however, that most criticisms of the Common Rule can be reduced to two broad categories. On the one hand are "complaints that the regulations impose a variety of burdensome bureaucratic procedures that seem to do little to protect research participants, yet consume substantial resources." Such criticisms, Emanuel and Menikoff note, are especially frequent in the context of "studies that pose few physical or psychological risks" to participants. On the other hand are complaints that "current regulations could be doing a significantly better job in protecting research subjects," presumably largely in "high-risk" studies (Emanuel and Menikoff 2011, 1145).

As suggested by its subtitle—"Enhancing protections for research subjects and reducing burden, delay, and ambiguity for investigators"—the ANPRM attempts to appease both camps of critics by shifting scarce regulatory resources from "low-risk" studies, where they unnecessarily burden research, to studies that "pose risks of serious physical or psychological harm" (Emanuel and Menikoff 2011, 2), which currently suffer from insufficiently rigorous review and thereby endanger participant welfare. That is, like regulators in many other sectors responding to charges of over- or underregulation (Black 2010, 189), the ANPRM's architects seek to render research regulation "risk based," by making the kind and extent of IRB review and agency oversight proportionate to the riskiness of the research. As discussed below, US research regulation is already risk based. But federal regulators seek to make it more tightly so, and in this respect, the ANPRM is just the US contribution to a global trend toward risk-proportionate regulation of a wide range of activities, including food safety, medicine, work safety, environmental protection, and financial regulation (Black 2010).

In pressing for increased risk-based research regulation, the ANPRM cleverly exploits what is perhaps the two camps of critics' only common ground: a shared faith in the possibility of regulators making objectively "correct" risk–benefit assessments, and their too-frequent failure to do the same, as demonstrated in part by widespread variation in IRB decisions regarding similar and even identical protocols (Meyer 2013a). Here the two camps part ways, with one camp emphasizing type I errors, in which "unreasonably risky" research is allowed to proceed, and the other emphasizing type II errors, in which important but "low-risk" research is rejected, altered, or delayed. Like the opposing camps of critics it seeks to appease, risk-proportionate research regulation assumes a meaningful way for regulators to distinguish "low-" from "high-risk" research. That is, it requires a basis on which some social planner can, in advance and with respect to all prospective participants in a particular study or category of research, deem some research-related harms insufficiently probable or significant to warrant the full panoply of protections afforded participants in other studies.

This chapter calls that assumption into question. Because prospective research participants are heterogeneous in their preferences and other circumstances, the same protocol will offer a different risk–benefit profile for different participants. IRB variation then should not surprise us in the least; much of it is likely simply a reflection of the fact that *all* individuals, including those who serve on IRBs, vary in their preferences regarding research risks, benefits, and trade-offs between the two. Before discussing this challenge from participant heterogeneity, I provide an overview of risk-based regulation and discuss two other notable challenges in applying such regulation to human subjects research: the challenges from research heterogeneity and from regulator bias. I conclude by suggesting an alternative way to redistribute scarce regulatory resources that embraces, rather than ignores, participant heterogeneity. Although I focus on US governance of human subjects research, the analysis is more broadly applicable in light of the fact that the United States has essentially exported this system to many other nations.

20.1 What Is Risk-Based (Research) Regulation?

Risk-based regulation is a decision-making framework used "to prioritise regulatory activities and deploy resources . . . based on an assessment of the risks that regulated [entities] pose to the regulator's objectives" (Black 2010, 187). The intended beneficiaries of the IRB system are research participants, and its primary goal is participant welfare.[1]

Risk-based frameworks typically divide regulated activities (or actors) into those that merit full assessment, those that merit limited assessment, and those that are excluded from assessment entirely (Black 2010). In the United States much industry and almost all academic research involving humans is subject to IRB review, either directly, through federal statute and regulations, or indirectly, through contract (Meyer 2013a).[2] Formally, the Common Rule sorts all of this research into three risk-based tiers of regulation. In practice, the reality is a bit different, as we will see.

First, six categories of human subjects research are (in theory) "exempt" from the regulations entirely (45 CFR 46.101(b) (2012)). In this first tier, risk proportionality is imposed by agency officials who drafted the regulations; IRBs are not responsible for determining how risky the activity is, or whether its riskiness is justified.

Ten categories of research published in the *Federal Register* comprise the Common Rule's second risk-based tier. To be eligible for "expedited" IRB review, one or more IRB members must find both that the proposed study involves only one or more of these ten categories of activity and that the study poses "no more than minimal risk" (ibid. 46.110(a)). Hence the division of labor is split: agency officials determine the categories of research that trigger eligibility for expedited review, and IRBs determine both whether a particular proposed study falls within one of those categories and whether its risks are "minimal."

Finally, at the other end of the spectrum is research that requires review by a fully convened IRB. Here the onus is entirely on the IRB to determine a study's riskiness, and hence to decide whether it should be permitted to go forward in its current proposed form, or at all. Agency officials' only contribution is the rather vague regulatory mechanism by which IRBs are to make this decision: namely, before they approve any individual study, IRBs must find that its "[r]isks to subjects are reasonable in relation to anticipated benefits, if any, to subjects, and the importance of the knowledge that may reasonably be expected to result" (ibid. 46.111(a)(2)).[3]

20.2 Challenges to Risk-Based Research Regulation

20.2.1 The Challenge from Research Heterogeneity

Critiques of research regulation are often linked to claims about the heterogeneity of research methods and disciplines. Certain disciplines or methods, it is said, pose more risk, and hence merit more scrutiny, than others (Gunsalus et al. 2007; Hamburger 2004; Oakes 2002). But when we look at data about how research participants fare, we find that a study's potential to set back or further the interests of participants does not depend on the discipline, methodology, or type of risk it involves. This poses an obvious challenge for attempts to engage in *ex ante* risk-based regulation of research at the relatively high level of abstraction one finds in statutes and even administrative regulations.

The riskiness of research does not, for instance, neatly correspond to any biomedical/nonbiomedical dichotomy, or to any other disciplinary divide. Biomedical research sometimes involves risky physical interventions, but often it involves no physical interventions, or only those we tend to think of as benign (e.g., allergy skin testing). Conversely, behavioral and social science research can involve physical intrusions (e.g., blood draws or ingestion of a radioactive substance for PET scan imaging for behavioral research). And even the most "benign" research methodology, such as talking, can pose nontrivial physical risks in both biomedical and nonbiomedical studies (e.g., panic attack resulting from sensitive survey or interview).

We might abandon disciplinary and methodological proxies and directly base risk-proportionate regulation on the kinds of risks themselves. But physical harms are not, as a rule, always greater in magnitude, more costly for the victim or society, more irreversible, or otherwise more important to avoid than are psychological, social, economic, and legal harms. Genetic research, for instance, may yield unwelcome news about paternity or predisposition to disease. Surveys and interview-based research with trauma victims can set back their recovery, leading to a cascade of psychological and economic harms.

Research benefits tend to get short shrift in both the research ethics literature and IRB risk–benefit analysis. But if what we care about is participant welfare, then we should care about both risks and expected benefits[4] (Meyer 2013a). It is worth noting then that the above analysis is equally true of research benefits: participants may benefit physically, economically, and psychosocially from participating in both biomedical and nonbiomedical studies, and there is no particular reason to categorically privilege physical benefits over other kinds of benefit.

20.2.2 The Challenge from Regulator Bias

It will be very difficult then to engage in significant risk-proportionate regulation at the level of statute or agency regulation. And indeed largely what we find in the current regulatory framework is that the overwhelming bulk of the work of risk-based regulation is delegated to IRBs. But this requires IRBs to take an unbiased view of research risks and expected benefits. As acknowledged even by Davis and Hurley, writing in this volume on behalf of PRIM&R, the well-known organization for IRB professionals, IRBs already have a "tendency . . . to err on the side of caution when evaluating potential risks," and so "spend more time reviewing minimal risk research than is appropriate". It is worth pausing to consider *why* this is the case, because the answer reveals that IRB risk aversion is not easily amenable to change.

Risk-based regulation "requires regulators to take risks. This is extremely challenging for a regulatory organisation. They have to choose which risks or levels of risk are they not prepared to devote the bulk of their resources to preventing" (Black 2010, 193). The "most common mistake" made by adopters of risk-based frameworks is assuming that local regulators will understand and accept the "philosophy of risk-based regulation" as opposed to a compliance-based approach (Black 2010, 207, 213–14).

IRBs, like most regulators, have asymmetric incentives to avoid type II errors, in which they inappropriately permit research to proceed, over type I errors, in which they inappropriately alter, delay, or block important research. It is critical to appreciate that the interests of research participants (and not only researchers, society, and future patients) can be set back by *both* types of error. Participating in research can feed participants' intellectual curiosity, serve as their mitzvah for the day, provide them access to cutting-edge diagnostics, or pay their rent (Meyer 2013a). Alas, type II errors are highly visible and often embroil the institution in bad PR, agency sanctions, and even litigation, while type I errors are hidden from most stakeholders other than researchers (Hyman 2007, 753–56; Zywicki 2007, 872–73). A study of risk-based regulation across several domains found that "[i]n practice, the political context is determinative" of which risks are tolerated in a risk-based system and which are not, rather than the risk model: "The higher the political salience of a sector or risk, the less will be the regulators' tolerance of failure in that particular area" (Black 2010, 193). IRBs face additional biases familiar to those who study bureaucracies and regulators, including capture, tunnel vision, self-selection bias, and cognitive dissonance (Meyer 2013b; Zywicki 2007, 892–95). IRBs' risk aversion tends to lead IRBs to err on the side of more, rather than less, review.

In addition to these more cynical explanations for IRB risk aversion is a more charitable explanation that is likely at least as much at play, and yet almost completely unnoticed in the research ethics literature. A meta-analysis of more than one dozen studies suggests that individuals tend to be significantly more risk averse when they make decisions whose consequences primarily fall on others, rather than on themselves (Atanasov 2010). This phenomenon, sometimes called "double risk aversion," has been observed in contexts highly relevant to IRB review. For example, subjects asked to predict how much discomfort would be involved in answering a sensitive survey predicted significantly more discomfort for others than for themselves. Double risk aversion is also more likely to occur when the decision maker perceives herself to be accountable or responsible for the decision, when she is uncertain about the beneficiary's risk preferences, and when the decision concerns health (Atanasov 2010; Meyer 2013b).

How do these biases play out under the current system? First, in order to determine whether a covered actor's activity constitutes human subjects research at all, IRBs must interpret and apply necessarily vague regulatory language pertaining to whether that activity is "generalizable" and "systematic," and whether it involves "interaction" or "intervention" with human subjects. IRBs must then determine whether the "human subjects research" it has identified is nevertheless "exempt." Although agency officials determine which abstract categories of research are exempt, someone must be responsible for determining whether a particular proposed study fairly fits one or more of these exempt categories, and in practice, that someone is associated with the IRB (Meyer 2013a). Moreover, because the regulations constitute a floor, not a ceiling (45 CFR 46.112 (2012)), even if an IRB determines that a protocol is exempt, it may subject what are more accurately called *exemptible* proposals to expedited or even full IRB review (Meyer 2013a). The well-regarded *Bell Report* commissioned by the NIH, for instance, found that 15 percent of proposals reviewed by IRBs were exemptible, and that fewer than half of IRBs regularly exempted from review such exemptible research as analysis of existing data, interviews, and surveys (1998, 28–30). Indeed some IRBs, by policy, simply subject all protocols to full review (Meehan and Davis 2005, 299, 309). As one commentator, himself an IRB member, put it: "There is no great gain in seeking [exempt] status" (Oakes 2002, 457).

Studies eligible for expedited review fare similarly. Currently, if the IRB chairperson or her designate finds that a protocol involves both only activities included in the DHHS Secretary's list and "no more than minimal risk," she "may"—but need not—review the study herself, rather than subject it to review by a fully convened IRB (45 CFR 46.110(b) (2012)). As the ANPRM notes, much expeditable research, like much exemptible research, receives full IRB review, presumably because reviewers find that they may pose more than minimal risk. The Bell Report found, for instance, that of those high-volume IRBs surveyed, only 52 percent regularly conducted expedited review of studies involving a simple blood draw, and only 60 percent did so for studies involving noninvasive data collection from adults (1998, 29–30).

The ANPRM proposes various ways of discouraging IRBs from "defining up" protocols into higher risk tiers. The regulations would state that when an IRB finds that a study involves only expeditable research activities, the IRB should presume that study to be "minimal risk." And researchers who believe that their study is exempt would simply register it with the IRB, and then be "excused" to proceed with the research, subject to possible audit. But—understandably, given the virtually infinite heterogeneity of research protocols—the ANPRM permits IRBs to depart from these default rules. The reviewer of expeditable research, for instance, "would have the option of determining that the study should be reviewed by a convened IRB, when that conclusion is supported by the specific circumstances of the study" (44516–17). And researchers working on "excused" studies would be able to proceed without delay — "unless the institution chose to review that filing and determined that the research did not qualify as Excused," a possibility the ANPRM contemplates encouraging by establishing a brief "waiting period" after registration before excused research could proceed (44520). Finally, the ANPRM leaves untouched what is perhaps the most significant opportunity for IRB risk-aversion to assert itself: the vague risk–benefit analysis that all nonexempt studies must pass in order to proceed.

One of the biggest design questions in risk-based regulation is the division of power in making risk assessments between regulators who establish and oversee the risk-based framework (here, OHRP) and local regulators or inspectors (here, IRBs). "[B]y its very nature, risk-based frameworks significantly curtail the scope for inspectors' discretion in determining how to plan inspections, who to inspect, and what to inspect for. It can also be difficult for inspectors to accept that they no longer need to spend too long on particular [actors or activities], as it calls into question the validity and usefulness of the way they have performed their roles previously" (Black 2010, 214). Thus removing too much of local inspectors' discretion is "a significant shift in practice and culture" that leaves many local regulators feeling "devalued," and which many have found "hard to accept" (Black 2010, 209).

But the ANPRM's opposite approach—retaining virtually all of the discretion currently held by IRBs, who have been trained to engage in searching inquiries for unnoticed risks while suddenly expecting them to knowingly disregard those risks as insufficiently important—is a massive shift in IRB practice and culture. A good example of how entrenched the current culture is comes from the first chapter in this volume. Writing on behalf of PRIM&R, a professional organization for IRB members and administrators, Davis and Hurley object that "IRBs should never be required to report or justify additional measures they adopt to augment protection of human subjects. Federal regulations are considered *minimum* standards for protection and to exceed those standards should be encouraged and supported even if they increase administrative burden and delay the research . . . . Efficiency itself is not a moral imperative or an ethical value, and . . . human subjects protections should never be compromised by a desire for increased efficiency."[5] Indeed, in other contexts, when central regulators have allowed local inspectors some measure of channeled discretion, "few categorisations . . . changed" from the inspector's past risk judgment, and in other cases, "risk scores went up, as everyone thinks their area is more risky than anyone else's." The "fundamental change" in culture, analytical approach, and skill set entailed by a shift to risk-based regulation tends to mean that it generally take at least two years for local regulators to adapt, sometimes "far longer," and in some cases, "in order to begin to change the inspection culture there has to be a shake out of the current supervisory staff, and new people hired" (Black 2010, 209–10).

20.2.3 The Challenge from Participant Heterogeneity

We have seen that heterogeneity among research protocols poses difficulties for risk-based research regulation, especially when combined with regulatory bias. But a much deeper—and almost entirely unrecognized—problem is that *participants* are different, and hence will have different expected outcomes, even when participating in the same protocol. Thus the heterogeneity problem for risk-based research regulation is not only heterogeneity across protocols within a given methodological or disciplinary category but also heterogeneity across participants within a single protocol. Such participant heterogeneity would remain a problem even if research regulators (legislators, agency officials, and IRBs) were perfectly unbiased in making risk–benefit decisions.

As I have explained at length elsewhere (Meyer 2013a), participant outcomes data reveal that both the probability and magnitude of risks and expected benefits depend significantly (though not exclusively) on the preferences and other personal circumstances of individual prospective participants. This is so moreover across each of the three major categories of research-related risks that the IRB system recognizes—physical, psychological, and informational (DHHS 2011, 44515)—as well as across all major categories of research benefits that the IRB system largely refuses to recognize—medical benefit, monetary and in-kind compensation, and a variety of intangible benefits, such as warm glow utility and satisfaction of intellectual curiosity. Risk–benefit heterogeneity in fact is so substantial that the same study can offer expected harm for one participant and expected benefit for another. One trauma victim, for instance, may be substantially set back in her recovery by recounting her traumatic experiences, while another might find the same interview or survey therapeutic. And indeed we find that like other individuals, IRB members differ dramatically in their risk assessments of the same protocol (Meyer 2013a).

Moreover, even if the same study offered the same risk–benefit profile to all participants, participants will often differ in their willingness to assume those risks in pursuit of benefits for themselves and/or others (Meyer 2013a). One trauma victim who expects to suffer some psychological and financial harm from setting back her recovery nevertheless rationally may be willing to assume these costs in order to help researchers gain a better understanding of trauma, while another participant rationally may not be so willing. Yet regulations require IRBs to assign a single risk–benefit profile to each study and then to determine, on behalf of *all* prospective participants, whether that risk–benefit profile is "reasonable" (45 CFR 46.111 (2012)). Higher up the regulatory chain, decisions made by legislators and agency officials about whole swathes of research activities mask even greater amounts of participant heterogeneity.

Notably, participant heterogeneity is on clear display in the study of participant outcomes reported by McDonald, Cox, and Townsend in chapter 7 of this volume. Although they urge that such data be used to inform IRB decision making—as does the ANPRM, when it suggests that the list of research activities eligible for expedited review be continually updated "based on a systematic, empirical assessment of the levels of risk" involved in various research activities (44516) — participant heterogeneity casts doubt on the usefulness of such data. Data alone cannot "determin[e] if the current system is, as some critics allege, overprotective or, as others contend, either underprotective or appropriately protective" (McDonald, Cox, and Townsend 2014) because such data will almost always reveal that the current system is overprotective for some and adequate or underprotective for others. No matter how well trained, intentioned, or de-biased, regulators are simply incapable of engaging in risk-based regulation that accurately reflects the preferences of all prospective participants.

Worse, absent the ability to honor everyone's preferences, IRBs' risk aversion leads them, through a broad understanding of research risk and a narrow understanding of research benefit, to make risk–benefit decisions that reflect the (imagined) preferences of the most vulnerable, risk-averse participants. But such risk aversion is benign only if we assume that individuals can only be harmed, and never benefited, by participating in research, a claim that is refuted by much of the empirical evidence on research outcomes (Meyer 2013a). Risk-based regulation is "a zero-sum game. Resources which are spent in one area are not spent somewhere else" (Black 2010, 186). Similarly decisions to protect some prospective participants *from* research come at the expense of denying others potentially welfare-enhancing opportunities to participate in research, and it is not immediately clear why we should prefer the former to the latter.

20.3 A Better Way to Achieve Risk-Proportionate Research Regulation

One alternative to skewing risk–benefit analysis toward the low end of the preference distribution would be to strive for research regulation that reflects the preferences of the "average" participant (whether mean, median, or modal). But this strategy of falsely deeming research participation "reasonable" for some participants when it is estimated to be reasonable for (more) others is uncomfortably similar to the kind of utilitarian thinking that the regulations were designed to prevent. As McDonald and colleages note in chapter 7, many other areas of risk regulation, especially in democracies, are based on average stakeholder preferences and ignore those of outliers. We can certainly adopt that approach here. But we should acknowledge that we're averaging, and not conceal that fact—to prospective participants and to ourselves—behind the seemingly objective language of risk-based regulation. In addition, we should recognize that outcomes data is "highly resource intensive to collect" (Black 2010, 203), that we will still need to find ways to de-bias IRBs from deviating from average preferences, and that it is only a rough proxy for even average preferences: data about participants' experiences in past studies will allow regulators to predict only roughly the average outcomes of a *different* cohort of subjects participating in a similar but ultimately *different* future study.

Or, we redistribute regulatory resources in a different way that avoids the challenges and costs of research heterogeneity and regulator bias and embraces, rather than ignores, participant heterogeneity—all without engaging in risk rationing that sacrifices the preferences of some to those of others. "While some people invoke autonomy as an objection to paternalism, the strongest objections are welfarist in character. Official action may fail to respect heterogeneity . . . " (Sunstein 2013, 1826). The fact that a costly problem like stakeholder heterogeneity exists elsewhere, where it may (or may not) be intractable, is hardly a reason not to address the problem in contexts where it can be addressed.

Happily, as I explain in more detail elsewhere (Meyer 2013b), research governance is such a context. For proposed research involving competent adults, IRBs would continue to prospectively review information disclosure and ensure risk minimization, but they would cede the time-consuming and hopelessly subjective task of risk–benefit analysis to individual prospective participants. Each prospective participant would make an individualized decision about whether participation would be "reasonable" — not in the abstract but *for her*. In fact this is precisely the task we already ask prospective participants to perform during the informed consent process: weigh the risks, the expected benefits to themselves and others, and the alternatives to participating, and then make a voluntary, informed decision about enrollment that is reasonable in light of their preferences and circumstances. The ANPRM itself hints at the rationality of this approach when it suggests expanding the categories of "excused" research activities when prospective participants are competent adults—if only it didn't also contemplate retaining IRBs' power to reclaim that risk–benefit decision from the prospective participants whose welfare is at stake.

Rather than attempt the ultimately futile task of transferring information about the diverse preferences of prospective participants to IRBs (and then asking prospective participants to reassert those preferences during an informed consent process that more closely resembles the process of asking children to assent to research or treatment), researchers and IRBs should transfer available population-level data about the outcomes of research participation to prospective participants.

Prospective participants might be told, for instance, that 15 percent of participants in an earlier cohort of the study (or, more likely, in prior similar studies) report having experienced X harm (or Y benefit). Each prospective participant would then use her local knowledge of her own preferences and experiences to engage in a quasi-Bayesian updating of this baseline prediction, roughly estimating her own individual odds of incurring the disclosed harms and benefits. For example, Sally might conclude that, although 15 percent of trauma survivor participants in studies similar to the one she is being invited to join report that their recovery was set back by recounting their traumatic experience, she has in the past found it therapeutic to tell her story, especially when the audience is educated and empathetic, and so it's more likely that she would be in the 85 percent of participants who don't report experiencing harm. Once a prospective participant has some sense of the likely costs and benefits of her participation, she can then decide whether enrolment would be reasonable for her. For instance, Harry might predict that he is relatively likely to experience some setback to his recovery but that he nevertheless feels so strongly about the need to better understand trauma that he is willing to accept that cost.

It is true that various failures of information and rationality conspire to render prospective participants, like all of us, suboptimal maximizers of their own interests. But, as we've seen, regulators suffer from several biases that make them, too, suboptimal maximizers of participants' interests. And many cognitive biases and heuristics, such as risk and uncertainty aversion, should tend to make it *less* likely that prospective participants will enroll in research. In any case, the significant role of bounded self-interest in decisions to enroll in research makes bounded rationality difficult to identify as such by third parties: precisely because decisions to enroll in research are often largely altruistic, it will be difficult to distinguish participation that reveals a genuine preference for altruism from participation that results from biased decision making. Instead of a crude, third-party risk–benefit filter through which IRBs have the power to conclude that a study is too risky, or its risks too complex to fathom, for all participants, a better way to protect individuals from biased decision making would be to shift these regulatory resources to monitoring the actual informed consent process, exploiting individual differences in comprehension by testing prospective participants' understanding of the study before permitting them to enroll (Meyer 2013b).

20.4 Conclusion

The future of human subjects research regulation is unclear. One thing, however, is not. Few think that the current system does a good job reflecting the interests of prospective participants. Yet heterogeneity among regulated research activities, regulator biases, and participant heterogeneity pose fundamental challenges to risk-based research regulation. It may be time to try another approach. Private ordering in research risks and benefits is more attractive, on the current regulatory framework's own participant-protective terms, than conventional wisdom would suggest.

Notes

1. Title II of the National Research Act of 1974 requires each covered institution to provide "assurances satisfactory to the Secretary" of the (then) Department of Health, Education and Welfare (DHEW) that it has established an IRB that will review proposed research "in order to protect the rights of the human subjects." National Research Act of 1974, Pub. L. No. 93–348, 212, 88 Stat. 342, 352–53 (1974). The Act also established a powerful ad hoc commission, the National Commission for the Protection of Human Subjects of Biomedical and Behavioral Research, to which Congress delegated most substantive policy questions regarding IRB review (ibid. 201(a)–(b)(1)). The Commission was to make recommendations about how IRBs should review research to the Secretary, who was then either to "undertake such action as expeditiously as is feasible," or else publish in the Federal Register an explanation of why the Commission's recommendations were not "appropriate to assure the protection of human subjects" (ibid. 204(b)). In other words, the Commission was charged with making recommendations for the protection of research participants, and HHS could only reject those recommendations for reasons that also sounded in human subjects protection rather than in, say, cost effectiveness or academic freedom. The resulting regulations are officially known as the Federal Policy for the Protection of Human Subjects.

2. Thus IRBs license everything from phase I trials of investigational new drugs to quality improvement activities and experimental economics and philosophy, to sociology surveys, oral history, and the studies that form the basis of the burgeoning empirical legal studies movement.

3. The FDA's human subjects regulations provide for an identical risk-benefit test (21 CFR 56.111(a)(2) (2012)). Outside of the United States, other regulatory and ethical guidelines governing human subjects research similarly call for risk–benefit ratios to be "proportionate," "favorable," or "justified" (Meyer 2013a, 274).

4. A "risk," as used here, refers to the magnitude of a harm or cost, discounted by its likelihood. The parallel concept is not benefit but "expected benefit": the magnitude of a benefit, discounted by its likelihood.

5. Elsewhere, the same authors oddly criticize the ANPRM for "overprotection" in proposing mandatory data security standards for all research (Davis and Hurley 2014).

References

Atanasov, Pavel. 2010. Double risk aversion. SSRN working papers series. http://ssrn.com/abstract=1682569.

Bell, James, John Whiton, and Sharon Connelly. 1998. Final Report. Evaluation of NIH implementation of section 491 of the Public Health Service Act, Mandating a Program of Protection for Research Subjects (The Bell Report).

Black, Julia. 2010. Risk-based regulation: Choices, practices and lessons being learned. In OECD, ed., *Risk and Regulatory Policy: Improving the Governance of Risk*. Paris: OECD Publishing, 185–224.

Department of Health and Human Services (DHHS). 2011. Advance Notice of Proposed Rulemaking. Human subjects research protections: Enhancing protections for research subjects and reducing burden, delay, and ambiguity for investigators. *Federal Register* 76 (143): 44512.

Emanuel, Ezekiel J., and Jerry Menikoff. 2011. Reforming the regulations governing research with human subjects. *New England Journal of Medicine* 365 (12): 1145–50.

Gunsalus, C. K., E. M. Bruner, N. C. Burbules, L. Dash, M. Finkin, J. P. Goldberg, et al. 2007. The Illinois White Paper. Improving the system for protecting human subjects: Counteracting IRB "mission creep." *Qualitative Inquiry* 13 (5): 617–49.

Hamburger, Philip. 2004. The new censorship: Institutional review boards. *Supreme Court Review* 2004: 271–354.

Hyman, David A. 2007. Institutional review boards: Is this the least worst we can do? *Northwestern Law Review* 101 (2): 749–73.

Meehan, Michael J., and Marleina Thomas Davis. 2005. Key compliance issues for institutional review boards. In John E. Steiner, ed., *Clinical Research Law and Compliance Handbook*. Burlington, MA: Jones and Bartlett Publishers, 299–334.

Meyer, Michelle N. 2013a. Regulating the production of knowledge: Research risk–benefit analysis and the heterogeneity problem. *Administrative Law Review* 65 (2): 237–99.

Meyer, Michelle N. 2013b. Research contracts: Towards a paternalistic market in research risks and benefits. Unpublished manuscript.

Oakes, Michael J. 2002. Risks and wrongs in social science research: An evaluator's guide to the IRB. *Evaluation Review* 26 (5): 443–79.

Sunstein, Cass R. 2013. The Storrs Lectures: Behavioral economics and paternalism. *Yale Law Journal* 122 (7): 1826–99.

Zywicki, Todd J. 2007. Institutional review boards as academic bureaucracies: An economic and experiential analysis. *Northwestern Law Review* 101 (2): 861–95.

21

Protecting Human Research Subjects as Human Research Workers

Holly Fernandez Lynch

The changes proposed to the Common Rule in the ANPRM were primarily intended to enhance protections for human subjects while reducing burden on researchers. However, due to a continued view of human subjects research as an exceptional endeavor that ought to be governed by exceptional rules (Sachs 2010; Miller and Wertheimer 2010; Wilson and Hunter 2010), the government and interested stakeholders have failed to take this once-in-two-decade opportunity to consider some enhanced protections that could be appropriately imported from a potentially unexpected but analogous setting—the workplace.

In this chapter I flesh out the analogy between human subjects in clinical research and traditional workers in order to demonstrate several ways in which their differential treatment is problematically inconsistent, with a focus on areas in which subjects are *less* stringently protected than their counterparts in customary workplace environments.[1] In particular, I argue that in some cases, human research subjects might actually be eligible for employment law protections without any regulatory change, and that in others, they ought to be "leveled-up" to worker-type protections. Thus clinical research subjects should at the very least not face regulatory limits on how much they may be paid for participation and should be entitled to no-fault compensation for research-related injury. Efforts to more fully integrate their perspective into the research endeavor, similar to the role of labor negotiations, should also be explored.

21.1 Genesis of Disparate Regulation

Today, researchers, ethicists, and regulators tend to see subjects as a class in need of special and substantial protection due to a history of research scandal and other (supposedly) unique characteristics, such as the nature of subjects' vulnerability, motivation, and risk taking. Indeed human subjects research regulation and US labor and employment law have always taken completely separate paths, such that those responsible for conducting and overseeing research rarely if ever consider whether it is necessary to comply with labor and employment laws, and labor and employment compliance agencies have been content to leave the research world to its own devices.

At first glance, this segregation makes sense. Research regulations are best understood as a response to a number of human rights tragedies that have been well-documented in this volume by Parasidis, Obasogie, Koski, and Feldman. The subjects of these experiments looked more like victims of torture and abuse, or at least like patients who had been subject to exploitation and neglect, than workers in the usual sense. And, of course, it seems obvious that victims and workers should be protected differently. The problem is that this mentality has stuck even though the world of human subjects research has dramatically changed.

Another factor is that research regulations were built on a predominantly medical model (Sachs 2010, 76). As a result investigators—like practicing physicians—have traditionally been expected to act protectively toward their subjects' interests as a matter of professional responsibility (PCSBI 2011, 70–74), in stark contrast to the often antagonistic relationship between management and labor. The reality is, however, that doctors engaged in research have fundamentally different goals and responsibilities than doctors engaged in medical practice, in particular, goals that focus on population-level health improvements and scientific advancement rather than improving the health of individual subjects (Brody and Miller 2003). Thus, while not necessarily adversaries, researcher and subject should not always be viewed as standing on the same side of the line.

Finally, perhaps the best explanation for the distinct paths of the two areas of law is simply that the clinical context in which biomedical research takes place seems to create an intuition that research participation cannot be work. Looking beyond that veneer, however, the analogy between subjects and other workers is actually quite strong.

21.2 Building and Clarifying the Analogy[2]

It is understandable how and why research regulation and labor and employment law have developed in parallel rather than together, but do the inconsistencies between them continue to make sense?

21.2.1 Participation as Work, Subjects as Employees, and Defining the Comparator

First, consider the claim that participation in human subjects research is itself a type of work. There are potentially compelling arguments in this regard, but also a great deal of disagreement (Wartofsky 1976). For example, can "work" entail being acted upon, or does it require one's own action? Are paid subjects selling their bodies or instead selling a service? Resolving these questions in such a way that would allow research participation to be defined as work, as I believe it should be, would certainly bolster the philosophical argument in favor of subject protection via labor and employment law standards. However, because the argument can also be made on the basis of analogy, the ontological question is flagged but not resolved here.

The analogy appears strongest for paid, healthy subjects involved in nontherapeutic research who are often motivated by money and may view their participation as a job (Abadie 2010; Helms 2002; Lemmens and Elliott 1999). Inconsistent treatment of these subjects and workers seems to be most difficult to justify. In fact it is possible that these subjects could satisfy applicable legal definitions of "employee" (Carlson 2001; Zatz 2008; Stone 2006) given the extent to which they are controlled by researchers and sponsors, such that they really are entitled to greater legal protections than they are currently granted by research regulations alone. Given the paucity of case law in this area,[3] however, subjects' precise status under labor and employment laws remains an open question.

In this regard it is important to note that legal protections do not extend to all traditional workers, but rather only to employees, as opposed to independent contractors or volunteers. Thus it is insufficient to suggest that research subjects are like workers in general without going further to demonstrate the ways in which they are like the *subcategory* of workers that is, or ought to be, covered by labor and employment laws. And although it complicates things, this "ought to be" caveat is important to include given the fact that even within the realm of traditional workers, many have suggested that legal protections do not extend far enough (Carlson 2001; Stone 2006).

Rather than applying existing legal definitions to human subjects, then, the best way to pursue the analogy between subjects and workers is to ask *why* the law extends certain protections to certain workers. If the same reasons apply to subjects, then it follows that the same protections should apply, unless we can identify some relevant reason to behave to the contrary.

21.2.2 Overlapping Rationale for Protection

The motivating rationale for labor and employment law protections is twofold: (1) there are some workers who are unable to adequately protect themselves due to divergent interests from those in positions of control and highly unequal bargaining power, and (2) there exists a party that can reasonably be expected to take responsibility for these workers' well-being (Davidov 2005, 13; Carlson 2001, 356). Taking the second factor first, it is perfectly reasonable to expect those sponsors and investigators that impose burdens on research subjects to also bear responsibility for their well-being; indeed this is currently what the regulations demand. And applying the first factor to human subjects research, it becomes apparent that the worker analogy applies beyond the realm of paid, healthy subjects.

Both workers and subjects of all sorts have interests that diverge from those of managers and researchers/sponsors, respectively. In many cases managers will offer only those benefits necessary to attract and retain an acceptable workforce, which may be very minimal. Similarly every added protection offered to research subjects influences how quickly recruitment can occur and adds to the expense of running a trial, affecting not only the sponsor's profit margins but also how much money is available for other important research. Even if a given researcher is not motivated by financial considerations, the inherent nature of research often demands the imposition of risks and burdens not for subjects' own benefit but for the good of others, as noted above.

These divergent interests would be unproblematic if workers and subjects could always protect themselves (Davidov 2005). However, they often also share the plight of poor bargaining power and collective action problems. As a matter of simple supply and demand, when there is a surplus of workers willing to do a job, competition among them can create a race to the bottom. In the research context as well, there is often competition to access studies for either therapeutic or financial reasons. Even if all workers or subjects would be made better off by holding out for improved terms related to things like payment and other benefits, compensation for injury, and a greater voice in management, individuals are unlikely to do so when faced with replacement and lack of equivalent or superior alternatives, resulting in dependency on a suboptimal job or trial.

The ultimate concern is that both workers and subjects will find themselves in circumstances of mutually advantageous, consensual exploitation in which they benefit enough to make participation worth their while, but are nonetheless treated unfairly because they deserve more given the burdens they are undertaking and value of their work (Wertheimer 2008). The baseline protections offered by labor and employment law help address this problem for workers, and the regulations applicable to research do the same for subjects. However, the research regulations inexplicably leave a number of important protections on the table.

21.2.3 Default Rule and Consistent Treatment

At root, many subjects—paid and unpaid, healthy and patient, involved in therapeutic and nontherapeutic research—are like those workers to whom the law does or should extend labor and employment law protections. Moreover the government is far from hands-off in the research context and subjects are widely viewed as in need of substantial protection. Against this background, it seems that as a default matter, subjects should be at least as well-protected as workers.

Of course, equivalent protection might be achieved by leveling workers down, eliminating some of the protections they currently enjoy, or leveling subjects up, granting them new protections borrowed from the workplace. Given the compelling rationales for worker protection described above, however, stripping workers of hard-won gains such as wage protections, workers' compensation, or collective bargaining rights seems inappropriate. Moreover, considering that we have substantially more experience with regulation of the workplace than with the regulation of research (which has only been regulated for a few decades), existing labor and employment law protections are likely to be a better reflection of social norms and agreement than the absence of such protections in the research setting (Sachs 2010, 75). And again, enhancing subject protection would be aligned with the goals of the ANPRM.

Thus only two options remain: level subjects up, or identify some relevant difference between subjects and workers in particular settings that would suggest a given workplace protection would be inappropriate to the research context. The remainder of this chapter will evaluate these two options in relation to subject payment, injury, and "voice"; there may be other types of worker protection also worth pursuing for subjects, such as oversight of the workplace itself, but these must be saved for another day.

21.3 Payment to Workers and Subjects

One of the most obvious areas in which workers and subjects are offered inconsistent protections is in the realm of payment for their efforts

(Lemmens and Elliott 1999). For example, protected workers are entitled to a minimum wage, whereas there is no regulatory floor for payment to subjects. However, this particular financial inconsistency is likely of little relevance to research subjects. This is because in addition to being lower than what subjects are generally paid (Latterman and Merz 2001), the minimum wage guaranteed by employment law is unrelated to the work performed and often too low to guarantee a decent standard of living. As such, it offers insufficient protection against exploitation, since workers may still be paid rates that are unfairly low (Phillips 2011).

The bigger problem for research subjects is that the regulatory system in some ways *encourages* their exploitation by effectively precluding high payments (Lemmens and Elliott 2001). Whereas workers legally may be paid as much as someone is willing to offer with no upper limit, the regulatory requirement to obtain consent to research under circumstances that minimize coercion and undue inducement (45 CFR 46.116) is generally interpreted as a bar on offering subjects "too much" money. Thus, even if a subject's efforts are quite valuable and/or burdensome, IRBs will often limit the amounts offered for participation in an effort to make sure subjects are not being made an offer "too good to refuse" (Lemmens and Elliott 2001; Largent et al. 2012).

This is intended as a subject protection, but the flip side is that eliminating concern for undue inducement would better protect subjects against exploitation,[4] and higher payments might even allow them to better self-insure against research risks. In other words, eliminating payment restrictions can still appropriately be cast as leveling up. Unless there is some reason to be more concerned about undue inducement in the context of human subjects research than in the employment setting—where it is not a legal concern at all—then it seems most appropriate to focus on avoidance of exploitation by allowing subjects to be paid as much as anyone is willing to offer.

So is there reason to be *uniquely* concerned about high payment in the research setting? In short, no. Many jobs involve substantial risks taken for others and entail uncertainty about risks. Indeed there is reason to be even less concerned about undue inducement of research subjects than other workers given that IRBs limit risks in critical ways and bear responsibility for ensuring that risks are appropriately balanced by research benefits. Thus an offer to participate in IRB-approved research ought to be viewed as inherently reasonable, rather than something one would accept only out of desperation (Emanuel 2005). There is also scant evidence to suggest that payment blinds subjects to research risks

(Halpern et al. 2004); in fact it might help signal risk levels in a way that allows subjects to make a more informed choice (Cryder et al. 2010). Each of these factors suggests that if we do not allow concerns regarding undue inducement to restrict worker payment, they should not be used to restrict subject payment.

Other concerns about high payment to subjects can also be dispensed with. For example, some argue that subjects motivated by money may lie or withhold information in order to enroll or stay in a trial or trials, leading to both methodological and ethical concerns (Tishler and Bartholomae 2003, 511–15; Abadie 2010, 154–55). However, the first solution to such a problem should not be to restrict payment, but rather to create registries to track subjects, impose mandatory washout periods, and implement tougher screening procedures (Tishler and Bartholomae 2003, 513, 517).

There might also be concern that without an upper limit on payment, some studies would be unable to compete for subjects or important research would become too expensive to conduct (Dickert and Grady 1999, 201; Phillips 2011, 243). This would be unfortunate, but we do not restrict payment in the workplace to make sure that important public sector and nonprofit projects are adequately staffed, and often they are not. Unless there is some argument that research is more important than these other projects, this concern seems to be just a fact of life, not a justification for differential treatment.

In the end, there is no social push to restrict worker payment (outside of the executive compensation realm, perhaps), and there is no compelling reason to restrict subject payment when worker payment is unrestricted. Thus the research regulations ought to be amended to clarify that high payments and substantial benefits to research subjects are perfectly acceptable, and may even be encouraged (Ackerman 1989, 3; Lemmens and Elliott 2001, 53; Shamoo and Resnick 2006, W10).

21.4 Compensation for Injury

Another glaring area of inconsistency between subjects and protected workers involves what members of each group are legally entitled to in the event of injury. In an oft-criticized approach,[5] the Common Rule demands only that subjects be told *whether* any compensation or treatment is available if they experience a study-related injury, but does not actually require such compensation or treatment (45 CFR 46.116(a)(6)). Injured subjects retain the right to sue but face a number of barriers in that regard, most critically that their injury may be no one's fault, but rather the unavoidable consequence of some experimental intervention. In contrast, workers covered by the workers' compensation system cannot sue but are guaranteed no-fault coverage of medical expenses and a portion of lost wages. This *quid pro quo* was motivated by the fact that litigation is slow, expensive, unpredictable, inconsistent, and generally inadequate to reliably or adequately protect the interests of injured workers (Peirce and Dworkin 1988, 652–55). Because litigation is, if anything, more problematic as a remedy for injured subjects who are unable to show fault, have explicitly consented to the risk of injury, and may face problematic governmental immunity in some contexts (IOM 2002, 188, 193; Pike 2012), a no-fault compensation structure similar to the workers' compensation scheme would seem to be an important subject protection. So again, we must ask, is there any reason not to level subjects up?

Perhaps it is the case that injured subjects are being adequately handled despite the regulatory gap, such that a government-mandated compensation system is unnecessary. However, the limited data that exists suggest otherwise. For example, a 2005 study of over one hundred academic medical center policies concluded that a subject's own health insurance serves as the "primary vehicle" for covering the cost of research-related injuries (Lewin Group 2005). Even if everyone had health insurance, policies vary in their inclusions and exclusions, copays, deductibles, and limits, and injured subjects would still be paying for their own care via premiums and copays. More important, health insurance does not cover things like lost wages, yet none of the institutions or sponsors reviewed prospectively offered such compensation (Lewin Group 2005). In fact even the most generous voluntary policies that fully cover the costs of medical care seem to leave out other economic losses that can impose a substantial burden and would be covered by a workers' compensation approach (Paasche-Orlow and Brancati 2005). Absent a clear showing that injured subjects are in practice at least as well protected as injured workers—a showing that has not been made—leveling subjects up cannot be avoided on the grounds that it is unnecessary.

Other possible rationales for differential treatment of injured subjects and injured workers are unconvincing as well. For example, arguments based on concern for overburdening the clinical research enterprise fail for the same reasons stated above, namely that even nonprofit employers doing socially valuable work may be subject to workers' compensation requirements. Moreover nearly every country that sponsors, hosts, or conducts substantial amounts of research—other than the United States—has implemented a no-fault compensation system for research-related injury, demonstrating feasibility (PCSBI 2011, app. IV). And it is true that demonstrating causation may be a challenge for injured subjects, since it will sometimes be necessary to tease apart symptoms associated with underlying disease from research-related harms. But causation determinations are already made in the course of adverse event reporting and institutional compensation policies (Pike 2012, 54–55). Causation may also be similarly challenging in the context of occupational diseases that are eligible for workers' compensation despite the difficulty of distinguishing whether they are related to one's work or instead a misfortune of ordinary life (Resnick 2006, 266). Finally, there is no need for concern that a compensation system would be viewed as a license to embark on riskier research, since the same safety and review standards would remain in place in any event.

Note, however, that consistency demands only that injured subjects be protected to at least the same *extent* as injured workers, not adoption of precisely the same *system* in both contexts. Thus subjects should be entitled to coverage without regard to fault, but should coverage also extend to unpaid subjects? Although, on the one hand, their exclusion may be consistent with the treatment of unpaid workers in some states, those jurisdictions that extend coverage to volunteers like interns and emergency workers seem to provide the more appropriate model. This is because unpaid subjects injured in the course of research participation might still lack bargaining power due to their pursuit of research benefits, and the truly altruistic subject has perhaps an even more compelling claim not to be left with the bill. On the other hand, it is unnecessary to adopt the workers' compensation approach of covering harms that arise out of and in the course of employment, which would create inappropriate windfalls in the research setting for subjects who might have experienced similar harms in clinical care (Pike 2012, 56), and might also have experienced some countervailing research benefits (PCSBI 2011, 69).

Ultimately there is no compelling reason not to treat subjects and workers similarly with regard to ensuring no-fault compensation for the costs of medical care and lost wages in the event of injury. Indeed there are several compelling reasons to do so, ranging from the problems associated with tort litigation to the value of limiting liability in the research setting to the symbolic importance of protecting those engaged in socially valuable activities. Here too the research regulations should be amended accordingly.

21.5 Gaining a Voice in the Workplace

As a final area of comparison, consider the differential legal protections afforded to the "voice" of research subjects and traditional workers. Although subjects are protected by IRBs, as Persad recognizes in chapter 10 of this volume, these boards certainly do not *represent* subjects. Moreover subjects who speak out against the terms and conditions of their research participation may be rejected, dismissed, or blacklisted from trials; even if the subject is not penalized, researchers and sponsors are under no obligation to negotiate. Labor laws, in contrast, protect workers' rights to organize unions, bargain collectively, and engage in other concerted activities, while requiring that employers at the very least come to the bargaining table in good faith (29 USC 151 et seq.). The bottom line is that workers have a right to have their voices heard, whereas subjects' voices may even be stifled by IRBs' paternalistic concerns.

Nevertheless, this is an area where offering subjects labor-type protections appears to be a poor fit. Subjects would likely face substantial difficulties organizing as a result of a variety of factors, such as not all being present in the same place at the same time, infrequent research participation resulting in no long-term investment in improving conditions, and unwillingness to sacrifice the potential benefits of research participation in hopes of negotiating for something better. Although some subjects may be willing to take that risk, it is unlikely that there would be a critical mass sufficient to effectuate change, particularly given legal restrictions intended to protect those whose choose not to engage in collective behaviors (29 USC 157).

At the very least, research regulations could make explicit that subjects may not be discriminated or retaliated against on the basis of attempts to advocate on behalf of subjects, inform subjects of their common interests and what they might be able to accomplish working together, and organize subjects for collective activity. However, since these problems are likely infrequent and unionization and collective bargaining are unlikely to be the most effective tools for research subjects to advance their interests, different options to promote subjects' voice should be pursued. For example, the regulations could mandate inclusion of subjects on IRBs, promote greater use of community advisory boards, and encourage subjects to join with other interested parties to form advocacy groups, rather than unions. Persad has also advanced several of these possibilities as a way to encourage democratic deliberation in human subjects research.

21.6 Conclusion

The similarities between subjects in clinical research and other workers have often been ignored, and the analogy certainly makes no appearance in the ANPRM's suggested revisions to the Common Rule. However, the fact that the regulators have expressed some willingness to "open the vault" and reconsider the current paradigm governing human subjects research makes this the perfect time to address the fact that a set of regulations that is intended to be strongly protective of human subjects actually leaves them less well-protected than their counterparts in the workplace.

While a subset may actually *be* workers, clinical research subjects of all sorts face precisely the same concerns that motivate (or should motivate) the extension of various legal protections to workers. Given the basic principle that like cases should be treated alike unless they are unlike in relevant ways, the regulations should be amended to level subjects up to the position of protected workers. In particular, subjects should be entitled to payment without concern for undue inducement, no-fault compensation for research-related injury, and strengthened protection of their "voice" in the research endeavor.

Notes

This chapter is based on my related law review article, which addresses these issues in substantially more detail: "Human research subjects as human research workers," *Yale Journal Health Policy, Law, and Ethics* 14 (Winter 2014).

1. Areas in which subjects are more protected than workers are also appropriate for reconsideration but are beyond the scope of this chapter given the ANPRM's focus on enhancing subject protection.

2. Other authors have also considered the analogy between subjects and workers; some of their relevant publications are included in the reference list. Speaking broadly, Abadie, Elliott, Lemmens, Resnick, and Shamoo take as their starting point the increasing commercialization of clinical research and the clear financial motivations of paid healthy subjects, arguing against the regulations' failure to recognize at least certain research relationships as nothing more than a business transaction. Dickert and Grady focus exclusively on payment to subjects, arguing that it ought to be treated as a wage commensurate to that paid for other unskilled labor. From there Anderson and Weijer assess the implications of treating paid subjects as wage-earners on a broader scale, ultimately addressing the moral obligations associated with "just" work. This chapter differs from the existing literature in several important ways: (1) it distinguishes between different types of workers under the law, (2) it considers the rationales for legally protecting workers and whether those rationales also apply in the research context, and (3)

it draws the analogy beyond paid, healthy subjects to all participants in biomedical research.

3. Relevant cases and administrative decisions include *Pharmakinetics Laboratories, Edward Lowe Industries, Inc. v. Missouri Division of Employment Security,* and *In re Qualia Clinical Service, Inc.*, all in the reference list.

4. Note that there is also a sense in which undue inducement involves a type of exploitation by taking advantage of another's circumstances to get them to do something they would otherwise prefer not to. But here the term exploitation is used to refer to taking unfair advantage by paying less than their efforts are truly worth.

5. A variety of commentators agree that as an ethical matter, injured subjects should not have to bear the costs of their own injuries: CIOMS (2002, 78–79; IOM (2002, 193); NBAC (2001, 123); and PCSBI (2011, 62 and app. IV) *on International and Transnational Requirements for Treatment and Compensation for Research Injuries.*

References

Abadie, Roberto. 2010. *The Professional Guinea Pig: Big Pharma and the Risky World of Human Subjects Research*. Durham, NC: Duke University Press.

Ackerman, Terrence F. 1989. An ethical framework for the practice of paying research subjects. *IRB: Ethics and Human Research* 11 (4): 1–4.

Anderson, James A., and Charles Weijer. 2002. The research subject as wage earner. *Theoretical Medicine and Bioethics* 23: 359–76.

Brody, Howard, and Franklin G. Miller. 2003. The clinician-investigator: Unavoidable but manageable tension. *Kennedy Institute of Ethics Journal* 13 (4): 329–46.

Carlson, Richard R. 2001. Why the law still can't tell an employee when it sees one and how it ought to stop trying. *Berkeley Journal of Labor and Employment Law* 22 (2): 295–368.

Council for International Organizations of Medical Sciences (CIOMS). 2002. *International Ethical Guidelines for Biomedical Research Involving Human Subjects*. Geneva: WHO.

Cryder, Cynthia E., Alex John London, Kevin G. Volpp, and George Loewenstein. 2010. Informative inducement: Study payment as a signal of risk. *Social Science and Medicine* 70: 455–64.

Davidov, Guy. 2005. The reports of my death are greatly exaggerated: "Employee" as a viable (though overly-used) legal concept. SSRN working paper series. http://ssrn.com/abstract=783484.

Department of Health and Human Services. Presidential Commission for the Study of Bioethical Issues (PCSBI). 2011. *Moral Science: Protecting Participants in Human Subjects Research*. Washington, DC: GPO.

Dickert, Neal, and Christine Grady. 1999. What's the price of a research subject? Approaches to payment for research participation. *New England Journal of Medicine* 341: 198–203.

Edward Lowe Indus., Inc. v. Missouri Div. of Emp't Sec., 865 S.W.2d 855 (Mo. Ct. App. 1993).

Emanuel, Ezekiel J. 2005. Undue inducement? Nonsense on stilts. *American Journal of Bioethics* 5 (5): 9–13.

Helms, Robert, ed. 2002. *Guinea Pig Zero: An Anthology of the Journal for Human Research Subjects.* New Orleans: Garrett County Press.

Halpern, Scott D., Jason H. T. Karlawish, David Casarett, Jesse A. Berlin, and David A. Asch. 2004. Empirical assessment of whether moderate payments are undue or unjust inducements for participation in clinical trials. *Archives of Internal Medicine* 164 (7): 801–803.

Institute of Medicine (IOM). 2002. *Responsible Research: A Systems Approach to Protecting Research Participants.* D. D. Federman, K. E. Hanna, and L. L. Rodriguez, eds. Washington, DC: National Academies Press.

Largent, Emily A., Christine Grady, Franklin G. Miller, and Alan Wertheimer. 2012. Money, coercion, and undue inducement: Attitudes about payments to research participants. *IRB: Ethics and Human Research* 34 (1): 1–8.

Latterman, Jessica, and Jon F. Merz. 2001. How much are subjects paid to participate in research? *American Journal of Bioethics* 1 (2): 45–46.

Lemmens, Trudo, and Carl Elliott. 1999. Guinea pigs on the payroll: The ethics of paying research subjects. *Accountability in Research* 7 (1): 3–20.

Lemmens, Trudo, and Carl Elliott. 2001. Justice for the professional guinea pig. *American Journal of Bioethics* 1 (2): 51–53.

The Lewin Group. 2005. Final Report. Care/compensation for injuries in clinical research. Contract Number HHS 100–03–0005. Prepared for the Department of Health and Human Services, Office of the Assistant Secretary for Planning and Evaluation, Falls Church, VA.

Miller, Franklin G., and Alan Wertheimer. 2010. Preface to a theory of consent transactions: Beyond valid consent. In Franklin G. Miller and Alan Wertheimer, eds., *The Ethics of Consent: Theory and Practice.* Oxford: Oxford University Press, 45–116.

National Bioethics Advisory Commission (NBAC). 2001. *Ethical and Policy Issues in Research Involving Human Participants.* Bethesda, MD: NBAC.

Paasche-Orlow, Michael K., and Frederick L. Brancati. 2005. Assessment of medical school institutional review board policies regarding compensation of subjects for research-related injury. *American Journal of Medicine* 118 (2): 175–80.

Peirce, Ellen R., and Terry Morehead Dworkin. 1988. Workers' compensation and occupational disease: A return to original intent. *Oregon Law Review* 67: 649–87.

Pharmakinetics Lab., Inc., No. 156-EA-94, 1994 WL 16865552, at ¶ 8469. November 14, 1994. CCH Unempl. Ins. Rep.

Phillips, Trisha B. 2011. A living wage for research subjects. *Journal of Law, Medicine and Ethics* 39 (2): 243–53.

Pike, Elizabeth. 2012. Recovering from research: A no-fault proposal to compensate injured research participants. *American Journal of Law and Medicine* 38: 7–62.

In re Qualia Clinical Serv., Inc., 2009 WL 2513820 (Bankr. D. Neb. 2009).

Resnick, David B. 2006. Compensation for research-related injuries: Ethical issues and legal issues. *Journal of Legal Medicine* 27 (3): 263–87.

Sachs, Benjamin. 2010. The exceptional ethics of the investigator–subject relationship. *Journal of Medicine and Philosophy* 35 (1):64–80.

Shamoo, Adil E., and David B. Resnick. 2006. Strategies to minimize risks and exploitation in phase one trials on healthy subjects. *American Journal of Bioethics* 6 (3): W1–13.

Stone, Katherine V. W. 2006. Legal protections for atypical employees: Employment law for workers without workplaces and employees without employers. *Berkeley Journal of Employment and Labor Law* 27: 251–86.

Tishler, Carl L., and Suzanne Bartholomae. 2003. Repeat participation among normal healthy research volunteers: Professional guinea pigs in clinical trials? *Perspectives in Biology and Medicine* 46 (4): 508–20.

Wartofsky, Marx W. 1976. On doing it for money. In *Appendix to Report and Recommendations: Research Involving Prisoners*. Washington, DC: National Commission for the Protection of Human Subjects of Biomedical and Behavioral Research..

Weijer, Charles. 2005. Meaningful work as due inducement. *Theoretical Medicine and Bioethics* 26 (5): 431–35.

Wertheimer, Alan. 2008. Exploitation in clinical research. In Jennifer S. Hawkins and Ezekiel J. Emanuel, eds., *Exploitation and Developing Countries: The Ethics of Clinical Research*. Princeton: Princeton University Press, 63–104.

Wilson, James, and David Hunter. 2010. Research exceptionalism. *American Journal of Bioethics* 10 (8): W4–6.

Zatz, Noah D. 2008. Working beyond the reach or grasp of employment law. In Annette Bernhardt et al., eds., *The Gloves-off Economy: Workplace Standards at the Bottom of America's Labor Market*. Champaign, IL: Labor and Employment Relations Association, University of Illinois at Urbana-Champaign, 31–64.

22

Getting Past Protectionism: Is It Time to Take off the Training Wheels?

Greg Koski

That human subjects research is a regulated activity in the United States and other countries is an interesting phenomenon. After all, how many areas of scientific inquiry are subject to governmental regulation? Peer review of research is common in virtually all fields of science, generally as part of the funding process and, of course, for publication, but prospective review and approval of research involving human or animal subjects is different—it is required by law.

In the second half on the twentieth century, public and governmental concern generated by media accounts of irresponsible conduct and unethical research conducted by legitimate scientists in major academic institutions and government agencies led to a national discussion of the ethical principles underpinning research on human subjects. As a direct result and with all good intentions, the government enacted legislation and eventually promulgated rules requiring that all such research be reviewed and approved prior to its initiation to ensure that it was justifiable, both scientifically and ethically.

This institutional review board (IRB) process, also known as the "human subjects protection process," has changed little since it was implemented in the mid-1960s, first by policy, and then by regulation in the 1980s. This apparent resiliency should not, however, be taken as a testament to its value or effectiveness. Many, indeed a rapidly growing number of scientists, institutional officials, and even the regulators themselves, are very much in the process of "rethinking" this long-standing regulatory framework, as many of the contributions in this volume aim to do.

This re-thinking, driven initially by dissatisfaction among scientists concerned with the excessively compliance-focused approach taken by many, if not most, IRBs, has now spread to many institutional officials, members of their IRBs and the staff who manage them, as well as the federal government itself. In reaction to these widespread concerns, and as discussed in greater depth by Davis and Hurley in chapter 1 of this volume, DHHS (with the cooperation of the Office of Management and Budget) offered seven basic proposals to amend the Federal Regulations for the Protection of Human Subjects in Research (DHHS 2011). The seven recommendations were largely obscured by the seventy questions posed to stimulate public comment on the proposals, raising in some minds concerns about the confidence of the authors about their own recommendations.

Since the ANPRM was issued, many individuals and organizations have weighed in on its perceived merits and shortcomings, and a number of them have included chapters in this volume presenting several innovative proposals about how the Common Rule might be modified, as the ANPRM says, "to both strengthen protections and reduce burdens, delays and ambiguity for investigators." While these are no doubt laudable goals, tinkering around the margins of our existing regulatory framework, as the ANPRM does, is not our only way, and perhaps not our best way, forward.

Rather than simply consider the future of human subject research regulations, we might do well to broaden our perspective, to challenge ourselves to look beyond rethinking of what we have as just a remodeling effort. Instead, we might begin by asking a more fundamental question: If we had an opportunity to start from scratch, would we build the same protective fortress today?

To answer this question, we might first consider, as many have before, the roots of our present approach and the goals to which it allegedly aspires. From the outset, as Carol Levine has said better than anyone, we have built a system that is "born in scandal and reared in protectionism" (Levine 1988, 167). Few can disagree with this apt characterization, and yet even as we nod our heads in agreement, we do so without evidence or good reason to believe that we are in fact achieving our goals or that there are no more effective alternatives available for consideration.

The regulatory approach that we have adopted over the last four decades for *protection* of human subjects in research is based on the implicit assumption, if not an explicit accusation, that left to their own judgment and without constant oversight, scientists will do harm to their human subjects—essentially we are taking the position that scientists are somehow irresponsible, bad people.

Surely, the oft-recited litany of events—tragedies, abuses, ethical lapses—however we might choose to characterize what happened at Tuskegee, Willowbrook, the Jewish Chronic Disease Hospital, the Fernald

School, the Human Radiation Studies, and so many others, is not something in which science or society can take pride (Brandt 1978; Beecher 1966; Jones1993; Goldby 1971; Katz 1972; ACHRE 1995). Nor will we count among the more glorious accomplishments of science the losses of Jesse Gelsinger, Ellen Roche, and others, tragedies that we claim will never be forgotten, even as too many already have (Raper et al. 2003; Steinbrook 2002). But ought we to use these events to justify continuation of an approach that even the Office for Human Research Protections, the very office responsible for oversight of IRBs and enforcement of the regulations we have created, now seeks to change them because they do not offer sufficient protections and impose excessive burdens and ambiguities for investigators and the human research endeavor?

In this time, nearly half a century or more after most of the tragic events cited above occurred, do we still truly believe that scientists are so untrustworthy, so irresponsible, so poorly trained or so selfish—choose whichever characterization you wish—do we truly believe that the risks to human subjects in research are so great that scientists cannot be allowed to design and engage in their scientific studies without prior review and approval by an oversight committee? If so, then surely we have failed miserably in our efforts to educate and train responsible investigators.

For the sake of discussion, consider an analogy—the approach that we have taken to protect our air transportation system and its passengers from terrorists. Because of a small number of admittedly horrific events, we have made an assumption that all passengers about to get on a plane are potential terrorists intent on blowing our planes from the sky. As a result we spend nearly $10 billion annually and cause endless hours of delays and inconvenience for passengers without even knowing whether or not the system we have built has actually done anything to make air travel safer. There have been several thwarted attacks in recent years, but none of them have been prevented by the TSA security screening process. Events have been prevented by effective intelligence activities and surveillance, while passengers with bombs in their shoes or their underwear have managed to get onto planes despite our best attempts and technology to prevent them from doing so.

Similarly the deaths of Ellen Roche and Jesse Gelsinger, and the terrible events in the TeGenero study in the United Kingdom, in which six young men narrowly escaped death by cytokine storm caused by a new biologic agent in a poorly designed phase 1 study, all occurred in research studies that had been *reviewed and approved* by IRBs or ethics committees (Suntharalingam et al. 2006; Wood and Darbyshire 2006).

If either the TSA security system or the "human subject protection system" were subjected to a thorough, rigorous analysis of their effectiveness as preventive programs, they would almost surely be abandoned on the grounds that they are simply not cost effective (Mann 2011). And yet we persist, more out of hope or desperation than out of any evidence-based reason, to believe that they are effective. It is as if doing something, anything for that matter, is better than doing nothing at all. While that is probably true, could we not being doing something better?

Imagine for a moment that a group of physicians were discovered doing abusive, unethical, and harmful things to their patients in the course of their medical practice. The events are reported in the media, and Congress, in its outrage, convenes a National Commission on Patient Safety and Protection of Patients from Medical Risks. The Commission meets for two years at the Petrie–Flom Center at Harvard Law School and eventually issues "The Cambridge Report" (Cambridge not being very far from Belmont). The report identifies several ethical principles for responsible conduct and oversight of medical practice to prevent patients from being harmed by irresponsible practitioners. Soon the Department of Health and Human Services issues new regulations requiring that every physician must submit a treatment plan to an Institutional Medical Practice Committee for prospective review and approval prior to initiation of treatment, except of in the cases requiring immediate, critical life-saving therapy.

While at first glance such an approach would seem completely disproportionate to the risk and inappropriate for the medical profession, is it in fact so very different from the approach we took to deal with reports of abuses in human subjects research? Such an approach, like our approach to research abuses, begins with an assumption that all physicians are irresponsible and cannot be trusted to take care of their patients. And we would therefore create a system for prospective review and approval of treatment plans that would pose huge impediments to the practice of medicine and timely delivery of care to patients in need, all at great cost to society with no commensurate benefits and no demonstrated effectiveness. Indeed the committees are not there when the care is delivered—ultimately the committees and the patients must rely on the professionalism of the physician. Extrapolating to the realm of human research, so too are the IRBs absent when investigators actually conduct their research, an observation duly noted by Henry Beecher (1966). We thus find ourselves confronted by a paradox in which the person best positioned to actually prevent harm is also the person most likely to do harm, and apparently the person we trust least to protect the rights and well-being of their research subjects—the investigator (Koski 1999).

Would society tolerate such a costly, inefficient, and ineffective approach to regulation and oversight of medical care? Of course not, but we do not simply allow doctors to run wild and do anything they want, and possibly harming their patients without oversight or discipline. In medicine we have started with a different set of assumptions and taken a different approach. We have begun with assumptions that physicians are caring, well-intended, well-trained, competent professionals who wish to take care of their patients, to "first do no harm"—to ensure their patients' safety, health, comfort, dignity, and privacy—even as they strive to treat and prevent disease.

How can this assumption be justified? The simple truth is that we have built a system to accomplish these goals using the tools of professionalism. Physicians are required to undertake a rigorous educational experience—college, medical school, residency, and specialty training, and at each step along the way, they are subject to objective examinations at accredited institutions. They are required to obtain professional certification, and before they are allowed to practice, they must be licensed and granted privileges to care for patients through a rigorous credentialing process. To maintain their privileges, they must receive continuing education. There are also well-developed, fully integrated processes for peer review, adverse event reporting, oversight, and discipline to ensure that physicians who fail to conduct themselves according to the standards of the profession are stripped of their privilege to practice medicine.

Ironically, in the profession of medicine, the only activity that is somehow exempt from these processes is clinical research—research involving human subjects. What if we were to apply the professional paradigm that we currently use for every other field of medicine to research?

It is interesting to note that the Food and Drug Administration and the Department of Health and Human Services, which oversee most biomedical research involving human subjects rely on rules and regulations to try to ensure responsible conduct, whereas in the rest of medicine, it is professionalism that regulates physician behavior—indeed it is the physicians themselves who embody the spirit of professionalism that guides their conduct, not the need to comply with regulations. As a backstop to this professional paradigm is, of course, a legal system that affords individuals who believe that they have been harmed or neglected by their physicians a right of individual recourse. Physicians who engage in substandard and/or irresponsible conduct or negligence are subject to medical malpractice lawsuits and claims of liability, but even here, there is a strong element of "peer review" to ascertain the prevailing standard of care and appropriateness of physician conduct. While the medical malpractice system may be a deterrent to irresponsible physician conduct, few would argue that fear of legal action is the primary motivator for a physician's professional behavior. Nonetheless, its potential impact is undeniable and capable of inducing unfortunate and costly consequences, namely the practice of "defensive medicine." Indeed the licensing and tort system for dealing with medical malpractice is itself problematic. Accordingly overreliance on the medical malpractice model in the research realm could well have an impact as detrimental to the responsible conduct of research as a rigid system of regulatory requirements, so a note of caution is warranted.

Development and implementation of a professional paradigm for research involving human subjects is likely to be at least as effective for ensuring responsible, ethical, safe conduct of clinical research as is the existing, compliance-focused approach, and it would be far less burdensome than the system for which so many are now calling for extensive reform. Reform is no longer a reasonable or appropriate goal. As has been said before, we cannot continue to do things essentially the same way, based on the same flawed assumptions and expect to have a different outcome. A complete redesign of the approach, a disruptive transformation, is necessary and long overdue.

Over the past thirty years, since the adoption of the Federal Regulations, our efforts to protect human subjects from research harms have focused on regulatory compliance achieved through education and oversight, not ethics. Each time the compliance paradigm has failed, we have intensified efforts to train investigators and hope for a better outcome. In essence we have done little more than put training wheels on the bike, with IRBs and HRPPs (human research protection programs) running alongside the investigators and research teams to keep them from falling down without fully appreciating what Henry Beecher said half a century ago, when ethical review and oversight were first adopted as a means of preventing harm to research subjects—that the only true protection of the safety, well-being, and rights of research subjects is the well-trained, well-intended, conscientious investigator (1966).

Jonathan Moreno (2001, 16) has written eloquently that what was once a system of "soft protectionism" has morphed into a rigid protectionist paradigm, and he believes that we have passed the point of no return—"Good-bye to all that," he says. But if we are to accept

Moreno's position, what does the future hold—more of the same? The very thought once again evokes Einstein's oft-quoted definition of insanity: "doing the same thing over and over again and expecting different results." With great respect for Moreno's opinion, I argue that not only *can* we change the failing protectionist paradigm, but that indeed, in the interests of science and society, we must. Rather than focus on how we should revise the current regulatory framework, we should focus on how we achieve the true goals of ensuring that research involving human subjects is done well and only by trained, certified professionals who take their responsibilities to ensure the well-being of their subjects as their highest priority. If we choose to take such a course, we will not abandon completely the current system for ethical and scientific review, which does indeed serve us well in many ways, but we could use it differently. All human research ought to be subject to peer review at any time, and certainly there are some types of highly risky or controversial research that might appropriately be subject to prospective review and approval. But moving forward, we should change our mindset and assumptions. Perhaps we can come to a realization that we have bred a new generation of investigators, better trained, more responsible, more willing to do the right thing not because they are required to do so by regulations but because it is the right thing to do. Perhaps we can reject our failing paradigm of protectionism and turn instead to the proven paradigm of professionalism.

Doing so, as we do in every other aspect of medical practice, would not be so very hard, as the tools already exist and their effectiveness is proven. Our greatest challenge is to find the will, as we already have the means. Yes, perhaps it is time to take off the training wheels!

References

Beecher, Henry. 1966. Ethics and clinical research. *New England Journal of Medicine* 274 (24): 1354–60.

Brandt, Allan M. 1978. Racism and research: The case of the Tuskegee Syphilis Study. *Hastings Center Report* 8 (6): 21–29.

Department of Energy, Office of Health, Safety and Security. 1995. Advisory Committee on Human Radiation Experiments: Final report (ACHRE). http://www.hss.doe.gov/healthsafety/ohre/roadmap/achre/report.html.

Department of Health and Human Services (DHHS). 2011. Advance Notice of Proposed Rulemaking. Human subjects research protections: Enhancing protections for research subjects and reducing burden, delay, and ambiguity for investigators. *Federal Register* 76 (143): 44512.

Goldby, Stephen. 1971. Experiments at the Willowbrook State School. *Lancet* 1: 749.

Jones, James H. 1993. *Bad Blood*. New York: Free Press. (Orig. pub. 1981.)

Katz, Jay. 1972. *Experimentation with Human Beings*. New York: Russell Sage Foundation.

Koski, Greg. 1999. Resolving Beecher's paradox: Getting beyond IRB reform. *Accountability in Research* 7 (2–4): 213–25.

Levine, Carol. 1988. Has AIDS changed the ethics of human subjects research? *Journal of Law, Medicine and Ethics* 16 (3–4): 167–73.

Mann, Charles C. 2011. Smoke screening. *Vanity Fair*, December 20. http://www.vanityfair.com/culture/features/2011/12/tsa-insanity-201112.

Moreno, Jonathan D. 2001. Goodbye to all that: The end of moderate protectionism in human subjects research. *Hastings Center Report* 31: 9–17.

Raper, Steven E., Narendra Chirmule, Frank S. Lee, Nelson A. Wivel, Adam Bragg, Guang-Ping Gao, James M. Wilson, and Mark L. Batshaw. 2003. Fatal systemic inflammatory response system in an ornithine transcarbamylase deficient patient following adenoviral gene transfer. *Molecular Genetics and Metabolism* 80: 148–58.

Steinbrook, Robert. 2002. Protecting research subjects—The crisis at Johns Hopkins. *New England Journal of Medicine* 346 (9): 716–20.

Suntharalingam, Ganesh, Meghan R. Perry, Stephen Ward, Stephen J. Brett, Andrew Castello-Cortes, Michael D. Brunner, and Nicki Panoskaltsis. 2006. Cytokine storm in a phase 1 trial of the anti-CD28 monoclonal antibody TGN1412. *New England Journal of Medicine* 355 (10): 1018–28.

Wood, Alastair J. J., and Janet Darbyshire. 2006. Injury to research volunteers—The clinical-research nightmare. *New England Journal of Medicine* 354 (18): 1869–71.

Appendix: Regulatory Changes in the ANPRM

For ease of reference, we have reproduced here the Office for Human Research Protection's summary table of key changes proposed by the ANPRM.

Comparison of Existing Rules with Some of the Changes Being Considered

Current rule	Changes being considered	Rationale for change
Issue 1: *There are no specific data security protections for IRB-reviewed research: regulations require IRBs to determine, for each study, "when appropriate [that] there are adequate provisions to protect the privacy of subjects and to maintain the confidentiality of data."*	*Specified data security protections would apply to such research, calibrated to the level of identifiability of the information being collected.*	*IRBs were not designed to evaluate risks to privacy and confidentiality, and often have little expertise in these matters. Setting uniform specific standards will help to assure appropriate privacy and confidentiality protections to all subjects, without administrative burden of needing a specific committee review of each study.*

Current rule	Changes being considered	Rationale for change
Issue 2: Research using existing biospecimens (clinical or from prior research) can be done without consent by stripping the specimens of identifiers.	Reforms would require written consent for research use of biospecimens, even those that have been stripped of identifiers. Consent could be obtained using a standard, short form by which a person could provide open-ended consent for most research uses of a variety of biospecimens (e.g., all clinical specimens that might be collected at a particular hospital). This change would only apply to biospecimens collected after the effective date of the new rules.	Changing technology in the field of genomics has dramatically increased the amount and nature of information about individuals that can be obtained from their DNA. Surveys indicate a desire on the part of most respondents to be able to decide whether their specimens can be used in research. Providing mechanisms for such control should enhance public trust in biomedical research.
Issue 3: Federal protections only apply to studies that are funded by certain federal agencies (Common Rule agencies), or to clinical investigations that involve products regulated by the FDA.	Regulations would apply to all studies, regardless of funding source, that are conducted by a US institution that receives some federal funding for human subjects research from a Common Rule agency.	Many have called for legislation to extend the Common Rule protections to all research with human subjects conducted in the US, regardless of funding source. This change would help narrow the current gap in protections.
Issue 4: Adverse events and unanticipated problems occurring in research are reported to multiple agencies and with various time-lines, with no central database as a repository for such data.	A single web site would be created for the electronic reporting of all such events: this would meet all federal reporting requirements and the collected data would be stored in a single database. Reporting requirements would be harmonized across agencies.	This reform would enhance the capacity to harness information quickly and efficiently to identify and respond to risks from experimental interventions, while also decreasing administrative burdens imposed by existing framework.

Current rule	Changes being considered	Rationale for change
Issue 5: *Current provisions of the Common Rule provide only basic information about the elements of informed consent and how consent documents should be written. Many consent forms are too long and hard to understand, and fail to include some of the most important information.*	*The regulations would be revised to provide greater specificity about how consent forms should be written and what information they should contain. The goal would be consent forms that are shorter, more readily understood, less confusing, that contain all of the key information, and that can serve as an excellent aid to help someone make a good decision about whether to participate in a study.*	*The informed consent of the subject is critical to the conduct of ethical research. The proposed changes will substantially enhance the quality of consent in many studies.*
Issue 6: *Each site in a study requires IRB review. Although the regulations allow one IRB to carry out the review for multiple sites, it is common for a single study conducted at multiple sites to have many IRBs separately reviewing the study.*	*For all of the US sites in a multi-site study, the changes propose a single IRB of record.*	*There is very little evidence that having multiple IRBs review the same study results in enhanced protections for subjects. By diffusing responsibility for that review, it might actually contribute to weakened protections.*
Issue 7: *Each Common Rule agency, and the FDA, is authorized to issue its own guidance with regard to interpreting and implementing the regulations protecting human subjects. That guidance may substantially differ from agency to agency.*	*The ANPRM does not propose a specific change but through questions, seeks to determine whether or not the differences in guidance from agency to agency are justified by differences in the applicable statutes or missions of those agencies, and if not, to determine how to make guidance more uniform.*	*If the differences in guidance are not justified, then it would be appropriate to eliminate those differences.*

Current rule	Changes being considered	Rationale for change
Issue 8: Research involving more-than-minimal risk requires review by a convened IRB.	*This requirement would remain unchanged.*	*Higher risk studies should be subject to the highest level of scrutiny.*
Issue 9: Research that requires review by a convened IRB requires continuing review at least annually.	Continuing review would generally not be required after all subjects in the study have completed all study interventions, and the only remaining procedures are standard-of-care procedures that are used to obtain follow-up clinical information (e.g., standard annual CT scans to detect any spread of the patient's cancer), and the analysis of the research data.	Since the research risks to subjects after completion of study interventions are limited to privacy and confidentiality concerns, which would be dealt with by the new uniform protections, this change would enable IRBs to focus attention on higher risk protocols.
Issue 10: Research that poses minimal risk and includes only research activities in a list approved by the HHS Secretary is eligible to be reviewed in an "expedited" manner (e.g., with one reviewer, instead of a convened IRB).	This list would be updated now, and at regular intervals, using appropriate data about risks to the extent possible.	Determinations about the risks imposed by various research activities should be based upon appropriate data.

Current rule	Changes being considered	Rationale for change
Issue 11: *Research that is eligible for expedited review requires continuing review at least annually.*	Continuing review would not be required of studies that are eligible for expedited review unless the reviewer, at the time of initial review, determines that continuing review is required, and documents why.	Research eligible for expedited review can involve only research activities that are included in the approved list. These activities are well-understood and it would be very unlikely that research involving such activities would lead to the new or unexpected risks with which continuing review is intended to deal.
Issue 12: *For a research study to be eligible for expedited review, an IRB member must determine that it is minimal risk.*	The "default" assumption will be that a study otherwise eligible for expedited review will be considered minimal risk unless a reviewer documents the rationale for classifying the study as involving more than minimal risk.	Since research that is eligible for expedited review can involve only research activities that are included in the approved list, very few such studies will involve more than minimal risk. This change will better assure that the level of review is well targeted to the level of risk.
Issue 13: *For a research study to be approved, even if it qualifies for expedited review, the same approval criteria must be met as for studies that are approved by a convened IRB.*	The ANPRM does not propose a specific change, but through questions seeks to determine whether some approval criteria do not meaningfully increase protections for subjects (i.e., in the case of studies that otherwise would qualify for expedited review).	Appropriate approval criteria may be different for studies that otherwise qualify for expedited review and those that do not.

Current rule	Changes being considered	Rationale for change
Issue 14: *Six categories of studies qualify as "exempt" from the regulations, meaning that they do not have to comply with any of the requirements of the regulations.*	*These studies would no longer be fully exempt from the regulations. In particular, they would be subject to the new data security protections described above; and for some studies (e.g., those using biospecimens) new consent requirements would apply.*	*Research that might pose informational risk to subjects should adhere to reasonable data security protections.*
Issue 15: *The categories of studies that qualify as "exempt" are not very clearly defined. As a result, it is sometimes difficult to determine whether a study qualifies as exempt.*	*The criteria for determining whether a study is exempt would be more clear-cut and less open to interpretation.*	*Clearer criteria will increase the transparency of the system and reduce the time and effort spent in determining whether or not a study qualifies as exempt.*
Issue 16: *Although the regulations do not require administrative review before a study is determined to be exempt, most institutions follow current federal recommendations and carry out such an administrative review.*	*The recommendation that all such studies undergo administrative review would be eliminated. Researchers would file a brief "registration" form with their institution or IRB, and would be permitted to commence their research studies immediately after filing the form. Audits of a small percentage of studies would take place to ensure appropriate application of and compliance with the revised regulation.*	*The major risk in most studies that might qualify as exempt is a breach of confidentiality. Given that there will be clearer criteria to determine when a study meets the standards for exemption, and that all studies will be covered under appropriate data security protections, there should be little need for or benefit from reviewing each study before it commences to determine that it meets the criteria for being exempt.*

Current rule	Changes being considered	Rationale for change
Issue 17: One of the six exempt categories applies to research using educational tests, survey procedures, or observation of public behavior, but not if both (i) information is recorded in a way that allows subjects to be identified, and (ii) disclosure of the subjects' responses outside of the research could reasonably place subjects at risk of criminal or civil liability or cause damage to financial standing, reputation, or employability.	This exempt category would be broadened by eliminating criteria (i) and (ii) for studies that involve competent adults (i.e., such research would be exempt even if the information was recorded in an identifiable way and the disclosure could pose such risks to the subject).	The new data security protections obviate the need for (i) and (ii).
Issue 18: Currently, research studies in the social and behavioral sciences that do not qualify for exemption category 2, but that involve certain types of well-understood interactions with subjects (e.g., asking someone to watch a video and then conducting word association tests), require IRB review.	The ANPRM does not propose a specific change, but seeks public comment on whether a broad subset of studies using common social and behavioral science methodologies can be identified that should be eligible for exemption 2 .	To identify areas of research that do not warrant the current degree of regulatory oversight so that review requirements are better calibrated to the level of risk.

Current rule	Changes being considered	Rationale for change
Issue 19: One of the six exempt categories applies to research involving the use of existing data, documents, records, and pathological or diagnostic specimens, but only if the sources are publicly available or if the information is recorded by researchers in such a manner that subjects cannot be identified, directly or through identifiers linked to them.	The requirements in this category that (1) all the data or specimens must exist as of the time that the study commences, and (2) the researcher cannot record and retain information that identifies the subjects, would be eliminated. If a researcher chooses to obtain and record identifiable information, the subject's consent would generally be needed (as required by the current rules), but that could be obtained at the time the materials are collected by using a general, open-ended consent to future research. With regard to studies using existing biospecimens, see Issue 2 above.	The new data security protections obviate the need for limitations in this exempt category.

Source: US Department of Health and Human Services, Office for Human Research Protections, "Regulatory Changes in ANPRM: Comparison of Existing Rules with Some of the Changes Being Considered," http://www.hhs.gov/ohrp/humansubjects/anprmchangetable.html.

Contributors

Adam Braddock
Health Sciences Assistant Clinical Professor (nonsalaried) and Associate Physician, Department of Pediatrics, Division of Academic General Pediatrics, Child Development, and Community Health, University of California, San Diego School of Medicine

Alexander Morgan Capron
University Professor, Scott H. Bice Chair in Healthcare Law, Policy and Ethics, Gould School of Law, Professor of Law and Medicine, Keck School of Medicine, and Co-Director, Pacific Center for Health Policy and Ethics, University of Southern California

Ellen Wright Clayton
Craig-Weaver Professor of Pediatrics, Professor of Law, Co-Founder, Center for Biomedical Ethics and Society, Vanderbilt University

I. Glenn Cohen
Professor, Harvard Law School, and Co-Director, Petrie–Flom Center for Health Law Policy, Biotechnology, and Bioethics

Susan Cox
Associate Professor, W. Maurice Young Centre for Applied Ethics, University of British Columbia

Amy L. Davis
Consultant (and formerly Senior Director for Programs and Publications), Public Responsibility in Medicine and Research (PRIM&R)

Barbara J. Evans
Professor of Law and George Butler Research Professor; Director, Center on Biotechnology and Law, University of Houston Law Center

Nir Eyal
Associate Professor of Global Health and Social Medicine (Medical Ethics) at the Harvard Medical School

Heidi Li Feldman
Professor of Law and Associate Professor of Philosophy, Georgetown University. Past Chair, Georgetown University Institutional Review Board C (Social and Behavioral Sciences)

Benjamin Fombonne
Cancer Diagnosis Program, Division of Cancer Treatment and Diagnosis, National Cancer Institute

Elisa A. Hurley
Executive Director, Public Responsibility in Medicine and Research (PRIM&R)

Ana S. Iltis
Associate Professor of Philosophy; Director, Center for Bioethics, Health and Society, Wake Forest University

Gail H. Javitt
Counsel, Sidley Austin, LLC

Greg Koski
Associate Professor of Anesthesia, Harvard Medical School, and Former Director, Office of Human Research Protections, US Department of Health and Human Services

Nicole Lockhart
Division of Genomics and Society, National Human Genome Research Institute

Holly Fernandez Lynch
Executive Director, Petrie–Flom Center for Health Law Policy, Biotechnology, and Bioethics

Michael McDonald
Professor Emeritus, W. Maurice Young Centre for Applied Ethics, University of British Columbia

Michelle N. Meyer
Assistant Professor of Bioethics, Union Graduate College, and Director of Bioethics Policy, Union Graduate College–Icahn School of Medicine at Mount Sinai Bioethics Program

Osagie K. Obasogie
Professor of Law, University of California, Hastings College of the Law with a joint appointment at UCSF Department of Social and Behavioral Sciences; Senior Fellow, Center for Genetics and Society

Efthimios Parasidis
Assistant Professor of Law and Public Health, The Ohio State University, Moritz College of Law, with a joint appointment in Ohio State's College of Public Health

Govind Persad
Visiting Scholar, Department of Medical Ethics and Health Policy, University of Pennsylvania, and PhD Candidate, Philosophy, Stanford University

Rosamond Rhodes
Professor, Icahn School of Medicine at Mount Sinai

Suzanne M. Rivera
Assistant Professor of Bioethics, Case Western Reserve University School of Medicine

Zachary M. Schrag
Professor of History, George Mason University. Editor, Institutional Review Blog

Seema K. Shah
Faculty, Clinical Center Department of Bioethics and Division of AIDS, National Institutes of Health

Hilary Shutak
Office of Communications and Public Liaison, National Institute of Diabetes and Digestive and Kidney Diseases

Jeffrey Skopek
Lecturer on Law, Harvard Law School, and Academic Fellow, Petrie–Flom Center for Health Law Policy, Biotechnology, and Bioethics

Laura Stark
Assistant Professor, Center for Medicine, Health and Society, Vanderbilt University

Patrick Taylor
Assistant Clinical Professor, Harvard Medical School; Director, Ethics Analysis and Applications, Children's Hospital Informatics Program, and Staff Scientist, Boston Children's Hospital

Anne Townsend
Research Associate, Department of Occupational Science and Occupational Therapy, University of British Columbia

Carol J. Weil
Program Director for Ethical and Regulatory Affairs, National Cancer Institute

Brett A. Williams
Attorney, Insley & Race, LLC, Atlanta, Georgia

Leslie E. Wolf
Professor of Law at Georgia State University College of Law and the Center for Law, Health and Society

Index

Abbo, Elmer, 165
Advanced Notice of Proposed
 Rulemaking (ANPRM), 2–4, 7–8,
 251, 342. *See also* Common Rule
 adverse event reporting system,
  16–17
 areas targeted for improvement, 46
 biobanks and, 210–11
 on biospecimen identifiability,
  194–95, 207
 on biospecimens and human subjects
  protection, 237–38, 246, 274
 criticisms of the Common Rule, 313
 data security standards and, 15–16
 disconnect between use of certificates
  and, 214–15
 ethical issues and, 129
 evaluating the proposed elimination
  of continuing review for previously
  expedited minimal risk studies,
  49–52
 federal regulations and, 17
 on generalizability, 291
 goals of, 12, 45–49
 harmonization of regulatory
  guidance, 17
 on hot spots of research risk, 121
 increased use of single IRB of record
  for multisite research, 15
 informed consent and, 15, 18–20
 Institutional Review Boards and, 12,
  13–15, 285–86
 mandatory general consent and,
  227–29
 nonconsensual access to data and
  biospecimens and, 267–69
 objective of, 9–10
 outcomes compatible with, 48–49
 on prisoners as human subjects, 93
 privacy provisions, 20–22, 252–55
 provisions of, 12–17
 Public Responsibility in Medicine
  and Research (PRIM&R)
  comments, 4, 17–18
 on regulator bias, 318–19
 responding to criticisms of research
  oversight practices, 52–54
 revised review framework to
  improve calibration of review
  process to risk of research, 13–15
 on secondary use distinctions,
  253–54
 specific regulatory changes, 351–58
Adverse event reporting system, 16–17
 Department of Defense and, 71, 75
American Academy of Pediatrics
 (AAP), 86
American Anthropological
 Association, 288, 291–292
Americans with Disabilities Act
 (ADA), 199
Amyotrophic lateral sclerosis, 70
Analogy between human subjects and
 human research workers, 328–31
Annas, George, 104
Anthrax vaccine, 69–71
Antiretroviral treatment (ART), 127
Assent, 86

Association of American Medical
  Colleges, 288
Atomic Energy Commission, 67
Atomic warfare, 66–68
Augmented Cognition program, 72
Autonomous authorization, 147–49,
  152–53

Bearder v. State, 243
Beauchamp, Tom, 148, 290, 291
Beecher, Henry, 130, 344
Belmont Report, 123n2, 137
  development, 10–11
  exempted research and, 166
  generalizability and, 290
  informed consent and, 146
  paradigm shifts in research ethics
    and, 282
  participatory inclusion and, 113
Beno v. Shalala, 165
Berger, John, 281
Bias, regulator, 316–20
Biobanks, 34–36, 38–39, 151
  current regulatory approach to, 208–10
  history and purpose of certificates
    and, 211–15
  informed consent and, 208–10
  public attitudes toward, 243–45
Biodefense and Emerging Infections
  Research Resources Repository
  (BEI), 36
Biological samples, discarded, 39–40
Biological warfare, 66–68
Biomedical Research Alliance of New
  York (BRANY), 179
Biospecimens, 189–191, 221–22,
  232–33
  case law, 238–43, 194, 222–23
  Certificate of Confidentiality and,
    207–208, 211–15
  challenges of mandatory general
    consent and, 227–29
  changes to consent of collection of,
    210–11
  consent process improvement
    via community education and
    engagement, 229–32
  defect in Common Rule's waiver
    provision and, 269–71
  human subjects protection and,
    237–38
  identification of research
    participation and, 197
  informed consent and, 225–27,
    246–48
  misjudging the likelihood and impact
    of identifiability of, 194–200
  need for appropriate, inclusive
    process for establishing policy on,
    273–76
  nonconsensual access to data and,
    266–69, 270–71
  OHRP on, 193
  placing too much weight on
    signatures and, 200–203
  problems with current regulatory
    framework and, 223–25
  as property, 245–48, 257–58
  rationale for mandatory
    consent for secondary uses of,
    recommendations for, 215–17
  re-identified for purposes of law
    enforcement, 199–200
  re-identified to access and reveal
    clinical information about an
    individual, 199
  re-identified to access and reveal
    more genomic data about an
    individual, 198–99
  right to privacy and, 245–46
Blanket consent model, 226, 227–28,
  253
Blustein, Jan, 167
Boilerplate provisions, informed
  consent, 20
Botulinium toxoid (BT) vaccine,
  69–70
Burdens of participation, 118–19

"Cambridge Report, The," 344
Cancer Genome Atlas Project, 231
Caplan, Arthur, 104
Case law on biospecimens,
  238–43

Centering Project, 115–16
  participants' experiences of benefits and burdens and, 118–19
  relevant findings, 116–19
Centering the Human Subject in Health Research: Understanding the Meaning and Experience of Research Participation, 115
Certificate of Confidentiality, 207–208, 211–15
  recommendations for, 215–17
Chemical warfare, 66–68
Children
  Common Rule and, 80–81
  community-based participatory research and, 81–82
  community pediatrics and, 79–80, 90
  defining community and research with, 87
  examples of research partnerships with, 87–89
  forming research partnerships with, 86–89
  institutional review boards and, 89
  as research partners, case for, 82–86
  risks of partnerships with, 85–86
  vulnerability and research partnerships with, 84–85
C.K. v. New Jersey Dep't of Health & Human Servs., 165
Clayton, Ellen Wright, 207
Clyde, David, 307–308
Cohen, Joshua, 162
Coleman, Carl, 174
Collegial review, 180–82
Combined DNA Index System (CODIS) database, 196, 198, 213
Common Rule, 2–3, 11, 16, 46, 113. *See also* Advanced Notice of Proposed Rulemaking (ANPRM)
  adverse event reporting and, 16
  on balancing risk with societal benefits, 37, 41–42
  biobanking regulations, 208
  biospecimens and, 237
  children and, 80–81
  on compensation for injury, 333–34
  definition of research, 33
  ethical issues and, 127, 128–29, 138n1
  expressive potential of law and, 134–36
  federal funding and, 17
  on information-based research, 265
  informed consent and, 35, 145, 146
  inherent defects in waiver provisions of, 269–71
  medical model and, 299–301, 309–10
  military personnel and, 72–73, 76
  need for appropriate, inclusive process for establishing policy on biospecimens and data, 273–76
  on nonconsensual access to data and biospecimens, 266–67
  types of research covered by, 285–86
  viewed as infallible, 31
  on vulnerable populations, 65
Community, defining, 87
Community advisory boards (CABs), 230
Community-based participatory research (CBPR), 81–82, 89
Community education and engagement, 229–32
Community pediatrics, 79–80, 90
  case for children as research partners in, 82–86
  defining community participation and, 81–82
Compensation of subjects and workers, 331–33
  for injury, 333–35
Compliance, 119–21
  ethical regulations and culture of, 131–32
Consistent treatment of subjects, 331
Consociationalism, 162
Continuing review, 49–52
Cooke, Robert, 292
Crane v. Matthews, 165
Criticisms of research oversight practices, 52–53

Data. *See also* Biospecimens
  need for appropriate, inclusive process for establishing policy on, 273–76
  nonconsensual access to, 266–69, 270–71
  security standards, 15–16
Data Analysis and Coordination Center (DACC), 36
Davis, Amy L., 4, 208, 211, 320
Decisional capacity, patients without, 32, 40
Decision repositories, 182–83
Declaration of Helsinki, 37, 144, 145
Default rule, 331
Defense Advanced Research Projects Agency (DARPA), 71–72
Defensive medicine, 346
De minimis risk, 27, 40–42
  confusion and inconsistency and, 33–34
  discarded biological samples and, 39–40
  exempted research and, 38
  genome and microbiome research and, 34–36, 38–39
  as new category of research risk, 36–40
  patients without decisional capacity and, 40
  research on populations and, 39
  surveys and, 40
Democratic deliberation, 157–58
  need for ethical review of public benefits research and, 164–67
  participatory inclusion as, 158–62
Department of Defense, 66
  additional safeguards for military personnel and, 72–75
  experimental use of medical products as prophylactic treatments by, 68–72
Department of Health, Education, and Welfare (DHEW), 286–87

Department of Health and Human Services (DHHS), 2, 9, 45, 65, 165, 344, 345. *See also* Advanced Notice of Proposed Rulemaking (ANPRM)
  on biospecimens, 189, 221–22, 274–76
  HIPAA Privacy Rule waiver provisions and, 271–72
  informed consent and, 146, 147
  military personnel and, 72–73
  prisoners as human subjects and, 94–95
Developmental reasons for children as research partners, 82–83
Dignitary harms, 252–53
Diminished consent, 152–53
Discarded biological samples, 39–40
DNA Identification Act of 1994, 196. *See also* Biospecimens
Doe v. Sullivan, 69

Educational materials for potential subjects, 19–20
Ethical Considerations for Research Involving Prisoners, 98
Ethical issues, 137–38
  Common Rule and, 127, 128–29
  culture of compliance as by-product of current regulations on, 131–32
  definition of subjects, 292–93
  democratic deliberation and, 157–58
  ethnography and self-experimentalism, 306–309
  and how regulations should address investigators and sponsors, 132–33
  objections to regulations on, 136–37
  overlooked by regulations, 130–31
  participant heterogeneity, 320–22
  principle of robust consent and, 301–304
  and reasons for addressing ethical responsibilities of investigators and sponsors, 129–32
  regulation enforceability, 133–36
  research heterogeneity, 315–16

review of public benefits research and, 164–67
separateness of persons and, 304–305
"Ethical Principles and Guidelines for the Protection of Human Subjects of Research," 10–11
Ethics Application Repository, The (TEAR), 183
Ethics creep, 180
Ethnography and self-experimentalism, 306–309
Evans, Barbara, 209
Evidence-based HRP, 114–15
Exaptation, 291
Exempted research, 38, 165–166
Expedited review of minimal risk studies, 49–52
Expressive potential of law, 134–136

Facebook, 256
Faden, Ruth, 148
Federal Policy for the Protection of Human Subjects, 80
Federal Register, 294, 315
Feldman, Heidi Li, 282, 284
Field testing, 66
Flynn, Laurie, 162–63
Føllesdal, Andreas, 162
Food and Drug Administration (FDA), 68, 69, 74, 75, 238, 345
on nonconsensual access, 268
regulations and ethical issues, 133

G (novel), 281
Gatter, Robert, 134
Gelsinger, Jesse, 343
Generalizability, 288–92
Genetic Information Nondiscrimination Act of 2008 (GINA), 198, 257
Genome research, 34–36
Genome-wide association studies (GWAS), 196
Governance and informed consent, 151–52

Greenberg v. Miami Children's Hospital, 240–41
Gulf War illness, 70
Gutmann, Amy, 158

Harmon, Amy, 223–24
Hastings Center Report, The, 2
Health Insurance Portability and Accountability Act (HIPAA), 13, 15, 16, 20–22, 194, 198–203, 211
standard as default in privacy issues, 254–55
waiver provision, 271–72
Heterogeneity
participant, 320–22
research, 315–16
Hitler, Adolf, 301, 303
HIV/AIDS, 127
Honberg, Ronald, 162–63
Honest broker model, 223
Hudson, Kathy, 258
Human Microbiome Project (HMP), 36
Human research protection (HRP) systems
Centering Project, 115–19
compliance and, 119–21
effectiveness of, 113–14
evidence-based, 114–15
getting past protectionism in, 341–47
limitations of participant-centered approach to, 122
participants' experiences of benefits and burdens and, 118–19
recommendations for practice and policy, 121
risk and, 116–18
Human subjects research
analogy with human research workers, 328–31, 337–38n2
biomedical and behavioral research regulation and, 286–88, 294–95
compensation for injury, 333–35
covered by Common Rule, 285–86
current regulatory framework for, 222–23

Human subjects research (cont.)
  default rule and consistent treatment of, 331
  deficiencies in regulation of, 1–3, 7–8
  defining subjects in, 33–34, 292–93
  ethnography and self-experimentalism in, 306–309
  gaining a voice in the research setting, 336
  generalizability, 288–92
  genesis of disparate regulation over subjects in, 327–28
  getting past protectionism in, 341–47
  heterogeneity, 315–16
  historical framework, 1, 10–12
  medical model in, 299–310
  oversight system, 52–53
  participation as work, 329
  participatory inclusion in context of, 162–64
  payment to, 331–33
  principle of robust consent and, 301–304
  protection and biospecimens, 237–38
  rationale for protection of, 330–31
  reasons for regulating, 46
  separateness of persons and, 304–305
"Human Subjects Research Protections: Enhancing Protections for Research Subjects and Reducing Burden, Delay, and Ambiguity for Investigators," 2, 9
Hurley, Elisa A., 4, 208, 211, 320

Iltis, Ana K., 4, 27–28
Immortal Life of Henrietta Lacks, The, 201
Individual autonomy, 1
Informed consent, 15, 18–20, 110, 143
  assent and, 86
  autonomous authorization and, 147–49, 152–53
  biobanks and, 35, 208–10
  biospecimens and, 246–48
  blanket, 226, 227–28, 253
  cumulative effects of exclusions, exemptions, and exceptions to, 145–47
  diminished, 152–53
  evolving status of human beings in research and, 150–51
  exceptions, 143–47
  lure of utility and, 149–50
  military personnel and, 73–74
  origin and evolution of, 143–45
  patients without decisional capacity and, 32, 40
  principle of robust consent and, 301–304
  public benefits exemption, 165–66
  reasons for slide away from, 147–51
  for secondary uses of biospecimens, 225–27
  traditional functions of, 151–52
Injury, compensation for, 333–35
Institute of Medicine (IOM), 11
  critique on recommendations by, 99–104
  on prisoners as human subjects, 93–105
Institutional Review Boards (IRBs), 12, 13–15
  Centering Project and, 115–19
  collegial review, 180–82
  Common Rule waiver and, 272
  compliance and, 119–21
  decision repositories and, 182–83
  definition of subjects and, 292–93
  differences in judgment across, 174
  ethical issues and, 127–38
  evidence-based and participant-centered process, 121
  expedited studies and, 49–52
  getting past protectionism in regulation of, 341–47
  impeding and limiting research, 31
  IRB creep, 282
  jurisdiction of, 285–86
  limitations of participant-centered approach with, 122

local precedents and, 174–84
military, 73
observations and audio recordings of meetings of, 110
oversight system, 52–53
PRIM&R and, 17–18
privacy and, 251
regulator bias and, 316–20
research partnerships with children and, 89
risk-based regulation and, 314–15
signatures on samples/data and, 200–203
study networks and, 178–80
thinking in cases, 174–76
types of research triggering review by, 289

Job Corps, 167
Joffe, Steven, 130
Jonsen, Albert, 285, 293, 295
Journal of the American Medical Association, 75

Kahan, Dan, 135, 136
Kipnis, Ken, 84
Koski, Greg, 130, 281, 283

Law enforcement, 199–200
Le Grand, Julian, 134
Levine, Carol, 342
Libertarianism, 305
Limited data sets, 21
Lindh, Anna, 197
Litigation for injury, 334
Local precedents
  collegial review, 180–82
  decision repositories and, 182–83
  defined, 174–76
  future of multisite studies and, 183–84
  research and findings on, 176–78
  review models to manage, 178–83
  study networks and, 178–80
Lynch, Holly Fernandez, 282

Man-break tests, 66–67
Mandatory general consent, 227–29

Mathews, David, 287, 288, 294
Medicaid, 165, 271, 288
Medical malpractice model, 346
Medical model
  ethnography and self-experimentalism, 306–309
  introduction to, 299–301
  principle of robust consent, 301–304
  separateness of persons and, 304–305
Medical products, experimental military use of, 68–71
Medical well-being, 166
Medicare, 165, 271
Medicine, defensive, 346
Menikoff, Jerry A., 2, 3
Metabolic Dominance program, 72
Meyer, Michelle, 281, 283
Microbiome research, 34–36
Milgram studies, 175
Military personnel, 65, 76
  contemplating additional safeguards for, 72–75
  development of biomedical enhancements for, 71–72
  experimental use of medical products as prophylactic treatments in, 68–71
  studies related to atomic, biological, and chemical warfare and, 66–68
Miller, Frank, 130
Moore v. Regents of the University of California, 238–40, 245
Moral reasons for children as research partners, 83–84
Moreno, Jonathan, 346–47
Multicenter Academic Clinical Research Organization (MACRO), 179
Multisite research, 15
Mustard gas, 66, 67

Natanson v. Kline, 145
National Bioethics Advisory Commission, 45, 150, 295
National Cancer Institute (NCI), 213

National Commission for the Protection of Human Subjects of Biomedical and Behavioral Research, 10, 96–97, 113, 285
  on defining human subjects, 292
  on generalizability, 288–89
National Commission for the Study of Ethical Problems in Medicine and Biomedicine, 269–70
National Commission on Patient Safety and Protection of Patients from Medical Risks, 344
National Institutes of Health (NIH), 36, 207, 227, 231
  study networks, 178–79
National Job Corps Study, 167
National Practitioner Databank, 136
National Research Act of 1974, 10, 145, 286, 287, 325n1
Naval Research Laboratory, 67
Nazi experiments, 1, 68, 95, 143–44, 150, 175, 299. *See also* Nuremberg Code
  principle of robust consent and, 302–303
Networks, study, 178–80
No-fault compensation system, 335
Nonconsensual access to data and biospecimens, 266–69, 270–71
Nuremberg Code, 37, 95, 96–97, 150, 299
  evolution of informed consent and, 143–45
  principle of robust consent and, 301–304

Obama, Barack, 2, 7
Office for Human Research Protections (OHRP), 110, 173, 193, 194
  on biobanking, 208–209
  on biospecimens, 200–203, 222–23, 265–66
  on Common Rule waiver, 272
  on generalizability, 291
  on nonconsensual access to data and biospecimens, 269, 274

Office for Protection from Research Risks (OPRR), 213, 293
Office of Science and Technology Policy (OSTP), 9
Off-label uses of medical products, 68–71, 75
1,000 Genomes Project, 231
Oversight system, 52–54

Paradigm shifts in research ethics, 281–84
Participant heterogeneity, 320–22
Participation, burdens and benefits of, 118–19
Participatory inclusion
  as democratic deliberation, 158–62
  in human subjects research context, 162–64
  models, 110
  protecting participants, 159–61
  reasons for, 162
  survey representation *versus* personal representation and, 161–62
Paternalism, 1, 85
Patient Protection and Affordable Care Act, 199
PatientsLikeMe (PLM), 257
Payment to workers and subjects, 331–33
  for injury, 333–35
Pediatrics, community, 79–80, 90. *See also* Children
  case for children as research partners in, 82–86
  defining community participation and, 81–82
Peer review, 346
Periodic random retrospective audits, 211
Photobiomodulation, 72
Pollack, Andrew, 258
Practical reasons for children as research partners, 82
Precedents, local
  collegial review, 180–82
  decision repositories and, 182–83
  defined, 174–76

future of multisite studies and, 183–84
research and findings on, 176–78
review models to manage, 178–83
study networks and, 178–80
Presidential Commission for the Study of Bioethical Issues (PCSBI), 157, 258, 274–75
Principle of robust consent, 301–304
Prisoners, 93–94
  contextual critique on IOM recommendations on, 101–103
  critique of IOM recommendations on, 99–104
  Institute of Medicine's recommendations on research using, 94–99
  IOM evolved ethical framework for evaluating, 98–99
  methodological critique of IOM recommendations on, 100–101
  substantive critique on IOM recommendations on, 103–104
Privacy
  blanket consent and, 253
  changing social norms about self-disclosure and, 256–57, 260–61
  dignitary harms and, 252–53
  existing paradigms in US research regulation, 251
  HIPAA standard as default in safeguarding, 254–55
  information and specimens as property and, 257–58
  potential for re-identification of de-identified data and, 258–60
  -related provisions contained within ANPRM, 20–22, 252–55
  secondary use distinctions and, 253–54
Privacy Protection Study Commission, 270
Professionalism, 345–46
Pronovost, Peter J., 33
Property, biospecimens as, 245–48, 257–58
Proportionality judgments, 54n2

Protectionism in human subjects research, 341–47
Psychotropic drugs, 66, 68
Public attitudes toward biobanking, 243–45
Public benefits research, ethical review of, 164–67
Public health surveillance (PHS), 32, 39
  defining research and, 33–34
Public Responsibility in Medicine and Research (PRIM&R), 4, 17–18, 23n1, 320
Puglisi, J. Thomas, 2–3
Pyridostigmine bromide (PB), 69–70

Quality assurance (QA), 32, 39
  defining research and, 33–34
Quality improvement (QI), 32, 39
  defining research and, 33–34

Race-based experiments, 66–67
Radiation experiments, 67–68
Reasoning in cases, 176
Regulation of human subjects research. *See also* Advanced Notice of Proposed Rulemaking (ANPRM)
  background on, 10–12
  biomedical and behavioral research regulations and, 286–88
  Common Rule system, 2–3, 11
  federal funding and, 17
  genesis of disparate, 327–28
  getting past protectionism in, 341–47
  harmonization of, 17
  Institutional Review Boards and, 109–11
  participant heterogeneity and, 320–22
  reasons for, 46
  regulator bias and, 316–20
  research heterogeneity and, 315–16
  risk and, 27–29, 313, 314–24
  technological changes and, 11–12
  voice of research subjects and workers in, 336

Regulator bias, 316–20
Re-identification of de-identified data, 258–60
Rempfer v. Sharfstein, 70–71
Report and Recommendations: Institutional Review Boards, 289
Repositories, decision, 182–83
Representation, survey *versus* personal, 161–62
Research. *See* Human subjects research
Research ethics boards (REBs), 113
 Centering Project and, 115–19
 limitations of participant-centered approach with, 122
Research ethics committees (RECs), 114
Responsible Research: A Systems Approach to Protecting Research Participants, 114
Review, continuing, 49–52
Rhodes, Rosamond, 4, 27–28
Risk
 benefit evaluation and ethical issues, 129, 314–22
 children and minimal, 80
 confusion and inconsistency and, 33–34
 defined, 325n4
 de minimis, 27–29, 32–42
 federal regulation and, 27–29, 313
 genome and microbiome research and, 34–36
 human research protection (HRP) Centering Project on, 116–18
 informed consent and, 32
 participant heterogeneity and, 320–22
 of partnerships with children, 85–86
 prisoners as human subjects and, 97–98
 proportionate research regulation and, 322–24
 proposed elimination of continuing review for previously expedited studies with minimal, 49–52
 regulation based, 314–22
 regulator bias and, 316–320
 research heterogeneity and, 315–316
Rivera, Suzanne, 210, 211
Roche, Ellen, 343
Roelcke, Volker, 299
Rogers, Joel, 162
Rosenblatt, Rand, 159, 161

Saghai, Yashar, 290
Samples, discarded biological, 39–40
Scalia, Antonin, 288
Schrag, Zachary, 282
Schuck, Peter, 152
Secondary use distinctions, 253–54
Secretary's Advisory Committee on Human Research Protections (SACHRP), 165
Self-disclosure, 256–57, 260–61
Self-experimentalism and ethnography, 306–309
Separateness of persons, 304–305
Shapiro, Harold, 295
Short tandem repeats (STRs), 196
Single nucleotide polymorphisms (SNPs), 195, 213
Smith, Scott M., 308
Social and Behavioral Science White Paper, 291
Social norms about self-disclosure and privacy, 256–57, 260–61
Soft protectionism, 346–47
Special Supplemental Nutrition Program for Women, Infants, and Children (WIC), 166
Stem cell research, 48
Study networks, 178–80
Sunnybrook Health Sciences Center, 182
Sunstein, Cass, 134–35
Surveys, 40

TeGenero study, 343
Thanatology, 302
Tiered consent, 226
Tri-Council Policy Statement, 294

TSA (Transportation Safety Administration), 343–44
Tuskegee syphilis study, 50, 95–96, 175

Uniform Code of Military Justice, 65
United Nations Convention on the Rights of the Child, 84
Utilitarianism, 305, 322

Veatch, Robert, 286
Voice of research subjects and workers, 336
Vulnerable populations, 61–62
  children as, 79–90
  defining, 61–62
  military personnel as, 65–76
  prisoners as, 93–105

Washington University v. Catalona, 241–42
Weindling, Paul, 299
Workers, human research
  analogy with human subjects, 328–31, 337–38n2
  compensation for injury, 333–35
  default rule and consistent treatment of, 331
  gaining a voice in the workplace, 336
  human subjects as, 329
  payment to, 331–33
  rationale for protection of, 330–31

Y-chromosome (Y-STRs), 195

Basic Bioethics
Arthur Caplan, editor

Books Acquired under the Editorship of Glenn McGee and Arthur Caplan

Peter A. Ubel, *Pricing Life: Why It's Time for Health Care Rationing*

Mark G. Kuczewski and Ronald Polansky, eds., *Bioethics: Ancient Themes in Contemporary Issues*

Suzanne Holland, Karen Lebacqz, and Laurie Zoloth, eds., *The Human Embryonic Stem Cell Debate: Science, Ethics, and Public Policy*

Gita Sen, Asha George, and Piroska Östlin, eds., *Engendering International Health: The Challenge of Equity*

Carolyn McLeod, *Self-Trust and Reproductive Autonomy*

Lenny Moss, *What Genes Can't Do*

Jonathan D. Moreno, ed., *In the Wake of Terror: Medicine and Morality in a Time of Crisis*

Glenn McGee, ed., *Pragmatic Bioethics*, 2d edition

Timothy F. Murphy, *Case Studies in Biomedical Research Ethics*

Mark A. Rothstein, ed., *Genetics and Life Insurance: Medical Underwriting and Social Policy*

Kenneth A. Richman, *Ethics and the Metaphysics of Medicine: Reflections on Health and Beneficence*

David Lazer, ed., *DNA and the Criminal Justice System: The Technology of Justice*

Harold W. Baillie and Timothy K. Casey, eds., *Is Human Nature Obsolete? Genetics, Bioengineering, and the Future of the Human Condition*

Robert H. Blank and Janna C. Merrick, eds., *End-of-Life Decision Making: A Cross-National Study*

Norman L. Cantor, *Making Medical Decisions for the Profoundly Mentally Disabled*

Margrit Shildrick and Roxanne Mykitiuk, eds., *Ethics of the Body: Post-Conventional Challenges*

Alfred I. Tauber, *Patient Autonomy and the Ethics of Responsibility*

David H. Brendel, *Healing Psychiatry:Bridging the Science/Humanism Divide*

Jonathan Baron, *Against Bioethics*

Michael L. Gross, *Bioethics and Armed Conflict: Moral Dilemmas of Medicine and War*

Karen F. Greif and Jon F. Merz, *Current Controversies in the Biological Sciences: Case Studies of Policy Challenges from New Technologies*

Deborah Blizzard, *Looking Within: A Sociocultural Examination of Fetoscopy*

Ronald Cole-Turner, ed., *Design and Destiny: Jewish and Christian Perspectives on Human Germline Modification*

Holly Fernandez Lynch, *Conflicts of Conscience in Health Care: An Institutional Compromise*

Mark A. Bedau and Emily C. Parke, eds., *The Ethics of Protocells: Moral and Social Implications of Creating Life in the Laboratory*

Jonathan D. Moreno and Sam Berger, eds., *Progress in Bioethics: Science, Policy, and Politics*

Eric Racine, *Pragmatic Neuroethics: Improving Understanding and Treatment of the Mind-Brain*

Martha J. Farah, ed., *Neuroethics: An Introduction with Readings*

Jeremy R. Garrett, ed., *The Ethics of Animal Research: Exploring the Controversy*

Books Acquired under the Editorship of Arthur Caplan

Sheila Jasanoff, ed., *Reframing Rights: Bioconstitutionalism in the Genetic Age*

Christine Overall, *Why Have Children? The Ethical Debate*

Yechiel Michael Barilan, *Human Dignity, Human Rights, and Responsibility: The New Language of Global Bioethics and Bio-Law*

Tom Koch, *Thieves of Virtue: When Bioethics Stole Medicine*

Timothy F. Murphy, *Ethics, Sexual Orientation, and Choices about Children*

Daniel Callahan, *In Search of the Good: A Life in Bioethics*

Robert Blank, *Intervention in the Brain: Politics, Policy, and Ethics*

Gregory E. Kaebnick and Thomas H. Murray, eds., *Synthetic Biology and Morality: Artificial Life and the Bounds of Nature*

Dominic A. Sisti, Arthur L. Caplan, and Hila Rimon-Greenspan, eds., *Applied Ethics in Mental Healthcare: An Interdisciplinary Reader*

Barbara K. Redman, *Research Misconduct Policy in Biomedicine: Beyond the Bad-Apple Approach*

Russell Blackford, *Humanity Enhanced: Genetic Choice and the Challenge for Liberal Democracies*

Nicholas Agar, *Truly Human Enhancement: A Philosophical Defense of Limits*

Bruno Perreau, *The Politics of Adoption: Gender and the Making of French Citizenship*

I. Glenn Cohen and Holly Fernandez Lynch, eds., *Human Subjects Research Regulation: Perspectives on the Future*